D0467634

CREATING THE COMMONWEALTH

Also by STEPHEN INNES

Work and Labor in Early America *(editor)*

Labor in a New Land: Economy and Society in Seventeenth-Century Springfield

"Myne Owne Ground": Race and Freedom on Virginia's Eastern Shore, 1640–1676 *(with T. H. Breen)*

Creating the Commonwealth

THE ECONOMIC CULTURE OF PURITAN NEW ENGLAND

STEPHEN INNES

W·W·NORTON & COMPANY

New York London

Copyright © 1995 by Stephen Innes
All rights reserved
Printed in the United States of America

First Edition

The text of this book is composed in Baskerville
with the display set in Cloister Open Face and Baskerville.
Composition and manufacturing by
the Maple-Vail Book Manufacturing Group
Book design by Jacques Chazaud

Library of Congress Cataloging-in-Publication Data

Innes, Stephen.
Creating the commonwealth : the economic culture of Puritan New England / Stephen Innes.
p. cm.
Includes index.
1. Work ethic—New England—History. 2. Entrepreneurship—New England—History. 3. Capitalism—New England—History. 4. New England—Economic conditions. I. Title.
HD8083.A11I56 1995
330.974'02—dc20 94–5616

ISBN 0–393–03584–0

W. W. Norton & Company, Inc., 500 Fifth Avenue, New York, N.Y. 10110
W. W. Norton & Company Ltd., 10 Coptic Street, London WC1A 1PU

1 2 3 4 5 6 7 8 9 0

For my parents

Louise Sherlock Innes

and

Stanley Ernest Innes

Contents

Acknowledgments

More than most, this book was a collaborative effort and I have many to thank. Peter Onuf and John Murrin each critiqued the manuscript—and encouraged the author—at a pivotal stage in its gestation. My debt to both is immense. The scholarship of Joyce Appleby, T. H. Breen, Stephen Foster, and Albert Hirschman provided (daunting) models of the kind of book I wanted to attempt to write, and their generosity and encouragement helped give me the will to try it. My colleagues at Virginia—Cindy Aron, Edward Ayers, Brian Balogh, Lenard Berlanstein, Everett Crosby, Carlos Eire, Martin Havran, Michael Holt, Melvyn Leffler, Allan Megill, Elizabeth Meyer, Erik Midelfort, Thomas Noble, Mark Thomas, and Olivier Zunz—showed time and again why this is the most stimulating as well as the most congenial of history departments. Those within the larger community of early modernists who had a hand in the shaping of this book include: William Abbot, Virginia Anderson, Phillip Benedict, Mark Bond-Webster, Bruce Coffey, Peter Coclanis,

J. H. Elliott, Robert Gross, Gloria Main, Donald McCloskey, John McCusker, Michael McGiffert, Theodore Porter, Agnes Sagan, Mary Schweitzer, Thomas Slaughter, Barbara Solow, Cinder Stanton, Lawrence Stone, William Taylor, and Lorena Walsh. The fact that I was able to profit from the earlier forays into New England's political economy by Christine Heyrman, John Frederick Martin, Darrett Rutman, and, especially, Daniel Vickers, made this project possible in the first place. An eleventh-hour dialogue with Karen Kupperman on the Puritan colony on Providence Island helped crystalize a number of important comparative issues for me. That Perry Miller had of course already said much of what follows will come as a surprise to few.

Research on this book began during my year as a fellow at the Institute for Advanced Studies at Princeton, and it's difficult to imagine a more ideal setting for embarking on a new project. Financial support came from the American Council of Learned Societies, the Ford Foundation, and the John Simon Guggenheim Foundation, for which I am deeply grateful. Multiple drafts of the manuscript, before its author finally mastered WordPerfect, were conscientiously and cheerfully prepared by Lottie McCauley, Kathleen Miller, and Ella Wood, all of whom I thank. Finally, I would like to thank the staff of W. W. Norton—Kate Brewster, Ann Adelman, and especially editor Steven Forman—for their professionalism and patience with an author who took twelve years to write a book whose subject is the Protestant work ethic.

CREATING THE COMMONWEALTH

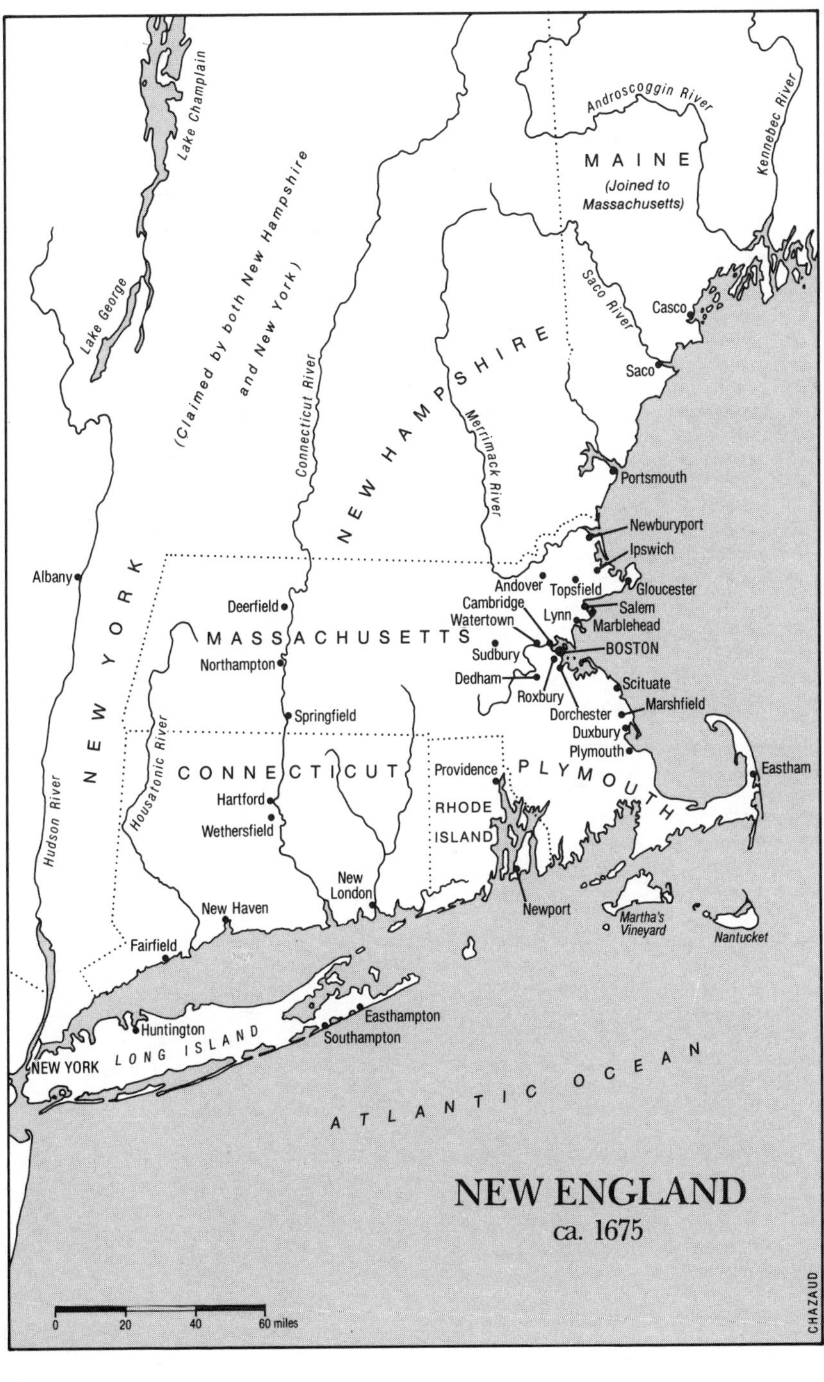
NEW ENGLAND
ca. 1675
Lake Champlain
Lake George
(Claimed by both New Hampshire and New York)
Connecticut River
NEW HAMPSHIRE
Merrimack River
Androscoggin River
Kennebec River
MAINE
(Joined to Massachusetts)
Saco River
Casco
Saco
Portsmouth
Newburyport
Ipswich
Andover
Topsfield
Gloucester
Cambridge
Salem
Lynn
Watertown
Marblehead
BOSTON
Sudbury
Dedham
Roxbury
Scituate
Marshfield
Dorchester
Duxbury
Plymouth
Eastham
Albany
NEW YORK
Deerfield
MASSACHUSETTS
Northampton
Springfield
Housatonic River
Hudson River
CONNECTICUT
Hartford
Wethersfield
Providence
PLYMOUTH
RHODE ISLAND
New London
Newport
New Haven
Martha's Vineyard
Nantucket
Fairfield
Easthampton
Huntington
Southampton
LONG ISLAND
ATLANTIC OCEAN
0
20
40
60 miles
CHAZAUD

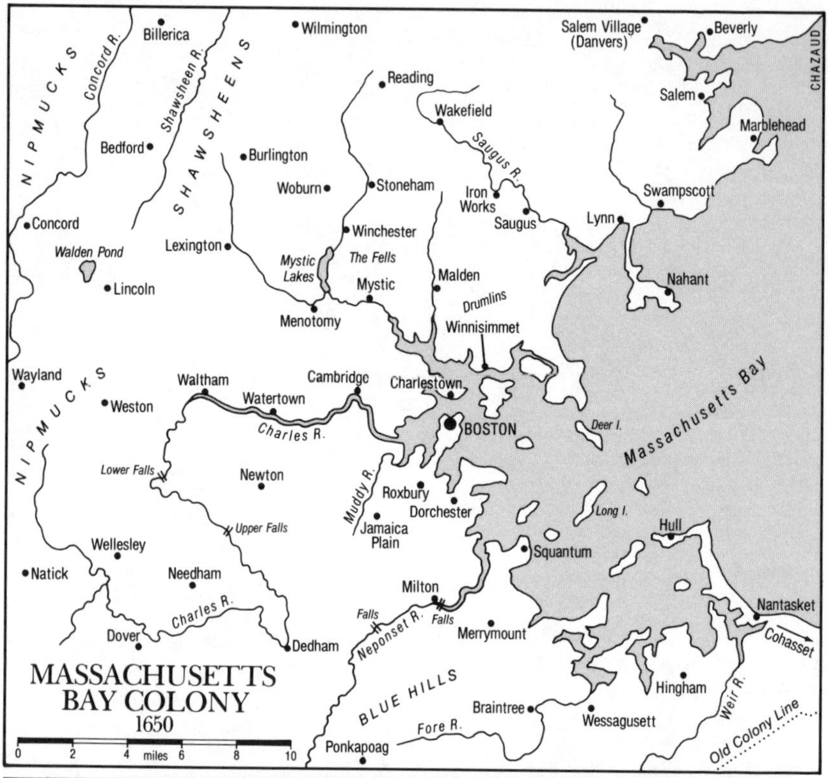

MASSACHUSETTS
BAY COLONY
1650
0 2 4 miles 6 8 10
CHAZAUD
Billerica
Wilmington
Salem Village
(Danvers)
Beverly
NIPMUCKS
Concord R.
Shawsheen R.
SHAWSHEENS
Reading
Salem
Wakefield
Marblehead
Bedford
Burlington
Saugus R.
Woburn
Stoneham
Iron
Works
Swampscott
Concord
Saugus
Lynn
Winchester
Lexington
Walden Pond
Mystic
Lakes
The Fells
Malden
Nahant
Lincoln
Mystic
Drumlins
Menotomy
Winnisimmet
Wayland
Waltham
Cambridge
Charlestown
Massachusetts Bay
Weston
Watertown
NIPMUCKS
Charles R.
BOSTON
Deer I.
Lower Falls
Newton
Muddy R.
Roxbury
Dorchester
Long I.
Upper Falls
Jamaica
Plain
Hull
Wellesley
Squantum
Natick
Needham
Milton
Nantasket
Falls
Falls
Charles R.
Neponset R.
Merrymount
Cohasset
Dover
Dedham
BLUE HILLS
Hingham
Braintree
Weir R.
Wessagusett
Fore R.
Old Colony Line
Ponkapoag

MASSACHUSETTS TRADE ROUTES 1640-1700
London
NORTH AMERICA
EUROPE
Boston
Naval stores, Furs, Lumber
Manufactured goods
Tobacco, Furs, Naval stores
Azores
Lisbon
Meat, Fish, Lumber
Madeira
Sugar, Molasses
Fish, Lumber, Livestock
Bahamas
Canary
Islands
Sugar, Molasses
Cuba
Hispaniola
Antigua
European goods
AFRICA
Jamaica
St. Christopher
Nevis
Montserrat
Barbados
Cape Verde
Islands
Trinidad
GOLD COAST
CHAZAUD
SOUTH
AMERICA

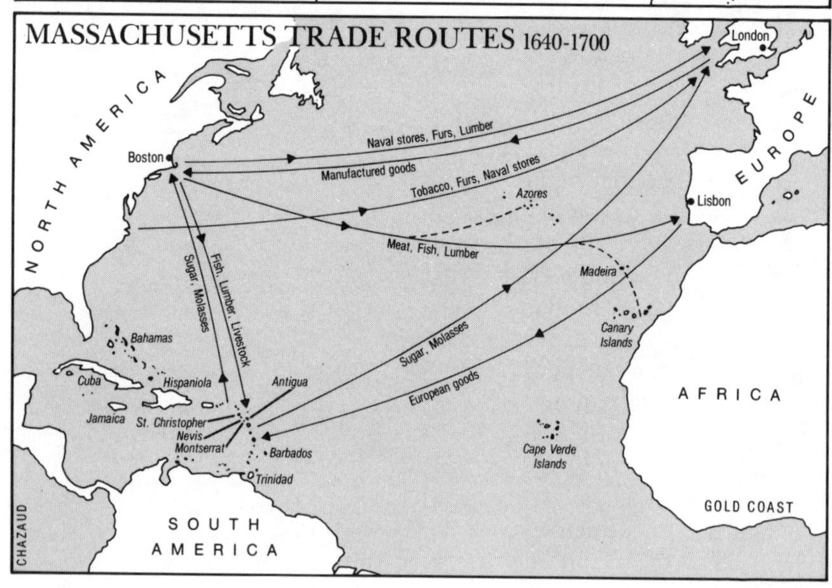

Introduction:

The Economic Culture of Puritan New England

This book examines the crucible of the original Puritan work ethic in America: seventeenth-century New England. There are several reasons for such a focus. The first is the common assumption—a correct one, I believe—that a distinctive productive ethic originated in some fundamental way among the men and women of Puritan New England. It was the result of a fortuitous combination in a New World setting of the Protestant concept of "the calling" with the emergent doctrines of mercantile capitalism, as expressed in the civic culture of the New England town. Or, to state things differently, it was the result of a potent blend of Puritan ideology and English culture at a particular—already relatively advanced—stage of that nation's economic and institutional development. Massachusetts Bay Colony, I will contend, succeeded for two overriding reasons: it freed the economy of anachronistic restraints; and it recognized the link between land ownership and productive labor.[1]

The women and men of Puritan New England created

what they called a "commonwealth." This was a commonwealth that successfully promoted *human* as well as economic development, that "improved" skills, initiative, and the social web as well as fields and fences. It did so by linking capitalism to redemptive community. Through their civic ecology, Protestant work ethic, and sense of communal purpose, seventeenth-century New Englanders created a stable, thriving, "middling"-rank society. This was a society that offered the mass of its inhabitants levels of prosperity, educational attainment, family stability, material culture, and life expectancy not duplicated elsewhere in British America. Settled primarily for religious purposes and meagerly endowed with natural resources, Massachusetts Bay Colony—against all odds—established a flourishing, diversified, family-based economy within a generation of its founding.[2] The Puritan colonists seeking to build their "Citty upon a Hill" in 1630 found themselves confronted by a land with thin, rock-filled soil, a short growing season, brutally cold winters, and few prospects of discovering either precious metals or a lucrative staple crop. Told by many that they could only be preserved "by miracle," a generation later the Bay Colonists were well on their way to becoming "the Dutch of England's empire."[3]

The early settlers of Massachusetts Bay helped turn their hard land into a prosperous colony by establishing a complex of social institutions—or civil society—grounded in the "federal" covenant. Civil society was the sphere of uncoerced association positioned between the patriarchal household and the state.[4] It was premised on the existence of the ethically autonomous (grace-bearing) individual as the fundamental constituent of society, rather than the order, guild, or corporation. It operated within a law-governed framework, and embraced local communities and institutions, townships, churches, and schools, as well as all that was market-regulated, voluntarily organized, or privately controlled.[5] This book will argue that the sources of Massachusetts Bay's success were in large part attributable to the colony's distinctive civic ecology, in which family, church, town, and commonwealth were bound together by a series of federal (collective or external) covenants. At the center of these was the "little commonwealth" of the family.[6] God, the Reverend John Cotton (1584–1652) declared, had appointed humankind "to live in Societies, first of Family, Secondly Church, and Thirdly, Common-wealth."[7] Upon the family's obligation to enforce good behavior rested all political and ecclesiastical authority in seventeenth-century New England. For the Puritans, the patriarchal family household represented the primary ethical realm, dependent in turn upon church, civil society, and the state in its task of inculcating the saints' potent "culture of discipline."[8]

Massachusetts Bay was a commonwealth that flourished in large part because its notion of redemptive community endowed economic development with moral, spiritual, and religious imperatives.[9] The settlers' providentialism—the belief that they were participating in the working out of God's purposes—made all labor and enterprise "godly business," to be pursued aggressively and judged by the most exacting of standards. As Max Weber later intuited, Calvinist social ethics—imagined in the Old World—decisively shaped the economic culture of this portion of the New. The formative dynamic was the link between outward success and inward conviction of being right with God. The doctrine of vocation embraced by the saints (Calvin's Elect) made labor sacred and grounded all striving behavior in communal obligation.[10] The Bay Colonists established a market economy and erected a moral-cultural system and civic society to supplement and control it. They authorized a regime of private property and freedom of contract but endeavored to see that it was checked and balanced by moral witness and civic restraint. Preachers such as Thomas Shepard (1605–1649) never tired of reminding the saints that self-interest was a "raging Sea which would overwhelm all if [it] have not bankes." In creating a culture of development that was at once metaphysically grounded and socially binding, the Massachusetts settlers fashioned a potent engine of economic and human development.[11]

The saints attempted to bridge what Emile Durkheim called the "duality of human existence," the co-existence in the same person of interest-motivated and altruistic-motivated action.[12] This work will contend that they were successful in establishing what some would call an oxymoron: moral capitalism. By conceiving of the godly as a mutual aid society,

Massachusetts Puritans fostered what theorists call "social capital"—networks, norms, and trust that enhance and amplify the benefits of investment in physical and human capital (tools and training).[13] Although firmly entrenched in the practices of commerce and exchange, contracts and debts, these avatars of the new capitalist world were anything but liberal. Worldly ends came from the most unworldly of motives. Believing that "the eyes of all people are uppon us," and ardently hoping that humankind "shall say of succeeding plantacions: the lord make it like that of New England," the migrants of 1630 wrought more than they knew.[14]

The Puritans settled in such an unprepossessing land in part precisely because its environment was more conducive to family farms than great plantations, more amenable to mixed farming than staple crop production. New England's rough land and fierce winters were unlikely to attract either gold-hunters or sluggards. Hence its attraction for many Puritan divines. As John White (1575–1648) declared, "If men desire to have a people degenerate speedily, and to corrupt their mindes and bodies too, and besides to tole-in theeves and spoilers from abroad, let them seeke a rich soile that brings in much with little labour."[15] New England self-evidently was not such a land. In fact, it appeared quite the opposite. The territory was, to the eyes of most observers, a rocky "desart Wildernesse," one that was "barren beyond belief," where "fearful famine and the misery that accompanieth it" appeared inevitable. It struck even the friends of Puritan colonization as a place where "rich men growe pore and poore men if they come over are a burthen." By all odds, starvation—not middling-rank prosperity—seemed in the offing for the migrants. One early settler declared that "if God discover not means to enrich the land, what shall become of us I will not determine [to say]." Oliver Cromwell was simply mouthing conventional wisdom when at midcentury he described New England as "poore, cold, and useless."[16]

Such attitudes persist today. Scholars continue to make references to "New England's economic backwardness" and the "protests of rural folk against mercantile capitalism," and to assert that "in its transition to a market economy," New England "may have been the least dynamic region of the British mainland colonies."[17] In fact Massachusetts settlers became the leading commercial people on the continent from the mid-seventeenth century onward. New England merchants dominated the Atlantic trading complex linking British America to the West Indies, Atlantic Islands, Southern Europe, and England. The Bay Colony's fishing and shipbuilding industries prospered beyond all expectations and fostered a synergistic form of "linked" development. Surplus production of agricultural provisions was characteristic from the 1630s onward.[18]

The main focus in the pages below is on the connection between Massachusetts Bay Colony's civic ecology, social capital, and rate of economic development.[19] The growth of economic and human development in seventeenth-century New England was promoted, first, by the distinctive civic ecology of Massachusetts Bay Colony, based on strong families and town organizations (as well as the existence of a vibrant public sphere at both the local and provincial levels); and second, by the creation of a religiously based "culture of discipline" that fostered industrious and "striving" behavior, communal responsibility, and a high ratio of savings and investment relative to income by its limitations on leisure. The development of capitalism in the early modern period required an ethic of disciplined work and self-denial in order both to maximize production and reinvestment and to attend to the needs of the economically vulnerable. It required that human beings "improve every bright and shining moment" while also ensuring that "the riche and mighty" not "eate upp the poore."[20] It required an ideology of social solidarity and trust to offset capitalism's ever present destructive capacities. Success in achieving this combination—as a Covenant People—allowed Massachusetts Bay to become the New World's first capitalist commonwealth.

Ascetic Protestantism shaped the Bay Colonists' "fundamentals," their education and aspiration. In the early modern period, no less than today, work and enterprise were cultural artifacts, the signatures of a particular array of attitudes and behaviors. As Max Weber postulated, economic growth derives from psychological and cultural wellsprings as well as material endowments. Skeptical over the presumed naturalness of "maximizing" behavior postulated, in their different ways, by both Marxists and neoclassicists, Weber declared categorically: "A man does not *by nature* wish to earn more and more money, but simply to live as he is accustomed to live and earn as much as is necessary for that purpose." Adam Smith, although the father of the naturalistic conception of economics, likewise regarded striving behavior as abnormal and culturally created; but, for Smith, in the right circumstances such behavior could prove economically decisive. "The difference between the most dissimilar characters, between a philosopher and a common street porter, for example, seems to arise not so much from nature as from *habit, custom,* and *education.*"[21] As Smith's remarks imply, culture—patterned behavior and institutions—shapes economic development, especially to the degree that it fosters the growth of both social capital (norms and cooperative networks) and human capital (education and training).

That cultural attitudes toward work and production should play a critical role in economic development is not really that surprising. Indeed, we should be more surprised by the opposite stance. Literary expressions of such social realities are both commonplace and telling. We know when Emerson writes, "A man is fed, not that he may be fed, but that he may work," that a distinctive attitude toward work is being invoked. The same, in reverse, goes for Faulkner's aphorism that "You can't eat for eight hours a day, nor drink for eight hours a day, nor make love for eight hours a day—all you can do for eight hours is work. Which is the reason why man makes himself and everybody else so miserable and unhappy." More negatively still, when a Barbadian slave declares that "The Devel was in the English-man, that he makes every thing work; he makes the *Negro* work, the Horse work, the Ass work, the Wood work, the Water work, and the Winde work," the bitterness that comes from unrequited labor is clearly in evidence.[22]

That whole cultures can be divided by such attitudes is suggested by Alexis de Tocqueville's famous voyage down the Ohio River, during which he found what amounted to two distinct work cultures. What divided them was the respective dignity accorded to labor:

> Upon the left bank of the Ohio [Kentucky], labor is confounded with the idea of slavery, while on the right bank it is identified with that of prosperity and improvement; on the one side it is degraded, on the other it is honored. On the [Kentucky bank] no white laborers can be found . . . all the work is done by slaves; on the [Ohio bank] no one is idle, for the white population extend their activity and intelligence to every kind of employment. Thus the men whose task it is to cultivate the rich soil of Kentucky are ignorant and apathetic, while those who are active and enlightened either do nothing or pass over into Ohio, where they may work without shame.

In Tocqueville's eyes, the South was the cultural mirror-opposite of the North, where the "spirit of freedom" and the "spirit of religion" allowed one to work without shame.[23]

Max Weber raised the cultural dimension of capitalism, and this book is heavily indebted to that insight. For Weber, Puritanism was instrumental in early modern economic development in part because its notion of "improvement" channeled individuals' behavior along capitalist paths. The doctrine of improvement led to the modern bourgeois-directed economy in which nature is "transformed into an instrument for the satisfaction of human needs, which multiply and diversify and can therefore no longer be understood as 'natural.' "[24] Certain aspects of Puritan belief, particularly the notions of the calling and improvement, harmonized with—and amplified—certain elements of capitalist behavior that many seventeenth-century English men and women, whatever their religion, already exhibited. Ascetic Puritanism helped make an already progressive people the more so.[25] In the orthodox Puritan colonies of Massachusetts, Connecticut, and New Haven, the vibrant civic culture of the New England town gave institutional expression to these impulses. In matters of property, trade, and labor, Puritanism served to legitimize (although not to engender) economic ideas and practices that were recognizably capitalist. The motive force of a free enterprise system—the drive to expand capital—grew naturally out of the Protestant notion of improvement. As Perry Miller averred, perhaps with some conscious oversimplification, "Devotion to business, accumulation of estates, acquisition of houses and lands: these were the duties of Christians." The need to improve one's talents led to the inescapable injunction to employ one's estate "so that it should become a larger estate."[26]

If the Calvinist work ethic was to be found anywhere in its most purely distilled form in the early modern world, that place was Puritan Massachusetts. The explanation for this is relatively simple. Nowhere else in the post-Reformation world did Calvinist social ethics find such full expression. While in Geneva, Holland, and low-country Scotland, Calvinist divinity was always qualified by pre-existing practices, in New England doctrine was the foundation for practice. New England represents the only historical case in which Calvinistic, sectarian Protestantism was institutionalized at the very founding of the social order.[27] It was the only place where ascetic Puritanism served as the governing cultural model. In England itself, the Puritan culture of discipline, having achieved revolutionary ends between 1641 and 1660, was forced into retreat after the Restoration. The vehemence of the reaction against Puritans—and all things Puritan—during the reign of Charles II eventually canalized the Protestant ethic into the more private realm of Dissent, where the Quakers and Presbyterians were its principal representatives. Within the Church of England, Puritans were also eventually defeated by the Arminian attempt to restore the mystery and majesty of the Henrician Church. Resacralizing the church, to a considerable degree, had the effect of desacralizing the workplace. The moment that "the railings went up around the communion tables in English churches the Protestant ethic was undermined; for in making altars and prayers especially holy and therefore worthy of special care, the Laudians made plows and shop counters less holy, less significant as means of glorifying God and working out salvation." In Massachusetts Bay, mothers, fathers, magistrates, and ministers all took upon themselves the responsibility for ensuring that plows and shop counters—not to mention spinning wheels, gristmills, and fishing boats—did indeed remain sanctified means for seeking God's glory.[28]

Here, special attention must be paid to the Protestant-humanist view that family life and work were the proper contexts of religious life—and to New England's unique demographic conditions that allowed these convictions full play. New England mothers and fathers were accorded what may have been a historically unprecedented length of time to socialize their children, who—in sharp contrast to Chesapeake youth—typically lived with their parents until achieving majority. The Chesapeake pattern of parental death and early inheritance was reversed in New England.[29] In tandem with Calvinist divinity, this allowed the Puritan family truly to become a "little commonwealth." New England parents impressed upon their children that work was at once an expression of their love of God and "the spontaneous relationship of man to the world around him." This was the mainspring of ascetic Puritanism and the principle that most distinguished it from monastic and medieval traditions, with their postulations of a higher morality for the monastery and a lower morality for everyday life. The end of ethical dualism endowed daily labors with sacred import. It was here, of course, that the saints were most firmly located within the broad mainstream of Reformed Protestant divinity. According to the Reverend Joseph Hall (1574–1656)), himself both a Calvinist and an Anglican bishop:

> Paradise served not only to feed [Adam's] senses, but to exercise his hands. If happiness consisted in doing nothing, man had not beene employed; all his delights could not have made him happy in an idle life. Man therefore is no sooner made, than he is set to worke: neither greatnesse, nor perfection can priviledge a folded hand; [Adam] must labor, because he was happy; how much more wee, that we may bee? . . . How much more cheerfully we goe about our businesses, so much nearer we come to our Paradise.[30]

In their successful efforts not to "priviledge a folded hand," the Bay Colonists achieved a degree of prosperity that always posed a threat to their Holy Commonwealth. Deeply ambivalent over the regime of economic freedom they had helped unleash, Bay Colonists—particularly in the vehicle of the clergy's special-occasion "jeremiad"—created a self-critical ideology that effectively interpreted material success as spiritual failure. The demands of living as a Covenant People almost invariably left hardworking women and men regarding themselves as "unprofitable servants." The New Englanders' narrative tradition, particularly their rhetoric of history, reinforced and reinterpreted these imperatives over a span of five generations.[31] The only region of British America to fashion a communally binding myth of its founding, as the providentially favored "New Canaan," New England also was the only region whose cultural interpreters—the governing magistrates and the Congregational clergy—tended to view most change and adaptation as forms of corruption, as actions that threatened the Bay Colonists' covenant with God.

Even before leaving England in April of 1630, the Massachusetts migrants were reminded of this charge by Governor John Winthrop (1588–1649) in words worthy of an Old Testament prophet:

> wee must Consider that wee shall be as a Citty upon a Hill, [and] the eyes of all people are uppon us; soe that if wee shall deale falsely with our god in this worke wee have undertaken and soe cause him to withdrawe his present help from us, wee shall be made a story and a by-word through the world; wee shall open the mouthes of enemies to speake evill of the wayes of god and all professors for God's sake; wee shall shame the faces of many of god's worthy servants, and cause theire prayers to be turned into Curses upon us, till wee be consumed out of the good land whither wee are going.[32]

Puritan social ethics always threatened to undermine Puritan divinity, as Winthrop may have intuited while still aboard the flagship *Arbella.* In New England the notion of the calling, one's service to God through service to the community in the realm of work, was powerfully articulated throughout the seventeenth century. Virtually every waking hour needed to be devoted to the improvement of one's talents in pursuit of the calling. The Puritans, like Locke, Emerson, and Lincoln after them, believed that it was labor that gave meaning to life and dignity to the worker.[33] They also believed that God worked through secondary causes and human labors were the principal manifestation of these causes. As Perry Miller has emphasized, that every man should have a calling and work hard in it was a first premise of Puritanism. Even

> the man who has an income must work. Everyone has a talent for something, given of God, which he must improve. Although poverty is not a sin if it be suffered for causes outside one's control, for any to accept it voluntarily is utterly reprehensible. God has so contrived the world that men must seek the necessities of life in the earth or in the sea, but the objects of their search have been cunningly placed for the finding. Coming to [this] momentous decision [John] Winthrop had reflected, "Whatsoever we stand in neede of is treasured in the earth by the Creator, and to be feched thense by the sweate of [our] Browes."[34]

Work in seventeenth-century New England was both a spiritual expression and an economic function. It was based on the Pauline injunction in I Corinthians 3:13 that "Every man's work shall be made manifest: for the day shall declare it, because it shall be revealed by fire; and the fire shall try every man's work of what sort it is." Work, for the saints, was at once individualistic and communal. It drew for its theological inspiration on both the Protestant idea of the calling—enshrined in the Shorter Westminster Confession—and the older Christian doctrine of the stewardship of wealth. As Reformed Protestants, the Bay Colonists labored "to entertain one another in brotherly affection." They, like all Christians in the early modern world, made common reference to "those Worldly Goods the Lord hath lent me."[35] Improvement, enterprise, and conservation in the use of God's gifts were their watchwords. Idleness and luxury were to be discountenanced by mother, minister, and magistrate, and on the grounds of utility as well as sanctity.

Paradoxes abound here. As seventeenth-century supralapsarians, the Bay Colonists rejected the "covenant of works" in favor of the "covenant of grace." They condemned as "Arminian" anyone who argued that "good works" could lead to salvation; yet the very culture so bent on destroying "works-righteousness" produced a work ethic unlike anything the early modern world had yet seen. They also created an institutional and civic culture to foster and amplify it. Their productive ethic was fostered through New England's distinctive civic ecology—through the interlocking efforts of the household, pulpit, meetinghouse, and assembly. Most unrelenting were the efforts directed against idleness, what Puritans called the "sin of Sodom." Few societies have legislated so frequently, so obsessively, and so effectively against idleness as did the orthodox New England colonies of Massachusetts, New Haven, and Connecticut.[36]

Also to be reckoned with here were the material expectations of the first settlers. New England men and women worked to establish a "comfortable" standard of living, to live in "box-framed" houses, wear woolen clothes, read printed books, farm with plows and oxen, and eat a diet of maize, pork, and beef.[37] In 1629 the Reverend Francis Higginson (1586–1630), a former lecturing Nonconformist from Leicestershire now living in the new settlement at Salem, testified to the high material expectations of the colonists. He advised prospective migrants to bring "all manner of carpenter's tools, and a good deal of iron and steel to make nails and locks for houses, and furniture for plows and carts, and glass for windows, and many other things. . . ." Recruited primarily from the solidly middling yeomanry and artisans of the commercially oriented mixed-farming (unenclosed or "champion") regions of East Anglia, the Bay Colony migrants showed little disposition to lower their standard of living once in America.[38] Nor did they. After surveying the probate inventories of seventeenth- and eighteenth-century New England, Jackson T. Main was moved to comment that "A Bible, a decent bed, and linen sheets were usual even among the poorer householders [of New England], and earthernware was common; these seem not just amenities but almost necessities."[39]

The colonists' improving ethic and material expectations had economic consequences. These were manifested in both the public policy of the local and provincial governments of Massachusetts and the work habits of individual women and men. Believing that it had an obligation to create the commonwealth, the Massachusetts General Court—particularly after the economic crisis brought by the end of the Great Migration in 1641—took legislative measures to foster enterprise and curtail idleness. Merchant-entrepreneurs were offered incentives by both the General Court and individual towns to establish the Bay Colony's material infrastructure: ironworks, fisheries, shipyards, mills, saltworks, glassworks, brick kilns, and clothmaking operations. Legislation was passed to augment human capital: to discourage idleness, bring vagrants into the workplace, and—most important in the long run—create an educated, literate, improvement-oriented populace. Schools were mandated for all towns of fifty families or more, and Harvard College and British America's first printing press were established in Cambridge. The effort to raise up a college-educated clergy and a literate laity—one of the Reformation's highest aspirations—was achieved more successfully in New England than anywhere else in North America. The success of Harvard (and after its establishment in 1705, Yale) in producing educated, ordained ministers gave New England what was possibly the lowest constant ratio of preachers to general population in the Protestant world.[40] By 1650, there was one minister for every 415 persons in Massachusetts; in all of Virginia in 1649 there were only six ministers, one for every 3,239 persons.[41] Of the 135 college-trained ministers in Massachusetts in 1660, no fewer than 116 were graduates of Harvard.[42] Protestantism also demanded changes in the calendar. The Old Calendar was purged of its red letter (holy) days and the 220 potential work days available in early modern Europe were increased to over 300 in Massachusetts.

Such efforts quickly bore fruit, particularly in the realm of commercial expansion. As the Puritan propagandist Edward Johnson (1598–1672) pointed out with obvious pride, even by the 1640s, merchants from "Holland, France, Spain, and Portugal [were] coming hither for trade." During the 1640s,

Massachusetts merchants and entrepreneurs developed broad connections in the West Indian and Atlantic trading complexes, often aided by ties to Puritan-minded London merchant houses. The town that became known to overseas traders as "Boston in New England" emerged as the principal entrepot not only for the settlements ringing Massachusetts Bay itself, but for those along Long Island Sound, Narragansett Bay, and the Connecticut River Valley as well. It also became the region's principal outlet for the provisioning and outfitting of ships, which developed into a major industry for Boston in the mid-1640s.[43] According to Johnson, not only had New England "fed their Elder Sisters, Virginia, Barbados, and many of the Summer Islands that were prefer'd before her for fruitfulness, but . . . even the firtil Isle of Great Britain." Despite early fears that no commercial crop could be found, "every thing in the country proved a staple-commodity, wheat, rye, oats, peas, barley, beef, pork, fish, butter, cheese, timber, mast, tar, sope, plankboard, frames of houses, clapboard, and pipestaves [and shortly] iron and lead is like to be also." As early as 1650, New England's ministers were interpreting the colony's unexpected level of prosperity in providential terms. Many clergymen, as did the post-millennialist Edward Johnson, saw in New England's flourishing economy, material comfort, and growing trade "the wonderful providence of the most high God toward these his new-planted Churches, such as was never heard of, since that Jacob's sons ceased to be a people."[44]

Johnson's town-by-town canvass revealed that in Dedham, the *locus classicus* of the "closed corporate peasant village," the inhabitants carried their surplus corn and livestock to Boston on a weekly basis. Dedham, Johnson declared, was a settlement "abounding with Garden fruits fitly to supply the Markets of the most populous Towne [Boston], whose coyne and commodities allures the Inhabitants of this Towne to make many a long walk." In Andover, according to Johnson, despite "the remoteness of the place from Towns of trade, [which] bringeth some inconveniences upon the planters," the townsmen continued to "carry their corn far to market."[45] Towns, early on, began to specialize in certain products, reflecting the resources at hand. In Hingham, our observer reports that "the people have much profited themselves by transporting Timber, Planke and Mast for Shipping to the Town of Boston, as also Ceder and Pine-board to supply the wants of other Townes, and also to remote parts, even as far as Barbadoes. They [lack] not for Fish for themselves and others also." It was by such means, repeated in every village, town, and port throughout early New England, that "this Wilderness should turn [into] a mart for Merchants in so short a space, Holland, France, Spain, and Portugal coming hither for trade."[46]

In 1660, in a document remarkable for its explicit detail about New England's commercial products and trading partners, John Winthrop, Jr. (1606–1676), observed that

> through the great blessing of the Lord upon the labours of the people heere, there is a comfortable supply of all sorts of corne and provisions necessary for subsistence, and that not only for themselves (the present inhabitants) but also for many others; so as it is not now as in our beginnings, when we were necessited to bring with us provisions sufficient for a long tyme, but now the country doth send out great store of biscott, flower, peas, beife, porke, butter, and other provisions to the supply of Barbados, Newfoundland, and other places besides the furnishing out [of] many vessells and fishing boats of theire owne. . . .[47]

That same year Boston Anglican Samuel Maverick, no friend to the Puritans, marveled over the productivity of the Bay Colony's livestock farmers, with many thousands of "Neate Beasts and Hoggs" being slaughtered every year for export to Newfoundland, Barbados, and Jamaica, and for the provisioning of ships. Increasingly important from the 1670s onward, with barberry rust devastating wheatfields in the eastern Massachusetts settlements, was the transshipment of goods from elsewhere. An official report on Newfoundland in 1678 provided a brief compendium of New England's place in the Atlantic trading complex. It noted that the island's inhabitants "chiefly consume the products of New England, the shipping of which Country furnishes them with

French Wine and Brandy, and Madera Wines in exchange for their Fish, without depending for any supply from England." For the remainder of the colonial period, Newfoundland would continue to be almost completely dependent on New England for its provisions and rum.[48]

Across the Atlantic, imperial officials took note of New England's swift economic rise, although with less pride than alarm. In 1689 Edward Randolph (1632–1703), royal agent in Massachusetts, went so far as to describe this once unprepossessing landscape as the main entrepot of British North America. In comments that emphasize New England's commercial as well as its productive capacity, he declared that

> The other *American plantations* cannot well subsist without *New England,* which is by a thousand leagues nearer to them than either *England* or *Ireland;* so that they are supplied with provisions, beef, pork, meal, fish, etc., also with the lumber trade, deal boards, pipe staves, etc., chiefly from *New England.* Also the Caribbee Islands have their horses from thence.

Randolph concluded by saying that "It is then, in a great part, by means of New England, that the other plantations are made prosperous and beneficial."[49]

New England's success in shipbuilding during the second half of the seventeenth century provoked the mercantilist Sir Josiah Child (1630–1699) to adopt the language of economic culture while warning that "Of all the American Plantations his Majesty has, none [are] so apt for the building of Shipping as New England, nor none more comparably so qualified for the breeding of Seamen." Child attributed both of these conditions to the "natural industry of that people."[50] This natural industry, far from bringing the intended benefit for the mother country, was helping to rear up a potent economic rival. It was through both legal and clandestine trade that Massachusetts by the 1680s had emerged as British America's main entrepot. Former governor Sir Edmund Andros (1637–1714) sounded the same themes as Child in 1690 while reporting to his imperial supervisors on the Glorious Revolution that had overthrown his regime on 18 April 1689. Andros informed the Lords of Trade that the Bay Colonists had the "smallest and poorest tracts of land" and produced "least of any of the other colonies for exportation." Yet, "by reason of the great number of artificers, particularly in Boston, shipwrights, smiths, etc., they build many ships and other vessels, some whereof they employ in trading with all sorts of provisions and lumber to other colonies and plantations, who bring home their produce and make Boston the store of all the plantation commodities."[51]

Although the wheat blight and New England's high rate of natural population increase ended the region's position as a net exporter of food well before the end of the seventeenth century, the shipment of substantial quantities of cod, mackerel, sawn lumber, barrel staves, cider, and—especially—ships served to shape work and settlement patterns for the remainder of the colonial period. From the early 1640s onward, when New England began to trade fish to Southern Europe and the West Indies, and use the credits thereby earned to meet its debts to British exporters of textiles, metalwares, and glasswares, the basic pattern of the region's commerce for the remainder of the colonial period was set.[52] Southern New England export centers such as Boston, Hartford, New London, New Haven, Providence, and Newport dominated the trade in grains, meat products, and pipestaves for the West Indies. Salem, Gloucester, Portsmouth, and Newbury in northern New England carried on the bulk of trade in fish, timber, and masts to both the West Indies and Europe.[53]

Geographically, the Atlantic coast region from Boston northward was dominated by cod fishing, timbering, shipbuilding, and naval stores production. The richer agricultural region along the Long Island Sound and Connecticut Valley provided the bulk of grains, preserved meat, and livestock for the export trade. Shipbuilding predominated in the towns of Boston, Charlestown, Salem, and Scituate during the period before 1700. By the time population growth outstripped the region's agricultural capacity in the 1680s, Massachusetts had become one of the major transshipment points in British America. Through Boston flowed increasing quantities of

British textiles and metalwares, West Indian sugar and molasses, Connecticut grain, New Hampshire lumber, New York furs, and Gulf of Maine fish.[54]

During the second half of the seventeenth century, New England's economic strengths were increasingly competitive rather than complementary with the mother country, a development that imperial officials viewed with mounting concern. The Earl of Sandwich, in his 1671 "comments upon New England," minced no words as to the likely consequences of such a rivalry: The New Englanders already were, he declared, "a numerous and thrivinge people and in twenty years are more likely (if civill wars or other accidents prevent them not) to be mighty, rich, and not at all carefull [to preserve] their dependence upon old England." Accordingly, the earl concluded—prophetically—that a coercive imperial policy would simply drive the colonists to independence. The "way of roughness and peremptory orders, with force to back them [would be] utterly unadvisable. For they are already too strong to be compelled. . . . And though I apprehend them yett not at that point to cast us off voluntarily and [by] choice: yett I beleeve if we use severity towards them in theire Government civill or religious, that they will (being made desperate) sett up for themselves and reject us."[55]

Sandwich's description of the New Englanders as a "numerous and thrivinge people" was an apt one. Through their work ethic and productivity, New Englanders helped create a populous and well-off society. Less edifyingly, it was the Bay Colonists' success in expropriating the Algonquians' land—while simultaneously building an export economy based on commerce with slaveholders in the British West Indies—that provided the resources and "vent for surplus" that allowed this economy to grow at impressive rates. Annual rates of economic growth for Massachusetts are estimated to have ranged from 1.6 percent to 2.0 percent during the years from 1640 to 1710, rates that were fast by seventeenth-century standards.[56]

Alone among New World colonies, Massachusetts Bay reproduced its population from the first decade onward. The Bay Colonists were the first British Americans to establish viable families.[57] While other mainland and Caribbean colonies invariably experienced fearsome mortality rates during the settlement period, Massachusetts increased its population 66 percent between 1640 and 1650—after the English Civil War had virtually stopped the arrival of new immigrants. Population increase in Maryland was not primarily generated by births until the late 1680s, and the colony did not produce a predominantly native adult population until the first decade of the eighteenth century.[58] With very little help from new migrants, the Massachusetts population grew from 9,000 in 1640 to 150,000 a century later.[59] Although during the seventeenth century some 150,000 men and women left Great Britain for mainland America—a figure that grew to 350,000 in the eighteenth century—New England received very few of these after the some 17,000–21,000 who arrived during the Great Migration (1630–41).[60]

In the Puritan colonies, population growth came almost entirely through natural means, a phenomenon that allowed New England to produce its own labor force virtually from the beginning. The natural growth rate of Massachusetts and Connecticut during the second half of the seventeenth century has been described by one demographer as "extremely unusual, if not unique in human history." A plentiful (if monotonous) diet of maize, rye, peas, pork, beef, and beer—along with a relatively balanced sex ratio, mixed economy, and the absence of killing tropical diseases such as malaria and typhoid—helped produce low infant mortality, a life expectancy near seventy for men and in the mid-sixties for women, and a low incidence of severe epidemics and famines.[61] The contrast with the Chesapeake colonies is arresting. Life expectancy in the "destructive demographic regime" of Maryland, where endemic malaria, typhoid, and dysentry took a grim toll throughout the seventeenth century, was roughly forty-three years for immigrant men; because of the dangers of childbirth, this figure was probably even lower for Maryland's women. In seventeenth-century Virginia, male life expectancy was in the late forties, female life expectancy in the late thirties.[62] Between 40 and 55 percent of the children born in Maryland during the seventeenth century could expect to die before reaching the age of twenty. While seventeenth-century New England couples had between six to eight children, all but one of whom could expect to reach maturity, Maryland couples produced three to four children, half of whom died in childhood. Most Maryland children lost at least one parent before reaching maturity.[63] The typical Virginia couple during the seventeenth century produced four to five children, one of whom would die in infancy.[64] Morbidity and mortality patterns—and hence patterns of population growth—were starkly different in New England. Although only about 5 percent of the settlers who crossed the Atlantic before 1700 came to New England during the Great Migration, by that year their descendants totaled more than 40 percent of the Old World population in the American colonies, not counting those who had migrated to New York and East New Jersey.[65]

The material prosperity undergirding this demographic expansion was, in comparison to the other New World colonies, widely shared. New England, even in Boston, lacked the fabulously wealthy merchants or planters to be found in Charleston, Kingstown, or along the James River; but a comfortable and independent existence was available to the vast majority of its population of farmers, fishermen, petty traders, and artisans by the end of the colonial period. Probate inventories reveal that the average real male wealth in southern New England by as early as 1650 stood as £260, a figure that rose to £395 (in pounds of constant sterling) by the end of the colonial period. By the 1690s, the median landholding of Connecticut men at death was 88 acres. As late as 1771, 80 percent of the families of rural Massachusetts owned and worked their own land. Even in the more densely populated towns surrounding Boston, this figure rarely dipped below 65 percent. The onset of the "consumer revolution" beginning in the 1690s raised material standards still higher. By the mid-eighteenth century, in New England as throughout British America, a richer and more varied supply of tablewares, clothing, and bedding was being purchased even by relatively humble householders.[66] When we measure colonial societies by their ability to offer economic autonomy and decent comforts to *all* their households (including servants and slaves)—when we focus on human as well as economic development—the New England colonies along with Pennsylvania demonstrably exceeded all others. While the Puritans came to America fired by an intense religious zeal, well before the end of the colonial period they had created societies that allowed some three quarters of their households to attain a "middling" standard of living, a far higher proportion than was found in Britain, the southern colonies, or the West Indies.[67]

In his depiction of New England as a quasi-republican society, the Earl of Sandwich indirectly acknowledged the connection between property-creating labor, middling-rank prosperity, and self-government. Through the long habit of self-government, the Bay Colonists were prepared to defend this society even against England itself. This they demonstrated in the Boston uprising of 18 April 1689, asserting that the challenge to land titles brought by the Dominion period (1686–89) threatened to deprive them and their forbears of "all their labor and Industry." With rumors reaching Whitehall that population growth had made New England capable of producing an armed force of some thirty thousand men, the Earl of Sandwich's earlier warnings were not to be taken lightly.[68]

As Perry Miller has shown so brilliantly, the very extent of New England's commercial success eventually produced a spiritual—and social—crisis for its people. Pious industry, many Bay Colonists believed as early as the 1660s, was wrecking the "Citty upon a Hill."[69] For the New England clergy, in particular, economic success seemed to produce—inevitably—spiritual failure. Industriousness and frugality brought wealth, which in turn brought temptation and worldliness, something we might dub the "Protestant dilemma." At the core of the Puritan ethic was a tension that was at once extraordinarily productive economically and tremendously difficult psychologically. The fundamental problem was something that the early modern world (with the conspicuous exception of Captain John Smith) had not yet come to grips with: social mobility. The concept of the calling, by demanding that every person pursue his livelihood relentlessly and methodically, always tempted him to get out of his place, to strive to grow richer, and eventually seek profit for himself and not for God and community. The Protestant ethic, in other words, always threatened to turn into the calculative rationalism that Max Weber called the "spirit of capitalism." For Weber, the Protestant ethic when divorced of its religious motive *became* the spirit of capitalism. In New England, the Protestant ethic—even while remaining firmly within its religious context—threatened to undermine the ancient notions of social hierarchy that all early modern people, Puritans included, believed essential for good order and stability. Not until the publication during the 1750s of James Burgh's *The Dignity of Human Nature* and Benjamin Franklin's *Poor Richard's Almanack* would the social mobility that was the almost inevitable result of the Protestant ethic in a New World setting be openly sanctioned.[70]

The classic American jeremiads, from John Cotton through such twentieth-century commentators as Reinhold Niebuhr and Daniel Bell, are all essentially variations on the Protestant dilemma: piety produces industry which produces wealth which produces status conflicts and worldliness. As Cotton Mather (1663–1728) declared of Plymouth during the 1690s, "Religion begot prosperity, and the daughter devoured the mother." In the mid-eighteenth century, John Wesley mournfully observed that "religion must necessarily produce both industry and frugality, and these cannot but produce riches. But as riches increase, so will pride, anger, and love of the world in all its branches." In 1819, John Adams asked Thomas Jefferson: "Will you tell me how to prevent riches from becoming the effects of temperance and industry? Will you tell me how to prevent riches from producing luxury? Will you tell me how to prevent luxury from producing effeminacy, intoxication, extravagance, Vice and folly?" By the twentieth century, this cycle would be secularized by Joseph Schumpeter into the process by which capitalism "destroys" the moral foundations upon which it is built.[71]

The most memorable—and influential—depiction of the early New England version of this jeremiad is of course Perry Miller's. Indeed, although not often recognized as such, Miller's *New England Mind* is at heart an arresting commentary on the region's culture of economic development. It was "pious industry," after all, that "wrecked the city on a hill."

The celebrated jeremiads of the clergy, upbraiding second-generation New Englanders for their worldliness, told the story of a "society which was founded by men dedicated, in unity and simplicity, to realizing on earth eternal and immutable principles—and which progressively became involved with fishing, trade, and settlement." A growing chorus of ministers lamented from the 1660s onward that economic growth had brought "a decay of godliness, class struggles, extravagant dress, and contempt for learning." Miller describes the process in a memorable passage: "The more everybody labored, the more society was transformed. The more diligently the people applied themselves—on the frontier, in the meadows, in the countinghouse or on the Banks of Newfoundland—the more they produced a decay in religion and a corruption of morals, a society they did not want, one that seemed less and less attractive."[72]

The central irony of the Protestant dilemma is that it was inescapable. The problem, says Miller, was that "the wrong thing was also the right thing." Industry, temperance, and self-discipline might well lead to the temptations of wealth, but a Puritan who foreswore these virtues was no longer a Puritan. Sloth, indolence, and idleness within the workforce could not be countenanced. And, neither could a lack of striving in the marketplace. Increasing material expansion after 1650 may well have signaled that New England was "deserting the ideals of its founders"—becoming a "plantation of trade" rather than a "plantation of religion"—but the clergy "would have deserted them even more had they not also exhorted diligence in every calling—precisely the virtue bound to increase estates, widen the gulf between rich and poor, and to make usury inevitable." At base, Miller declares, the jeremiads represent "a chapter in the emergence of the capitalist mentality, showing how intelligence copes with—or more cogently, how it fails to cope with—a change it simultaneously desires and abhors."[73]

The developmental public policy of the Massachusetts General Court is a compelling illustration of this ambivalence. Pious industry may have "wrecked" the city on a hill, but it had plenty of help from the political economy fashioned by the same magistrates, clergymen, and selectmen who so fervently denounced the materialism and oppression in their midst. In assessing the capitalist mentality he finds reflected in the sermon literature, Miller calls attention to one remarkable fact: "while the ministers were excoriating the behavior of merchants, laborers, and frontiersmen, they never for a moment condemned merchandizing, laboring, or expansion of the frontier. They berated the consequences of progress, but never progress; deplored the effects of trade upon religion, but did not ask men to desist from trading; arraigned men of great estates, but not estates."[74]

Even as the Massachusetts General Court (with help from individual towns) was actively promoting commerce, fisheries, ironworks, sawmills, and shipyards—as well as banning feudal land tenure and establishing a contractually based legal system—it was deploring the rise of materialism and self-seeking in its midst. A strikingly unconscious rendering of the juxtaposition of the need for piety and the need for commodities is found in the General Court's call for a "solemne day of humiliation" in October 1652. Prominent among the reasons adduced for fearing that the avenging hand of God was about to fall on New England was the "worldly mindedness, oppression, and hardhartedness" feared to be rampant in the land. Yet in the subsequent charge to the inhabitants the Court asked the churches to pray "that God would supply us with such commodities as are wanting."[75] Likewise, in 1671 the Reverend John Oxenbridge (1608–1674), even while warning that the General Court was not in the "merchandising business," urged it to promote the development of staple commodities which "may command supplies from abroad."[76] The New Englanders, it seems clear, wanted both a godly community *and* a commercialized society. And, despite their ambivalence, that is precisely what they got.

The Puritans were moving "crab-like" into the new capitalist world—looking backward in alarm even as they were advancing forward with dispatch.[77] Intent on replacing a corrupt modern order with the true primitive order, the saints ended up accomplishing something quite like the reverse.[78] They created an economy increasingly based on the principles of economic freedom, even as they ferociously denounced the cupidity that was the engine to that system. Despite their "Augustinian strain of piety," the Bay Colonists' theological beliefs in the end acted as a solvent on corporatist forms of human society. Pivotal in this regard was their conviction that each individual consciousness potentially contained within it an element of the divine. By endowing the individual with a particular notion of grace, the saints created what has been called "inner-worldly individualism," based on the postulate that the individual man (and, much later, woman) stood at the center of moral and ethical judgments. By radically restructuring the relationship between the elect and the unregenerate, they transformed existing notions of collective identity and social solidarity.[79] In effect, by constructing a polity based on grace, they established a quasi-republican society. By portraying sin as an internal matter—emphasizing conscience over positive law—the saints unwittingly endorsed a world of greater economic freedom. By stressing conscience as the arbiter of personal behavior, they advanced the separation of church and state. By demanding a new form of piety based on the doctrine of the calling, they (again, unwittingly) sanctioned a new type of profit making. In seventeenth-century New England, Protestant salvation theology helped create the ethically autonomous (male) individual even as it rooted all labor and enterprise in communal and other-worldly obligation. This, of course, was emphatically not the case of "individualism" rising at the expense of a declining "communalism." The New England individual was imbedded in community.[80] Inner-worldly individualism emerged as a consequence of, not at the expense of, a revived collective identity and social solidarity within the community of the elect.[81]

As I shall attempt to show in the pages below, these dualisms—along with the Puritans' narrative mythology—proved sources of cultural strength, not weakness, of community, not individualism. In the vehicles of the weekly sermons, as well as the special-occasion jeremiad, the Congregational clergy—with the support of their increasingly female-majority congregations—ensured that there would be some moral check on capitalist excess. In establishing what would become a venerable American tradition, Puritan sermons served as modes of public exhortation joining spiritual renewal to social criticism.[82] John Dod and Robert Cleaver had warned Elizabethan Puritans that God "favours a fair bargainer" and that "He would have commerce and traffic to proceed from love." Portraying economic behavior as a special realm for Christian responsibility, the English divine William Perkins (1558–1602) wrote that "it is the dutie of every Christian man to remember, in all his bargains and dealings, that his manner of dealing must not onely be warranted by the lawes of the land, but even by God's word also."[83]

The same admonitions, the same demands for both moral and marketplace discipline, were voiced continuously throughout the life of the Bay Colony. In 1657, Richard Mather (1596–1669) warned his Dorchester congregation that "experience shows that it is an easy thing in the midst of worldly business to lose the life and power of Religion." In similar vein, Richard's grandson Cotton Mather advised the Massachusetts General Assembly in 1709 that "the business of the City [must] be managed by the *Golden* Rule. The things that used to be done in the market-place, shall be done without *corruption.*"[84] No matter how vigorous a "pretender of religion" a man might be, Mather averred, "if he be not a fair-dealer [in the marketplace] THAT MAN'S RELIGION IS VAIN." Mather promised eternal woe to all "Hypocrites, who can make a show of this and that piety, and *purity,* but can *cheat,* and *cozen,* and *oppress,* and wrong other people in [their] dealing with them."[85] Invoking the Pauline injunction to "Let no man seek his own, but every man another's wealth" (I Corinthians 10:24), Mather grounded economic effort in communitarian motives. As David Levin has aptly observed, Mather "was not marketing religion, but bringing religion into the market."[86]

The chastising efforts of ministers such as Cotton Mather helped increase the likelihood that the Bay Colony would remain a capitalist *commonwealth*—a society that demanded both deferred gratification and a link between individual and collective well-being. The ministers' sermons, as well as the daily devotional labors of mothers and fathers within the New England household, provided a cultural counterweight to unbridled capitalistic behavior, the moral ballast of the developmental state. They helped ensure that the ethics of the marketplace were never unchallenged, never became those later identified with—and castigated as—social Darwinism. The ministers' efforts, along with those of magistrates, church elders, and parents, ensured that if New England was to be a capitalist society, it would attempt to be a just one.

The issue of gender warrants attention here, particularly with respect to women's role in exercising charity (personal responsibility for one's neighbors) and inculcating Puritan social ethics in the young.[87] John Cotton III, in his 1694 sermon *A Meet Help: Or, a Wedding Sermon . . .*, used the language of improvement to advise the Puritan mother to "keep at home, educating of her children, keeping and improving what is got by the industry of the man."[88] The family was the mainstay of New England's civic culture—not least because of prevailing demographic patterns—and the day-to-day responsibility for inculcating the tenets of the culture of discipline perforce laid heavy claims on the energies of mothers and older daughters. Throughout the colonial period, Massachusetts females were praised by clergy and laypeople alike for their maternal role as interpreters and inculcators of Puritan norms. When Dorothy Dudley died in 1643, Anne Bradstreet (1612–1672) memorialized her for being "pitiful to [the] poor, Whom oft she fed, and clothed with her store," a woman who was "A true Instructer of her Family . . . which she ordered with dexterity."[89]

While barred from formal power, in church as well as state, women had played a prominent role in the Puritan movement since its inception. During some of the earliest Elizabethan prosecutions of Puritans in the late 1560s, more females than males were jailed on accusations of separatism. Lay patronesses such as the Countess of Lincoln and Lady Arbella Johnson were highly visible suppliers of financial support and hospitality in the period leading up to the Great Migration.[90] Women were disproportionately represented among the ranks of Puritan radicals and Quakers during the Civil War years of the 1640s. Those constructing London's ramparts and fortifications in 1643 in the face of an expected royalist attack included "Ladies, women, and girles . . . carrying buckets to advance the labour."[91] Women also played a role in reclaiming for Massachusetts Bay Colony the "auncient priviledges" of the first Massachusetts charter after it was vacated by a writ of *scire facias* in 1684. The Reverend Increase Mather (1639–1723), in England from 1688 to 1692 seeking to ensure that "property, liberty, and Our Colledge should all be confirmed to us," credited the intervention of high-born patronesses for the success of his efforts. The Countess of Sutherland, "a very pious and admirably prudent lady," agreed to "sollicit both the King and Queen [William and Mary] with great Importunity to be kind to New England." The Countess of Anglesey, Lady Ann Clinton, and Martha Lockart, "all of them Ladyes of honor belonging to the Court, did . . . pray the Queen's favor to her subjects in New England." That the second provincial charter (1691–1774) retained enough of the Bay Colony's "peculiar priviledges" to prevent it from being "in the same case with New York, Virginia, and the other plantations," Mather ascribed to the advocacy of these high-born dissenting women.[92]

More concretely, there is the issue of the progressive feminization of New England Congregational churches during the second half of the seventeenth century. During this time, New England women were entering communion and owning the covenant in greater numbers than men—and were doing so at an earlier age. From the 1660s onward, church membership in most New England towns became progressively feminized; no first-generation church admitted more men than women in any single decade from the 1660s to the end of the century. Of the churches with extant records, 70 percent registered substantial female majorities of new members during the 1690s.[93] By the closing decades of the seventeenth century, women members outnumbered men by more than two to one in New England congregations, and ministers were taking note of this in rhetoric that later would be associated with the doctrine of separate spheres. In a sermon entitled *Ornaments for the Daughters of Zion* (1692), Cotton Mather declared that "There are far more *Godly Women* in the World than there are *Godly Men;* and our *Church Communions* give us a [practical] Demonstration of it. I have seen it without going a Mile from home, That in a Church of between *Three* and

Four Hundred *Communicants,* there are but few more than *One* Hundred *Men;* all the Rest are Women. . . ." And in a funeral sermon preached for Katharin Willard, Mather memorialized those "Handmaids of the Lord, who tho' they ly very much Conceal'd from the World, and may be called The Hidden Ones, yet have no little share in the Beauty and the Defense of the Land." Mather found this to be true "in many parts of these American Regions . . . in the Cotteges of the Wilderness, as well as in our Capital city."[94]

Conscience, for New England Puritans, was defined as the voice of God speaking within. It was axiomatic among the saints that "an upright Conscience must be the clerk of the Market." For men as well as women in seventeenth-century New England, the acts of producing, buying, or selling were judged according to the same—or higher—moral calculus applied to all behavior in a covenanted society. Treating one's neighbor as oneself demanded fair, not hard, dealing, good, not shoddy, workmanship.[95] John Winthrop began the Puritan enterprise by insisting that each New Englander conform to the ancient Christian injunction to "love his neighbor as himselfe." The leading political theorist of his colony, Winthrop is best remembered today for declaring to his fellow settlers:

> wee must be knitt together in this worke as one man, wee must entertaine each other in brotherly Affection; wee must be willing to abridge ourselves of our superfluities, for the supply of others' necessities; wee must uphold a familiar Commerce together in all meekenes, gentleness, patience, and liberallity; wee must delight in eache other, make others' Conditions our owne, rejoice together, mourne together, labour and suffer together, allwayes having before our eyes Our Commission and Community in the worke, our Community as members of the same body. . . .[96]

New England, of course, never lived up to such Olympian aspirations, and the colony's treatment of Indians, Quakers, and accused witches periodically made a positive mockery of the concept of Christian brotherhood. Even fellow Puritans in England during the 1640s were embarrassed by the ferocity of religious intolerance in Massachusetts Bay.[97] A Covenant People, the Bay Colony's leadership believed, was answerable only to themselves and their God. Indeed, the very potency of the colonists' economic culture—as with capitalism always—brought great destruction to some forms of life even as it was creating a higher standard of living for others. In seventeenth-century Massachusetts the native peoples, not to mention all indigenous flora and fauna, bore the brunt of the saints' mandate to "increase and multiply," to "subdue" and "improve" the land. As early as 1642, Miantonomo, chief of the Narragansetts, was calling on all Indians to unify and defend themselves against the New England settlers: "for you know our fathers had plenty of deer and skins, our plains were full of deer, as also our woods, and of turkies, and our coves full of fish and fowl. But these English having gotten our land, they with scythes cut down the grass, and with axes fell the trees; their cows and horses eat the grass, and their hogs spoil our clam banks, and we shall all be starved." Not for the last time, those who stood in the way of the American economic juggernaut faced the choice of moving aside or risk being crushed. The very strength of community in Puritan New England brought a higher level of exclusiveness—or worse—toward outsiders.[98]

Those within the commonwealth of saints, however, were in part shielded from the excesses of the economic dynamism that ascetic Puritanism fostered. Much of the explanation for this is found in the hermeneutics of "typology"—the belief that Old Testament events prefigured Jesus Christ and the establishment of the New Jerusalem. The communitarian rhetoric of Winthrop's lay sermon, "Modell of Christian Charity"—echoed for a century and a half in ministers' sermons, and enforced by church discipline—provided a powerful and oft-used check on economic individualism. Clerical injunction, church discipline, and parental precept continuously reinforced these principles. By 1640, some seventy-seven practicing ministers had made their way to New England.[99] Cultural brokers par excellence in colonial

America, the ministers' role in representing society to itself and reinforcing its norms was a potent one. The clergy's sermons were—by far—the dominant form of public discourse in Puritan New England. It has been estimated that the average New England churchgoer heard approximately seven thousand sermons in her or his lifetime, totaling some fifteen thousand hours of listening. Sermons were the main vehicles for articulating and preserving the colonists' collective self-consciousness, their self-created mythical identity as a Covenant People. Each Congregational church, some 720 in number in New England by the end of the colonial period, helped impart and reinforce the saints' potent culture of discipline. The three major forms of church discipline—public rebuke; admonition (depriving the accused of the sacraments); and excommunication (preventing the accused from taking the sacraments and voting in church)—gave teeth to the injunction that all walk in "brotherly love and Holy *watchfulness* to the building up [of] each other in the fellowship of Christ." The Congregational ministers' sermons, with their perennial demands for repentance and regeneration, for putting neighbor before self, grounded all economic behavior within a communal context. The clergy's pronouncements consciously tied the ordinary labors and dealings of New Englanders to the colonists' communal identity as God's Elect—and to the salvational drama of New England's mission.[100]

The Bay Colonists' collective self-narrative, particularly with respect to their consciousness of being the "New Israel," was a communal memory that acquired greater, not lesser, potency with the passage of generations. Granted that all peoples construct world views that give meanings to their actions—and employ language to signify these meanings—the federal covenant was an unusually potent form of symbolic expression. The Massachusetts colonists were constantly reminded that they were "the People of Christ" who "ought to behave themselves in War-like Discipline."[101] No other British colony was so self-consciously engaged in the ongoing task of fashioning and refashioning a myth of itself as a community "outside of the world."[102] New Englanders, who hoped to escape the history of human corruption by building a pure church and commonwealth, became the most historically minded of peoples. To a striking degree among New World populations, New Englanders used their "history," their "past," to construct—and reconstruct—their sense of collective purpose and destiny. More than any other New World population they mediated daily behavior through the prism of history—conceived as the hand of God working through secular as well as sacred time. Through ordinary sermons and special-occasion jeremiads, with their distinctive array of tropes, narrative techniques, and rhetorical strategies, New England ministers linked even the humblest woman or man in the commonwealth to the Bay Colony's larger redemptive mission.[103] The *lifelong* conversion process—with its continuous cycles of humiliation and exaltation—made individual saints "zealous in love and labor" in their daily activities. The problem of—always imperfect—assurance of grace was confronted by Congregationalists in the day-to-day actions of faith, repentance, and obedience. Communally, the saints' collective self-consciousness as the covenanted church of visible saints served to spur enterprise, dignify labor, and temper marketplace behavior.[104]

The Massachusetts inhabitants were told by five generations of ministers that they could remain God's New Israel only by restraining avarice and cupidity, by always behaving as one "Community as members of the same body. . . ."[105] Self-criticism was central in this mythology. No other colony was so obsessed with God's "controversy" with its settlers, devoured tracts on the impending "Day of Doom," or accepted at face value ministers' pronouncements that "Degeneracy" was "a greater Evil in us than in any people."[106] Their peculiar confessionally based experience both bound New Englanders together and set them apart from the larger mainstream of British North America. The belief that they were acting according to providential design, revealed in the books of Daniel and Revelations, gave New Englanders their identity and much of their sense of purpose. In Puritan New England, work, enterprise, and social obligation were rooted in a constantly reinforced rhetoric of remembering, cultivating, and passing on a distinctive communal identity. It was in fashioning a self-identity based on the probational nature of the federal Covenant—in creating a "we"—that the Bay Colonists created their distinctive economic culture.[107]

The Puritan clergy's continuous admonitions to their congregations to return to the purported moral rectitude of the founding generation both reaffirmed civic identity and reanimated the colonists' work ethic. The clergy's declarations that personal piety and devotion to the Word were the preconditions for Chosen status endowed economic behavior—and indeed all human activity—with sacred import. While the rhetoric of the ministers' sermons, particularly the more lacerating jeremiads, has too often been taken for reality, their overriding function—in Weberian terms—was to prevent the Protestant ethic (hard work and enterprise) from turning into the "spirit of capitalism" (calculative and secularized rationalism). The jeremiads served to broker, in Perry Miller's terms, the tension brought by a capitalist world the New Englanders simultaneously desired and abhorred.

Within the civic context of seventeenth-century New England, ascetic Protestantism proved to be a splendid instrument for coping with the risks and uncertainties of early modern capitalism. Its social psychology, no less than its religious institutions and social networks, provided seventeenth-century saints with advantages others did not have.[108] It fostered ambition and enterprise and a peculiar orneriness always characteristic of New Englanders. In preaching the fundamentally irreconcilable doctrines of unconditional election and the autonomy of the willing self, Congregational divinity upheld the dialectical foundation of the Reformed tradition. In mythologizing themselves as an "embattled people of the Word," commisssioned by the Almighty to uphold a sacred, exclusive Covenant, New Englanders embraced the culture of discipline. This foundation myth gave meaning to individual lives and meaning collectively—the conviction that each woman and man's life was part of a greater effort, was connected to both the local community and the larger assemblage of the faithful. The covenanted church took isolated individuals and "gathered" them together into one "spiritual and mystical body."[109] Within this corporate community, the saints were constantly reminded that life was a pilgrimage, a struggle to overcome obstacles and resist temptation. Trials, tribulations, even disasters, were burdens to be borne, obstacles to be surmounted. Hard work, enterprise, and frugality were means to these ends. But all genuine rewards would only come in the afterlife. The core of this book's argument is that it was the culture of discipline, based on striving, sobriety, and self-denial, in tandem with the communal myths and civic institutions peculiar to seventeenth-century New England, that gave the Bay Colonists their true comparative advantage.

1

Puritanism, Capitalism, and the "Human Capital" Question

To say that Puritans were capitalists—even of the communal variety—is, of course, to engage in a form of anachronism. The term "capitalism" entered into social analysis primarily as a reaction to the nineteenth-century Industrial Revolution. And, as a consequence of the social depredations brought by that process, the term entered into scholarly discourse primarily by way of hostile critics.[1] Adam Smith, although the founder of classical capitalist theory, never used the term at all in *Wealth of Nations.* And while Karl Marx himself often spoke of "capital," he rarely used "capitalism" as a noun. It was not until the publication in 1902 of Werner Sombart's *Der moderne Kapitalismus* that the word acquired its modern usage. Because Marxism appropriated the communitarian tradition of Western Christianity—with its ideals of social justice and spiritual equality—the development of the market has often been equated with the decline of community. And the transition in New England from the seventeenth-century Puritan community to the nineteenth-century factory town has often served as a paradigm for this process.[2]

Yet even as this interpretation was first being articulated in the late nineteenth century, powerful dissenting voices were being heard, initially within German scientific sociology itself. Max Weber, in what became one of the most influential theories ever offered by a social scientist, contended that by fostering an ethic of systematic acquisition, Puritanism served as midwife to seventeenth-century entrepreneurial capitalism.[3] At points, Weber came perilously close to arguing that without Calvinism—by which he meant English Puritanism—the "capitalist spirit" *(Geist des Kapitalismus)* never would have emerged in a historically viable form.[4] In Weber's formulation, the spirit or "ethos" of that age, in turning from the immanent to the material world, embodied a new concern for economic enterprise. The underlying cause lay not in the rise of secularism or skepticism but in the development of a new kind of religious motivation. Weber coined the term "inner-directed worldly asceticism" *(innerweltliche Askese)* to explain the shift from the conspicuous splendor of Renaissance humanism to the "rational calculating" ethic of the sixteenth and seventeenth centuries. The gravamen of his argument was that anxiety over salvation drove Calvinists to seek assurance in unrelenting work and enterprise, all the while eschewing the temptations of luxury and enjoyment. He declared that "When the limitation of consumption is combined with [a] release of acquisitive activity, the inevitable practical result is obvious: accumulation of capital through ascetic compulsion to save." Only after such an ideological shift had been accomplished could the main lineaments of a capitalist economy—wage labor-capital relationships, reinvestment of surplus, and constantly expanding accumulation—fully emerge.[5]

Scholars of English Puritanism, in contrast to their American counterparts, have traditionally emphasized the individualistic rather than communal dimension of Calvinist social ethics. R. H. Tawney, a Christian socialist, associated the Puritan ethic with the commercialization of agriculture in England in the sixteenth century and the growth of capitalist industry during the seventeenth and eighteenth centuries. Viewing the social consequences of that ethic with considerably more scorn than did Weber, Tawney indicted it for sanctifying riches, degrading poverty, undercutting traditional social obligations, and legitimizing an individualist, competitive, acquisitive capitalist society. Both Weber and Tawney ascribed the so-called "Puritan" virtues—hard work, temperance, self-discipline, thrift—to the renunciatory ethos imposed by predestinarian theology. Updated brilliantly by Michael Walzer as the "disciplined man," steeled for revolution in an age of disorder, the Weberian ideal type reached its apogee in the early 1960s—only to be completely overturned by the new social historians during the 1970s and 1980s.[6]

Refusing to follow Weber, Tawney, and Walzer in viewing religion in instrumental terms, or to accept Louis Hartz's assumption that all of colonial America was "born modern," the new social historians portrayed early New England as a covenanted society in which neighborliness and self-effacement outweighed the claims of the marketplace. The lineal family, patriarchy, ethical consensus, and localism—all imbued with Puritan covenantualism—were presented as the society's dominant values. The seventeenth-century inhabitants of such towns as Dedham, Andover, Ipswich, and Concord were portrayed as communitarian localists, even peasants—unacquisitive, group-oriented, and backward-looking. The most beautifully rendered and influential of these community studies spoke of a society of "One class, one interest, one mind."[7]

There is a large measure of truth in this new view, particularly when compared to the more extreme Weber-Tawney interpretations, or with the work of Progressive or neo-Progressive scholars such as J. T. Adams, Sacvan Bercovich, and William Cronon.[8] Colonial New Englanders *were,* by any measure, more consistent and determined in discountenancing worldliness and self-seeking than their post-Revolutionary successors.

On the face of things, early New England seems to have lacked many of the criteria essential for a capitalist economy. In seventeenth-century New England, modes of conflict resolution—as well as economic dealings generally—were intended to reflect the rule of love as well as the rule of law.

Throughout New England's first century, most conflicts were resolved through arbitration and church discipline, not lawyers and the courts. Informal, face-to-face methods of deciding disputes prevailed, rather than a formalized legal system that treated neighbors and strangers alike. The legal form of the presentment (the opening motion of court proceedings) had not yet taken over from the ecclesiastical form of repentance (the practice of church members resolving disputes among themselves).[9] In the common law courts, plaintiffs still employed the more flexible and open-ended "general issue" rather than more technical forms of pleading. Book debt (kept in merchants' and farmers' account books) and casual loans predominated over more sophisticated financial instruments such as promissory notes, conditional bonds, and bills obligatory. In contrast to the Chesapeake colonies, where fully negotiable sterling bills of exchange were early a central element of local finance, colonial Massachusetts—even by the eighteenth century—relied on depreciable promissory notes for its instruments of exchange. In the Bay Colony, paper money was nonexistent for most of the seventeenth century, as were land banks and speculative bonds. Short-term book debt normally was interest-free. In 1641 the Massachusetts General Court, following English standards since 1624, placed an 8 percent limit on the price of commercial credit. This legislation was complemented during the next decade by a host of (what proved to be short-lived) regulatory laws impeding people's rights to buy, sell, or wear whatever they pleased.[10]

Much appears to support a "pre-capitalist" portrayal of early New England. The primitive state of accounting procedures, the continuation of medieval restrictions on the free use of property, and the absence of banks, a reliable currency, and general incorporation laws, meant that Bay Colonists could not have been full-blown Weberian "rational calculators" even if they had so desired. Perhaps *the* most important "diagnostic of market penetration"—synchronicity and convergence in the behavior of prices—did not emerge until the late eighteenth century in Massachusetts.[11] When compared to a modern finance-capitalist economy, with its stock, bond, and money markets, and its array of such recondite instruments as risk analysis, ratio analysis, pro forma statements, discounted cash flow, derivatives, and dynamic hedging, New England's economy seems almost laughably primitive. Still more important, the Bay Colony remained on the front side of the larger divide between early modern and modern society with respect to the great changes brought by industrialization and urbanization.

This was a society, after all, in which land tenure was in the semi-feudal form of "free and common socage," not allodial property (conveying absolute dominion); and countless legal restrictions curtailed the free alienation of both real and personal property. Wage and price controls and class-based sumptuary laws, although mostly honored in the breach, were found on the statute books of the Massachusetts General Court and the bylaws of most towns until the 1670s. Various bans on imports and exports—like most economic regulation in early New England—were enforced by the use of informers who were paid for their efforts by fines on the offending party. Public authority enjoyed vastly greater *formal* power over production and exchange than it would possess after the ratification of the Constitution. To talk about the economic freedom that is the essential precondition of a fully capitalist economy in the context of such a society seems patently impossible.

As emphasized in the Introduction, the Puritans' very reason for being in New England—their "errand into the wilderness"—was in the service of God, not Mammon. It was the vaulting hope of escaping worldliness, corruption, and licentiousness—in short, of building the New Jerusalem—that propelled the bulk of New England's settlers to America in the first place. Even before they departed for the New World, the General Court of the Massachusetts Bay Company publicly affirmed that "this business might be proceeded in with the first intention, which was chiefly the glory of God."[12] The migrants' own comparison of themselves to the ancient Jews, along with the use of typology, gave a larger cosmic significance to the settlers' need to eschew materialism and cupidity.[13] The need for "weaned affections" lay at the center of Puritan social ethics. Governor Winthrop explicitly warned his fellow migrants against allowing "our pleasures, and proffitts" to usurp God at the center of their lives. Indeed, few states in the early modern world were less receptive to profit seeking for individualistic rather than communal purposes than was seventeenth-century Massachusetts. Those prospective immigrants hoping to come for worldly and self-regarding ends were told candidly to seek their fortune elsewhere.[14]

All this said, there remain compelling reasons to think that Perry Miller's famous allusion to the New England Puritans' "capitalist mentality" is more right than wrong.[15] Even taking into account the issue of historical anachronism, the weight of evidence—particularly in light of the English background of the early migrants—stands squarely on the capitalist rather than pre-capitalist side of the ledger. Either designation, to be sure, involves a degree of arbitrariness and semantic hair-splitting; but when one focuses on the civic institutions and economic culture of Puritan New England, the strong presence of capitalist forms seems undeniable. The Puritans were not "like us"; nor were they "modern" in any meaningful use of that term. Women and men regarded by their contemporaries as atavistic exotics, the saints inhabited a psychological, cosmological, and spiritual universe utterly foreign to late twentieth-century sensibilities. They believed in Providence, not impersonal forces, the soul, not the self. They were intolerant—indeed, bigoted—Calvinists who offered to those who disagreed with their godly vision "free Liberty to keep away from us."[16] They made approved godliness a prerequisite for citizenship and demanded that their civil magistrates punish sinners as well as criminals.[17] In the Bay Colony, the courts dealt with adultery, fornication, "night-walking," non-attendance at church, sleeping during sermons, card playing, and idleness, as well as the traditional array of criminal offenses adjudicated in English common law courts. Although not technically a theocracy, the Massachusetts government had deeply authoritarian tendencies when it believed the federal covenant endangered. Only in seventeenth-century New England was it possible for a man to be banished, as was one Hugh Bewett in 1640, for "holding publicly and maintaining that he was free from original sin and from actual [sin] also for half a year before. . . ."[18]

Yet in economic affairs and the creation of a civil society, the saints' progressive tendencies are unmistakable. There is ample evidence that in their productive activities, exchange ethics, and political economy, the Bay Colonists were discernibly and irrevocably capitalists. In their behavior in the marketplace, in their public policies regarding property, law, contract, and (especially) land tenure, as well as in their Weberian virtues of industry, enterprise, and prudence, the New Englanders, I will argue, had clearly crossed the threshold that separates a pre-capitalist from a capitalist society.

Defining precisely the nature of this capitalist threshold in an early modern setting is an exercise worth doing. Much of the disagreement over whether or not early America was a "capitalist" society derives from the various interlocutors' failure adequately to define the terms being used. Indeed, coping with confusing or contradictory definitions of capitalism has for some time been the principal occupational hazard of the "transition-to-capitalism" debate.[19] Some portray capitalism primarily as an economic system that respects the natural rights of property; others view it principally as a system in which some exploit the labor of others. On the one hand, we have a definition of capitalism that is based on an enterprising ethic and the division of labor; on the other, a definition based chiefly upon an exploitative system of social relations, divided between property-owning capitalists and propertyless and deskilled proletarians.[20] Those hewing to this latter, neo-Marxian interpretation disparage attempts to define "pre-industrial" societies such as colonial America as capitalist. The aim of this theoretical assault, in the pungent words of Fernand Braudel, "is to reduce everything to a post-Marxian orthodoxy: we are not allowed to talk about capitalism before the end of the eighteenth century, in other words before the industrial mode of production."[21]

It would be fruitless to try to establish a historically precise etymology of capitalism; but some working benchmarks may be established to illustrate the kind of economic culture the first English migrants brought to Massachusetts Bay. When, in Greece during the sixth century B.C., coined money came into general use for the first time, it allowed men and women to conceptualize their fields, bushels of grain, and cattle in terms of the exchange value of so many pounds of silver. The use of money as a medium of exchange also allowed all possessions and transactions to be recorded. The Greeks developed a private, money-changing type of banking, and through their imperial and commercial expansion diffused it to Egypt, Israel, India, and Italy. What many would describe as the spirit—and practice—of a form of capitalism was clearly evident in the classical world from the time of Periklean Athens onward. In the *Republic,* Plato described—and disparaged—usurers as those who "multiply their capital by usury." Although the Greeks and Romans developed advanced institutions in the fields of property law and commercial exchange, their bookkeeping practices remained primitive. They thought in terms of receipts and expenditure, not credit and debit. In a departure from Greek practices during the classical and Hellenistic ages, the Republican Romans developed a respect for legal documents, inscribed on *tabulae,* as reliable and final acts. In Roman law the word "capital" referred to the principal of a loan, as distinct from interest or other carrying charges.[22]

The ancients, however, lacked a genuinely transnational market. Not until the papacy gave support for a single, transnational market following the coronation of Charlemagne in A.D. 800 could such an entity be said to be coming into being. The Europeans' self-conception of themselves by A.D. 1000 as the "People of Peter" helped foster the spread of market relationships because people thought of themselves as a single community. By the time of the period of papal decline during the first half of the eleventh century, an international market centered in Italy had developed. By the twelfth century, the growth of capitalist forms was unmistakable. The term "capital" (from Late Latin *caput,* "head") by the mid-twelfth century had come to denote funds, merchandize stocks, coin, and money carrying interest. By the early fifteenth century, we find such theologians as Bernardino of Siena (1380–1444) speaking of "that prolific cause of wealth we commonly call capital."[23] In the writing of Bernardino, arguably the most brilliant economic thinker produced by classical scholasticism, we also discover an embryonic version of the theory of marginal utility, one that would not be substantially improved upon until the work of Bernardino's fellow countryman, Ferdinando Galiani (1728–1787) four centuries later.[24] The sources of value for Bernardino were threefold: utility *(virtuositas),* scarcity *(raritas),* and pleasurableness *(complacibilitas).* The word "capitalist" itself, in Braudel's view, likely dates from the mid-seventeenth century.[25]

The "transition-to-capitalism" question originated with Adam Smith's theory of the self-developing division of labor. This theory postulated that Continental and English feudalism transformed itself into capitalism by way of the division of labor, catalyzed by the growth of trade and competition. The division of labor, for Smith, was the main source of economic growth and technological innovation in commercial societies. The widening of the market, he contended, increased the division of labor and hence both the productivity of labor and the wealth of the nation (or, in the language of neoclassical economics, productivity was increased by overcoming indivisibilities). The genius of *Wealth of Nations* was its elaboration of this insight. Smith's opposition to mercantilist doctrines favoring state aid to a nation's merchants and manufacturers against foreign competition was based on the premise that such policies led to the contraction rather than expansion of the market.[26]

During the early seventeenth century, Smith argued, the two main components of capitalism—individual private property and widespread wage labor—became conspicuous features of the English economy as a result of the progressive division of labor. For Smith, the division of labor reflected—and heightened—the level of development in the productive forces. Promoted by constantly growing world trade, the division of labor reshaped the social relationships of class and property by the beginning of the seventeenth century. Under the self-ordering economic system, economic growth occurred when individuals used their savings ("funds") to pay wages to workmen who produced commodities to be sold on the market, thereby augmenting the fortune of both the individual saver and the larger society. The result was a tripartite division of economic interests ("the three great, original, and constituent orders of every civilized society") based upon the particular means of production: those deriving incomes from rent; those living off the profits of stock or capital; and those reliant on wage labor.[27]

Generalizing at a high level of abstraction, Adam Smith clearly exaggerated the decisiveness of this transformation. Neither by land tenure law, nor social structure, nor any other category was England *feudal,* even by the reign of Henry VIII (1509–47). Political and social changes dating back before the Angevin period, particularly with respect to the precocious nature of state building, had ensured as much. Central government in England dated from the reign of William I (1066–87) or earlier. Political and economic feudalism was declining from the twelfth century onward, although social and legal feudalism lasted much longer. (Land law, in particular, continued to be based on the quasi-feudal arrangements of tenures in fee simple.) Since the reign of Henry I (1100–35), no English baron was legally entitled to erect a castle without a license signifying the King's consent, and central government began to replace the system of local military power introduced by the Normans. The great judicial reforms of Henry II (1154–89), particularly the expanding use of itinerant judges, grand juries, and the extension of royal justice generally to parties in civil disputes, provided the lineaments of the modern civil state (although the only social groups who had access to royal courts were monied freemen). The English monarchy, in sum, was "the only lay power in Western Europe to establish a common law by the beginning of the thirteenth century."[28]

Central government facilitated the expansion of a national market. As early as the ninth century, English monarchs had apparently established an extensive network of marketing centers. By the late thirteenth century, patterns of wages, rents, and agricultural specialization reveal the strong presence of market forces in England.[29] Between a third and a half of English villagers during the thirteenth and fourteenth centuries worked less than three acres of land; they thus derived much or all of their livelihood from wage work.[30] At least in the short run, the peasants profited by the imbalance between land and people brought by the Black Death in 1347–48. By the time of the Great Revolt of 1381, the peasantry was in the throes of a major transformation. Peasant holdings were being redistributed, mobility in the labor market was increasing, and copyhold tenure was replacing bond tenure. Even this early, the working population significantly exceeded the number of peasant holdings. Individual private property as well as widespread wage labor were extant in England by the early sixteenth century, well before the reign of James I (1603–25). Likewise, Adam Smith's emphasis on England's constantly growing trade is undercut by the serious trade depressions of 1594–97, 1604–08, 1615–17, 1619–23, and 1626–31. Not until 1660 can it be said that England's world trade underwent a quantum expansion. Smith was correct, however, in his contention that by the early seventeenth century, England—unlike France, Spain, Poland, and Germany—had no peasantry in the Continental European sense.[31]

What is commonly called the transition to capitalism, therefore, began well before the early modern period (1500–1800). It was the product of long-term changes that even before the twelfth century had been taking place in the enclaves of capitalist activity—trading towns, merchant houses, and guilds.[32] With the late medieval shift of Europe's economic center from the Mediterranean littoral to northwest Europe, the way was paved for the emergence of mercantile capitalism. When, in the sixteenth century, the Atlantic finally supplanted the Mediterranean as the center of the international trading economy, much of the transition to capitalism had already been accomplished. Some locate the origins of both mercantile capitalism and the Enlightenment in the forced migration of Protestants from the older centers of commerce and Erasmian humanism such as Flanders, northern Italy, and southern Germany during the sixteenth and early seventeenth centuries.[33] Others, more persuasively in my view, point to the rise of the slavery-based "Atlantic system," with its potent—and unprecedented—combination of African labor, European capital and technology, and American land. One scholar states categorically that from the sixteenth to the nineteenth centuries, what moved along Atlantic sealanes "was predominantly slaves, the output of slaves, the inputs to slave societies, and the goods and services purchased with the earnings on slave products." Either scenario, however, helps account for the dramatic capitalist surge at the beginning of the seventeenth century, first in Holland and second (and more decisively) in England.[34]

The patrimonial mercantilism destroyed by capitalism's rise was, in the main, not a regime favorable to laboring men and women. As Adam Smith was among the first to see, the traditional, aristocratically dominated society that capitalism undermined was something other than hospitable to laboring folk. Appalled to discover during his sojourn in France (1764–67) that the peasants there paid a killingly high proportion of their income to the state, Smith believed that his "system of natural liberty" could not help but allocate resources in a more equitable manner.[35]. Some estimate that as late as the eighteenth century, France suffered in excess of sixteen general famines, as well as local famines on virtually an annual basis.[36] Smith ascribed such suffering to the traditional corporatist "system of Europe" and looked to British America for a practical vindication of this belief.

England's "precocious" transition to capitalism gave grounds for optimism on this issue. Although both Prussia and France as late as the eighteenth century remained traditional juridically defined "societies of orders" (divided into those who pray, those who fight, and those who work), by the seventeenth century England already exhibited Smith's "constituent orders" of wage laborers, rentiers, and merchant-capitalists. The hallmarks of traditional society still being visited upon the European peasantry—confiscatory taxation, arbitrary law enforcement, and chronic malnutrition—were for the most part absent from the English countryside. Secular fluctuations of wages and prices could—and during the late sixteenth and early seventeenth centuries, did—wreak great hardship among laboring women and men, but Continental-style exploitation was a thing of the past for most English people.[37]

As Max Weber noted, it was during the Reformation era

that the rational-legal state played a decisive role in breaking patrimonialism and the remnants of feudalism. It did so by freeing land and labor for the capitalist market and by incorporating a formalistic legal code based on due process. Weber's principal criterion for distinguishing pre-capitalist from capitalist production was a labor force that was free from control by guild, village, or municipality. Such freedom allowed for the private appropriation of the means of production, and their allocation and use according to calculations of maximal efficiency. Only the state can legitimate the activities and institutions—profit seeking and property—that make possible a capitalist society.[38] For Weber, state action and Calvinist social ethics had the effect of making an already progressive people the more so. Protestantism, Weber rightly insisted, was a significant agent of modernization. Along with the Dutch during their Golden Age, the seventeenth-century English had clearly made the transition from a patrimonial to a modern state, or, in Weberian terms, from patrimonial capitalism to rational capitalism.[39]

Seventeenth-century England, by a number of criteria, was more highly evolved and politically progressive than any nation in Europe. It was almost unique in the early modern world for its lack of tolls and trade barriers between cities and between provinces. It was the only nation-state embracing a large territory with a single, unified coinage. It was also deeply influenced by the widely shared and culturally potent concept of the "freeborn Englishman," dating back to Runnymede (or indeed in some ways back to the *gens Anglorum* of the Venerable Bede [ca. 673–735]), as well as by the absence of a Continental-style Roman law tradition. The English were famous—or infamous—throughout the early modern world for their desire for personal and economic freedom and for their generally anti-authoritarian ways. The relative weakness of the absolutist tendency in England, the absence of a parasitic "tax-office" state doling out sinecures to royal favorites, the comparative smallness of the English court, and the early prominence of liberal free trade doctrines, all made a social crisis on the order of the French Revolution unlikely in England's transition to capitalism.[40]

During the sixteenth and seventeenth centuries, England

experienced a virtually unprecedented political evolution, one that heavily stamped the kind of civic and religious institutions—and attitudes—brought to Massachusetts Bay by the Puritan migrants. This evolution included the early and rapid development of a unified national state; the establishment of Parliamentary rule and the concurrent restraints on the growth of absolutism (both inspired by a rising fear of popery); the reduction of the "bastard feudal" local magnates; and the monopolization of the legitimate use of force by the central government.[41] It included such benchmarks as the Petition of Right in 1628. With the power of royal authority increasing in Europe, "only in England did another coherent rhetoric—the rhetoric of law, liberty of the subject and the common welfare—emerge durable enough effectively to hold its ground not against but alongside the rhetoric of monarchical glory and grandeur."[42] Similar claims could be made for the Poor Law of 1601. When Elizabeth's government accepted, however reluctantly, responsibility for the relief of suffering, a major step was taken toward the development of the modern bureaucratic state. English policymakers were among the first to understand, however embryonically, that the growth and expansion of the market economy demanded the creation of counteractivities in the public realm.[43] Moreover, these needed to focus less on regulating economic activity (wage and price laws, statutes against forestalling, regrating, hoarding, and the like), and more on providing a safety net for those displaced by market forces. By the beginning of the eighteenth century, England had experienced the rise of a powerful legal-bureaucratic state designed to function in a capitalist economy, with the full apparatus of an outdoor relief system, national bank, deficit financing, and a permanent civil service. In less than a century and a half after 1530, England had experienced a conversion to Protestantism; revolutions in statecraft, agriculture, commerce, and printing; a dramatic growth in the metropolis of London; and an even more dramatic expansion of the rate of literacy.[44]

While the reasons adduced for England's priority are legion, the rise of literacy sparked by the realm's conversion to Protestantism seems the most compelling. An economic backwater by the time of the dissolution of the monasteries in the late 1530s, England was threatening to become a colossus a century later. Because the Renaissance, Reformation, and Enlightenment occurred almost simultaneously in England during the period between 1530 and 1630, the realm's conversion to literacy and scientific naturalism came with astonishing speed. Much of this change may be accounted for by the shift from script to print, fueled in large part by the Reformation. Before 1500, the total number of books printed throughout all of Europe and the British Isles was approximately 35,000, the vast majority in Latin. There followed a communications revolution unmatched until the present age of computers, electronic mail, videocassettes, and desktop publishing. From the 1530s onward, England experienced a dramatic expansion in the number of Bibles, almanacs, pamphlets, and broadsheets printed. The result was the creation of the early modern world's first reading public.[45]

The fact that the Puritan upsurge coincided with, and indeed was fostered by, the first era of mass communication through print needs to be underscored. Protestant reform and the newly developed print culture fed off and reinforced each other, as we shall see at greater length in Chapter 3. The link between Protestantism and the printing revolution was immediate and unmistakable. During the 1520s in the Lutheran regions of the German principalities, four times as many books were published as were printed during the preceding decade. The determination of William Tyndale (?1494–1536) and Miles Coverdale (?1488–1569) to translate the Bible from the Greek and Hebrew so that even "the boy that driveth the plough" could read the Scriptures bore fruit in the Great Bible of 1539. It, along with the Geneva Bible of 1560, served as the mainstay of English Protestantism until the publication of the King James Version in 1611. By the mid-seventeenth century an astonishing 600,000 Bibles had been printed and sold in England, along with nearly a million psalters and New Testaments. English Puritans discovered that they could use devotional literature to socialize their children and instill confessional identity and loyalty. The English saints, according to John Sommerville, "were the first to write books exclusively for children and the first to show an awareness of the difficulties involved in communicating with them."

Equally significant was the rapid expansion of schooling spurred by Protestantism. It was during the seventeenth century, particularly within English-speaking populations, that formal training in the use of pen, ink, and paper became readily available in cities and large market towns.[46]

During the seventeenth century, almanacs competed with the Bible in sales, providing much astrological nonsense, but also uniform tables for computing the costs of goods and payment of wages, conversion tables for weights and measures, and distance estimates between trading towns. Printed arithmetics, practical manuals, and maps joined with the proliferating devotional works and martyrologies. Double-entry bookkeeping, although originally developed in thirteenth-century Italy (apparently aided by the introduction of Arabic figures), did not penetrate the rest of Europe until the printing revolution made cheap manuals widely available. Moreover, printing, typefounding, publishing, and bookselling—in England no less so than on the Continent—remained overwhelmingly Protestant preserves. It was the printing revolution, when coupled with the Protestant determination to substitute scriptural reading for the Mass as a person's decisive encounter with God, that helped produce the first vernacular-reading public.[47]

The new field of political economy was witnessing changes of an equal magnitude. By the early seventeenth century, wealth was increasingly being redefined into the more dynamic terms of productive capital. The great pamphlet debates in England during the 1620s among Gerard de Malynes (1586–1641), Edward Misselden (1608–1654), and Thomas Mun (1571–1641), occasioned by the realm's severe trade depression and currency shortage, brought many of these issues before a larger reading public for the first time.[48] The focal points of these debates—foreign exchange rates, international trade policy, and currency depreciation—helped redirect English trade policy away from its earlier preoccupation with the accumulation of treasure for its own sake and toward the means by which to encourage international commodity exchange.[49] It was during the 1620s, largely through the advent of the mercantilists' "balance of trade" theory (which held that the state should promote a favorable balance of trade, particularly in manufactures), that debates over the distinctions between wealth, capital, and currency found popular expression. In *England's Treasure by Forraign Trade* (written during the 1620s and published posthumously in 1664), Thomas Mun distinguished between "natural" and "artificial" wealth. The "one is naturall, and proceedeth of the Territorie it selfe: the other is artificiall and dependeth on the industry of the inhabitants." National prosperity, for Mun, was achieved by combining a minimum of natural with a maximum of artificial wealth in the creation of commodities for sale abroad. He attributed the dramatic economic rise of the Dutch Republic to the use of this formula, particularly in its herring industry. Mercantile exchange was also increasingly defended as a positive social good. Edward Misselden, in his writings from the 1620s, asserted that commercial exchange was pleasing to God because it bound people to one another. Merchants were portrayed (by mercantilist writers who were often themselves merchants) as "Stewards" of the nation's wealth.[50] Ethical issues, for most of the new mercantilist writers, were relegated to the individual conscience, and the state's role became that of superintending the general economy. While in 1571 Parliament passed a law against the "sin" of usury, in 1624 it regulated interest rates for the public good.[51] In a parallel but distinct body of thought from the mercantilists, natural law philosophers such as Hugo Grotius (1583–1645) and Samuel Von Pufendorf (1632–1694) provided the nucleus of value and price theory. In Adam Smith's terms, such dynamic conceptions of wealth were what separated the "stationary" (static) economy from the "progressive" (expanding) one.[52]

Sanctioned gain also achieved normative status. The intellectual justification for the pursuit of gain—for the purpose of bettering oneself and the community—was in part provided by the revolution in rationalism and in moral and political philosophy carried out in the sixteenth and seventeenth centuries. The rationalist revolution, which was largely the work of Machiavelli, Spinoza, Erasmus, Bacon (and eventually Hobbes and Locke), helped redefine unlimited acquisition from a sin to a "public-spirited excellence."[53] In addition, the religiously based notion of "improvement" led naturally to the eighteenth-century concept of "betterment." Not for the last time, Protestant religion and secularizing philosophy worked through opposite means to accomplish similar ends. Acquisitiveness, previously regarded as a socially destructive vice, was openly defended by Edward Misselden and Thomas Mun during the economic policy debates of the 1620s. Misselden averred that gain always has a public as well as a private dimension. He asked rhetorically, "What else makes a Common-wealth, but the private wealth?" The ethic these writers endorsed was *not* raw economic individualism, but—as the history of Puritan New England illustrates—an acquisitiveness disciplined by an awareness of communal obligation.[54]

The creation of a literate, urban-based "middling class" which was embracing the new political economy, along with the peculiar social structure of early modern English agriculture, with its large landholdings and tripartite class divisions between landowners, capitalist tenant farmers, and wage laborers, made Tudor-Stuart England a distinctive society. The contrast with France, with its proliferation of smallholdings (and with its much slower rate of industrialization) is especially telling. With an average holding of 100 acres, in contrast to France's 30, seventeenth-century English landowners found it much easier to accumulate the capital necessary to develop industrial and semi-industrial enterprises. The French were also much slower than were the English to adopt the Dutch-inspired "New Husbandry" (consisting of new crops, the elimination of fallowing, and the stall feeding of cattle). It was the sum of all these conditions that laid the basis for the eighteenth-century industrial revolution in England. Robert Brenner's convincing argument for England's "precocious transition from feudalism to capitalism" suggests that the founders of Massachusetts Bay Colony were bearers of a culture that was already capitalist when they arrived in the New World.[55]

The commercialization of English agriculture during the period from 1550 to 1660 permanently ended, although at great social cost initially, the ancient demographically based cycle of abundance and dearth.[56] While a combination of poor harvests and trade depressions brought periods of genuine dearth to Tudor-Stuart England—especially in 1594–97, 1604–08, 1615–17, 1619–23, and 1626–31—the overall trajectory of change was toward sufficiency. Parish rolls for the County of Essex between 1560 and 1599 show a significant surplus of births over deaths. Disregarding migration, natural increase would have brought a doubling of the population during Elizabeth's reign.[57] England had escaped the Malthusian cycle. Early seventeenth-century English men and women had "crossed a barrier which divided them from their own past and from every other contempory society."[58] The ancient restrictions on the free disposition of one's grain—the laws against forestalling, engrossing, and regrating—began to fall by the wayside, as food abundance eliminated the older rationale for public control of work and production (in the name of the subsistence needs of society). Without the regulatory and protective restrictions justified by food scarcity, grain—the only product ever systematically subjected to price controls—could simply be regarded as an interchangeable, market-priced commodity. The public recognition of this fact had taken place by the mid-seventeenth century.[59]

Here, it is important to take note of the role of serendipity in capitalism's rise. The intellectual and institutional changes being described here depended to a great extent upon the triumph of mechanical philosophy over the Scholastic Aristotelianism and Neoplatonic theory that had preceded it. As the writings of Governor John Winthrop reveal clearly, the Puritan movement emerged amidst the larger intellectual transition from an organic image of the universe to a mechanistic one, from scholasticism to Baconian science, indeed, from custom to contract.[60] The abrupt collapse of Scholastic economics after a reign of some five hundred years was brought about not by the Reformation or the rise of capitalism but by the revolution in natural science. When the Aristotelians refused to accept the new discoveries in experimental science, their economic philosophy became as discredited as their antiquated astronomy, cosmology, physics, and medicine.[61] The Scholastic doctors, Aquinas, Albertus Magnus, and John

Duns Scotus, had viewed economic problems primarily from the vantage point of ethics and social justice. They were much less concerned with the actual operation or efficiency of the economic system. With the collapse of the ethically based Scholastic economics, the amoral principles of mercantilism filled the vacuum. Responding to Gerard de Malynes's condemnation of merchants for seeking their private gain *(Privatum Commodum),* Edward Misselden openly defended the merchants' right "to seeke their *Privatum Commodum* in the exercise of their calling."[62]

As Misselden's wording suggests, sanctioned gain was given an additional—historically decisive—stimulus by the Puritan doctrine of the calling. The Puritans, arch foes of all forms of worldliness, created a work ethic that, at least in a New World setting, was almost certain to expand one's worldly goods. In one of Puritanism's apparently inexhaustible store of ironies, the New World settlers most openly and militantly disdainful of "works-righteousness" ended up creating a work regime more rigorous than was found in those societies believing that work *could* be meritorious (could lead to salvation). Indeed, Weber and his followers argued that it was the calling, as much as anything else, that helped shift English people inexorably toward the new capitalist order. In the language of the period, the calling demanded that Christian men and women devote virtually all their waking hours to "improving their time and talent" for the greater glory of God.[63]

By the early seventeenth century, Puritan writers' emphasis on stewardship and the positive duties of the Eighth Commandment had created a powerful imperative to increase one's estate.[64] The colonization of New England itself was justified on such grounds by clerical and lay writers alike. In such cases where piety and profit "jump[ed] together," Plymouth Governor Edward Winslow (1595–1655) declared in 1624, the will of God was clear:

> Not that we altogether, or principally propound profit to be the main end of that [which] we have undertaken; but the glory of God, and the honour of our country, in the inlarging of His Majesty's dominions. Yet wanting out-

> ward means to set things in that forwardness we desire, and to further the latter by the former . . . hoping that where religion and profit jump together, which is rare . . . it will encourage every honest man, either in person or purse, to set forward the same.[65]

As Winslow's careful distinctions reveal, this was something quite different from raw economic individualism. The doctrine of stewardship mandated that profit seeking be firmly grounded within a communitarian setting. Acquisitiveness needed to be tempered and disciplined—although not officially controlled—by a respect for communal obligation. This indeed was the essence of communitarian capitalism.

The greater one's surplus, the more there was to share with one's church and community. In 1619 the Reverend Jeremy Dyke rejected the idea that "men having enough should give up their calling and receive in no more." Rather, they should endeavor to accumulate additional wealth—for the good of the community. They should "make the overflow of their cup serviceable" to their neighbors.[66] In 1616, in a tract entitled *The Plea of the Poore,* the Reverend John Downame laid out an especially comprehensive rendering of this argument. He declared that "because Scriptures require that we should be bountiful and plentiful in good-works, this should increase our care and diligence in preserving and increasing of our estates, by all lawful meanes, in acquisition and getting by our honest and painefull labours in our callings, and by our frugall husbanding and thriftie spending of our goods, that so having greater plentie we may be the richer in good workes." John Preston (1587–1628), Master of Emmanuel College, Cambridge, and a man deeply revered by the Massachusetts settlers, bluntly declared that "to have blessed opportunities, and not to use them, is a signe [that] we [lack] love to Christ."[67] Defending the principle of stewardship even more forthrightly, Presbyterian divine and former army chaplain for Cromwell Richard Baxter (1615–1691) provided as pithy a rendering of the Protestant ethic as one could hope to find: "If God show you a way in which you may lawfully get more than in another way (without wrong to your soul or any other), if you refuse this, and choose the less gainful way, you [violate] one of the ends of your calling, and you refuse to be God's steward, and to accept His gifts and use them for Him when he requireth it: you may labour to be rich for God, though not for the flesh and sin."[68]

Spurred by the doctrine of the calling, the rationally calculating profit motive gained a much wider general acceptance in both secular and sacred discourse. The mid-sixteenth-century author of *A Discourse of the Common Weal* frankly declared that every man seeks "where most advantage is." In 1621, nine years prior to the Puritan migration, Thomas Culpeper, Sr., could confidently assert that "private gaine is the compass men generally saile by." During the debate in the Bay Colony in 1639 over censuring merchant Robert Keayne for price gouging, Governor John Winthrop admitted that the impulse to buy cheap and sell dear was universal, even within the commonwealth of saints. In 1656, in a pamphlet entitled *A vindication of a regulated enclosure,* the Anglican minister Joseph Lee asserted the "undeniable maxime, That every one by the light of nature and reason will do that which makes for his greatest advantage." Gain for the purpose of personal advancement, as well as for the good of the community, was now explicitly condoned, even by the clergy. Lee asked rhetorically, Why are God's glory and "our own gains and advancement of our estates . . . alwaies incompatible?" Moses himself, Lee averred, even while leading the children of Israel to the promised land, "had an eye also to the recompense of reward."[69]

Such cultural changes represented if not the triumph of a "bourgois" mentality, then at least emergence of a "middling-rank," anti-aristocratic sensibility. It was this "advanced" and enterprising cast of mind that both Adam Smith and Karl Marx regarded as the most distinctive feature of British migrants to colonial America. Adopting the language of economic culture, Marx and Engels went so far as to attribute the rapid economic development of English America to this collective *mentalité.* In the *German Ideology,* they describe the colonists as individuals whose "consciousness can sometimes appear further advanced than the contemporary empirical relationships. . . ." Furthermore, in

> countries which, like North America, begin in an already advanced historical epoch, their development proceeds very rapidly. Such countries have no other natural premises than the individuals, who settled there and were led to do so because the forms of intercourse of the old countries did not correspond to their wants. Thus they begin with the most advanced individuals of the old countries, and therefore with the correspondingly most advanced form of intercourse, *before this form of intercourse has been able to establish itself in the old countries.*[70]

The social background and resources of the first English emigrants to Massachusetts Bay suggest that Marx and Engels were correct in this assessment. The Puritan migrants to New England were drawn predominantly from the most commercial regions of the mother country. These were areas in which the trade structure of the larger provincial cities had shifted from relatively unskilled industrial production toward skilled crafts, with attendant gains in administrative and marketing efficiency. Some 60 percent of the immigrants during the Great Migration hailed from either provincial market towns or large commercial centers such as Norwich, Salisbury, or Canterbury. These migrants regularly participated in the diversified market economies common in the region between the Stour and Humber river valleys. The larger English towns contained a wide spectrum of occupations and, in the cases of Norwich and Canterbury, supported major textile industries as well as myriad commercial activities. Far from being wedded to a "household mode of production," the migrants—both as producers and consumers—daily participated in local economies of considerable scope, scale, and sophistication.[71]

Likewise, the non-urban immigrants were drawn overwhelmingly from the commercially oriented wood-pasture agricultural communities and the "champion" (unenclosed) mixed-farming areas. No region in England, however, was a self-contained world. Even the most remote parish was touched by seventeenth-century England's system of open markets, fairs, and private trading.[72] The wood-pasture emphasis on cattle and pig raising—a practice that intensified in Massachusetts—necessitated daily access to local and regional markets, both for the sale of meat and dairy products and for the purchase of foodstuffs for household consumption. These were also areas in which manorial institutions such as the courts leet and baron were particularly weak and thus exercised minimal control over farming practices. East Anglia, in general, witnessed some of the greatest increases in the authority of the ecclesiastical parish in the wake of the decline of the manor and village courts.[73]

The East Anglian heartland of the Puritan migration (Norfolk, Suffolk, Essex) was not only the most agriculturally innovative region of England but also one of the centers of both the textile trade and rural industries in general. With its mixed economy, partially enclosed farm system, and wood-pasture agriculture, East Anglia was well suited to become the cradle of capitalism in England. Indeed, some scholars believe that East Anglia had possessed a distinctively innovative culture for several centuries. Past center of Lollardy (with its Puritan-like pietism, use of the vernacular Bible, and anticlericalism) and future recruiting ground for the Eastern Association (heart of the New Model Army), East Anglia had been England's most progressive region since at least the end of the fourteenth century.[74] Its New World descendants carried on this tradition.

Thomas Barnes has aptly noted that "The wilderness was primaeval, but Massachusetts society was not primitive." The Massachusetts Bay Company itself was a creation of the Puritan-minded London commercial class, a significant number of whom brought their skills and contacts to Boston, Salem, or Ipswich, there to carry on their oceanic trade with many of the same commercial contacts as before. Also numbered among the some seventeen to twenty-one thousand settlers who came to Massachusetts Bay during the Great Migration were a disproportionate number of university matriculates, most of whom were clergymen. Between 1630 and 1650, some 104 matriculates from Cambridge and 29 from Oxford had made their way to New England. But ministers were not alone in the possession of a high level of learning and skills. A number were highly trained in the law: Governor John Winthrop was an attorney in Wards; Nathaniel Ward and John Humfrey were barristers; Richard Bellingham was a counsellor and recorder; the younger Winthrop and several others had been at the Inns of Court. In addition to the fact that many Bay Company officials were merchants, most settlers were urban artisans from market-oriented regions. Their endowment of physical assets was also impressive. Uniquely with the settlers of that other Holy Commonwealth, Pennsylvania, the Massachusetts migrants liquidated large amounts of property in England—farms, shops, businesses—to finance their move to the New World. These monetary resources enabled the settlers to transport thousands of cattle, pigs, sheep, horses, and goats to Massachusetts during the 1630s. The livestock not only provided the initial basis of the Bay Colony's domestic economy but ensured that the saints would escape the starving time common to the founding period of other colonies.[75] The New England settlers also arrived in generally intact social units. Instead of the solitary, youthful, and impecunious adventurers who made their way to the Chesapeake and West Indian colonies, Massachusetts' migrants were drawn largely from the middling classes and they came in nuclear families or even entire communities. The age structure of the emigrant population almost exactly mirrored that of the mother country. More indefinably, Puritans were drawn overwhelmingly from what contemporaries called the "industrious sort," men and women whose self-discipline and striving behavior had already marked them off from what they described as the "mixed multitude." The Renaissance gentleman—defined by his aversion to manual labor—was conspicuous by his absence.[76]

The Bay Colony's first settlers, like most early modern Englishmen (and the Scholastics and Platonists before them), equated a "good economy" with contentment with one's station. Gerard de Malynes, the one pamphleteer from the economic debates of the 1620s that we know the Massachusetts General Court officially consulted, defined a good economy as one in which every member "should live contented in his vocation." But in early Massachusetts, it did not take long for the combination of the Protestant ethic, labor shortage, and land abundance to undermine such hierarchical prescriptions.[77] It did not take long for it to become evident that labor, a painful necessity in the Old World, could lead to increased productivity—and social mobility—in the New.[78]

2

An "Honest Gaine": John Smith, John Winthrop, and the Political Economy of Colonization

It was Captain John Smith (1580–1631), the self-styled "Admirall of New England," who first grasped the region's potential as a "middling"-rank society. While sailing along the stark but hauntingly beautiful New England landscape in 1614, Smith remarked that it lacked but "the long labor and diligence of industrious people and Art." In constructing what proved to be New England's first "culture of development" argument, Smith asserted that the trilogy of work, industry, and enterprise would make the region the equal of "any of those famous Kingdomes, in all commodities, pleasures, and conditions." Throughout his colonial writings, Smith spoke frankly of the material well-being that successful settlement would produce. If "New England"—as Smith named the region during his voyage—were "cultivated, planted and manured by men of industrie, judgement, and experience," it would equal, if not surpass, the fertile isle for which it was named. With mixed farming and fishing both likely to thrive in the region, Smith confidently predicted that a middling-rank standard of living would quickly be attained. And at the heart of Smith's ethic—unlike Governor John Winthrop's—lay a vision of social mobility. Those who would enjoy the fruits of this society, the captain believed, would be England's hardpressed people of "small meanes." Indeed, for Smith, providing a haven for such men and women was very close to the whole point of New World colonization.[1]

In his "note for men that have great spirits, and smal meanes," the captain declared his wish to "finde imployment for those that are idle, because they know not [where to find work]." Smith asked rhetorically: "Who can desire more content, that hath small meanes; or but only his merit to advance his fortune, then to tread, and plant that ground hee hath purchased by the hazard of his life? If he have but the taste of virtue, and magnanimitie, what to such a minde can bee more pleasant, than planting and building a foundation for his Posteritie, gotte from the rude earth, by God's blessing and his owne industrie. . . ?" It was Smith's passionate belief that, in New England, "every man may be master and owner of his owne labour and land; or the greatest part in a small time."[2] With a substantial portion of England's laboring men and women working for the local gentry in a condition of quasi-vassalage, Smith's aspiration was a genuinely radical one.[3]

Few questions were so compelling to Englishmen in the early modern era as the ownership of one's own labor. The growing disrepute of wage labor during the early seventeenth century was a direct result of the general economic crisis of that period. If, in an era of declining real wages, such work led only to poverty and dependency, then only men and women who controlled their own labor could be regarded as free. To lose control over one's labor was inevitably to compromise one's liberty and security along with everything else bound up in the ancient but potent notion of "freeborn Englishman." Not even the radical Levellers during the Civil War period favored granting the franchise to wage laborers.[4]

And, as the propagandists of colonization well knew, the prospects of controlling one's own labor as a waged worker, craftsman, or husbandman appeared to be growing more—not less—precarious by the early seventeenth century. The period from 1590 to 1650 witnessed a succession of some of the worst employment crises ever experienced by the British Isles. Population growth was behind much of this. From a population of 2.25 million in the 1520s, England grew to some 4 million souls by 1603. A 1607 report to the House of Lords declared the need for the government to find "vent" for the realm's apparently surplus population, "either by transferring to the wars or [the] deducing of colonies." Earlier improvements in diet had spurred a dramatic growth in the laboring-age population, and the "multiplication of hungry mouths" in turn stimulated commercial farming. In 1564, the County of Essex had shipped 1,086 quarters of grain to London's market; by 1625, this figure had risen to 12,765. A greater reliance on commercial agriculture led to greater social shocks when population growth outstripped food supply. Increasingly by the 1590s this began to happen. A rapidly expanding population outran the supply of both food and work; and a series of bad harvests—together with textile depressions, enclosures, estate consolidations, rising prices, and falling wages—brought hardship to laborers and small producers alike.[5]

The rise in commercialized agriculture, with its resort to larger holdings and economies of scale, eventually produced sufficient long-term gains in efficiency by 1660 to enable England to feed most of its population. By this time, copyholders were being replaced by commercial tenants who adopted crop specialization, invested their surplus income, and embraced improved agricultural methods. Throughout the eastern counties especially a "proliferation of middlemen—higglers, badgers, poulterers, fishmongers"—now helped link the individual producer and the larger market. Commercial expansion brought considerable social dislocation, but also raised the general standard of living. Edward Chamberlayne (1616–1703) could assert in 1669 that England's laboring ranks lived as well as did husbandmen (tenant farmers) elsewhere: "The lowest member, the feet of, the body politic, are the day labourers, who by their large wages given them, and the cheapness of all necessaries, enjoy better dwellings, diet, and apparel in England than the husbandmen do in many other countries."[6] England suffered virtually no food crises from 1650 to 1725, a period in which France experienced a succession of regional and general famines. Whereas in France oat and barley prices invariably rose following a failure of the wheat crop, this was not true in England.[7]

But, in the transitional period leading to this improvement, the social costs were exceedingly high. Laborers, cottagers, and artisans whose wages had earlier allowed them to keep their families above the subsistence level could no longer do so. The result was the infamous era of Hugh Make-Shift, with its proliferation of masterless men, vagrants, beggars, drunkenness, and criminality. By some estimates, unemployment and underemployment had brought nearly one quarter of England's laboring population to the edge of starvation. After a decade and a half of relative prosperity and peace following the Anglo-Hispanic treaty of 1604, England's economy went into a nearly forty-year-long crisis. Some have contended that the decades of intermittent extreme hardship from 1616 to 1650—culminating in the indiscriminate pillaging by both Royalist and Parliamentary armies during the Civil War—were among the most difficult years through which the country ever passed. In Cambridgeshire, the real value of the wages of agricultural laborers stood at its lowest point by the second decade of the seventeenth century, only 44 percent of its fifteenth-century level. Estimates are that between a quarter and a half of the population of Stuart England was chronically impoverished. Skilled artisans and the yeomanry did not belong to this group, but it most likely included a majority of both unskilled and semi-skilled workers: cottagers, agricultural laborers, and industrial workers such as weavers.[8] Although the general crisis of the early seventeenth century was doubtless less severe than the medieval famines of 1360–90, 1405, 1413, and 1422–23, to those living through it the very disintegration of the social order seemed at hand. In particular, the commercialization of agriculture had disentangled both farming and industry from the myriad bonds of social obligations of manor, village, and guild.[9]

These socioeconomic dislocations were especially acute in the "wood-pasture" regions from which the majority of the Puritan migrants derived. Unlike the "sheep-corn" regions of communal settlements organized according to open-field principles, the dispersed dairy-farming regions such as John Winthrop's south-central Suffolk were buffeted by one severe economic dislocation after another. It was in these regions that the price revolution, the decline in real wages, and the depression of the woolen cloth industry brought by the Thirty Years War caused the greatest social shocks. The need for a culture of discipline had social as well as religious roots.[10]

Remedies for the general crisis, as John Smith's vision makes clear, centered on the problem of unemployment. Such a focus was inevitable, given prevailing conceptions of political economy. Early seventeenth-century English economic theorists continued to define a healthy economy by the level of employment, not the level of productivity. The extent of "full" employment, not comparative advantage in the allocation of capital, served as the measure of productive efficiency. Although pamphleteers during the economic policy debates of the 1620s were beginning to shift the focus to capital accumulation and investment, prosperity was still largely equated with the amount of spending necessary for full employment. For those concerned with public policy, although no longer for individual entrepreneurs, profit was calculated by net spending on labor, not by returns in productivity. An employment crisis produced an economic crisis, not the other way around. Work, in this soon-to-be-abandoned view—like bullion, like wealth generally—was still usually seen in zero-sum terms. It was not expandable; the more for some, the less for others. It is here that we find the logic for restrictions against multiple occupations and early entry of apprentices in the regulatory legislation of Tudor England. Even the enterprising "projectors," who were aware of the new capitalist world that was aborning, remained wedded to the equation of employment with prosperity. The risk-oriented merchant-entrepreneurs who were creating new industrial and business enterprises in Caroline England measured the success of their schemes "only by the amount of work they created."[11]

Likewise, the writers of the economic tracts that proliferated during the seventeenth century—Edward Misselden,

William Petty, and Nicholas Barbon in particular—bewailed England's lack of employment opportunities and portrayed work, including make-work, as the foundation of prosperity and stability. In *The Circle of Commerce* (1623), Misselden found the main causes of England's economic distress in the forced idleness of the poor and the excessive consumption of the rich. He called for the creation of a publicly funded "stock" by which the poor could be set to work creating commodities for export. Anticipating a proposal later made in Massachusetts by the Reverend Hugh Peter, Misselden suggested that a fishery be established by such means, both to increase the food supply and to decrease England's dependence on foreign nations.[12]

Unemployment, as a result, was used as one of the principal rationales for colonization. Imperial propagandists (such as Smith and the Hakluyts) and Puritan advocates such as John Winthrop and John White alike portrayed America as a haven for England's surplus laborers. A stanza from the Puritan epic poem *Good News from New-England* invited the distressed English wage laborers to seek their fortune in Massachusetts:

New rais'd from sleepe, another cries, my earnings are but small,
I'le venter to this new-found world, and make amends for all.[13]

For a nation so militantly Protestant as was Stuart England, the unemployment brought about by the general crisis was a spiritual as well as a practical issue. A people that defined earthly labors in terms of the calling could hardly brook massive unemployment. It was for this reason that we find John Winthrop, as one of the leaders of the newly organized Massachusetts Bay Company, arguing for colonization in 1629 in terms remarkably similar to John Smith's. Colonization would represent, Winthrop declared, "Charity to our neighbors impoverished by decay of Trade and left destitute of hope of imployment in tyme to come, who may comfortably be sustayned by their labours in [America] yielding them sufficient matter of imployment and meanes of recompense."[14]

With both eloquence and compassion, Winthrop sketched out what amounted to the Puritans' political economy of labor recruitment. Like John Smith, Winthrop directed his major concerns toward the plight of men and women of small means, although for Winthrop this group denoted the small husbandmen more than the laboring poor. For the Puritan theorist, self-sufficiency was the key. When, in the "Modell of Christian Charity" (1630), he wrote that divine Providence "rancked [humankind] into two sortes, rich and poore," Winthrop did *not* define the former as the truly opulent, but rather "all such as are able to live comfortably by their owne meanes duely improved."[15] The most lamentable consequence of the general crisis, accordingly, was the cost in stunted lives and stifled hopes brought by England's twin scourges of overpopulation and underemployment. So grim was the situation, he averred, that the worth of human beings had been reduced to that of animals. England had grown "weary of her Inhabitantes, soe as man whoe is the most praetious of all creatures, is here more vile and base than the earth we treade upon, and of lesse prise among us than an horse or a sheepe." "Our shops [are] full of rich wares," Winthrop complained, yet "under our stalls lie our own flesh in nakedness." The vagabondage and beggary produced by the general crisis had so reduced normal feelings of communal and familial obligation to the less fortunate that the state had been compelled to intercede. Masters, Winthrop asserted, "are forced by authority to entertaine servants," and "parents [had to be ordered] to maintaine there owne children." The towns, too, "complaine of the burthen of theire poore, though we have taken up many unnessisarie yea unlawfull trades to mainetaine them."[16]

Objecting yet again to the intrusive nature of Crown regulation brought on by the general crisis (and sounding a theme that would be repeated in Adam Smith's *Wealth of Nations*), Winthrop directly attacked the labor settlement acts deriving from the 1601 Poor Law (which barred those on relief from moving to another parish in search of work). Restricting the mobility of labor was objectionable on both ethical and utilitarian grounds. Once in New England, Winthrop would help see to it that such practices were not adopted by the Bay Colony. On the eve of his departure, he explicitly decried the fact that "we use the authoritie of the Law to hinder the increase of our people, as by urginge the Statute against Cottages, and inmates." Summing up his general indictment of the human cost brought by the widespread lack of opportunity, he attacked England's labor settlement laws head on: "thus it is come to passe, that children, servants, and Neighboures, especially if they be poore, are [counted] the greatest burthens, which if things weare right would be the cheifest earthly blessinges."[17]

The Reverend John White (1575–1648), one of the founders of the fishing-oriented Dorchester Company, joined Smith and Winthrop in portraying colonization as a "mercy" to laboring folk. The fishing plantations projected for coastal New England were inspired by "Compassion towards the Fisherman" of England's distressed West Country, as well as "some expectation to gain." In his influential *The Planter's Plea* (1630), White contended that while voyages to Newfoundland "prove more beneficial to the merchants," those to New England "are farre more profitable to poore Fisherman."[18] For White, as for John Smith, it was the envisioned combination of fishing and farming—in a free labor economy—that promised to make New England a haven for those of small means.

Undergirding, and in part inspiring, the pronouncements of Winthrop, Smith, and White was the Protestant redefinition of the concept of Christian charity—a concept that had undergone a major transformation during the Reformation. By the late sixteenth and early seventeenth century, particularly in the writings of William Perkins, William Ames, and Lancelot Andrews, charity had come to be seen as a reciprocal responsibility rather than a paternal obligation. A theology based upon notions of universal depravity and the priesthood of all believers had scant use for the Platonic-Scholastic world of essences and immutable hierarchies. Protestant Christianity, by teaching that all men and women are equal in the eyes of a God who surpasses all worldly authority, helped subvert notions of hierarchy that dated back to the ancients. Indeed, it was precisely this cast of mind that Weber saw as producing the democratic and entrepreneurial element of Calvinism.[19]

Charity, in the new dispensation, ceased to be an obligation of a superior human essence to an inferior—and needy—

human essence, and became instead an assertion of "the love that spontaneously seeks out a brother's misfortune and acts to relieve on a principle of equal regard."[20] The new theological egalitarianism of the Protestant world could no longer accept the inevitability that the poor would always be with us. Paternalism had always rested on the immutability of a society of orders. The rich had been obliged to offer charity and succor to the poor, who in turn were expected to be content with their social station and deferential toward their superiors. In the eyes of Puritan reformers, both these expectations were rendered problematical. Measures needed to be taken, from both an Enlightened and a Reformed perspective, to give men and women the means to pull themselves out of poverty—and to keep middling-level folk from falling into it. The 1601 Poor Law reflected not only the principle that all Christians have a *duty* to labor but the corollary that all men had a *right* to work.[21] For seventeenth-century Protestants, equal regard meant equal opportunity to work.

Few groups grasped the social implications of this ideological shift more fully than did the English Calvinists, especially those bound for Massachusetts Bay. For these theorists, genuine charity must consist of the gift of dignified work that alone could signify a state of justification. Charity that consisted simply of alms and relief would not do—it harkened back too much to the idealist traditions of Thomistic and Dantean Christianity. Worse still, anticipating the argument made by Benjamin Franklin in *On the Labouring Poor* (1768), such succor was represented as confirming the recipient in his idleness. As the preachers intoned, "beggars commit sacrilege who abuse the name of Christ, and make their poverty a cloak to keep them idle still." According to the English divine Lancelot Andrews (1555–1626), the only form of charity that genuinely benefited the destitute was work. It was charitable "to employ them in such sort [of occupation] as they may do good." The sturdy poor could thereby be physically and spiritually rehabilitated and restored to membership in the commonwealth.[22] Charity demanded that the poor be weaned from any tendencies toward idleness and moral waywardness by requiring them to embrace the dignity of work. Beneath all of these formulations, however, was the assumption that there was sufficient work to go around. And in early Stuart England, all believed, there was not.

For Puritans, as for Captain John Smith, the New World was a sign of God's Providence for His Chosen. It would offer, as England no longer could, a sufficient reward for their labors. And this applied to the yeomanry and substantial artisans as well as husbandmen and laborers. While the majority of the 70,000 Britons who left their homeland for America and the West Indies during the 1630s were drawn from the laboring classes, as we have seen, the 17,000–21,000 migrants to Massachusetts included disproportionate numbers of urban artisans and substantial farmers. With these in mind, John Winthrop asked rhetorically on the eve of his departure from England: "why then should we stand striving here for places of habitation etc. (many men spending as much labour and coste to recover or keepe sometimes an acre or twoe of Land, as would procure them many [hundred] as good or better in another Countrie [America]) and in the meane time suffer a whole Continent as fruitfull and convenient for the use of man to lie waste without any improvement?" In a similar vein, Salem minister Francis Higginson lamented to his former neighbors in Leicester, England, "Great pity it is to see so much good ground for corn and for grass as any is under the heavens, to lie altogether unoccupied, when so many honest men and their families in old England through the populousness thereof do make very hard shift to live one by the other."[23]

Artisans faced similar pressures, particularly in the depressed villages of the textile regions of East Anglia. The onset of the Thirty Years War in 1618 deprived the cloth-manufacturing counties of many of their European markets, resulting in lower prices for English cloth and higher unemployment for those directly and indirectly involved in the textile industry.[24] In recounting the reasons why he migrated to New England, the Ipswich tailor John Dane pointed to the depression-related "conservation of work" philosophy embraced by English tailors. His testimony also underscores the resentments striving behavior could provoke in a constricted economy. As a young man, Dane had gone "to live in the chief place in Hatfield town, and [taken] an apprentice and kept a journeyman." Yet "the [existing] tailors were so disgusted at it that they made [complaints to the local gentry] to get me out of the town; for, said they, 'he takes up all our work, and we know not how to live.' "[25] The Reverend John Cotton, in a sermon preached at the departure of the Winthrop fleet in April 1630, pointed to the population pressures on artisans as one of the main justifications for emigration. The saints, Cotton declared, needed to "settle a Citty or Commonwealth elsewhere" because "Nature teacheth Bees to do so, when as the hive is too full, they seeke abroad for new dwellings." For Cotton, it was clear that "when the hive of the Commonwealth is so full, that Tradesmen cannot live one by another, but [rather] eate up one another . . . it is lawfull to remove."[26] Honest labor in Caroline England, in John Winthrop's view, promised some artisans less reward than did chicanery. English tradesmen could not expect an adequate recompense for their time and labor "except falsehood be admitted to equall the ballance."[27]

In economic terms, what all these observers were saying was that increasing population in England had produced diminished returns on both labor and capital investments. As labor-land ratios increased, both average and marginal returns to labor effort fell to progressively lower levels. In America, as Smith and Winthrop had foreseen, these ratios would reverse themselves. It was that reality, when combined with the settlers' work ethic and civic institutions, that led to the Bay Colony's swift economic development.

In the eyes of Protestant reformers, New England was well suited to serve as a haven for England's displaced workers on both practical and moral grounds. Fish, John Smith correctly predicted, would serve as the "maine Staple," allowing settlers who had "nothing but [their] hands" to "set up a [fishing] trade, and by industrie quickly grow rich; spending but halfe that time well, which in England we abuse in idelness, worse or as ill." Most important of all, said Smith, fishing—in contrast to tropical staples requiring slavery and the exploitation of unfree labor—would "return an honest gaine." He, like Winthrop, wanted a world where workers earned their bread through the sweat of their brow. In particular, Smith was at pains to avoid the nakedly exploitative European colonization of Mesoamerica and Peru where what "the Spanyard got was chiefely the spoyle and pillage of [the Indians] and not the labours of their own hands." This form of enterprise was known to contemporaries as "present profit" (raw greed). It sought immediate wealth at any cost rather than gradual and moderate returns on sustained investments of capital and labor. To a considerable degree, this distinction between honest gain and present profit is the principle that animates the entire corpus of Smith's colonial writings.[28] It was a distinction grasped by both a self-made yeoman like Smith and a Puritan gentleman like John Winthrop.

At the heart of this principle, at least for John Smith, lay a distinctive attitude toward work and the disciplines of upward mobility. Smith was among the first to recognize that America offered the promise of a new type of middling-class society, one in which workers could expect to keep the fruits of their labors—and thereby better their condition. The promise of freehold property would foster individual industriousness and general economic prosperity. And the basis of this middling-class society was the dignity of labor. As his reference to "the long labor and diligence of industrious people and Art" suggests, for Smith the promise of America was a bourgeois society.[29] Expressing a political economy that would extend through John Winthrop, William Petty, John Locke, John Wise, Tom Paine, John Adams, Waldo Emerson, Abraham Lincoln, and John Dewey, Smith envisioned a world where everyone who labored would receive the fruits of his labor. It was to be a world where work was dignified and where there were no feudal barriers to trades—or secure land tenure. In New England, Smith predicted confidently, there would be "no hard Landlords to racke us with high rents, or extorted fines to consume us." Above all, in New England—indeed this was the whole point of the enterprise—"by industry" settlers might "quickly grow rich," but "Riches [would be] their servants, not their Masters."[30]

This was to be a fishing and farming republic populated by improving citizens and governed by enlightened entrepreneurial elites. Men would fish in the morning and tend their farms in the afternoon. Their leaders would be "no silvered idle golden Pharisies, but industrious honest hearted Publicans." Leaders would seek "provisions and necessaries for their people" rather than "jewels, ease and delight for themselves."[31] For John Smith, like John Winthrop, early New England was to be a world of dignified and disciplined work—for everyone.

Smith's and Winthrop's respective visions for America highlight the difficulty of distilling "Puritan" from "English" influences in the forging of the Bay Colony's political economy. What such a comparison yields is a broad basis of agreement—except over social mobility and the "Errand into the Wilderness." All across the board, the parallels between the economic visions of Winthrop and Smith are manifest. In agriculture, industry, commerce, public policy, even the ethics of exchange, the two men saw virtually eye to eye. Where they did differ was in the captain's overt endorsement of social mobility and the governor's determination to build a "Citty upon a Hill." Both of these fixations, however, had developmental consequences.

Smith and Winthrop embraced what could be described as a form of moral capitalism, the philosophical keystone of communal capitalism. They advocated an "honest gaine," to be achieved through regular and orderly returns on investments of labor and capital. Risk taking there would be—why else would Smith build his enterprise on a foundation of "men of great spirits"?—but this risk taking would be, in Max Weber's terms, of the rational calculating, not adventurous Venetian, variety.[32] Both men discountenanced the lust for "present profit" achieved through get-rich schemes and gold hunting. Both believed that New England should be formed as a commonwealth in which men and women would work in order to "entertain one another in brotherly affection." Both contended that New England's future lay in a mixed fishing-farming-extractive economy, complete with such fully industrial enterprises as ironworks and shipyards. Because of the region's minimal resources, both men believed that the Bay Colony settlers would have to learn commerce or perish. Both understood that real financial incentives for the settlers would be required if New England was to develop properly.

The point of departure for both men was that wealth was to be achieved "by labour." And that applied to everyone. New

England was to be a society without drones and without queen bees. Merchants, ministers, magistrates, even the governor, were expected to perform manual labor when necessary. This was to be a society with laborers but without a distinct laboring class. While in Virginia, Smith had remarked that if colonies were to succeed, they needed "neither more Masters, Gentlemen, Gentlewomen, and children than you have men to worke, which idle charge [will be found] very troublesome, and the effects dangerous." Smith's bitter experience with the large number of feckless gentlemen among Virginia's first settlers led him to conclude that "one hundred good laborers [would be] better than a thousand such Gallants as were sent [to] me, that could do nothing but complaine, curse, and despaire."[33] But with one hundred good laborers, Smith believed, anything was possible.

More than is sometimes appreciated, John Smith's traumatic experience in Virginia—culminating in his being forced out of the colony in 1609—shaped his plans for New England. The two and a half years of death, disease, disorder, and chaos had persuaded Smith that only settlers with a strong work ethic should be allowed to colonize the New World. His trials in trying to get work out of idle dilettantes and roistering street urchins, not surprisingly, left no appetite for further contact with either group. It is even possible that he conveyed these convictions to John Winthrop when the two men met briefly on the eve of the Great Migration.

What these "loyterers" and "roarers" had in common, Captain Smith believed, was an almost complete aversion to disciplined labor. Indeed, Smith declared, far too many men for Virginia's survival "would rather starve than worke."[34] Together, the loiterers and roarers were the targets of the captain's oft-quoted "President's order for the drones." With the infant Virginia Colony on the brink of starvation and collapse because of the idleness and disorderliness of the populace, Smith informed the settlers that "since necessitie hath not power to force you to gather for your selves those fruites the earth doth yeeld, you shall not only gather for your selves, but those that are sicke." Echoing St. Paul's injunctions in II Thessalonians 3:10, Smith declared that those who would not work would not eat.[35] Moreover, in a gesture that one suspects would only have been made in English America, Smith established his own labor as the standard the "drones" would have to emulate. The captain ordered that "he that gathereth not every day as much as I doe, the next day shall be set beyond the river, and be banished from the Fort as a drone, till he amend his conditions or starve." This order, Smith observed, "many murmered was very cruell." But "it caused the most part so well [to] bestire themselves, that of 200 [settlers] . . . there died not past seven" that winter.[36]

Greed no less than idleness could destroy a colony, as again Smith had learned in Virginia. The London Company's lust for present profit instead of an honest gain had resulted in a labor force composed of "Refiners, Gold-Smiths, Jewellers, Lapidaries, Stone-cutters, Tobacco-pipe-makers, Imbroders, Perfumers, [and] Silkemen, with all their appurtenances."[37] With such a proliferation of impracticable luxury craftsmen dispatched to Virginia between 1607 and 1609, it came as no surprise to Smith that the young colony soon found itself gripped by a gold fever. Ordinary work and essential tasks for survival in the wilderness were shirked in a vain rush to find precious metals or exotic crops. With visions of the Spanish silver mine at Potosi dancing in their heads, the colony's settlers ran after every mad scheme to find instant enrichment. The worst, reported the captain, were "our guilded refiners with their golden promises [that] made all men their slaves in the hope of recompenses." There was, Smith lamented, "no talke, no hope, no worke, but dig gold, wash gold, refine gold, loade gold, such a bruit of gold, that one mad fellow desired to be buried in the sands" in order that the sand would "make gold of his bones."[38]

For Smith, the lust for present profit was what destroyed the Virginia Company. And it was a lust shared by investors, merchants, Company officials, the King, and the settlers themselves. Immediate rather than long-term returns on investments of time or money were sought and no sense of working for the greater collective good was recognized. Corporatist checks on destructive individualism were weak or nonexistent. Most important, the Virginia experience violated Smith's sovereign prescription for an honest gain—that all profits come "in tyme by industry." There was in early Virginia neither deferred gratification nor a linkage between individual and collective well-being. It was in the realm of civic ecology that the contrasts between Virginia and Massachusetts would be the most pronounced. In Virginia there were no town meetings to forge and express the public will. Appointed commissioners at the county level, not elected selectmen at the town level, governed day-to-day life in the Old Dominion. The institutions that so successfully produced Massachusetts' abundant store of social capital—strong families, churches, townships, schools, colleges—were weak, embryonic, or nonexistent in seventeenth-century Virginia.[39]

Virginia's fixation was on economic, not human, development; on present profit, not honest gain. Captain Smith emphasized that those London merchants and investors who expected present profit from New World colonization were doomed to disappointment (as, more poignantly, were the settlers whose lives depended on them). "Hastie hopes" for present profit, Smith declared, invariably led to failure, even disaster. This, the captain recounted for all who would listen, was exactly what had happened in Virginia. During the Company period, that colony had violated an essential principle of Smith's political economy: a secure material basis needed to be laid before attention could be turned to the major profit-producing commodities desired by investors. In prose burning with indignation and sarcasm, Smith attacked the shortsightedness of the Company's directors. Responding to criticisms that he failed to provide instant returns on the adventurers' investments, Smith replied:

> whilst I and my company tooke our needlesse pleasures in discovering the Countries about us, building of Forts, and such unnecessary fooleries, where an Egge-shell (as they writ) had beene sufficient against [the Indians]; neglecting to answer the Merchants expectations with profit, feeding the Company only with Letters and tastes of such commodities as we writ *the Country would afford in tyme by industry,* as Silke, Wines, Oyles of Olives, Rape, and Linsed, Raisons, Prunes, Flax, Hempe, and Iron; as

> for Tabacco, we never then dreamt of it. Now because I sent not their ships full fraught home with those commodities, they kindly writ to me, if we failed the next returne, they would leave us there as banished men.[40]

Smith reserved his greatest outrage for the investors' failure to acknowledge the tremendous labor required for successful colonization. They acted "as if houses, and all those commodities did grow naturally, only for us to take at our pleasure." Not hiding the deep bitterness beneath his sarcasm, the captain observed that "we did admire how it was possible [that] such wise men could so torment themselves and us with such strange absurdities and impossibilities, making Religion their colour, when all their aime was nothing but present profit."[41]

This tragic and self-defeating scenario was what Smith and John Winthrop were determined to avoid repeating in New England. Smith's political economy reflects such a determination. Neither will-sapping communalism nor egotistic individualism would be permitted. As a son of the Lincolnshire yeomanry, he doubtless endorsed the seventeenth-century English saying that "everyone's work is no one's work." As Smith knew, the greatest hardships and starving times in both Virginia and Plymouth occurred before the conversion from communal to private land ownership. The Puritan colony on Providence Island (1630–41), where land tenancy and rigid control from London prevailed—in part to avoid the Virginia experience—would tell a similar story.[42] The best guarantee of personal industry, Smith believed, was a link between labor and land ownership. Indeed, the link between land ownership and productive labor came close to being the centerpiece of John Smith's vision. The captain's writings make it clear that he understood, at least in inchoate fashion, that the engine of capitalism—the drive to expand one's capital—rested most firmly on a foundation of private property. Without the promise of freehold property, the motivation necessary to spur workers to the requisite effort would be lacking. This Smith was determined to provide. The early histories of both Virginia and New Plymouth had shown the futility of sharp oscillations between excessive communalism and excessive individualism. Directly echoing Captain Smith, Plymouth's Edward Winslow warned in 1624 that the "vain expectation of present profit" was nothing less than the "overthrow and bane" of plantations. The London merchant Matthew Cradock, in his proposals for creating a fishing industry in Massachusetts, declared that it would only succeed if it were established "without expectations of present proffit only."[43]

Laying out a carefully calibrated formula for economic advancement, Captain Smith had shown the prospective New Englanders how to avoid both the Scylla of lassitude and the Charybdis of greed. Emphasizing that "many hands make light worke," he repeatedly called for a society in which all were required to perform manual labor. In order to encourage honest gain instead of present profit, he built in incentives for land clearing and cultivation. This was to be a society where the labors of those of small or moderate means would produce an almost revolutionary measure of mobility. The captain declared his intention to

> let every man so it bee by order allotted him, plant freely without limitation so much as hee can, bee it by the halfes or otherwayes. And at the end of five or six yeares, or when you make a division, for every acre he hath planted, let him have twenty, thirty, forty, or an hundred; or as you finde hee hath extraordinarily deserved, by it selfe to him and his heires for ever; all his charges being defrayed to his lord or master, and publike good.[44]

In calling for up to a hundredfold recompense for the number of acres planted—and for linking the sum of individual productivity to the "publike good"—Smith made profit-based mobility the engine of his economic system. Smith, like Thomas Mun in *England's Treasure by Forraign Trade,* overtly conceptualized wealth in dynamic, expansionary terms. Each producer in pursuing his own interest would add to the nation's aggregate wealth. By expanding one's capital, society's capital would expand correspondingly.[45]

Like most of the pamphleteers in the economic policy debates of the 1620s, Captain Smith made material incentives—particularly the lure of private property—the centerpiece of labor recruitment. The lessons of the Virginia experiment were twofold for Smith: The search for short-term profit leads to failure; and the link between productive labor and land ownership must be recognized. The desire to provide oneself and one's family with a comfortable level of subsistence Smith regarded as natural and even commendable—so long as acquisitive instincts were tempered by ethical scruples and respect for the public good. And not the coercive hand of state regulation, but the normative values inculcated by families, churches, and schools, were to be the principal means for achieving this end. Conscience, for John Smith, no less than for the Puritans, was to be the most efficacious way of regulating economic behavior. These cautionary warnings were, of course, staples of seventeenth-century Protestant rhetoric, whether of the Puritan variety or not. As Boston minister John Cotton would emphasize, it was the *motive* behind accumulation that was all-important. The great Puritan casuist William Ames had declared that "not every desire of riches is covetousnesse, but only the inordinate love of them; and that love is inordinate which is repugnant to the love which we owe to God, or our Neighbor."[46]

The very distinction between present profit and an honest gain suggests that working for one's "own benefit and comfort" had a legitimate place in Smith's political economy. In his *Description of New-England* (1616), Smith wrote candidly that "I am not so simple, to thinke, that ever any other motive than wealth will ever erect [in New England] a Commonweale; or draw companie from their ease and humours at home, to stay in New England to effect my purposes."[47] The captain said that "hee is double mad that will leave his friends, meanes, and freedome in England, to be worse there [in America] than here." In the most evocative expression of this view, Smith based the appeal of New World colonization on the promise of upward mobility. He asked what person with "judgement, courage, and any industrie or qualitie [of] understanding, [would] leave his Countrie, his hopes at home, his certaine estate, his friends, pleasures, libertie, and the preferment sweete England doth afford to all degrees [of people], were it not to advance his fortunes by injoying his deserts?"[48] In Smith's world, it was to be the lure of gain, not the pull of tradition or the whip of authority, that brought men and women to their labors.[49]

And by enjoying one's deserts Smith meant acquiring land. If his acreage compensation formula was faithfully followed, he predicted, even the humblest, most indigent migrant would significantly "advance his fortune." "A servant," Smith boldly declared, "that will labor within foure or five yeares may live as well [in New England] as his master did here [in England]."[50]

John Smith's writings, as well as his experiences in Virginia, may have influenced the actual settlement of Massachusetts Bay more than we have realized. The captain himself had little doubt that the founding of both Virginia and Massachusetts were the fruit of his own efforts. At the time of Jamestown's settlement in 1607, New England was known as the "North Part of Virginia." In 1624, with a characteristic lack of modesty, Smith had declared that Virginia and New England were "but [two] pigs of my owne Sow." In the year of Massachusets Bay's founding, he wrote to the Bay Colonists, "I am ready to live and dye among you, upon conditions suting my calling and profession to make good, Virginia and New-England, my heires, executors, administrators, and assignes."[51] Smith's *General Historie of Virginia, New-England, and the Summer Isles* (1624) provided one of the most comprehensive and accurate guides to the Indians, natural resources, and topography of Massachusetts Bay, in addition to its riveting portrayal of the trials of early Virginia.

The planners of the Puritan migration could not have avoided, even if they had wished, the lurid stories about Virginia—provided by John Smith and many others—that circulated in London on the eve of the Great Migration. But there are more palpable clues to this potential influence. We know that Smith took considerable heart from his meeting with Winthrop shortly before the latter's departure for Massachusetts Bay in 1630. We also know that as he lay dying a year later, Smith publicly consoled himself with the belief that at least in New England, his dreams for proper New World development would be realized. The captain described himself as "over glad" to see the New England Puritans—who he described as "Industry her selfe"—"adventure now to make use of my aged endevours."[52]

And make use of them they apparently did. As Massachusetts governor, John Winthrop constantly held up Virginia as a counterexample. To Winthrop, Virginia represented the inevitable fate of an uncovenanted people, governed by the sinfulness of "natural liberty," and driven almost entirely by worldly motives. Like Smith, Winthrop ascribed the failure of the Virginia Company to the lust for "present profit"—although his interpretation of this deformity was shaped in part by the specific Puritan concept of the covenant. Winthrop declared his determination to avoid the three "great and fundamental errors" committed by Virginia's labor recruiters. First, Winthrop was persuaded that the many misfortunes experienced by the London Company settlers could only be explained by their spiritual impoverishment. The fact that "their mayne end was Carnall and not Religious" doomed the colony from the start, he believed. The London Company's organizers sought worldly profit from staple crops, precious metals, or new trading routes to the East; the prospect of creating a Holy Commonwealth and pure churches beckoned them not at all.

The second error, and the one Winthrop dwelt most upon, was the lack of disciplined probity in the Virginia labor force: "They used unfitt instruments, a multitude of rude and misgoverned persons, the very scumme of the Land." Instead of relying on godly, sober, and disciplined laborers, the Virginians accepted profane, licentious, ungovernable folk: street urchins from London, vagrants from the countryside, and luxury craft tradesmen. (It is here, of course, that one discerns most clearly the famous Elizabethan distinction between the worthy and unworthy poor.) With Virginia's notoriously weak civic, religious, and familial institutions, the one thing that bound this motley crew together was extreme acquisitiveness. The results, for Winthop, were predictable. The reports of starvation, brutality, and chaos that emanated from Jamestown confirmed the Puritan leader's views on the social consequences of natural liberty unchecked by church or community. Unshackled by what Winthrop defined as "civil liberty," the freedom to do *only* that which was "right and just" in the eyes of civil authorities, Virginia's first settlers turned on the Indians, their leaders, and each other. In so doing, they turned their Eden into a charnelhouse.

The unloosening from customary cultural moorings that New World colonization entailed demanded a culture of discipline. It meant that the settlers needed to be more than naturally self-regulating and self-disciplined. More to the point, a settlement that in the eyes of most of its early inhabitants was designed to advance the Protestant Reformation—or even bring on the Second Coming—needed to be composed of "fit instruments." The fate of the Covenant People, as several generations of mothers and fathers, ministers and magistrates never tired of intoning, depended upon it. To avoid provoking the wrath of God, and ultimately forfeiting the covenant, the New Englanders (as Winthrop declared in "Modell of Christian Charity") would need to prevent licentiousness and materialism from "breaking out" among them. They would need to build their entire society on the culture of discipline. Virginia's failure to establish a culture of discipline, along with the third "great and fundamental" error—the failure to "establish a right form of government"—boded certain destruction for the colony.[53]

Virginia's mistakes in labor recuitment were precisely the ones the Puritans were eager to avoid. Indeed, both the chosen method of labor recruitment and the structure of the Massachusetts Bay Company itself were designed to prevent their repetition. The underlying principles of the Puritans' labor recruitment efforts were based on the need for disciplined probity. These principles were spelled out by Winthrop in 1629 in a series of axioms:

(1) It is granted by all that this intended plantation is a worke both lawfull and honorable.

(2) It must be advanced by persons gifted for such a worke.

> (3) Every one that is fitt hath not a minde to the worke and noe bond of conscience cann ordinarilie be imposed uppon him that hath noe desire to it.[54]

Winthrop's assertions that men and women needed to be "gifted for such a worke" and that "noe bond of conscience" could be imposed on the unregenerate suggest the predestinarian interpretation of the work ethic. Skills, in the absence of "a minde to the worke," were not enough, Winthrop believed, to qualify a settler for membership in the Puritans' New Sion. Those who lacked motivation and incentive, as John Smith had discovered in Virginia, made the very process of colonization impossible. They were drones instead of workers; instead of creating the commonwealth, they destroyed it.

It would be a mistake, however, to see Winthrop's comments as implying that *only* Visible Saints possessed the requisite work ethic. Indeed, the Protestant notion of the calling mandated precisely the opposite stance. In their understanding of the calling, the Protestant reformers displayed their greatest confidence in the malleability of human nature. Nowhere did the saints sound less Augustinian; nowhere did they display greater charity toward the unregenerate. In the preachers' use of the ideal of the calling, there is surprisingly little concern with human frailty. In "no other area of dogma is there such generous treatment of the reprobate; all men are not only capable of a calling, but must follow one. Work is the godly in prayer, but in the ungodly, too, it is regarded as creative, essential to society, and worthy of reward."

The New England settlers took seriously both sides of the injunction that "work is the godly in prayer, but . . . the ungodly, too." The Protestant advocacy of proper and legitimate pleasure in both work and the rewards of work applied to the visibly godly and the visibly ungodly alike. Turning away from the penal and Thomistic understandings of work, Anglo-American Protestants believed that work was "at once an expression of salvation and also of the spontaneous relationship of man to the world around him." Work was done for one's God, one's fellows, and—only after these needs were met—for oneself.[55]

The Protestant dignification of labor helps explain why

what appeared to be New England's greatest handicaps—the rough quality of its land and the harshness of its winters—were actually sources of attraction for some Puritans. Since the failure of George Popham's colony on the Sagadahoc (Kennebec) River in 1607–08, New England had been widely regarded as unsuitable for colonization (a perception John Smith had done his best to counter).[56] Upon his arrival in the Bay Colony, John Winthrop affirmed that "only hard labour would transform the wilderness into settled lands." The settlers encountered, said one of Winthrop's compatriots, "A very difficult worke, [which] requires much hard Labour, to subdue so Ruff and woody A wilderness." Pamphleteer William Wood averred that all New Englanders needed to be "workers in some kinde." One early arriving minister wrote back to his flock in England that only "industry and selfe denyall" would allow men and women to "Subsist as well here as in any place."[57]

The Puritan propagandist Edward Johnson wrote that the first settlers found a "remote, rocky, barren, bushy, wild-woody wilderness, a receptacle for Lions . . . and all kind of wild creatures, a place that never afforded the Natives better [than] the flesh of a few wild creatures and parch't Indian corn incht out with Chestnuts and bitter Acorns."[58] In 1636, the Reverend Richard Mather informed a correspondent in England that "The land [in Massachusetts] looks not pleasant to the eye in many places, being a rude and unsubdued wilderness. . . ."[59] He cautioned that only with the greatest physical exertions could such land be made to yield "sufficient sustenance for men of moderate minds." A youthful workman on Governor Winthrop's estate wrote candidly to his father back in England that "the country is very rocky and hilly and some champion [open] ground, and the soil is very fleet [shallow], and here . . . is no Michaelmas [autumnal] spring . . . we do not know how long we may subsist, for we cannot live here without provisions from ould eingland."[60]

For John Winthrop, the difficulty in subduing such an inhospitable land meant that successful colonization of Massachusetts could only be accomplished by near-heroic, God-inspired labor. Indeed, so widespread were perceptions of the difficulties in subduing the New England landscape that

Winthrop was forced to deny that success could only come "by miracle." Drawing repeatedly on covenantal language, Winthrop assured the more timorous among the prospective migrants that God would inevitably "bless the labors" of an enterprise He favored—particularly those of His Chosen. Responding in 1629 to critics who asserted that "We must . . . be praeserved by miracle if we [are to] subsiste," Winthrop invoked the language of the covenant. Though "miracles be now ceased, yet men may expecte a more than ordinarie blessing from God upon all lawfull meanes where the worke is the Lord's . . . *for it is usuall with him to encrease or weaken the strength of the meanes as he is pleased or displeased with the Instruments and the action. . . .*"[61]

Ascetic Puritanism, in perhaps its greatest contrast to the Renaissance ideal of the leisured gentleman, imposed its work ethic on high-born and low-born alike. Winthrop, as did Smith during his leadership of Virginia, made a conspicuous example of his own willingness to perform manual labor. As an early settler informed a friend in England, "So soon as Mr. Winthrop was landed, perceiving what misery was like[ly] to ensue through their idleness, he presently fell to work with his own hands and thereby so encouraged the rest so that there was not an idle person to be found in the whole plantation [so that the Indians] admired to see in what short time they had all housed themselves and planted corn for their subsistence." Although doubtless done primarily for didactic purposes, the governor's actions in taking up the hoe signaled that in New England encomiums on the dignity of labor would apply to everyone.[62]

The daunting process of setting up farms in a harsh region like New England clouded the Bay Colony's future for over a decade. The end of the somewhat artificial prosperity of the 1630s, brought by the constant influx of eager customers for cattle, grain, and lumber, caused many Bay Colonists to despair. Some surmised that God was telling them that they were wrong in having chosen such an unpropitious habitat for their New Canaan.[63] In 1640, Winthrop was forced to acknowledge the growing lure of Virginia and the Providence Island Colony (not destroyed by the Spanish until the next year): "Many men began to inquire after the southern parts;

and the great advantages supposed to be had in Virginia and the West Indies, etc." Ten years of coping with bitterly cold winters, wet springs, rocky soil, and periodic infestations of caterpillars and pigeons had disillusioned more than a few of the godly. The economic collapse of 1640 was the final straw. After making reference to the "bitter storms this place is subject unto," Edward Johnson declared that the Lord had been "pleased to hide from the Eyes of his people the difficulties they [were] to encounter . . . [so] that they might not thereby be hindered from taking the worke in hand." In countering those who looked to the more temperate southerly climes, John Winthrop declared time and again that—like the Old Testament Jews—New Englanders had already found the New Canaan, had reached the Promised Land. But its milk and honey would only flow after the application of the "sweat of our browes." Indeed, in standard Puritan fashion, Winthrop contended that the very unfruitfulness of Massachusetts would reduce the threat of worldliness that prosperity would bring. In his initial answers to objections that English migrants would regret departing from a "fruitful land with peace and plenty," he pointed to "the advantage of a meane condition" that would allow "more freedom to dye . . . [to] the things of this world . . . [and] to laye up treasure in heaven."[64]

The sheer difficulty in subduing New England's landscape as well as the need to choose "fit instruments" for the endeavor placed a high premium on the Massachusetts workforce. There was a goodly portion of England's population that was unlikely to respect the power of disciplined probity and thus was not to be allowed into the farming-fishing commonwealth. Not surprisingly, for John Smith, these were the same gentlemen, sharkers, and drones who had almost brought Virginia to ruin. As one of the primary characteristics of Renaissance gentlemen was a disdain for manual labor, Smith's dismissal of them as "useless parasite[s]" is to be expected.[65]

The goal of the culture of discipline was to attract only industrious and sober folk to the New World. John Smith, as well as other influential seventeenth-century observers, believed that early Virginia had been settled largely by the "mixed multitude." The mercantilist pamphleteer Sir Josiah

Child wrote that, in contrast to New England, "*Virginia* and *Barbados* were first peopled by a sort of loose vagrant People, vicious and destitute of Means to live at Home (being either unfit for Labour, or such as could find [no other way] to employ themselves [except by] Whoring, Thieving, or other Debauchery, [so] that none would set them on to work)." Similarly, in describing Barbados during the early 1650s, Henry Whistler wrote that "This Island is the dunghill whereon England doth cast forth its rubbish: Rogues and whores and such like people are those which are generally brought here." Plymouth Governor William Bradford (1590–1657) ascribed the early difficulties of his colony to the presence of the "mixt multitude," who "came for gain, or worse ends" and who quickly grew "loose and profane."[66] While the sober and industrious were driven to migrate primarily through economic forces beyond their control—rising prices, falling wages, enclosures—Smith, Child, Whistler, and Bradford believed that the mixed multitude were undone by their own sloth, licentiousness, profligacy, and drunkenness. These men agreed that colonizing by means of a "loose vagrant People," particularly in a semi-tropical climate, was a recipe for disaster.[67]

The pronouncements on labor made by Winthrop and Smith reveal the degree to which the labor theory of property developed in William Petty's *Verbum Sapienti* (1665) and John Locke's *Second Treatise* (1690) had its roots in ascetic Puritanism.[68] Work for the saints was the warrant and source of all wealth: God gave the use of the world to the industrious and rational; title to property came principally from work; the fruits of labor belonged to the worker; men and women only had a right to what they actually could use. The first source of wealth was God's bounty, but men and women were not expected to be passive. The emergence of civil society brought the labor theory of property. According to John Winthrop's writings, wealth—once the natural law was supplanted by the civil law—was to be the consequence of labor. Locke, himself of Puritan origins, likewise based property ownership on acts of improvement. He declared that the right to property began whenever a person "mixed" his labor with something—an acorn, an apple, a fish—by removing it from its natural state. Labor conveyed possession. For early modern Englishmen, political liberty itself rested on the individual's control over the fruits of his own labor. Slavery, the obverse of liberty, was the condition of those men and women who lacked this control. Having himself briefly been held as a slave in the Middle East, John Smith regarded this dichotomy as anything but an abstract one.[69]

John Winthrop's justification for colonization had rested on such premises from the very beginning. It was distilled in the Puritan doctrine of improvement, based on the Book of Genesis. What the vision of social mobility was for John Smith, the doctrine of improvement was for John Winthrop: the main spur to industry and enterprise. While neither Luther nor Calvin could be accused of intending such, there proved in practice to be a near-inexorable connection inhering in the "elective affinity" between the doctrine of improvement, the calling, the doctrine of stewardship, and economic freedom. In 1629, Winthrop wrote that "the whole earth is the Lords garden and he hath given it to the sonnes of men with a general Commission: Gen:I:28: increase and multiplie, and replenish the earth and subdue it." He proceeded to emphasize that "the end is double and naturall, that man might enjoy the fruits of the earth, and God might have his due glory from the creature."[70] By subduing the earth, Winthrop meant clearing the land and building farms, shops, smithies, shipyards, bridges, forts, and ironworks; in short, economic development. Moreover, and this too became a centerpiece of communal capitalism, the principles of utility and conservation also needed to be adhered to. In 1639, drawing on the same scriptural warrant, Winthrop declared that because "God gave the earth etc. to be subdued . . . a man can have no right to more than he can subdue."[71]

In 1634, when Boston's "generality" demanded the allocation of all remaining land on an equal basis, Winthrop emphasized his unwillingness that "the people [of Massachusetts] should have more land in the bay than they might be likely to use in some reasonable time. . . ." He explained that many already "had much [land], and could make no use of it, more than to please their eye with it." In invoking God's promise to bless the labors of the worthy, Winthrop declared:

"Noe place of it selfe hath afforded sufficient [living] to the first Inhabitants, such thinges as we stand in neede of are usually supplied by God's blessing upon the wisdome and industry of man, and whatsoever we stand in need of is treasured up in the earth by the Creator, and to be feched thense by the sweate of our browes."[72]

As with so much else in the New England Way, John Winthrop's labor theory of property derived from the legend of Adam's Fall. Indeed, the very distinction between a prelapsarian covenant of works and a postlapsarian covenant of grace rested on the transformation of man's relationship to God brought by Adam's disobedience. For Winthrop, man lived in a state of primitive communism before the Fall—a state of innocence in which all things were held in common and the ruling principle was that of love. Only after Adam rent himself—and his posterity—from the Creator was universal love replaced by self-love. Hence acquisitiveness, in Winthrop's view, was not innate to humankind but entered history with the Fall, of which it was both cause and consequence. The Fall of man ended the period of primitive communism, and men and women in their corruption acquired an insatiable acquisitive propensity.[73]

Thus the economic motive, what became the drive to expand capital, originated in Adam's sin. For Calvinists, it could only be kept in check by the (unmerited) infusion of divine grace, which "takes possession of the soule and infuseth another principle, love to God and our brother." This principle, rooted in the Beatitudes and the Last Judgment scene in Matthew 25, was the animating source of countless seventeenth-century Puritan sermons. Ideologically, it was what distinguished communal capitalism from the more predatory forms of capitalism found in the Chesapeake and West Indies. The voluntaryism of the federal covenant gave it institutional expression. The voluntary covenant was the basis for the extraordinary civic ecology of the orthodox Puritan colonies. In the "Modell of Christian Charity," Winthrop laid out the social obligations brought by acceptance of this principle.[74] The "Lawe of Grace" (or, the gospel law), which had superseded the "Lawe of nature" (or, the moral law), mandated that men and women "lay upp [worldly goods] as Joseph did, [so as] to have ready uppon such occasions, as the Lord (whose stewards wee are of them) shall call for them from us" in order to provide for the needy.[75] In seeking wealth through "the sweate of our browes," men and women both gave God His due glory *and* provided sustenance for their brethren.

* * *

"By the sweate of our browes"—an Old Testament phrase that became the moral basis of New World labor. At least for those laborers who were free. From the time of the founding of Puritan New England until the American Civil War, this included the majority of white American males. In Lincoln's 1858 debates with Stephen Douglas and his Second Inaugural Address, it would—for the first time—be applied to African Americans as well.[76] For the founding generation, the generation of Winthrop and Smith, this work ethic meant the bonding of all one's energies into a singleminded dynamic that one imagines has rarely been attained before or since. It provided the motive energy to, among other things, prepare some 12,000 acres for tillage during the first decade of settlement and clear some 700,000 acres of New England's daunting landscape between 1630 and 1720. It endowed settlers with the brute strength (and eventual capacity for ecological destructiveness) to cut down a total of 260 million cords of wood between 1630 and 1800.[77] It provided the initiative and enterprise necessary to establish the Bay Colony's impressive infrastructure: gristmills, sawmills, ironworks, smithies, wharves, and drydocks, as well as clapboarded and cellared houses, framed outbuildings, and five-rail fences. It also helped build during this period a shipping fleet of over two thousand vessels, not counting fishing craft. It helped fashion a capital city that by 1720 "had the finest highway system in the colonies, superior to that of most English cities, and a sewer system that provided the best drainage of any town in America or England."[78] This productive ethic allowed an agricultural region renowned for its rockiness and infertility to become the means by which "the other plantations are made prosperous and beneficial." These accomplishments were not unconnected. As both Winthrop and Smith had recognized, the Protestant work ethic needed to be harnessed to a commercial economy if New England were to survive. Farmers as well as fishermen needed "vent" for their surplus. Living in a land devoid of tropical staple crops and precious metals, New Englanders had to learn commerce or perish.[79] This would demand a significant export trade in fish, grains, meat products, and ships.

For both Winthrop and Smith, a highly diversified quasi-industrial economy was deemed essential. The political economy of both men rested on a vision of active commercial exchange and enterprise. The colony would need to develop major export commodities to exchange for the large stores of textiles, metalwares, and medicine it planned to import from England and the Continent. And both had only to look across the North Sea for an example of the kind of society they were seeking to build.

For both thinkers, the Dutch were the people to emulate. Smith and Winthrop, like contemporary English economists such as Malynes, Misselden, and Mun, took note of the United Provinces' astonishing rise to national prosperity and commercial dominance during the late sixteenth and early seventeenth century.[80] Since its revolt against the Spanish Crown in 1566, the Northern Netherlands had emerged as the third carrier in the economic race that took capitalism from twelfth-century merchant ventures through Renaissance banking to the international staple economy of the Atlantic system.[81] A small republic eternally vulnerable to incursions from the sea and lacking such elemental natural resources as iron ore, timber, coal, or precious metals, Holland by the beginning of the seventeenth century had emerged as the principal middle carrier in the European economy. The Dutch success seemed to beggar the imagination. As Joyce Appleby puts it: "Without mines, how did the Dutch come to have plenty of coin? With few natural resources for export, how could the Dutch engross the production of other countries? How did the Dutch have low interest rates and high land values? How were high wages maintained with a burgeoning population? How could high prices and widespread prosperity exist simultaneously in the Low Countries?"[82]

Max Weber found an answer for these questions in the culture of ascetic Protestantism, with restrictions on consumption serving to promote capital formation. Many of the "liberal mercantilists" in England pointed to more mundane factors such as a fluid land market, low interest rates, low customs duties, efficient banks, land registers, labor specialization, liberty of conscience, and an advantageous geographic location during an era when commerce was shifting from the Mediterranean to the Atlantic.[83] But John Smith emphasized two factors above all: the herring industry and shipbuilding. The former allowed the Dutch to create exports in a society without significant natural resources; the latter stimulated commerce and helped foster a highly skilled and specialized workforce. Smith asked rhetorically:

> who doth not know that the poore Hollanders, chiefly by fishing, at a great charge and labour in all weathers in the open Sea, are made a people so hardy, and industrious? and by the venting this poore commodity to the Easterlings [Hanseatic League] for as meane [a commodity], which is Wood, Flax, Pitch, Tarre, Rosin, Cordage, and such like (which they exchange againe, to the French, Spainards, Portugales, and English, etc. for what they want) are made so mighty, strong and rich. . . .

The message was clear for Smith: If a people wished to be clothed in pearls, diamonds, and velvets, they needed to trade in codfish, tar, and pipestaves. And this, of course, is exactly what New England eventually did. A firm believer in what would today be described as export-led economic growth (as well as what developmental economists now refer to as "backward" and "forward" linkages) Smith declared that "Herring, Cod, and Ling, is that triplicate that makes [the Hollanders'] wealth and shippings multiplicities, such as it is, and from which (few would thinke it) they yearly draw at least one million and a halfe of pounds [sterling]."[84]

During his 1614 voyage, Smith listed for his readers "What

merchandize and commodities for their labour they may finde. . . ." Whales and precious metals were the first commodities sought; but if, as Smith intuited, these were either lacking or prohibitively expensive, then "Fish and Furres [will be] our refuge." Smith fully recognized that New England's unprepossessing soil meant that the local economy must rest on the fishing industry. The "maine Staple" to "bee extracted for the present to produce the rest," he asserted, "is fish," which "however it may seeme a mean and a base commoditie: yet [it will be] well worth the labour." Indeed, as the Dutch had shown with their herring fisheries, not just individuals but whole societies could grow rich by means of the fishing trade. The Dutch, Smith contended, had become rich "as no State but Venice, of twice their magnitude." Where else but the United Provinces could one find "so many faire Cities, goodly Townes, strong fortresses, and that aboundance of shipping and all sorts of merchandize?"[85]

Smith and Winthrop agreed that New England was best prepared to develop three major commodities: fish, wood products, and livestock. As his list of "grosse commodities" suggests, shipbuilding closely followed fishing in Smith's productive vision. As with fishing, New England would enjoy a clear comparative advantage over its competitors. Raw materials would be no problem. Unlike the timber-short mother country, "in New England the trees are . . . [of] much thicker and firmer wood, and more proper for shipping." In what proved to be his most prophetic observation, Smith wrote that shipbuilding would become "the chiefe engine wee are to use" in establishing New England's productive economy. Waxing rhapsodic over the glories of shipbuilding—and the role it would play in training skilled woodworkers—Smith intoned that, "Of all fabricks, a ship is the most excellent, requiring more art in building, rigging, sayling, trimming, defending, and moaring" than any similar endeavor.[86]

Smith showed a clear willingness, even enthusiasm, to depart from the Old World's guild-based craft tradition. Like the contempt Adam Smith famously displayed against the ancient apprentice-based artisanal "corporations," John Smith disdained the cumbersome and anti-competitive guild system as the most appropriate means for training craftsmen.

Like Adam Smith, the captain believed that the requisite skills for even the most recondite craft could be quickly acquired by willing and able workers through on-the-job training. The seven-year apprenticeship system, John Smith believed, primarily functioned to protect masters against competition for—and eventually from—their workers. The captain declared confidently that an experienced shipwright would be able to "direct an unskillful Carpenter or Sailor to build Boates and Barkes sufficient to saile those coastes and rivers" of the New World. That Smith endorsed such a pragmatic approach to a craft he regarded as "the master-peece of all the most necessary workemen in the world" spoke volumes about his aversion to guild-based production. Not surprisingly for a man who had risen from humble yeoman origins to a position as one of the preeminent colonizers in the early modern world, John Smith disdained institutions of inherited privilege—especially if they blocked mobility for "men that have great spirits and small meanes." Like such later bourgeois radicals as Tom Paine and John Wilkes, Smith objected to any Old World institutions that thwarted the disciplines of upward mobility.[87] Guilds, like entry fines, labor settlement laws, and rent-racking leaseholds, were to have no place in his vision for the New World.

The colonization model for early New England outlined by John Smith, with its particular emphasis on fishing, shipbuilding, and industry, was shared by virtually all the organizers of the Massachusetts Bay Company. The Winthrop family's own forays into ironmaking, glassmaking, and graphite mining are cases in point. The Winthrops' trading partner Richard Saltonstall predicted in 1632 that "we shall raise good profit not only by our fishing trade (which is sufficiently known) but by hemp, flax, pitch, tar, potashes, soap ashes, masts, pipe staves, clapboard (and iron as we hope)."[88] Similarly, the elder Winthrop, after calling attention to the opportunities in New England for fishing, fur trading, and commercial husbandry, predicted large earnings from "making pitch, Tarr, Pottashes, and sope ashes . . . cutting of masts . . . making of Iron, [and] what other mines there are we know nott." On the eve of his voyage to New England, the governor underscored the opportunities for fishing, fur trading, and commercial husbandry, as well as "making pitch, Tarr, Pottashes, and sope ashes. . . . Cuttinge of masts . . . makeing of Iron, [and] what other mines there are wee know nott." Winthrop expressed the hope that the "Trade of Furres" alone "may be Brought out of that Continent to the valew" of no less than "£30,000 per annum at least. . . ." Once in New England, Winthrop displayed a shrewd eye for what economists call comparative advantage, advising Connecticut's Thomas Hooker that "you must turne your Cowes into flaxe and hempe, by which Course you may soone outstrippe [Massachusetts]; for that is a merchantable Comodity, and one acre with you will yield more than 4 [in Massachusetts]. (Provided allways that you secure [the river port of] Say brook)."[89]

Although the most religious of men, Winthrop was every bit the rational calculator when it came to things economic. Piety and profit, he believed, if properly channeled through civic institutions and conscience, could go hand in hand. An undiversified, household-based agricultural economy, New England—in the eyes of its principal founders—was not to be. A diversified, industralizing economy (like the one from which they were departing) was the goal from the very beginning.

Such a highly diversified economy, of course, would demand a highly skilled labor force. Governor Winthrop himself, at the very time he was mandating the need for a sober and pious workforce, penned a detailed list of the variety of skills the colony's first settlers needed to possess. From a Company subscription of £10,000, Winthrop hoped to recruit "200 Carpenters, Masons, Smiths, Coopers, Turners, Brickburners, Potters, Husbandmen, [and] Fowlers. . . ."[90] The Puritan author of *New England's Prospect* reflected the saints' concerns for what they called a "better Art, and the way of thriving," when he endorsed the recruitment of

> an ingenious carpenter, a cunning joiner, a handy cooper, such a one as can make strong ware for the use of the country and a good brick-maker, a tiler and a smith, a leather dresser, a gardener, and a tailor. One that hath good skill in the trade of fishing is of special use and so is a good fowler; if there be any that hath skill in any of

> these trades, if he can transport himself, he needs not fear but he may improve his time and endeavors to his own benefit and comfort.[91]

* * *

"To his own benefit and comfort"—these were the sentiments that made New England what later would be called a "bourgeois society." While it would take another three centuries for these concepts to be leached of much of their communitarian and familial content, they did betoken a real departure from Old World ways. The writings of Smith and Winthrop suggest why "traditional society," however one wishes to define it, did not get transmitted to the New World. Indeed, it could not. Trying to recreate traditional forms is at bottom the very opposite of traditional behavior. And it would be exceedingly unlikely that the Puritan migrants—the highly educated beneficiaries of Renaissance humanism and the scientific revolution—would undertake such an effort. The New England Way would be based on both Scripture and reason (although a reason made "right" through the infusion of God's saving grace). New England's Puritans consciously rejected scholasticism and turned to the emerging natural sciences for the foundation of their cosmology. Like their intellectual kinsmen the Quakers, the Bay Colonists rejected the older deductive Scholastic science in favor of the new experimental methods.[92] The collapse of Aristotelianism and the world views of the Christian Middle Ages, as we have seen, left little choice but to embrace these progressive philosophies. This was the cast of mind that was brought to Massachusetts Bay by an extraordinarily talented collection of theologian-intellectuals. As Adam Smith, Karl Marx, and Max Weber all understood, emergent tendencies in England were—by this very process of colonization—distilled and crystallized in the New World. Puritanism, and the freedom of experiment afforded by colonization, made an already progressive people the more so.

The wide ambit of agreement between the economic philosophies of John Winthrop and John Smith illustrates the potent combination of Puritan and English influences. Puritanism's role was limited but decisive. As Perry Miller and Thomas Johnson declared some years ago: "about ninety per cent of the intellectual life, scientific knowledge, morality, manners and customs, notions and prejudices [of the Puritans] was that of all Englishmen. [But the] other ten per cent, the relatively small number of ideas upon which there was dispute, made all the difference between the Puritan and his fellow-Englishmen. . . ."[93] And nowhere was this difference more critical than in the realms of economic culture and civic institutions.

Like today's Hutterians, the early New Englanders eagerly innovated in the material realm even as they sought to turn the clock back to the medieval (or even apostolic) era in the spiritual realm. Bitter foes of the materialism and display of Tudor-Stuart England, the Puritans embraced with fervor its Baconian spirit of experiment and innovation. The New Englanders, as the public policies of the Massachusetts General Court reveal, put both the English enlightenment and liberal mercantilism into practice. The Calvinist mandate to "improve every bright and shining hour" merged with and accelerated the larger enlightenment project of improving the physical world. Their narrative of history created an economically potent "community of meaning," one that bound all New Englanders into a sacred cause with daily claims on the energy and enterprise of each woman and man. The conflating of prophecy and history—the belief by at least some settlers that on this tiny Puritan outpost rested the responsibility for fulfilling God's plan for human redemption—fused all Puritans' daily labors with a millennial zeal. (John Winthrop went so far as to describe the founding of New England as the final act of the Reformation; the City upon a Hill would serve as a model for Christ's promised earthly kingdom.) The saints' progressive view of history, as the unfolding of God's plan for humankind, harmonized with and to a degree accelerated the larger intellectual shift from organic to mechanical ways of thinking, from hierarchically defined to contractually defined relationships. For the Puritans of Winthrop's generation, improvement was always a spiritual ideal, the means by which the regenerate woman or man made the daily journey on the road from sin to redemption.[94] In Massachusetts Bay, however, these ideals would have material and institutional, as well as spiritual, consequences.

Puritanism played a key role in the transition to capitalism by channeling and legitimating the striving behavior increasingly common among seventeenth-century Englishmen of all religious persuasions. The Puritan ideals of the calling, improvement, and stewardship harmonized with the new political economy, with its principles of economic freedom with respect to property, trade, and labor. The Protestant ethic helped to both spiritualize the workplace and methodize time.[95] Although deeply Augustinian when it came to human perfectibility, the New Englanders behaved like Erasmian humanists in the realm of economic behavior.[96] Committed to a view of human depravity straight out of St. Augustine's *City of God,* Puritans of Winthrop's generation also knew that God "smiles on the labors of His faithful." Their goal was to make New England a flourishing and productive society as well as a godly one. To achieve this end would require the judicious labor recruitment of enterprising and hardy folk and the acquisition of sufficient investment capital from the London commercial community. It would also require, and produce, something which John Winthrop at least was not prepared to accept: John Smith's vision of social mobility.

Adam Smith had understood, according to his friend Dugald Stewart, that "It was the general diffusion of wealth among the lower orders of men, which first gave birth to the spirit of independence in modern Europe, and which has produced under some governments, and especially [Britain's] a more equal diffusion of freedom and of happiness than took place under the most celebrated constitutions of antiquity."[97] We can discern a few revealing glimpses of this spirit of independence produced by an "augmentation of fortune" among early New England's humbler settlers. The Puritan economic ethic, as we shall see in greater detail in Chapter 3, contained features that subverted the social order it was designed to sustain—in particular, a degree of economic mobility inconsistent with the ideal of an ordered social hierarchy.[98]

In 1633, a scant three years after the arrival of the Winthrop fleet in Massachusetts Bay, the General Court was complaining that workmen were using their high wages for the purpose of getting drunk and disorderly. The Court responded by reimposing previously rescinded wage and price controls. It also publicly condemned the workmen for the "greate extortion used by dyvers persons of little conscience, and the greate disorder which grewe hereupon. . . ." The magistrates had little doubt where the cause of this disorderliness lay: in the "vaine and idle waste of much precious tyme, and expense of those immoderate gaynes [from the workmen's wages] in wyne, stronge water, and other superfluities."[99] The following year, the General Court attempted to clip the pretensions of uppity workmen by using a device that had been banned in England the first year of James I's rule, class-based sumptuary legislation. Taking alarmed note of the "greate, superfluous, and unnecessary expenses occasioned by reason of some newe and immodest fashions," especially the wearing by ordinary settlers of "silver, golde, and silke laces, girdles, [and] hatbands," the Court banned the wearing of such fashions by ordinary men and women on pain of forfeiture.[100] In 1639 the General Court's fulminations on declension approached self-parody, contending as they did that the infant colony was rife with "Novelties, oppression [profiteering], atheisme, excesse [of apparel], superfluity, idleness, [and] contempt of authority."[101]

Again in 1651, while noting "those blessings which, beyond our expectation, the Lord hath been pleased to afford unto us in this wilderness," the General Court bewailed that these same economic blessings were causing the lower sort to forget their station, particularly in their dress and social comportment. Using the earnings from what must have seemed to be astonishingly high wages, laboring men and women were apparently aping the costume and behavior of their betters to a degree that the Court found genuinely alarming. "We cannot but to our greife take notice," the magistrates declared, of "that intollerable excesse and bravery [that] hath crept in uppon us, and especially amongst people of meane condition." In especially revealing phrasing, the magistrates pronounced their "utter detestation and dislike that men or women of meane condition, educations, and callinges should take uppon them[selves] the garbe of gentlemen, by the wearinge of gold or silver lace, or buttons, or poynts at theire knees, to walke in greate bootes; or women of the same ranke to weare silke or tiffany hoodes or scarfes." Such dress was allowable only "to persons of greater estates, or more liberall education."[102]

Discovering for the first—but not the last—time the socially radical force of the free market, the General Court took steps to quash the spirit of independence brought to the Bay Colony's common people by material prosperity. Commending unto "all sorts of persons a sober and moderate use" of their newfound prosperity, the Court banned the wearing of gold and silver lace, great boots, knee points, silks, and tiffany hoods by any person whose estate was worth less than £200. Again in 1662, while passing yet another sumptuary law, an increasingly exasperated Court declared that "the rising generation are in danger to be corrupted and effeminated" if there were not a return to simpler and more modest patterns of dress. Yet New England was not to see such a return to simplicity and contentment with station—in the seventeenth century or thereafter. In 1714, in language strikingly reminiscent of the General Court's 1633 admonition, Attorney General Paul Dudley complained of "the great Extravagance that People, and especially the Ordinary sort, are fallen into, far beyond their Circumstances, in their Purchases, Buildings, Families, Expenses, Apparel, and generally in their whole way of Living."[103]

Correspondence between the Reverend John Eliot and Sir Simonds D'Ewes (then contemplating migration to New England) suggests how quickly some Bay Colonists grasped the socially subversive nature of the Protestant ethic in a New World setting. Eliot frankly told the baronet "to bring not many servants, for they [will] be a sure charge and trouble and an uncertain gain." Those servants who did come to New England—far from wanting them to be robust and enterprising—should rather be "poor and such as cannot work, and then you shall keep them." For, "if they be either rich [or] workful, they will desire freedom" and become "ill members in our young commonwealth."[104] In similar vein, John Winthrop, while discussing in 1645 the fact that former servants "could not be hired when their times were out [except] upon unreasonable terms," related the following exchange between master and servant in Rowley (whether or not the governor was amused by the story's denouement is not indicated):

> The master, being forced to sell a pair of his oxen to pay his servant his wages, told his servant [that] he could keep him no longer, not knowing how to pay him the next year. The servant answered [that] he would serve him for more of his cattle. But [what] shall I do (saith the master) when all my cattle are gone? The servant replied, you shall then serve me, and so you may have your cattle again.[105]

Social mobility, both upward and downward, produced shocks that were profoundly unsettling to New England's first governing classes. The explanation for this lies in the high land-labor ratio, the direct reverse of Old World patterns. While many—including Adam Smith—have assumed that cheap land would lead automatically to higher levels of economic development, the opposite was more likely to be true, particularly in a colonial setting. The reason is that one of the principal requirements for capital accumulation, surplus labor, is likely to be missing in the absence of coercion. In colonial societies possessing an abundance of land expropriated from Native American proprietors, hired labor was inevitably in short supply. The logic behind this is self-evident: Few settlers proved willing to share the fruits of their labors as either waged workers or a tenants if they could capture them all by themselves.[106]

As a result of the high land-labor ratio in British America, the choices for labor systems were stark: a reliance on coerced labor (indentured servants or slaves) or dependence on the family labor characteristic of the owner-occupied farm.[107] British America's eventual division into "plantation colonies" and "farm colonies" rested primarily on this division between bonded and free labor. For both cultural and economic reasons, New Englanders chose the second form of labor. But this choice was not foreordained. On the contrary, some in

John Winthrop's circle openly questioned whether the mobility available to servants and laboring folk generally would not necessitate a conversion to racially based slavery. While proposing to Winthrop in 1645 that captured Narragansett Indians be exchanged for African slaves, Salem magnate Emmanuel Downing declared: "for I doe not see how wee can thrive untill wee gett into [Massachusetts] a stock of slaves sufficient to doe all our business." Downing's reasoning is illuminating, fearing as he did that "our Children's Children will hardly see this great Continent filled with people, soe that our servants will still desire freedome to plant for themselves, and not stay [as workers] but for verie great wages." He predicted that "wee shall maynteyne 20 Moores cheaper than one Englishe servant."[108]

The General Court's early sumptuary laws reveal in an especially direct fashion some of the early dilemmas posed by social mobility. This was also a dilemma that was partly of the Court's own making. The magistrates, by the time of the 1651 sumptuary legislation, had been vigorously promoting economic development for over a decade. What the General Court failed to see was what Adam Smith—and John Smith before him—saw so well: that the improved material conditions economic growth brought the laboring classes often caused them to forget their "condition, educations, and callinges." Few leaders of Winthrop's generation appear to have realized that many of their own policies were fostering this social mobility. One of the first men fined under the sumptuary law of 1651 was Jonas Fairbanks of the Hammersmith Ironworks in Lynn. A highly skilled forge helper at Hammersmith, Fairbanks was presented before the Essex Quarterly Court in November 1652 for "wearing great boots." The Lynn ironworks, utilizing the highly advanced Walloon indirect process of iron fabrication, was founded under General Court sponsorship in 1643. Fairbanks may well have been one of the ironworkers whom John Winthrop, Jr., recruited in a 1641 circuit of English ironworks. Ironworkers—like the clanging, belching, firelit forge where most of them labored—proved to be a trial to orthodox Puritans. But Jonas Fairbanks, like the industrial plant in which he was employed, was in New England at the direct initiative of the Bay Colony's leaders. The colony's commitment to an industrializing and commercialized economy had brought Fairbanks, clearly no Puritan, to Massachusetts. His use of the high wages garnered by forge helpers at Hammersmith to purchase a pair of gentleman's riding boots may or may not have signified a conscious slight to the Bay Colony's system of social hierarchy. But as the Puritan leaders discovered in the 1670s when they abandoned class-based sumptuary laws permanently, it was the "general diffusion of wealth among the lower orders of men" that finally broke the "Great Chain of Being."[109]

John Winthrop in 1630 had confidently declared that God had "disposed of the Condition of mankinde, as in all times some must be rich, some poore, some highe and eminent in power and dignitie; others meane and in subjection." Well before the governor's death in 1649, the social reality of the Bay Colony had given the lie to these pronouncements. New England had become a society in which even settlers of "small meanes" could legitimately aspire to become "owners of their own labour and land." Much of the explanation for this phenomenon lies in the saints' creation of a new anthropology of work and a new calculus of expectations, what Max Weber baptized—and immortalized—as the Protestant ethic.

3

The Protestant Ethic and the Culture of Discipline

Whether work or rest is the natural state for human beings is a topic long debated by philosophers and social scientists alike. The very origin of the Protestant ethic thesis derived from Max Weber's conviction that unrelenting activity and enterprise was unnatural—that it was a peculiar and historically contingent form of behavior.[1] Locke, the founder of liberalism (an ideology of work), declared that "the chief, if not the only, spur to human industry and action" was the emulative-driven "uneasiness" that roused men and women from their natural lethargy. Adam Smith averred that rest, not work, was the natural and ideal human condition, synonymous with freedom and happiness. In the *Theory of Moral Sentiments* (1759), Smith followed Locke's emulative interpretation by rooting the pursuit of wealth, as well as "all the toil and bustle of the world," in the need to "be observed, to be attended to, to be taken notice of with sympathy, complacency, and approbation."[2] Alexis de Tocqueville likewise believed that human beings had a "natural passion for idleness." More negatively, the Reverend Thomas Malthus declared that so innately slothful was humankind that only the goad of starvation drove the masses to their labors. In his *Essay on the Principle of Population* (1798), Malthus spoke unblinkingly of "Man as he really is, inert, sluggish, and averse from labour, unless compelled by necessity." Drawing the obvious political economic lesson from such a perception, the agricultural reformer Arthur Young contended that "Every one but an idiot knows, that the lower classes must be kept poor, or they will never be industrious."[3]

Hegel and Marx, by contrast, saw work as the most natural and creative, indeed the most basic and sustaining, of human activities, a stance that they shared with the Puritans. Both men defined history as largely the creation of humankind through labor. Drawing on the materialist philosopher Ludwig Feuerbach, Marx regarded productive work as the highest expression of the human "essence" or "species-being." Work was the natural and free exercise of the activity of human beings.[4] In the *German Ideology* (1845–46), Marx and Engels declared that while men and women "may be distinguished from animals by consciousness, by religion or anything else you like," human beings in fact "begin to distinguish themselves from animals as soon as they begin to produce their means of subsistence." In the *Economic and Philosophical Manuscripts* (1844), Marx declared that the purpose of socialism was to allow humankind to reappropriate its long-forfeited essence. Otto Rank and Henri Bergson, defining man as *Homo faber* (man the maker), made work synonymous with human life itself. For Rank, it was the creative or work instinct, not the sexual instinct, that was the primal human drive. Thomas Carlyle went even further in this direction in his "theosophy of toil." Seeing God's essential being as diffused throughout the material universe, Carlyle believed that whenever a person transforms matter, "he is doing nothing less than altering—however minutely—the face of the Almighty."[5]

Most assessments of the naturalness of work turn on whether manual labor is regarded as a blessing or a curse. It was the historic achievement of ascetic Puritanism to help decide this question decisively in favor of the former view.

Classical antiquity, while not denigrating labor per se, viewed wage labor as degrading because it resembled the servile work performed by slaves (an attitude eventually duplicated in the American South). Greek attitudes toward labor and work were also affected by the existence of two distinct moral codes as postulated by Plato, the non-competitive, altruistic one of the "guardians" (the government) and the competitive, self-interested one of the marketplace. The guardians were banned from the world of commerce and trade as well as the ownership of property in general. They provided the moral glue to an otherwise atomized society. For both Plato and Aristotle, the philosophic life and the happiness it entailed derived from the *vita contemplativa,* not the *vita activa.* Leisure *(schole)* and fame *(kleos)* were for the ancients the transcendent social ideals. To the Aristotelians and their followers the goal of life was happiness, and leisure was the prerequisite for achieving it. In his *Nicomachean Ethics,* Aristotle declared that the purpose of work was to provide human beings with leisure: "happiness, it seems, requires leisure; for the object of our business is leisure, as the object of war is the enjoyment of peace." Indeed, Aristotle claimed that leisure was the only fit life for a man and, like Plato, he endowed with political power only those untainted by production or commerce. The civic ecology of fourth-century B.C. Athens, accordingly, differed markedly from that of Puritan New England. Civic virtue for Aristotle was primarily embodied in the political citizen, not the farmer, artisan, or laborer. Republicanism began—and until the seventeenth century remained—an ideology of leisure.[6]

The ancients, of course, did not deprecate all hard work or endorse the idle life. During the archaic period, the moral-didactic poetry of Hesiod (written about 700 B.C.) sounded themes that would not have been out of place in the mouth of Benjamin Franklin: the need for industry and frugality; a disdain for aristocratic leisure; and a belief in healthy competitiveness. In his *Works and Days,* Hesiod distinguished between two goddesses of Strife, one reprehensible, the other not. The younger, negative deity "promotes ugly fighting and conflict." But the "elder born of gloomy Night" is "much the better for man." The spirit of competitiveness responsible for making people work, the elder Strife, "rouses even the shiftless one to work. For when someone whose work falls short looks toward another, towards a rich man who hastens to plow and plant and manage his household well, then neighbor vies with neighbor as he hastens to wealth. . . ."

So potter is piqued with potter, joiner with joiner,
beggar begrudges beggar, and singer singer.

Elsewhere in the poem, Hesiod advises his wastrel brother Perses: "Do not put things off till tommorrow and the next day. A man of ineffectual labor, a postponer, does not fill his granary"; "if your spirit in your breast yearns for riches, do as follows, and work, work upon work." "Hunger," the poet declared, "goes always with a work-shy man." Gods and men alike "disapprove of that man who lives without working, like in temper to the blunt-tailed drones who wear away the toil of the bees, eating it in idleness."[7]

During the classical period, the philosophical pronouncements of Plato and Aristotle were often counterpoised by the everyday realities of Athenian life. Sokrates, who made his living as a stonemason, spoke glowingly of artisans, and many Athenian citizens worked as farmers or craftsmen. Much of the unskilled labor in the Hellenistic city-states was indeed performed by slaves, and resident aliens such as the Athenian metics carried on much of the mercantile activity. But the principal division in the classical world was not between workers and thinkers, but between citizens and non-citizens. And among the non-citizens, the labors of the most conspicuously excluded group—the slaves—had the effect of discrediting and degrading wage labor as simply another form of dependency.[8]

By the late republican period of Rome, such figures as Cato the Younger and Cicero, both of whom (not surprisingly) became the Romans that early Americans most revered, privileged the worthy farmer over the scheming aristocrat.[9] Virgil, who consciously modeled himself on Hesiod, declared in the *Georgics* that "*Labor omnia vincit improbus* (Hard work overcomes all difficulties)." Where the Greeks and Romans were most distinguishable from sixteenth-century Protestants was in their failure to develop an anti-idleness ethos (or ideology) and in their belief that the high-born should not labor for *profit.*

Augustinian Christianity likewise stopped well short of outright celebration of manual labor. One of the founding doctrines of the church—*Conceptio culpa,* the theology of original sin—defined work in penal terms, as a punishment for Adam's disobedience. Labor became the "curse of Adam," proof and punishment of man's original sin. Postlapsarian men and women were condemned to toil all the days of their lives and to earn their bread by the sweat of their brows. Christian ethics of the patristic period, like the Stoic teachings that emerged with the breakdown of the Greek city-state, devalued worldly distinctions (and, to a degree, all earthly labors). Legitimate social distinctions needed to be recognized and individuals were required to accept their roles and play them well; but ultimate meanings lay elsewhere.

In his *Summa theologica* (1266–73), Thomas Aquinas built the grand edifice of scholasticism on the distinction between the liberal (mental) and the servile (manual) arts. Seeking to reconcile Christian theology with Aristotelian philosophy, faith with reason, Aquinas resuscitated much of the old classical ideal. The medieval *summum bonum,* the life of prayer and contemplation, thus bore important similarities to the civic humanist ideal of Periklean Athens. Where the Scholastics did break new ground was in their contention that labor was the principal source of human wealth and thus the "chief claimant to remuneration." (This was the adumbration of the labor theory of value that allowed R. H. Tawney to declare that "The last of the schoolmen was Karl Marx.") By the late Middle Ages the new awareness of the importance of labor brought with it a renewed emphasis on the duty of every person to work, a stance once primarily associated with the Cistercians, Benedictines, and Lollards.[10]

It was the much-maligned mercantilist theorists who, in tandem with ascetic Puritanism, brought the value of labor fully to center stage by the early seventeenth century. The mercantilists' fascination with Holland's commercial rise led to a preoccupation with methods for best utilizing a nation's resources, particularly its most important resource—its labor force. Even while celebrating the merchant's skill in linking farmers and artisans to international markets, writers such as Edward Misselden, Thomas Mun, and William Petty recognized that such skill was useless without the employment of labor. In *Verbum Sapienti,* Petty used the principle of illustrative numbers to argue that a larger fraction of the national income was produced by labor than by capital.[11] Not least of the many ironies associated with this belated recognition of labor's importance as a factor of production was that it came about during the embryonic stages of the Industrial Revolution when, for the first time, labor was no longer the most important item in direct production costs in industries with heavy fixed capital equipment such as ironworks and paper manufacturies.[12]

By the early seventeenth century, especially in the newly Protestant portions of Holland, England, Scandinavia, Germany, France, and Austria, an overtly positive attitude toward work—akin to Marx's labor theory of value—began to emerge. *Homo faber* (man the maker) now took precedence over man the contemplator and, for some, even man the sinner. Summing up the myriad social consequences of such a mental shift—particularly for the lower sort—Joyce Appleby writes: "When work was no longer seen as part of an unending drudgery that just kept people alive, it took on a new value. Work created surpluses for exchange, work created wealth. In reevaluating work, those who marveled at the world's new productivity were enhancing the worth of labor—what ordinary men and women did."[13] Implicit, although not yet explicit, in this redefinition of work was the assumption that it would foster the disciplines of upward mobility.

The Catholic Church for centuries had included in its ranks such progressive and labor-oriented groups as the Benedictines and Cistercians. (Or at least before ca. 1300, when an evident moral and productive lassitude within these houses helped give rise to the mendicant orders.) The guiding principle of the sixth-century Rule of St. Benedict was *Orare est laborare* (To pray is to labor); and (especially important for my concerns) it was in Western monasticism in general that work routines were first systematized and rationalized according to the clock. Monks, particularly in the Cistercian Order, prayed, ate, and worked according to the strict regimen of the monestary's bells.[14] The invention of double-entry bookkeeping, for many the touchstone of capitalistic enterprise, took place in either Genoa or Pisa some three centuries before the Reformation. Moreover, what Weber called "occidential capitalism" was itself a product of the Christian Middle Ages. Techniques we once believed uniquely characteristic of the capitalistic age, including joint liability, partnerships, letters of credit, deposit and exchange banking, bills of exchange, double-entry bookkeeping, and marine insurance, all originated during or before the Middle Ages. Investors in Catholic Florence by the early fifteenth century had available to them such sophisticated legal devices as *accomandita* contracts (allowing limited-liability investment in partnerships) and time deposits (paying a fixed rate of interest for capital kept in the firm for a specified period). Florence's public debt was held by individuals in the form of negotiable instruments paying—in the case of the Seven Percent Fund—up to 7 percent per annum.[15]

Within canon law itself, a more positive (quasi-egalitarian) stance toward labor and striving behavior was emerging by the late medieval period. The tradition of radical Conciliarist thought associated with Pierre d'Ailly and Jean Gerson in the early fifteenth century and such radical jurists as Bartolus of Sassoferrato and Salamonio challenged the legitimacy of the three-ordered, labor-degrading society—with those who pray, those who fight, and those who work arrayed in descending order.[16] In the Catholic humanism of Erasmus and Montaigne, such challenges became almost indistinguishable from Protestant dissent. By the later seventeenth century, one could fairly describe French Jansenism as represented by Pierre Nicole (1625–1695), with its predestinarian theology, ascetic ways, and striving ethic, as a form of Calvinistic Catholicism.[17]

Still, it fell to radical Protestants to bring about the full dignification of labor. It was the Reformers' dual emphasis on the positive merit of hard work and the duty of all men and women to perform it that signaled a real break with the past. Calvinist desires to glorify God in pursuing one's daily work and the conviction that all work should be productive—the doctrine of vocation—became distinctively Protestant characteristics by the early seventeenth century. The abandonment of ethical dualism—the separation of humankind between the *consilia* (religious orders) and the *praecepta* (sinful masses)—eliminated the distinction between the higher morality of the monastery and the lower morality of the everyday world. With the elimination of the intercessory class, living the godly life became the responsibility of every woman and man, not the prerogative of the cloistered few. Regardless of station, one's principal obligation was the glorification of God through earthly labors. Universalizing the obligation to work, sacralizing the workplace, and rationalizing time, Protestants both spiritualized labor and collapsed the ancient and Scholastic bifurcation between workers and thinkers.[18]

And for the first time in the West, *ordinary* work was celebrated. As Huldrych Zwingli wrote, "In the things of this life, the laborer is most like to God." Martin Luther advised his congregation: "Even though [your work] seems very trivial and contemptible, make sure you regard it as great and precious, not on account of your worthiness, but because it has its place within that jewel and holy treasure, the Word and commandment of God." Drawing on the same Pauline doctrine that later would animate John Smith, Luther declared: "It is not fitting that one man should live in idleness on another's labor, or be rich and live comfortably at the cost of another's hardship, as it is according to our perverted custom. St. Paul says, 'whoever will not work shall not eat.' "[19] The Reverend Joseph Hall, effectively inverting Thomistic categories, preached that it was not the kind of work that was critical, but rather whether or not it was being done to glorify God: "The homeliest service that we doe in an honest calling, though it be but to plow, or digge, if done in obedience, and conscience of God's Commandment, is crowned with an ample reward; whereas the best workers for their kinde (preaching, praying, offering Evangelicall sacrifices) if without respect of God's injunction and glory, are loaded with curses. God loveth adverbs; and cares not how good, but how well." Laying out the theological underpinnings of communal capitalism, Reformed preachers told the faithful that "A cobbler, a smith, a farmer, each has the work and office of his task, and yet they are all alike consecrated priests and bishops, and every one by means of his own work or office must benefit and serve every other, that in this way many kinds of work [may] be done for the bodily and spiritual welfare of the community."[20]

For Protestants, daily labors—however humble—were nothing less than the "masks of God." Like the Old Testament Jews, they rooted all labor in a single Creator, who called all men and women to participate in His creative work as history unfolds.[21] Reformed theologians believed that God worked through secondary causes, through the material labors of individual men and women. Through the workings of the order of redemption, they believed, God had created both a social system that included the means of grace *and* the faculties of the self that would express it in daily behavior.[22] Luther put it most directly, and he put it in language that both John Winthrop and the Reverend Richard Mather would later echo. He also expressly included women as well as men within the ranks of the godly laborers:

> What else is all our work to God—whether in the fields, in the garden, in the city, in the house, in war, or in government—but . . . a child's performance by which He wants to give his gifts in the fields, at home, and everywhere else? These are the masks of God, behind which He wants to remain concealed and do all things. . . . He joins man and woman [in labor] so that it appears to be the work of man and woman, and yet He does it under the cover of such masks. We have a saying: "God gives every good thing, but not just by waving a wand." God gives all good gifts; but you must lend a hand and take the bull by the horns; that is, you must work and thus give God good cause and a mask.

In exhorting men and women to "lend a hand and take the bull by the horns," Luther baptized the new order of striving and enterprise. In arguing that God had given each person a particular station in life in which he was to labor for his material necessities—and thus be a burden to none—Luther both undercut the rationale for the mendicant orders and endowed daily labors with a new moral urgency.[23]

But it was John Calvin (1509–1564), the only systematizer among the Reformers, who made Protestantism a genuinely revolutionary creed. He did so by wedding to Lutheranism the Old Testament prophetic tradition of personal responsibility. The ethical centerpiece of Calvinism was the belief—paradoxical for a predestinarian theology—that all men and women were totally responsible for their own behavior.[24] This conviction, as much as anything else, is what made possible New England's culture of discipline. Calvin himself, and those who reinterpreted his systematics thereafter—Theodorus Beza, Martin Bucer, William Perkins, and John Cotton—made obedience to the law and fulfillment of one duties to others preconditions for elect status. This is not simply a question of conversion anxiety. A loving God inspires reciprocal affection among the saints, which they manifest in their labors. *Agape,* as well as anxiety, thus drives the saints to their labors. The hope of salvation "flowed from and reinforced an ethic of self-discipline."[25] The seeking of the transcendent in this world—that specifically Protestant form of illuminism—was rooted in the immediacy of grace, available directly to individual men and women.[26] No longer mediated through the sacraments and ecclesiastical institutions, grace "became present in the immediate historical present."[27] In forging the Calvinist-Puritan, answerable only to God and to his or her own conscience, Calvin created what was arguably the first "disciplined" human type, and laid the basis for the culture of discipline's fixation with personal responsibility. It is in Calvin, as Herbert Lüthy has emphasized, that the Old Testament prophetic desire to conform word and deed, doctrine and practice, emerged in its starkest form. It was this cast of mind, not simply a legitimization of usury or a more friendly attitude toward acquisitiveness, that most linked Calvinism to capitalism. Calvinists were the catalysts for the emerging order of commercial capitalism because they built their theology on a notion of personal accountability.[28]

Both products and purveyors of the new values of industry

and enterprise, Calvinists such as the early Bay Colonists saw the world as malleable—not fixed—and attempted to shape it in their own image. The creation of ascetic Puritanism was, from a cultural perspective, a revolutionary act. These "free" men and women, who were, as Lüthy points out, "responsible to themselves and their own conscience and—unlike the inner-directed Lutherans—active in the world, spread their effect far beyond the realm even of the Calvinist diaspora and far beyond the time of the initial intensity of belief, to become a yeast in the Western world, the most active agents of the development toward a modern Western society in which 'capitalism' . . . is but one strand among many." From both old Geneva and the Puritan settlements of New England, a "revolution in the truest sense set forth."[29]

The core of this revolution was what Weber called a "transvaluation of values." Calvinism, as the history of early New England reflects, contributed to the rise of capitalism most directly by rendering the daily labors of men and women at once sacred and routine. It made humankind's work God's work. It made cobblers, smiths, and farmers "consecrated priests and bishops." It endowed mothers and fathers with the sacred task of inculcating the habits of "holy conversation." It provided an inner compulsion to maximize labor and the returns from labor, producing a zeal for work unlike anything the world had yet seen. It applied to ruling-class males the same strictures against idleness and self-indulgence that had traditionally been directed exclusively at laboring women and men. It created a rhetoric of discipline *and* the religious and civil institutions to enforce it. Puritan lecturers, exhorters, and pamphleteers between the 1580s and 1640s constructed both an ethical code for the conduct of daily life and the communal institutions necessary to compel obedience among the faithful. In New England, the reliance on testified regenerate membership—what became known as the "New England Way"—put this code into practice in Congregational churches from the mid-1630s to the end of the seventeenth century. Calvinism endowed the standard virtues with a religious imperative, as important in their six days of the week as were prayer, sermons, and the sacraments on the seventh.[30]

Obedience to the law and the fulfillment of one's duties to

others was reinforced by the experiential and affective dimension of the Reformed tradition. Until the mid-eighteenth century—far longer than in England—the calling remained a mainstay in the American colonists' conception of work.[31] The calling, as we have seen, was the belief that God had called every person to serve Him—and the community as well—by working in some useful and productive occupation. Before entering an occupation, craft, or profession, a person was required to determine whether he (and originally the opportunity to choose was confined to males) had a calling to undertake it. One's talents, inclinations, and station were all assessed in answering this question. What was not acceptable was a life of leisure, a life of prayer, or a life devoted to "vicious" luxury—any life, that is, that was unproductive, that failed to contribute to the common good. One's occupation was one's "particular calling," which needed to be in accord with the "general calling" of seeking redemption. After being called to a given occupation, a person's task was to labor in it with the same single-minded devotion, relentlessness, and enterprise that one was expected to display in the larger task of seeking salvation.[32]

Idleness, sloth, and shoddy workmanship were to be shunned, as were such unproductive or morally suspect professions as acting, fortunetelling, and making playing cards. Thrift, time-consciousness, and frugality were to be encouraged, as was rationalized planning in all facets of one's life. The doctrine of stewardship—the belief that all earthly possessions were temporary gifts from God—demanded a rational expansion of one's resources. The Parable of the Talents taught people to use the capital and skills temporarily in their possession aggressively and entrepreneurially. Production was encouraged; consumption beyond the level of moderate comfort discouraged.[33] Self-indulgent, luxurious living meant fewer surplus goods available for supporting church and community. Thereby was God dishonored.

The emphasis throughout was on socially beneficial productivity. The Protestant rejection of such Catholic vocational preferences as asceticism, sacrament, and status meant that the most godly calling was the most obviously economic and productive one: that of the husbandman, the artisan, the tradesman, and—in a departure from earlier practices—the merchant. In contrast to Scholastic theory, merchants were seen as the benefactors of humanity by mercantilist writers and most Puritans by the early seventeenth century. Whereas merchants' activities had not been equated with moral turpitude in the Christian West since the twelfth century, outright celebration of the life of commerce awaited the early seventeenth century. Substituting the principle of usefulness for older aristocratic notions of public virtue, mercantilist writers hammered home the message that men in commerce served the public. In the *Circle of Commerce* (1623), Edward Misselden declared that the merchant's profession was noble because he increased the nation's wealth. Misselden and most mercantilist writers, except for Gerard de Malynes, praised the members of even such monopolistic enterprises as the Merchant Adventurers, Levant Company, and India Company as "Stewards of the Kingdom's wealth."[34]

By contrast, the Scholastic writers had believed that usury, cheating, and mendacity were common—and frequently indulged in—mercantile temptations. Until the late twelfth century, many theologians had come close to equating the very act of trading *(negotium)* with the sin of covetousness. Such views were manifest in the pronouncement of St. Bonaventure: "*et de hoc rarissime evadunt mercatores* (and very rarely do merchants escape from this [sin])." The Scholastics, like the physiocrats and Jeffersonians of the eighteenth century, almost without exception preferred agriculture to trade, and this view colored their perception of the usefulness of merchants. (The seventeenth-century mercantilists' encomiums to merchants also stood in sharp contrast to Adam Smith's openly scornful view of overseas traders. Believing, with the physiocrats, in the superiority of agriculture to trade and industry, Smith spoke contemptuously of the "mean rapacity [and] monopolizing spirit of merchants and manufactures.") Some English Puritans, including the colonial organizer John White, occasionally gave voice to such anti-mercantile sentiments. Writing to John Winthrop in 1637, the Reverend White declared that "it is high time that a Magazine [communal warehouse], out of which needful provisions might be had at a reasonable [rate], were erected, and shopkeepers [be] made unuseful, who [otherwise] will prove [to be] soe many moaths to their neighbors." But in Massachusetts Bay itself, such anti-mercantile comments were notable for their rarity. While some individual merchants such as Robert Keayne were denounced as "moaths" and "Cormorants," outright condemnations of the act of trading were infrequent, even among clergymen.[35]

Although English-speaking Protestants retained a belief in the Great Chain of Being—the conception that God had appointed viceregents to order and instruct society—the activities of magistrates and preachers as well as merchants were increasingly justified on the grounds of utility, not cosmology. According to Richard Baxter, the English divine who was for Weber the most representative Puritan, plowmen and shepherds were to be given the same status as magistrates and ministers:

> The callings most useful to the public good are the magistrates, the pastors, and teachers of the church, schoolmasters, physicians, lawyers, etc., husbandmen (ploughmen, graziers, and shepherds); and next to them are mariners, clothiers, booksellers, tailors, and such others that are employed about things most necessary to mankind; and some callings are employed about matters of so little use (as tobacco-sellers, lace-sellers, feather-makers, periwig-makers, and many more such), that he may choose better [and] should be lothe to take up with one of these, though possibly in itself it may be lawful.

In emphasizing the religious and psychological importance of work done for the community's good, Baxter laid out the animating principle of communal capitalism: the link between individual and collective well-being. It was, he averred, "a great satisfaction to any honest mind to spend his life in doing the greatest good he can; and a prison and constant calamity to be tied [spending] one's life in doing little good at all to others, though he should grow rich by it himself."[36]

Even before the Puritan migrants set foot in America, the particular calling was being enforced by official Company policy. The "General Letter" circulated through the Massachusetts Bay Company in the spring of 1629 mandated that all persons resident in Massachusetts Bay Colony must "apply themselves to one calling [or more] and no idle drone [shall] be permitted to live among us." In 1642, the colony passed a law that went so far as to threaten families with the loss of their children and apprentices if they were not brought up in a legitimate calling. The selectmen of each town were empowered to remove from households any children or apprentices insufficiently trained in "some honest Lawfull calling, labor, or imployment, either in husbandry or some other trade profitable to themselves or the Common-wealth." Those children without a warrantable calling were to be taken away from their parents or masters and bound by the quarterly court to new masters until they were twenty-one if boys, eighteen if girls.[37]

The same logic, that all inhabitants should be constantly employed in a productive calling (although always allowing "due recreation" and rest), applied to legislation directed against fishermen in 1673. Heretofore a favored group of workers because of the economically vital nature of their trade, the fishermen had since the 1640s been exempted from the obligations of militia drill. But, when the General Court learned of some mariners' penchant for spending their shoretime hours "ideling, gaming, or spending their time unprofittably," especially on days when others were at militia drill, it revoked the exemption. In order to prevent the discouragement of those men who discharged their militia duties faithfully, the Court ordered that "all fisherman . . . when they are at home, (and not imployed necessarily, and so judged by the cheife officers,) shall attend publick traynings, or else be fined five shillings."[38]

As John Winthrop and Captain Smith both prophesied, New England proved singularly inhospitable to men and women regarded as drones. Living in the Puritan commonwealth meant working to support it with a relentlessness that may indeed have been historically aberrant. Weber's assertion that the calling was at the heart of the Protestant ethic is documented by its centrality in the ministerial rhetoric throughout the seventeenth century. Equally beyond doubt is the peculiar salience of the doctrine of the calling in the New England colonies. Nowhere else in the early modern world, including Pennsylvania, was the rhetoric of the calling so all-pervasive in public and ecclesiastical discourse.

What may be questioned, however, is the supposition by Weber—and many who have followed him—that a rationalized workplace (the Protestant ethic) invariably gave way to calculative rationalism (the spirit of capitalism). As a committed atheist, Weber found it difficult to treat religion in other than functionalist terms; and the almost routine conflation of the Protestant ethic with the spirit of capitalism in the subsequent literature shows the continuation of this tendency.[39] Weber defined the spirit of capitalism as "calculative rationalism"—what the Protestant ethic became when it was divorced of its religious motive. He, and most of his disciples (Tawney, above all others) portrayed the one as following almost inexorably upon the other. The writings of early New England's most renowned theologian, the Reverend John Cotton, suggest the difficulty with such an interpretation. To a striking degree, we have been all too ready to believe the Puritans' own denunciations of the "worldliness" growing in their midst. Among the most dangerous thing one can do on this issue is to take the Puritan Jeremiahs at their word.

What is commonly regarded as the finest exposition of the Protestant ethic in New England literature is found in Cotton's *The Way of Life* (1641). It epitomized the demand that people should devote themselves to profitmaking—*without* succumbing to the temptations of profit. That human labors were efficacious only if performed within the context of the communally obligated calling was the linchpin to Cotton's thought. If "thou beest a man that lives without a calling, though thou hast two thousands to spend, yet if thou hast no calling, tending to [the] publique good, thou art an uncleane beast." For Cotton, it was axiomatic that all Puritans needed to be "setled in a good calling, though it be but of a daylabourer." But, unless this was a productive calling that served to increase the colony's material wealth, it was—quite literally—ungodly work: "Seek one another's welfare," Cotton enjoined, because "it will not onely serve [one's] owne turne, but the turn of other men. Bees will not suffer drones among them, but if they lay up any thing, it shall be for them that cannot work."[40]

The central tension within the rhetoric of the calling—indeed, some believe it to be the central tension within Puritanism itself—was the need to show "diligence in worldly business and yet deadness to the world." Considerably understating the psychological pressure involved in mediating this tension, Cotton spoke of the "combination of virtues strangely mixed in every lively holy Christian." Motive, that most elusive of all human qualities, was quite literally everything. To all outward appearances, the diligent saint (working for God's glory only) was indistinguishable from the diligent worldling (working for himself or herself only):

> Say not therefore when you see two men laboring very diligently and busily in the world, say not, here is a couple of worldings, for two men may do the same business, and have the same success, and yet [there is] a marvelous difference between them: the heart of the one may be dead to these things, he looks at them as they be; indeed, *but crumbs that fall from the children's table.* He looks not at them as his chiefest good; but *the bread of life,* the spiritual good of his soul, that is the thing which he chiefly labors after. And another man places his happiness and felicity in them and makes them his chiefest good, and so there is a manifest difference between them.[41]

This was such a mystery as none can read but they that know it themselves:

> For a man to *rise early, and go to bed late, and eat the bread of carefulness,* [is] not a sinful but a provident care, and to avoid idleness, cannot endure to spend any idle time, takes all opportunities to be doing something, early and late, and loseth no opportunity [to] go any way and bestir himself for profit—this will he do most diligently in his calling. And yet [he must] be a man dead-hearted to the world.[42]

Saints needed to improve every bright and shining hour on this earth, to go any way and exert any effort to make a profit, and to do so with verve and innovativeness, and yet never avert their eyes from things celestial. Such a cast of mind was precisely the "marvelous difference" between saint and sinner, between the elect and the reprobate. The brethren were enjoined to be "busy like ants, morning and evening, early and late, and labor diligently with their hands, and with their wits, and which way soever as may be the best improvement of a man's talent, it must be employed to the best advantage." Yet the saint's "heart and mind and affections" always had to be directed above.[43]

Aside from time spent in sleep or in lawful recreation, the "lively holy Christian" was enjoined to spend all his hours in the performance of the two callings. Thomas Shepard stated flatly that "for as it is a sin to nourish worldly thoughts when God set you a work in spiritual, heavenly employments, so it is, in some respects, as great a sin to suffer yourself to be distracted by spiritual thoughts, when God sets you on work in civil (yet lawful) employments." Richard Baxter advised the faithful to ensure that "the time of your Sleep be so much only as health requireth; For precious time is not to be wasted in unnecessary sluggishness."[44] Baxter, more so than the American Cotton, was not averse to reminding his followers that time-thrift paid material as well as spiritual dividends. "Remember how gainful the Redeeming of time is," he declared, "in Merchandize, or [in] any trading; in husbandry or any gaining course, we use to say of a man that hath grown rich by it, that he hath made use of his Time."[45] Making an hourly calibration of his obligations, Boston's Increase Mather wrote in his diary that "I am not willing to allow my self above Seven Hours in Four and Twenty for Sleep: but would spend the rest of my Time in Attending to the Duties of my personal or generall Calling." The merchant Robert Keayne, censured and fined by the Massachusetts General Court in 1639 for price gouging, took refuge in such time-stewardship while defending his actions. Composing his last will and testament during the 1650s, the import merchant vigorously denied that "I have had in my whole time either in Old England or New many spare hours to spend unprofitably away, or to refresh myself with recreations. . . ."[46]

That such a rationalized approach to one's daily labors was itself a form of irrationality has perhaps been Weber's most abiding insight. An ethic that enjoined men and women to labor incessantly with their hands as well as their wits, that told them to improve every talent to the best advantage, and all the while to eschew the temptations of worldliness, made psychological demands of a wholly new order on Western men and women. As Stephen Foster declares, "if Christians had been under orders to die daily for sixteen hundred years before a European even set foot in New England, at least they had not always been told to pursue their mundane affairs with a truly holy violence in the process." The right thing was simply too close to the wrong thing. The difference between "covetous affection" and "diligent zeal," writes Foster, "could be grasped only by a mental contortionist." And while the genuine worldling was likely to spend his terrestial existence blithely ignorant of the consequences of his ungodly conduct, the saint was likely to be self-questioning, no matter how virtuous his daily life. Given that each Puritan had to judge his attitude by a standard which "almost always required him to bring in a verdict of guilty," it is not difficult to account for the answering calls the clergy's jeremiads invariably provoked.[47]

In the place of the old legal and economic compulsion to work, the Puritans substituted a sense of duty and the force of habit. During a time when coercive forms of labor mobilization such as slavery and indentured servitude were taking root elsewhere in British America, New England's Puritans relied on the inner compulsions of worldly asceticism.[48] Although during the 1640s, as we have seen, prominent Bay Colony leaders such as Emmanuel Downing called for the importation of slaves, the future health of New England's economy would ultimately rest on the diligence and enterprise of the sons and daughters of Puritan householders. The ethical tenets imposed on New England's young included: diligence in one's calling; strict asceticism in the use of material goods or enjoyment of earthly pleasures; and an acute time-consciousness. That such a cultural shift toward asceticism was the necessary correlative of the larger egalitarian thrust of Protestantism was the insight of one of the greatest modern-day critics of "puritanical efficiency," the Italian political theorist Antonio Gramsci. It is not at all difficult to see seventeenth-century New England as "a state where the working masses are no longer subject to coercive pressure from a superior class and where new methods of production and work have to be acquired by means of reciprocal persuasion and by convictions proposed and accepted by each individual." This process was aided in North America by the fact that the colonies began with a settler population notably short of the groups Gramsci dubbed "pensioners of economic history"—aristocrats, courtiers, functionaries, and all those living off inherited wealth.[49]

At the center of the process of reciprocal persuasion was a war on idleness. To a large degree, of course, the contempt for idleness was the necessary correlative for the respect for labor. In a nation that, through William Petty and John Locke, helped formulate the labor theory of property, idleness was castigated precisely because labor was so highly valued.[50] Moreover, Gramsci's comments aside, there was an egalitarian thrust to the saints' prescriptions against idleness, one that became an integral feature of communal capitalism. As we have seen, in a real departure from earlier practices, these injunctions included the idle rich as well as the idle poor. Governor Winthrop's public willingness to take up the hoe was the literal embodiment of the Weberian cultural transformation. The late sixteenth-century shift within the Reformed tradition from a passive to an active view of faith helped lay the groundwork here. Theodorus Beza and Heinrich Bullinger restored a dimension of human agency—of justification for worldly effort—seemingly lacking in Calvin's own formulations. The Heidelberg Catechism (1562) of Zacharius Ursinus and Kaspar Olevianus, with its teaching that good works were done in faith as signs of humankind's thankfulness, passed into English Protestantism—and eventually New England—through the writings of William Perkins.[51] Perkins, in his *Treatise of Callings* (1605) and elsewhere, fashioned a practical divinity. He castigated the idleness not only of rogues, beggars, vagabonds, and monks, but also of rich gentlemen who "spend their days in eating and drinking, in sports, and in pastimes." Perkins's student, William Ames, made as the centerpiece of his teachings the notion that both rich and poor needed to recall that "man is made for Labour and not for Idleness." "God sent [all men and women] into this world," declared another preacher, not "as a Play-house, but a Work-house." Richard Mather, founder of New England's most famous ministerial dynasty, echoed Perkins's and Luther's pronouncements on the dignity of even the most humble labor of both women and men and the need for all to perform it. In his 1657 "farewell sermon," Mather advised members of his Dorchester congregation that "you must perform your religious duties" amidst

> your eating and marriage . . . your buying and selling, your plowing and hoeing, your sowing and mowing and reaping, your feeding cattle and keeping sheep, your planting orchards and gardens, your baking and brewing, your building houses or outhouses, your fencing in ground or [what] other business ever.

All Christians, declared John Cotton, must be "setled in a good calling, though it be but of a day-labourer. . . ." Christ himself "stooped to a very low employment, rose up from Supper, and girded himselfe with a Towell, and washed his Disciples feet."[52]

Such was the vision of Puritan asceticism—a vision that made washing feet, digging ditches, feeding cattle, and baking and brewing God's work. The heart of the Protestant ethic for Weber was a form of (irrational) rationalization of effort, especially in work. It inspired men and women to work in a methodical, sustained, and diligent fashion—to "improve each bright and shining hour," as the painful preachers put it. And because this was done for God, not man, there could be no surcease of effort. Indeed, it was the spiritual, not material, component of the Protestant ethic that gave it its insatiable quality. As Stephen Foster notes, it was "precisely *because* men labored for God and *not* for gold (or status or honor)" that they "had to continue working in their callings constantly: material needs or even the desire for riches might be satisfied at some finite point, God never." This insatiable quality of the Protestant ethic was what led Weber to contend that Puritanism—because of the doctrine of Election—led to the psychological drive to expand capital and hence to the development of capitalist society. It was at this point, for Weber, that the Protestant ethic *became* the spirit of capitalism. The source for both industriousness and accumulation, according to Weber's (most-contested) formulation, was anxiety over predestination. Reformed Protestantism's rejection of the Catholic system of rituals and sacraments, he famously argued, came at the price of lacerating personal anxiety about assurance.[53]

It was here that Weber veered off course. He correctly argued that conversion anxiety was a leading component of the Protestant ethic because it provided the psychological basis for striving behavior. But in presenting conversion anxiety in Arminian (or "works righteousness") terms—implying that the saints worked hard in order to *prove* their election—Weber critically misrepresented English Calvinism. He did so by conflating the covenant of works and the covenant of grace. In part through the influence of Beza and the Heidelberg theologians, the distinction between these two covenants emerged clearly within English Puritanism after the 1580s—with significant consequences for the future. Weber left the impression that Puritans believed in works righteousness rather than justification by faith alone—what the saints called "unmerited free grace." Drawing on Calvin's understanding of the testimony of expectant faith resulting from grace, he declared that Puritans "held [it] to be an absolute duty to consider oneself chosen," because the lack of such self-confidence was seen to be "the result of insufficient faith, hence of imperfect grace." Weber contended that "the religious valuation of restless, continuous, systematic work in a worldly calling, as the highest means of asceticism, and at the same time the surest and most evident proof of genuine faith, must have been the most powerful conceivable lever for the expansion of that attitude toward life which we have here called the spirit of capitalism." Abandoning his characteristic subtlety in dealing with Calvinist divinity, Weber flatly asserted that intense worldly activity "alone disperses religious doubts and gives the certainty of grace."[54]

But proving one's faith—achieving *certainty* of grace—through striving behavior was never a feature of Reformed thought in the post-Dortian period (i.e., after the twin doctrines of the total depravity of humankind and its complete dependence on divine grace had been systematized at the synod held at Dort, Holland, in 1618–19). Indeed, the impossibility of achieving salvation through good works was close to the main point of Puritan theology. From the 1580s onward the theological keystone to Reformed Protestantism was the distinction between the two covenants: the prelapsarian covenant of works and the postlapsarian covenant of grace. It was during the 1570s that Reformed divines, with Heidelberg theologians taking the lead, began to reformulate the relationship of nature and grace in God's treatment of humankind in terms of the two covenants.[55] The fruit of this reformulation was what American Puritans would call the "New Covenant," the successor to the Abrahamic covenant between God and the Jewish nation, as set forth in Genesis 17:10 (in which God established "my covenant, which ye shall keep, between me and you and thy seed after thee," and which was sealed by the circumcision of all male children). Under the New Covenant theology of the 1590s, as William Stoever writes:

> God originally entered into a "covenant of works" with Adam, promising mankind everlasting life in return for obedience to the divine law. After the fall, God entered a "covenant of grace" with Adam, which became fully effective when Christ's active obedience and atoning death fulfilled the requirements of the law. In the covenant of grace, salvation is offered mankind in return for sincere faith in God's promise to justify the believer in virtue of Christ's work, and God himself undertakes to enable the elect to believe. Adam's fall, Puritans held, destroyed mankind's ability to apprehend the ultimately true and to will the truly good, *thereby rendering human beings incapable of achieving blessedness by their own efforts under the covenant of works.*[56]

Puritan theology was based on the distinction between "saving faith" (God's free gift to the predestined elect) and historical faith (intellectual acceptance of Christian doctrine).[57] In typically dialectical fashion, it contained elements of both conditionality and absoluteness. It taught any striving individual that in the absence of God's freely—but arbitrarily—offered grace, he or she was incapable of obeying the law and was therefore damned. Conversion brought sanctification, the regimen of continuous, disciplined behavior that every saint needed to exhibit. Sanctified behavior was the basis for New England's culture of discipline. While no amount of diligent labor could prove election, the *failure* to strive was conclusive evidence that one had not yet been offered saving grace. The ambiguity in the conversion experienced energized New Englanders. Sanctification, the gradual, day-by-day improvement of a person's behavior in obedience to God, was a consequence, not a cause, of justification. Moreover, the conversion experience itself brought not a surcease from effort but the opposite: "no sooner was faith kindled than a combat began in which the soul must fight against doubt and despair by 'fervent, constant, and earnest invocation for pardon.' This combat never ceased. . . ." The preachers invariably described salvation as a work of "unconceiveable difficulty."[58]

Preaching that "A Christian's real Work begins when he is Converted," Samuel Willard (1640–1707), minister of the Third Church in Boston, advised his parishioners that conversion "is a principle of spiritual life which must have some act and exercise and that is doing the will of God, whether in pulpit or countinghouse."[59] Willard's 1,000-page *Compleat Body of Divinity* (1688), the most systematic exposition of Puritan theology ever published in New England, proclaimed:

> *there is but* one Way, in *one* Covenant, *according to which* God *hath engaged to make Man happy.* It is true, there are two Covenants, in which God hath been concerned with Man: the Covenant of *Works* and the Covenant of *Grace;* and these have their *several* ways and rules. In the *first,* Man was to be made happy by *Works;* in the second, by *Grace.* The former depended upon man's *personal Obedience;* the latter upon *Christ's.* The former called for *doing,*

> the other for *believing*. But each of them have their *limited* way. And man being *fallen* from the first Covenant-Condition, and set it against him, and having lost his strength, it can *no more* be a Rule of Happiness to him. It is now only by the *New Covenant,* that he can ever hope to obtain Life & Salvation.[60]

Under the covenant of grace, salvation came through God's free—but arbitrarily offered—grace. Saving faith produced good works (and thus, happiness), not the other way around. But, as New England's history makes evident, such a formula did not become grounds for lassitude and debilitating paralysis. Quite the opposite. Told that their actions could have no impact on their prospects for salvation in the absence of saving grace, Congregational men and women were warned that the best prophylactic against the sin of despair was unrelenting effort in all daily activities.

By eliding the critical distinction between the covenant of works and the covenant of grace, Max Weber turned the real Protestant ethic on its head. The main—and undeniably potent—link between the Puritan work ethic and conversion anxiety was negative, not positive. No Reformed Protestant, from Theodorus Beza and Hieronymus Zanchius (and their English popularizer, William Perkins) through John Cotton and Jonathan Edwards, believed that it was possible to demonstrate elect status through striving behavior—or the corollary that worldly success invariably denoted the presence of saving grace.[61] Sanctified behavior, vitually all Reformed preachers agreed, did not prove a justified state. But, in a typical Puritan double-bind, the *absence* of sanctified conduct was viewed as prima facie evidence of reprobation. While it was not possible to prove one's election by exhibiting diligence, conscientiousness, and moral seriousness, the failure to display these qualities, all agreed, signified reprobation. Even under the exquisitely calibrated machinery of the federal covenant, any New Englander who believed that he or she deserved to be saved was deemed guilty of the sin of pride, or worse.[62]

The key element of the conversion experience was its ambiguous combination of conditionality and absoluteness.

This was an ambiguity that had the effect of fueling striving behavior. True assurance was always imperfect. In order to be sure, one had to be unsure. As Edmund Morgan declares: "Though God's decrees were immutable and no man whom He had predestined to salvation could fail to attain it, the surest earthly sign of a damned soul was security." Indeed, it was the acceptance by the Arminian Caroline bishops of the heresy of works righteousness (the belief that salvation was achieved through human, not divine, effort) that helped drive English Puritans to Massachusetts Bay in the first place. During the Antinomian crisis of 1636–37, John Winthrop declared that the claim by Anne Hutchinson (1591–1643) to immediate revelation "tended to slothfulness, and to quench[-ing] all indevour in the creature" because the prospective saint needed only to wait passively for the Holy Spirit to take possession of her. Without some element of "preparation" for grace, should it eventually be offered, there was much less incentive for striving behavior. Why should a settler exert himself if he could "stand still and waite for Christ to doe all for him"?[63]

Despite his misconstruction of conversion anxiety, Weber's larger insights as to its consequences remain valid. Manifestly, there *was* something distinctive about the Protestant ethic, as the history of communal capitalism in New England suggests. While the continued existence of pre-Reformation practices blocked the full implementation of the culture of discipline in the Old World, Massachusetts afforded an opportunity to build an entire society on such principles.[64] It was in the Bay Colony that the Calvinist culture of discipline took deepest root. In their annual work calendar, public policy, family governance, and doctrine of the calling, the New Englanders made the Protestant ethic the very core of their ecclesiastical and civic identity. Whereas in England, Scotland, Holland, and the Swiss cantons the culture of discipline could only be imposed selectively, on individual congregations, Massachusetts Bay Colony was founded on such principles from the beginning.

The most distinctive feature of the culture of discipline was a preoccupation with immiserating vices. Here it is important to remember that Puritanism (and Protestantism in general) began as a countercultural revolt. Reformers were exercised not only over communion rails, stained-glass windows, tithes, annates, Crusaders' and Peter's pence, but also over the public tolerance of immiserating vices. "The vices that were most bitterly denounced from the pulpit and on the floor of the House of Commons during the late sixteenth century," declares William Hunt, "were those that caused poverty: avarice and oppression on the part of the propertied; envy, sloth, and sensuality on the part of the poor." Ascetic Puritans, as we have seen, rejected Scholastic dualism in ethics, and assessed spiritual and moral conduct by the same highly calibrated and recondite standard. At the heart of both stood the notion of personal responsibility. Self-government and self-denial were the means to free oneself from the slavery of sinful and impoverishing addictions. English and, later, American Puritans defined "freedom" and "liberty" primarily in terms of the personal virtue that flowed from the possession of grace. St. Paul had admonished the Galatians (5:1), "Stand fast therefore in the liberty wherewith Christ hath made us free."[65] Hunt describes sanctification as "an elaborate problem of detoxification." The saints were enjoined "to rid themselves of [all] debilitating addictions—to luxury, prestige, sex, and alcohol." In this way Puritanism began as, and always remained, a demand for what contemporaries called a reformation of manners.[66]

Theological shifts played a key role here. By the late sixteenth century, in England no less than on the Continent, the reformation of doctrine accomplished by Luther and Calvin was followed by demands for a second reformation, a reformation of life. From the time of the Presbyterian movement of the late sixteenth century onward, dogmatic positions within confessional groups became less important than the improvement of the practical conduct of daily life. Disciplinary measures needed to be taken to educate and indoctrinate the faithful, aided by the mass production of devotional literature and the systematics and polemics of Reformed apologists. Within Calvinist populations these tendencies were quickened by a new narrative of history predicting that the

"End Time" was at hand, that the age-old conflict between Christ and Antichrist had reached its climactic phase. As the derogative term "Puritan" given to the saints by their opponents suggested, they hoped to escape into the "End Time" purity promised in the New Testament. Protestantism's recovery of the true gospel was said to herald the final defeat of the Beast of the Apocalypse (Roman Catholicism), an event in sacred time that was expected to usher in the Second Coming of Christ and the thousand-year rule of the righteous. Such eschatological speculation became especially pronounced in England after the outbreak of the Thirty Years War in 1618, and led to the intensification of longstanding popular fears of "popery" in the realm.[67]

With Protestants on the Continent afflicted by war, famine, persecution, and the forceable reconversion of some 6 million of their members between 1580 to 1640, the absolute need to work hard and eschew vice and luxury seemed self-evident. Some believe that it was the millennialism brought by the new emphasis on eschatology, not predestinarian theology itself, that was most responsible for the Calvinist demands for a reformation of manners. For English Puritans, the fulfillment of the millennial prophecies of Isaiah and Revelation depended upon the preparationalist self-discipline of the individual believer. Thus for some it was the "concrete reality of the apocalypse, rather than the abstract theory of predestination, which propelled Calvinist preachers to praise and teach the virtues of asceticism." Those confessional groups like the English Puritans that embraced covenant theology placed renewed emphasis on the need for personal discipline, humility, and self-denial as measures to restore the favor of an angry God toward His Chosen People. This eventually became the dominant trope in seventeenth-century New England clerical (and, one supposes, parental) rhetoric.[68]

The preoccupation with immiserating vices helps explain the continuous efforts made in Parliament from the 1570s through the 1620s to outlaw drunkenness, fornication, blasphemy, and sumptuary excess. There were, as both John Smith and John Winthrop recognized, secular as well as religious reasons for regarding certain behaviors as vices and seeking to eradicate them. As William Hunt explains the Puritans' sociology:

> Drunkenness, [the saints believed] led to sloth and dishonesty; fornication left bastards on the poor rates. Blasphemy brought bad luck—both to the blasphemer and the community that tolerated it—and one may assume it was highly correlated with other undesirable social traits. Excess of apparel was a symptom of the competition for status. Conspicuous consumption depleted the charitable resources of the well-to-do and inspired humbler folk with self-destructive envy.[69]

Although a fear of illicit sexual behavior is commonly regarded as the quintessential Puritan concern, drunkenness was in fact a greater preoccupation. From the vantage point of my argument, there were few vices more destructive of the formation of "human capital." There is considerable evidence that many observers—Puritan and non-Puritan alike—believed that drunkenness was becoming an increasingly acute and even dangerous social problem in England by the beginning of the seventeenth century. The availability of cheaper, more potent beer, along with a trend toward more public and less socially regulated drinking, helped to produce the notorious "alehouse culture."[70] Such a culture, many Puritans believed, was about to bring England to ruin not only because it invited the wrath of God, but also because it systematically undermined the personal discipline required for survival in difficult economic times. This was particularly true for the laboring poor. The ability to plan, to consider alternative views of the future, to assign probabilities—in short, to calculate rationally—depended on the possession of a mind unclouded by alcohol.[71]

Indeed, as Hunt discovered from his study of Tudor-Stuart Essex, for the painful preachers, drunkard and saint came to represent the opposite poles of the human spectrum. It was widely believed that alehouses were dangerous to the poor themselves, and there can be no doubt that alcoholism, then as now, dragged many folk down from moderate hardship to utter destitution. In an economically (and often socially) tumultuous period, the man or woman who was diligent, thrifty, and sober, who could think clearly and work hard, was more likely to make it than those who were drunken and feckless. Character counted, something no Puritan preacher was likely to forget. They knew that especially for the day laborer, cottager, or poorer artisan, "the quickest and surest way for a man to improve his economic as well as spiritual, condition was to stay out of Mother Tibbald's alehouse."[72]

In Puritan New England, the program of spiritual detoxification was enforced by a powerful combination of institutions that formed New England's distinctive civic ecology. These included the family, church, board of selectmen, and quarterly court. All were designed to foster those personal virtues that ever since have defined the Puritan work ethic: industriousness, diligence, temperance, workmanship, prudence, rectitude, thrift, independence, the desire for betterment, and (perhaps most important) the capacity for deferred gratification.[73]

What unifies and animates all these traits is the second element of the culture of discipline, a peculiar attitude toward the use of one's time. Puritans objected to drunkenness on the grounds that it led to idle minds and begging hands—in short, to the wasting of "God's precious time." The conviction that time is precious and must be used methodically was a mainstay of Protestant social ethics. It was this belief that helped accelerate that larger cultural shift by which time was conceived not as a succession of agricultural cycles, festivals, and cataclysms, but as a chronological net or template over one's daily life. Indeed, it is not an exaggeration to say—as many have—that Protestantism helped bring time-consciousness out of the cloistered monastery and into the workaday world of ordinary men and women. Anglo-American Puritanism in particular "saturated its believers with an acute sense of the dangers of idleness, enjoining them to guard against the misspence of time and to improve the passing moments, each of which, in the end, had to be accounted for in heaven." Each saint was told that virtually every waking hour should be devoted to "redeeming the time" by improving one's talents. The Reverend Joseph Hall declared categorically that "Nothing is more precious than time." Nothing shall "abide a reckoning more strict and fearfull." The Almighty "plagues the losse of a short time, with a revenge beyond all times. . . ."[74] Cotton Mather observed in equally declamatory fashion that the seeming innocuousness of idleness made it the more pernicious. It was, he wrote, nothing less than the gateway to Hell:

> the most *concealed,* and yet the most *violent,* of all our *passions,* usually is that of IDLENESS. It lays *adamantine chains* of death and of darkness upon us. It holds in *chains* that cannot be shaken off, all our other, though never so impetuous inclinations. . . . We have usually more *strength* to *do good,* than we have *will* to lay it out. Sirs, *Be up, and be doing!* 'Tis too soon yet sure for an *Hic situs est* [Here is the place he rests].[75]

For Mather, as for Hall, every waking moment needed to be saturated with pious action: a willful effort to glorify God through activity. In eulogizing his younger brother Nathaniel, Mather wrote that he "apprehended that the *idle minutes* of our lives were many more than a short liver should allow: that the very filings of *gold,* and of time, were exceeding *precious. . . .*" By the mid-eighteenth century, a more secularized version of these sentiments would be provided by Ben Franklin: "Our time is reduced to a Standard, and the Bullion of the Day [is] minted out into Hours . . . [so that] he that is prodigal of his Hours is . . . a squanderer of money."[76]

The methodization of time brought by ascetic Puritanism, if you will, represented a shift from pre-industrial time to bourgeois time (although such meta-historical categories often conceal as much as they reveal). Time for medieval Christians was an essence, belonging to the community and to God. The original religious injunctions against usury were based on the belief that time could not be "sold" precisely because it belonged to God.[77] Under the scientific scholasticism of the fourteenth century and Italian humanism of the early fifteenth, the concept of time as an essence was supplanted by a view of time as a conceptual construct.[78] The results of this shift were considerable, particularly when combined with technological advances in clockmaking. The medieval workday, like that of the ancients, had been divided into four parts: *tiérce* (from sunrise to midmorning); *sext* (from midmorning till midday); *none* (from midday to midafternoon); and *vespers* (from midafternoon till nightfall).[79] Mechanical advances in clockmaking allowed for the division of the day into the now universal segmentation of twenty-four hours. It was during the fourteenth century that the spread of the mechanical clock and the escapement system allowed for the hour to be calibrated as the twenty-fourth part of the day.[80]

William Perkins acknowledged the cultural potency that the clock had attained by the end of the sixteenth century during one of his admonitions against self-pride. In constructing what would eventually become the "Divine Clockmaker" metaphor, Perkins condemned the

> follie of that man who, having a costly clock [conscience] in his bosome never extolleth or thinketh on the wit and invention of the clock-maker, but is continually in admiration of the spring or watch of the clocke by whose meanes all the wheeles have their swifter or slower, their backward or forward motions, and by which the whole clocke keepeth his course.[81]

Likewise, the Reverend Richard Eaton of the textile community of Coventry emphasized the transitory nature of life by preaching: "we have a great taske and a short time allowed; we had need to listen to the clocke and to counte the houres."[82] In 1630, John Preston made the connection between clocks and religion still more explicit: "in this curious clocke-worke of religion, every pin and wheel that is amisse distempers all." That same year, in his "Modell of Christian Charity," John Winthrop wrote that to love one's brother is to "sett all the faculties on worke in the outward exercise of this duty as when wee bid one make the clocke strike. . . ."[83]

While time-consciousness, not to mention watch-wearing,

was doubtless correlated with social status in early New England, there is evidence in the Massachusetts court records of a popular time framework based on mean, not solar, time. There are a number of suggestions that ordinary settlers in the Bay Colony—including women—conceptualized time in hourly terms. In an Essex County deposition dating from January 1641, one Goodwife Hardy declared that "I saw Mr. Pester, his hose unfastened, between 8 and 9 in the morning and he seemed to me as if he had Laine all night there." Goodwives Felton and Pride likewise deposed that the "Moon rose about eleven or twelve o'clock at night." Two men had been seen leaving the house "at eight o'clock."[84] In Hampshire County in 1686 the widow Sarah Barnard discovered a drunk who had invaded her bedroom and collapsed on her bed and "lay [there] about a quarter of an Houre."[85] In 1690 two men were accused of "abusing the watch about or after Ten of the clock at Night." Even for those not fully liberated from diurnal rhythms, hourly estimates were not uncommon. In a 1660 Essex County deposition regarding events during the morning of an alleged crime, John Jackson declared that "I did rise out of my bed and looked out of my windoe and saw the sonn was up almost an hour hie."[86]

New England's was a new form of asceticism. It looked forward to the time-and-profit calculus of commercial and industrial society rather than backward to the flesh-mortifying desert hermits of Western monasticism. The rise of time-consciousness required by the calling demanded not only that all New Englanders work but that "they work in a profoundly new way: regularly, conscientiously, and diligently."[87] During the seventeenth century, such systematization was done for the glorification of God, in order not to squander His precious time. The worldly, as well as otherworldly, benefits accruing from such rationalized behavior were there for even the saints to see. Missionary John Eliot admonished his Indian charges that "if you were more wise to know God, and obey his Commands, you would work more than you do. . . ." If the Indians followed God's command—

and English example—to labor six days a week, Eliot predicted that God would provide them with "clothes, houses, cattle, [and] riches, as [the English settlers] have. . . ."[88]

The New England Puritans' first, and perhaps most decisive, step in the direction of methodizing time was to purge and rationalize the Old Calendar. Ascetic Puritanism's exaltation of the Word over mystery and majesty left no place for sacred places and sacred days—or rather, made *all* space, time, and work holy.[89] Cromwell's soldiers during the Civil War removed altars from the east end of churches and tore down communion rails around the sanctuary in accordance with this principle.[90] So too with respect to time. The pre-Reformation parish had observed an elaborate array of feast days and collective rituals. One late sixteenth-century observer estimated that under the Pope, nearly half the days of the English year were in some way holy. In addition to Sunday Mass, there were festivals to mark the agricultural cycle and processions to avert disaster, as well as the myriad church-ales, bride-ales, dirge-ales, annual wakes, revel feasts, and perambulations of the bounds. Along with the fifty-two Sabbaths, there were ninety-five feast days and thirty *profesti* (saints' eves). Then there were the more secular breaks from work—craft holidays, Morris dancing, "Saint Monday," wassailing, stoolball matches, pitching the bar, and maypoles.[91] If one of the marks of a capitalist economy is a rationalized and production-oriented weekly calendar, it is clear that pre-Reformation England had not yet crossed that threshold.

Under the logic of the culture of discipline, holidays, sports, dancing, and village festivals were not regarded as sinful in themselves, but because they wasted God's precious time. By the 1570s, Protestant reformers had accomplished a substantial rationalization of the Old Calendar. Puritan William Harrison took considerable satisfaction that the "saints' days, superfluous numbers of idle wakes, guilds, fraternities, church ales, help-ales and soul-ales . . . [particularly the] heathenish rioting at bride-ales" had been "well diminished and set aside."[92] While Elizabeth I was no Puritan, she was not unsympathetic to the reforming goals of the culture of discipline.

This changed under James I. Indeed, it was the King's tolerance of the Old Calendar—and the traditional culture it sustained—that helped rekindle English Puritanism in the late 1610s. Despite his Calvinist upbringing, James proved willing to sponsor extravagant luxuries such as court masques, and he allowed the profaning of the Sabbath by state-encouraged games and revelry. In 1617, James issued his Book of Sports ("Declaration concerning Sports"), giving the royal imprimatur to traditional Sunday games and festivities. The King feared that the Puritan war on Merrie Old England was causing many subjects to relapse into popery. Such dangers were especially acute in economically backward areas such as Lancashire and Cumberland where the Reformation had been less enthusiastically received. To the Puritans, however, James's policy of accommodation was tantamount to a surrender to the Antichrist. The King forbade the Puritan-influenced Parliament of 1621 from even discussing the Book of Sports. Once the Elect Nation, England now began, as Edward Johnson later put it in *Wonder-Working Providence,* "to decline in Religion, like lukewarme Laodicea." The King's proclamations encouraged "lewd and prophane persons to celebrate a Sabbath like the Heathen to Venus, Baccus and Ceres."[93] Charles I's open alliance with the Arminians in 1626 fractured the quasi-Calvinist religious consensus within the Church of England that had prevailed for over sixty years. Moreover, Charles—unlike James I—levied taxes without Parliamentary consent and arrested members of Parliament without showing cause.[94] When in 1633 the Book of Sports was reissued and William Laud became primate, many saints determined that the Antichrist had in fact triumphed in England.[95] Massachusetts, in the view of John Winthrop, had been provided as a haven.

Upon arrival in America, New England's settlers stripped the Julian Calendar of as much of its pagan and specifically Catholic heritage as possible. The result was an American calendar that was surely among the plainest in the Western world.[96] Saints' days, carnivals, and festivals all went by the boards, as did dancing, card playing, gaming, the theater, most instrumental music, football, and shuffleboard. Gone were the major feasts of the Christian calendar—Christmas, St. Valentine's Day, Easter, and Michaelmas—as well as a whole host of more minor red letter (holy) days. Cognizant of the sheer amount of labor that would be required to reestablish an English standard of living in the New World, the Massachusetts General Court in 1643 emphasized the "necessity of husbanding men's time in this country."[97]

The Bay Colonists also instituted a much clearer division between work and leisure—an essential precondition for a rationalized economy—by means of a strict Sabbatarianism. As with much of their social ethics, the Puritans in their Sabbatarianism were following the precedent of the Old Testament Jews. According to the Book of Deuteronomy, the first absolute ban of work of any kind on the Sabbath was instituted as a commemoration of Israel's escape from Egypt. (The etymological root of the Hebrew *shabbat* is the verb "to stop," and it is work from which one is stopping.) "We under the New Testament," the colonists declared, "follow God's will in acknowledging no holy-days except the first day of the week only." For the Reverend Thomas Shepard (1605–1649), the Sabbath was the very embodiment of the Puritan culture of discipline: "It's easie to demonstrate by Scripture and argument as well as by experience that Religion is just as the Sabbath is, and decayes and growes as the Sabbath is esteemed: the immediate honour and worship of God which is brought forth and swadled in the three first Commandements, is nurst up and suckled in the bosome of the Sabbath."[98]

Hard, productive work for six days was to be followed by one day of almost complete surcease. The social consequences of this Sabbatarianism are suggested by the grumblings of a non-Puritan traveler, stuck in Boston on a Sunday:

> All [the New Englanders'] religion consists in observing Sunday by not working or going into the taverns on that day; but the houses are worse than the taverns. No stranger or traveler can therefore be entertained on a Sunday, which begins at sunset on Saturday and continues until the same time on Sunday. At these two hours you see all their countenances change. [On] Saturday evening the constable goes round into all the taverns of

> the city for the purpose of stopping all noise and debauchery. . . .[99]

The list of activities banned on the Sabbath was a long one: all farming, artisanal, mercantile, and professional work; all domestic labor (including cooking, brewing, sweeping, bed-making, haircutting, and shaving); all traveling, hunting, drinking, running, and all walking (even in one's garden), except "reverently to and from meeting."[100] The New England Sabbath also afforded an official day of rest for servants and slaves. In 1668 the General Court mandated that "no servile worke shall be donn on that day, namely such as are not workes of piety, of charity, or of necessity."[101]

As with the culture of discipline generally, Sabbatarianism was enforced by a potent combination of family, church, and court. The Puritan notion of collective accountability—under the covenant of grace—meant that heads of families were responsible for the obedience of their entire household. Thomas Shepard called on fathers to see that discipline was imposed on three classes of dependents in particular:

> our children, servants, strangers who are within our gates, are apt to profane the Sabbath; we are therefore to improve our power over them for God, in restraining them from sin, and in constraining them (as far as we can) to the holy observance of the rest of the Sabbath, lest God imputes their sins to us, who had power (as Eli in the like case) to restrain them and did not; and so our families and consciences be stained with their guilt and blood.[102]

No one was immune to punishment for violations. This the constable of Wenham discovered when he was presented to the Essex quarterly court in 1647 for "sending a prisoner from Wenham to Salem on the Lord's day."[103] In 1661, Northampton's Francis Hacklington, although a valued brick-maker for the Springfield magnate John Pynchon, was judged culpable by Pynchon and his fellow magistrates on the Hampshire county court for "breach of the Sabbath in working by carrying of bricks at his kilne . . . to the profaninge [of] that holy tyme."[104] Even the most humble offense was likely to bring a swift rebuke. Aquila Chase and his wife were presented to the court for the simple act of "gathering pease on [the] Lord's day."[105] John Hussy was fined 20 shillings "for working [on] a fast day in March last, notwithstanding he was minded of it." Those who, like David Wheeler, Mathew Coe, Morris Somes, and John Wakely, were discovered "hunting and killing a raccoon in the time of [Sunday] exercise," were subject to whippings or a heavy fine.[106] So too were those who, like Allester Grimes, were seen "hoeing corn" on the Sabbath. In a scene that one suspects could only have been enacted in Puritan New England, the culprit, when discovered, "dropped his hoe and molded the earth with his hands."[107]

The necessity of providing fodder for livestock—or, indeed, any crop-related labor—was an insufficient excuse for Sabbath-breaking. Like all farm or housework, such labor needed to be integrated into the discipline of a six-day week. In 1648, Marblehead's Thomas Bowin was fined "for sailing from Gloster harbor on the Lord's day, when the people were going to the morning exercises, having hay in his boat."[108] When Bowin's fellow townsman Archibald Thompson drowned while "carrying dung to his ground in a canoe upon the Lord's day," John Winthrop detected the avenging hand of God, especially in that the accident occurred "in fair weather and [on] still water."[109] The same Sabbath ban held true for domestic tasks that remained unfinished as Saturday evening approached. Elizabeth Lambert of Lynn was "admonished for brewing on the Lord's day." She had—culpably—"left some things from her brewing on the last day to finish on the Lord's day."[110]

An especially graphic, indeed tragic, illustration of the psychological pressure brought by the Saturday twilight moratorium is provided by a 1649 journal entry from John Winthrop. As Winthrop relates the story, a miller and some hired hands had been repairing a leaking milldam on Saturday afternoon. With the likelihood that the entire dam would collapse unless it was quickly shored up, the laborers presumably worked with great celerity. However, "night came upon them before they had finished what they had intended." The miller's conscience "began to put him in mind of the Lord's day, and he was troubled." Yet, despite these stirrings of conscience, the workers "went on and wrought an hour within the night." The following day, in what was seen as a horribly swift visitation of God's retributory wrath, the miller's five-year-old daughter was found drowned. Called to stand in contrition before his church, the father "freely in the open congregation, did acknowledge [his child's death] as the righteous hand of God for his profaning his holy day against the check of his own conscience."[111]

In seventeenth-century Massachusetts, the only work-less days were the Sabbath, election day, Harvard commencement day, and periodic days of public thanksgiving and "days of humiliation." The result was a working year of over 300 days, instead of the traditional 240 or so. The Puritans thereby significantly altered the shape of the working year as it had existed in a wide variety of historical settings. In the place of the nearly universal 2:1 work-to-rest ratio, Puritan New England adopted an almost 4:1 ratio. The 2:1 work-to-rest ratio has prevailed in cultures as diverse as ancient Rome, medieval Europe, pre-revolutionary China, and late twentieth-century America.[112] New England's was apparently among the most leisureless calendars ever adopted. It was quite literally a template for the Puritans' culture of discipline.[113]

Not surprisingly, the new calendar was not to everyone's taste. Governor William Bradford, in his *Of Plymouth Plantation* (1620–47), shows that the non-Puritan members of New England bridled at the loss of the Old Calendar's many holidays. A revealing incident in Plymouth Plantation on December 25, 1621—or, in the disapproving words of Governor Bradford, "the day called Christmas Day"—shows the clash between Merrie Old England and the culture of discipline. Expunged from the Puritan calendar as a pagan remnant, Christmas had long been a traditional day of revelry in Elizabethan England, especially among the laboring classes.[114] When Bradford tried to lead a work detail out into the woods that morning, he discovered that some recent arrivals wanted to honor this ancient tradition. They expressed scruples about working on Christmas Day. As Bradford relates the scene in his history:

> On the day called Christmas Day, the Governor called [the settlers] out to work as was [usual]. But the most of this new company excused themselves and said it went against their consciences to work on that day. So the Governor told them that if they made it [a] matter of conscience, he would spare them till they were better informed; so he led away the rest and left them.

But when the governor and his laborers "came home at noon from their work," they found that those who had been left behind were "in the street at play, openly; some pitching the bar, and some at stool-ball and such like sports." Pitching the bar, stoolball, and shuffleboard, along with other traditional alehouse pastimes such as "diceplaying, cards, tables, shovegroat, scales, dancings, hobbyhorses, and such unseasonable dealings," had been banned by the Plymouth General Court as sinful uses of God's precious time. Accordingly, Bradford "went to [the revelers] and took away their implements and told them that [their playing sports] was against *his* conscience, that they should play and others work." He informed them that "If they made the keeping of [Christmas] [a] matter of devotion, let them keep [to] their houses; but there should be no gaming or reveling in the streets." The governor followed this entry in his *History* with the wry observation that since that time, "nothing hath been attempted that way, at least openly."[115]

In addition to rationalizing the calendar, Massachusetts took steps at both the local and provincial levels to enforce the culture of discipline through civil and ecclesiastical institutions. Town government, the county courts, and the Congregational churches were the principal instruments in this process of social control. Even before leaving England, Bay Colony leaders made prohibitions on idleness official Company policy. "In the infancy of the plantation," they declared in May

1629, all settlers would have to "apply themselves to one calling or other, and noe idle drone [would] bee permitted to live amongst us." The chapter on idleness in the Massachusetts *Book of General Lawes and Libertyes* of 1648 mandated that

> no person, Housholder or other, shall spend his time idlely or unprofitably under pain of such punishment as the Court of Assistants or County Court shall think meet to inflict. And for this end it is ordered that the Constable of everie place shall use speciall care and diligence to take knowledge of offenders in this kinde, especially of common coasters, unproffitable fowlers, and tobacco takers.[116]

Under New England's decentralized and communally oriented government, town meetings, boards of selectmen, and county courts took responsibility for policing the use inhabitants made of their time. In 1640, the Essex quarterly court ordered that "If any of the Towne[s] shal know any person that shall live out of a particular calling [they] shall informe the Grand jury [in order] that they may proceed against them." After Thomas Oddingsall was "presented for idleness," the Essex magistrates (in good Weberian fashion) ordered him "to bring in a weekly account of his employment to Mr. Hathorne." When Dedham's selectmen were informed that John Littlefield "runs up and down misspending his time" and was likely not only to "bring ruin to himself" but also become a charge upon the town, they responded by ordering Littlefield to "dwell with Thomas Aldridge [for] two, three, or four weeks" in the hope that living with a sober householder would bring Littlefield to mend his ways. Similarly, Plymouth's Thomas Higgins, having "lived an extravagant life," was "placed with John Jenny for eight years to serve him as an apprentice." In Springfield, after the cooper John Mathews's wife was killed in an Indian attack on the town during King Philip's War, leaving the demoralized (and often inebriated) Mathews with sole responsibility for his infant son, the town meeting took remedial action. It "voted and Agreed [that] the Select men shall take Care of John Mathews and have an inspection over him, that hee [shall] follow his employment and make improvement of his time: and to settle him in a way that he may doe it."[117]

As well as banning outright such unprofitable uses of one's time and energy as dancing, card playing, the theater, and shuffleboard, the General Court licensed and regulated taverns and inns to prevent excess "tippling" (anything longer than half an hour). Constables were instructed to prevent "night meetings" and "night walking" after the 9:00 P.M. curfew, and were also enjoined to inspect individual households for idlers or anyone prone to "mispend precious time." In 1673, Springfield canoeman Samuel Terry and eight other men were fined by magistrate John Pynchon for "an uncivill play acted," which the court characterized as "Immodest and beastly."[118] Town constables were also enjoined to "inspect particular families and present a list of the names of all idle persons to the selectman. . . ." Single men were forced to live in a church member's household, under the belief that the family was a little commonwealth—the basic institution for inculcating the culture of discipline. By the 1650s, a county-based house of correction was added to this institutional array. Magistrates were empowered to commit "idle persons, stuborne persons against them that have authoritie over them, runawayes, common drunkards, pilferers, common night walkers, and wanton persons." After being subject to a punishment of ten lashes, the inmates were set to work on such experimental industrial crops as hemp and flax.[119]

Husbands and fathers who failed to provide for their wives and children felt the coercive hand of civil authority. In 1668, the General Court amended the earlier mandates on the House of Correction to take account of "complaints that there are some persons in [Massachusetts] that have families to provide for, who greatly neglect their callings or mispend what they earne, whereby their families are in much want and are thereby exposed to suffer and to neede relief from others." To remedy what they characterized as "these great and insufferable evils," the magistrates declared that they would treat "in a speciall manner" those who neglected their families.[120] By the same logic, to permit settlers—especially male heads of households—to remain inebriated and idle in a colonial setting was to invite almost certain hardship on the wife and children dependent on their labors. Communal obligations outweighed individual rights in such instances. The welfare of the family, not the liberty of the freeholder, was the town's overriding concern.

The gendered implications of the culture of discipline are reflected in litigation against Salem's James Davis in 1640. He was accused of being a "drone" on the "honey of his wife's labor." The Essex County magistrates, in attempting to describe to John Winthrop their (to date unsuccessful) attempts to impose the culture of discipline on Davis, offered "a word or two concerning his life when he was with us."

> It was scandolus and offensive to men, sinfull before god; and towards his wife. In stead of puttling honour upon her as the weaker vessell, he [lacked] the natural affection of a reasonable creature. We also found him Idle and indeed a very Drone sucking up the honey of his wife's labour, he taking no pains to provide for her, but spending one month after an other without any labour at all. It may be sometimes one day in a month [that] he did something [after] being put upon it, being threatened by the government here . . . besides he is given very much to lying [and] drinking strong waters.

In a similar case from 1643, Thomas Chubb was "presented for misspending his time idly to the prejudice of his family." In 1657, John Tilison was released from a sentence to the house of correction by the Essex justices on condition that he "live with his wife and provide for her according to his place, as a husband ought to." In 1679, the local office of "tithingman" was created to ferret out persons who endangered their family's well-being by spending "their time or estates, by night or by day, in tipling, gaming, or otherwise unproffitably. . . ."[121]

The culture of discipline also reflected the Reformed tradition's heavy reliance on the book as an instrument of both faith and acculturation. Anglo-American Puritans, to a striking degree even among Reformed Protestants, were a "people of the Word." The extreme biblicism of Elizabethan Puritans was reflected in their central demand for free access to the Word of God—in English. The newly developed print culture both reflected and reinforced such tendencies. Because of their belief that salvation was achieved *sola scriptura,* through the encounter with the Word of God as revealed in the Bible, saints required that all ages and ranks be taught to read. New England was to embody the Protestant authority of the trained intellect.[122] Because Scripture and (right) Reason were the twin pillars of the New England Way, the godly needed to be educated to think for themselves. Social practice in Massachusetts Bay Colony followed these precepts. For seventeenth-century Puritans, knowledge and learning, instead of being the special privilege of a sacerdotal caste, were to be made available to everyone. In the *Areopagitica* (1644), his great plea to Parliament for unlicensed printing, John Milton testified to the Puritans' view of the power of the printed word, even while acknowledging its potentially subversive nature: "For Books are not absolutely dead things, but doe contain a potencie of life in them to be as active as that soule was whose progeny they are; nay they do preserve as in a violl the purest efficacie and extraction of that living intellect that bred them. I know they are as lively, and as vigorously productive, as those fabulous Dragon's teeth; and being sown up and down, may chance to spring up armed men." The Massachusetts Reforming Synod of 1679 declared that books were "talents in God's service." In their recommendations for the revitalization of education, the assembled ministers asserted that "the interest of Religion and good Literature have been [accustomed] to rise and fall together."[123]

New Englanders, as a result of such sentiments, attempted to establish a college and publicly supported schools during the first two decades of settlement. The General Court promoted literacy not only by authorizing the establishment of Harvard College in 1636 (followed by its technically illegal incorporation in 1650), but by banning the illiterate from serving as Congregational ministers. When in 1654 the Boston Second Church sought to elevate its ruling elder—a man "illiterate as to academical education"—to the position of pastor, the General Court refused its assent. The Court reasoned that "if such men intrude themselves into the sacred functions [of the pastorate] there [would be] danger of bringing the profession [of the ministry] into contempt."[124]

Although efforts to establish the grammar schools that would prepare youths for Harvard initially proceeded in fits and starts, particularly in outlying regions, by the end of the seventeenth century a publicly supported school system was coming into being across the Bay Colony. In their determination to promote literacy by founding locally based free schools and Harvard College, the New Englanders were not pioneers, but rather were continuing the educational revolution begun a century earlier. Reformation spirituality and Renaissance scholarship combined to produce in England, as on the Continent, a seemingly irresistible desire to found schools.[125] But, in large part because of the strong civic culture fostered by the New England town system, such efforts bore greater fruit in New England than elsewhere.

As part of the legislative program of the 1640s, the Massachusetts General Court enacted a series of laws to ensure universal literacy and provide for publicly funded grammar (Latin) schools. Education was the chosen method for inculcating the ideals of the culture of discipline in the colony's youth, particularly with respect to work habits. Acknowledging that older migrants would find it more difficult to convert to the new ways, the Reverend John White advised Governor Winthrop in 1637 to follow the Dutch example:

> you have the Low-Country's [as] a patterne for Industry. I wish I could present you any other [example] for family discipline [because] A greate parte of your body [of colonists] hath been unaccustomed to laborious courses who will very hardly be brought unto them in their [advanced] age; all hope is in the training up the youth in time.[126]

Aware of the necessity to "train up" the colony's youth, in 1642 the General Court took action to establish publicly supported schools. Taking into consideration "the great neglect in many parents and masters in training up their children in learning, and labor, and other employments which may bee profitable to the common wealth," the Court ordered the selectmen in every town to "take account from time to time of their parents and masters, and of their children, concerning their calling and employment of their children, especially of their ability to read and understand the principles of religion and the capital lawes of the country." In 1647—noting that it was a "cheife project of that ould deluder, Satan, to keepe men from the knowledge of the Scriptures, as in former times by keeping them in an unknowne tongue"—the Court mandated that all townships with fifty or more households "forthwith appoint one within their towne to teach all such children as shall resort to him to write and reade, whose wages shall be paid either by the parents or masters of such children, or by the inhabitants in generall." The minimum number of families was later reduced to forty. Towns possessing one hundred or more families were ordered to "set up a grammar schoole . . . to instruct youth so farr as they may be fitted for the university."[127] Although all of the eight towns with a hundred or more families in fact established grammar schools, initially only one third of the communities required to maintain reading and writing schools did so. To ensure local compliance with its 1690 law mandating that all children and young servants be taught to read English, the Connecticut General Assembly authorized grand jury visits to suspected families and fines of 20 shillings per uninstructed child or servant.[128]

The key to New England's success in achieving widespread literacy, as elsewhere, was its mix of institutions—a main characteristic of a strong civil society. The high levels of literacy achieved by Massachusetts and Connecticut were attributable to the combined efforts of the family, free schools, "dame" schools, printing presses, apprenticeships, and Harvard College. The rudiments of reading and writing were learned at home through the use of such pedagogical devices as the famous New England primer. At schools, one learned to write, cipher, and—at least for those boys headed for Harvard—the basic skills of Latin and penmanship as well. Privately funded dame schools, increasingly common after the mid-seventeenth century, were unregulated, home-based institutions that operated on contractual principles. During the seventeenth century, formal instruction for females was usually limited to several years in a dame school learning the principles of reading, writing, and religion. In Springfield, Pentecost Mathews (the cooper John Mathews's wife) earned £8 2s. 9d. in 1653 for "worke schooling" the child of magnate John Pynchon. Goodwife Mathews also took 35 shillings for schooling Elizur and Hannah Holyoke, children of another of Springfield's elite families. In neighboring Northampton by 1673, between a fourth and a fifth of those attending the town school were females. Schoolteaching was the first professional calling available to New England women. Asserting that "the frontier . . . stretched women's roles," Richard Melvoin notes that Deerfield's first known schoolteacher was a woman, Hannah Beaman.[129] Under New England's system of apprenticeship, masters were usually responsible for teaching at least the rudiments of reading and ciphering to their young charges. Masters who failed to provide such skills could be, and were, sued for non-performance of contract by the apprentice's family.

New England's federally organized civil society shaped educational practices. Although the Massachusetts General Court from the 1640s onward mandated the establishment of publicly supported schools in towns with sufficient numbers of families, it was the townspeople themselves who voted to use their resources of land and tax monies to implement such goals. In Dedham, during the town's founding decades, the town meeting granted land to support a school as well as the church. In Dedham, as elsewhere, local taxes supported the minister and the schoolteacher and local officials set attendance policy. In 1651 in New Haven—an independent colony from the time of its founding in 1639 until it joined Connecticut in 1662—the General Gourt authorized payment of up to £40 to pay a schoolmaster to teach male children to read, write—and, if they were capable of it—learn the rudiments of Latin. When Springfield established a grammar school in the town center in 1679, children living in the outlying settlements of Long Meadow, Skepnuck, and the west side of the Connecticut River were excused from compulsory attendance. While compliance with the Massachusetts law requiring towns of forty or more families to provide formal education was always far lower in the outlying settlements, it became more general near the end of the century. Outlying settlers also displayed a willingness to utilize creative policymaking for educational purposes. War-torn and once-abandoned Deerfield voted in 1698, after many years of irregular schooling at several sites, that "a School House be built upon the Town's Charge," with the dimensions of eighteen by twenty-one feet. Deerfield taxed all townspeople to pay for the new school and teacher; but all families with children aged six to ten, "whether male or female," were levied an additional tax. The town also created a school committee to see to the hiring of a schoolmaster, repair of the schoolhouse, and provision of firewood for the scholars.[130]

During its founding period the Bay Colony also established and subsidized the first (and until 1675, the only) printing press in British America. Located at Harvard College, and worked by Stephen Day and his son Matthew, the press printed its first book in 1640: *The Whole Book of Psalms, Faithfully Translated into English Meter.* Reflecting the saints' insistence on the "plain style," its motto was "God's Altar needs not our Polishings." That year the General Court ordered that Stephen Day, because he had been "the first that set upon printing," was to receive a 300-acre land grant from the colony. Day and his successors Samuel Green and Marmaduke Johnson turned out an imposing list of publications at the Harvard press, including devotional literature, almanacs, the 1648 *Lawes and Libertyes,* and John Eliot's 1663 translation of the Bible into the Algonquin language. When the General Court licensed a second printing press in 1675, to be located in Boston, the result was vigorous competition between Cambridge's Samuel Green and Boston's John Foster. Foster's press, located in the seat of both government and commerce, was destined to win out, and by the 1680s Boston had emerged as the center of book publishing in North America.[131]

Particularly important among the publications turned out by the Massachusetts presses were almanacs, which constituted almost one third of the imprints between 1639 and 1660. These pamphlets were profitmaking enterprises funded by local merchant-investors. The almanacs were written by such personages as Samuel Danforth, whose *A Brief Recognition of New England's Errand into the Wilderness* (1671) provided the Bay Colony with what proved to be its most enduring metaphor. Almanacs, along with free schools, played a large role in fostering literacy. Publication of the almanac was part of a determination by the General Court and the Puritan clergy to educate and edify the Bay Colony's ordinary settlers. It reflected the Protestant Reformation's determination to raise up a literate laity, as well as a university-trained clergy. In playing this role, almanacs quickly achieved a wide circulation within the colony. Despite the mass audience sought by almanac writers, material of a recondite nature was not uncommon. In the 1674 Cambridge almanac, Watertown minister John Sherman published an essay recounting Johannes Kepler's theory of planetary motion. The 1675 issue contained a woodcut by John Foster illustrating the Copernican heliocentric system.[132]

The importance of literacy was upheld by virtually all public institutions in the Bay Colony. The General Court and town boards of selectmen, in addition to regulating those institutions that fell within their respective jurisdictions, kept up a constant drumbeat of encouragement and admonition lest "that old deluder Satan" keep the unlettered from the Word of God. Already highly literate by early modern standards at the outset of colonization, New Englanders chose to divert time and resources away from the always pressing tasks of commercial development and setting up farms to raise these standards still higher.

A literate and numerate populace was coming into being in New England by the beginning of the eighteenth century. The creation of publicly supported schools, the widespread circulation of such publications as almanacs and devotional literature, and the household instruction provided by mothers and fathers, all helped change New England from a society with a male literacy rate of roughly 50 percent at the time of the colony's founding to a position of near-universal male literacy by the time of the American Revolution. New

England literacy rates were always higher in the more urbanized areas of Boston and its vicinity. Substantial gains were eventually made in female literacy rates, especially after the 1690s, when public schooling became more available to girls. With women, as with men, more could read than could write, but from the earliest period, women played a key role in fostering literacy. Puritan mothers were expected to read the Bible all the way through at least once a year. "Serious reading and godly writing" were expected from Puritan females, including the keeping of spiritual journals and taking notes during ministers' sermons.[133]

The initial foundations for literacy were invariably laid in the household, because of the saints' belief that early reading of the Bible was essential to save the child from damnation. With Locke, Bay Colonists believed that "When he [or she] can talk, 'tis time he [or she] should begin to learn to read."[134] Mothers apparently were responsible for teaching reading and fathers for writing. Increase Mather, a second-generation New Englander, recalled in his autobiography that "I learned to read of my mother [Katherine Holt Mather]. I learned to write of my father, who also instructed me in grammar learning, both in Latin and Greeke tongues." When Sarah Stiles began work as schoolmistress in Windsor, Connecticut, in May 1717, she was expected to teach only reading, leaving instruction in writing and arithmetic to the male teacher who came during the winter.[135]

By the time of the American Revolution, as John Adams proudly proclaimed, even in the more rural areas illiterates were as rare in New England "as Catholics or Jacobites." Kenneth Lockridge contends, persuasively in my view, that it was "an intense Protestantism" rather than changing patterns of wealth and mobility that catalyzed the movement toward mass literacy. From an overall adult male-signature literacy rate of under 50 percent by the mid-seventeenth century, the New England men born around 1700 exhibited a signature rate of almost 85 percent. Female literacy rates achieved their greatest gains after the 1690s; in Windsor, Connecticut, they rose from 27 percent for those born in the decades of the 1660s and 1670s to 90 percent for those born in the 1740s.[136] Literacy rates were always higher in the more urbanized, commercialized regions, with the Connecticut Valley exhibiting the highest levels (as measured by male-signature rates). Of the 378 men who made deeds in Boston-dominated Suffolk County during the years 1653–56 and 1686–97, only 11 percent signed with a mark.[137] Overall, some one third of the wills left by Massachusetts women during the seventeenth century were signed. Female will-signature rates in Revolutionary-era Massachusetts ranged from 88 percent in Boston to 60 percent in rural Suffolk County.[138] At the end of the colonial period, 90 percent of men throughout Massachusetts could sign their names and 50 percent of females recorded signatures in their wills. By the 1790s, young women in New England were achieving near-universal literacy.[139]

Institutions played a central role in fostering New England's high literacy rates. It was not Protestantism per se but rather the local educational policies, household initiatives, and civil society it inspired that were most responsible for expanding literacy. Comparisons from other colonies help illustrate this point. By the end of the colonial period, in New England the "meanest orders of men were three-quarters literate and yeoman farmers were near universal literacy." In Pennsylvania and Virginia, despite the existence of charity schools, itinerant schoolmasters, paid private tutors, and laws mandating the education of apprentices, the absence of a locally based public school system kept overall male literacy rates only slightly above eighteenth-century England's rate of approximately 60 percent. By the late 1790s, some 32 percent of free male Virginians were still using marks rather than signatures, more than double the proportion of male illiterates in New England (including the frontier settlements of Maine and New Hampshire). In Pennsylvania, where the impact of radical Protestant dissent was closer to the New England pattern than in Virginia, nearly a third of adult males were illiterate by the end of the eighteenth century.[140]

When the Reverend Andrew Burnaby, the English Vicar of Greenwich, traveled through Pennsylvania and Massachusetts in 1760, he found the Pennsylvanians more aggressively commercial, the New Englanders more literate and reflective. Burnaby described the Pennsylvanians as "by far the most enterprizing people upon the continent," while in Massachusetts the vicar discovered that the "Arts and Sciences seem to have made a greater progress here than in any part of America."[141] Pennsylvania and Virginia did not benefit from a civil society-based public school system that, in Lockridge's characterization, "moved most of New England into a class by itself." For Lockridge, it is clear that "a uniformly and intensely Protestant society and, above all, the systematic state action which emerges from such a society were essential to moving male literacy the last large step to universality."[142] The strong correlation historians have discovered between literacy, population density, and commercialization likewise underscores the importance of New England's town-based civil society.[143]

John Milton, who wrote the *Areopagitica* at the height of the English Civil War and knew first hand that books could indeed "spring up armed men," rightly underscored the socially subversive nature of the spread of literacy. Like the socially radical potential of the free market economy, rising literacy rates served to undermine older notions of social hierarchy. Although even by the eighteenth century, many Continental *philosophes* balked at educating the servant class, a century earlier, as Elizabeth Eisenstein points out,

> English Puritans, harking back to Lollard traditions, wanted books placed in the hands of serving maids and simple folk. They encouraged low-born men to defy the high and mighty and to fight as Christian soldiers against papists and monks. Successive editions of [John] Foxe's *Book of Martyrs* [orig. 1563] were progressively enriched by dramatic accounts of fishermen, tailors, housewives and the like, who confounded learned churchmen and bested their persecutors before going heroically to face torture and death.[144]

Thomas Cartwright, one of the founders of English Puritanism during the 1570s, cast the widest possible net in demanding that "all ought to read the scripture . . . all ages, all sexes, all degrees and callings, all high and low, rich and poor, wise and foolish have a necessary duty therein." The Word of God, Cartwright declared, needed to be made known to "doctors and masters but [also to] tailors, smiths, weavers, and other artificers, [not only] of citizens alone but of country-folk, ditchers, delvers, [cow-herds], and gardeners," so that all—regardless of gender or station—would be capable of "disputing even of the Holy Trinity." Elizabethan Puritans explicitly demanded books addressed to "such Men and Women of Trade, as Taylors, Weavers, Shopkeepers, [and Seamstresses]. . . ."[145]

Crown officials and colonial governors were not unmindful of the connection between free schools, printing presses, and anti-authoritarian—particularly republican—sentiments. Virginia Governor William Berkeley (1608–1677), arch foe of the Puritans, rejoiced in 1671 that in his colony, unlike Massachusetts, "there are no free schools nor printing, and I hope we shall not have these [in a] hundred years; for learning has brought disobedience, and heresy, and sects into the world, and printing has divulged them, and [produced] libels against the best government."[146] Unlike Virginia and Pennsylvania, where a close correlation existed between literacy rates and social status, New England was not divided between a literate gentry elite on the one hand and a mass of illiterate agriculturalists on the other. In the Bay Colony, as was typically true for New England's culture of discipline, institutions made a critical difference. They helped form the human capital upon which the region's swift economic development depended.

The very success of the Protestant ethic in fostering time-consciousness and striving behavior—in producing wealth as well as fostering literacy and strong civic institutions—raised a larger moral problem, one that New England ministers' sermons and published tracts returned to indirectly again and again: how to draw the line between industrious enterprise and self-regarding acquisitiveness. The social and psychological tension brought by the saints' attempt to keep the Protestant ethic from turning into the spirit of capitalism are perhaps best revealed by the celebrated case of merchant Robert Keayne.

4

The Ethics of Exchange, Price Controls, and the Case of Robert Keayne

In 1639 Robert Keayne, a pious and well-connected import merchant, was fined the enormous sum of £200 by the Massachusetts General Court for the crime of "oppression" (price gouging). By modern standards, Keayne's offense seems pitifully innocuous—and his severe punishment a powerful testament to the pre-capitalist nature of the Bay Colony's business ethics. Keayne was found guilty of "taking above six-pence in the shilling profit; in some above eight-pence; and, in some small things, above two for one." Keayne's violation had been to sell a bag of nails that cost him sixpence at a mark-up price of eightpence. Similar "oppressive" prices had been paid by the customers at his Boston shop for "great gold buttons," a skein of thread, and a bridle. After the civil sword fell, the ecclesiastical followed. In addition to his £200 fine by the General Court (eventually reduced to £80), Keayne was censured—and nearly excommunicated—by the Boston First Church for "selling his wares at excessive Rates, to the Dishonor of God's name, the Offense of the Generall Court, and the Publique scandall of the Country." The merchant was compelled to stand before his congregation and "with tears, acknowledge and bewail his covetous and corrupt heart."[1]

For taking between 50 and 100 percent profit on his business transactions, Robert Keayne became a pariah. The man who was Boston's wealthiest merchant, brother-in-law to the prominent clergyman John Wilson, and founder and captain of the prestigious Ancient and Honorable Artillery Company, was forced to grovel in the dust for selling sixpenny nails at eightpence. With Keayne in mind, Rowley minister Ezekiel Rogers went so far as to propose a "Law to hang up some [merchants] before the Lord; they deserve it, and it would to him be a sacrifice most acceptable." Keayne's name became—as it was intended to become—a byword for cupidity and hard dealing in the Bay Colony.[2]

So unpopular was Keayne that in the famous but unrelated case of Goodwife Sherman's sow in 1642, litigation against the import merchant so deadlocked the Massachusetts General Court that it was forced to convert to bicameralism as a means of breaking the constitutional crisis. The creation of the House of Deputies was the consequence. Even as civil war was engulfing England, the Massachusetts General Court spent—in the words of John Winthrop—"the best part of seven days" debating whether Keayne was guilty of stealing innkeeper Elizabeth Sherman's errant swine.[3] When a majority of the (pro-Keayne) Assistants attempted to thwart the majority of (anti-Keayne) Deputies by resorting to the "negative voice" (veto), the General Court separated into two independent houses. The Assistants (magistrates) sat as the upper house, while the Deputies (representatives) sat as the lower. For Governor Winthrop, the magistrates' loss of the negative voice was a portentous event. In his view, it threatened to convert Massachusetts from a "mixt aristocratie" into a "mere Democratie."[4] (Keayne's role in the colony's conversion to bicameralism prompted a whimsical Samuel Eliot Morison to propose: "If, as is claimed, this was the first full-fledged bicameral legislature in the English colonies, a monument on Beacon Hill to Goody Sherman's sow, as the mother of Senates, would seem to be in order.")[5]

The focal point for two of the young colony's greatest *causes célèbres* within the space of three years, Robert Keayne's tribulations were not yet over. As a man who was of "ill report in the country for [being] a hard dealer in his course of trading," a veritable "Cormorant" who preyed on the weak, Keayne continued to provoke controversy.[6] He was fined in 1646 for non-attendance at (and contempt for) the House of Deputies. In 1652, after having been recently elevated to a judgeship on the Suffolk County bench, Keayne was forced to resign his commission in disgrace after having been found "three times drunke, and to have drunke to excesse two times." Some of his neighbors jumped into the fray to denigrate him for "company keeping," wantonness, and general profligacy.[7]

It seemed impossible to believe anything but the worst of a man who had twice brought Massachusetts to an uproar since his arrival from London in 1635. Even family matters spilled over into the public realm. Keayne's only surviving son Benjamin married the mentally unstable Sarah Dudley (sister of the future poet Anne Bradstreet), who was subsequently banished from the church in 1647 for "Irregular prophecying" and for "falling into odious, lewd, and scandalous uncleane behavior with one Nicholas Hart, an Excommunicate person of Taunton."[8] The couple were eventually divorced and an irate Robert Keayne cut his former daughter-in-law out of his will, despite the fact that she had borne him a granddaughter. Several importuning, but ungrateful, relatives spread stories of the import merchant's lack of charity in his dealings with in-laws. The accretion of all these trials provoked Keayne, in his last will and testament, to go so far as to compare his afflictions at the hands of his fellow New Englanders to those of Jesus Christ.[9]

By any measure, even though his stay in New England had been financially prosperous (he left an estate valued at over £4000), it had been psychologically harrowing. When Robert Keayne died in 1656, he was a tortured and embittered soul. His experience as a merchant trying to live by the ethical code of the Puritan commonwealth indeed seems a cautionary tale. And so historians have read it.

Since the 1920s, Robert Keayne's trials have been intrepreted as evidence of the anti-capitalist nature of New England's business ethics. The Keayne affair has become the *locus classi-*

cus of the "just price" interpretation of New England's economic policy—the putative touchstone of the Bay Colony's anti-acquisitive exchange ethics. Keayne's censure has been held up as proof that the principle of the governmentally regulated economy, based on the tradition of the moral economy, shaped all business dealings in colonial New England. The Keayne affair has been offered as evidence that economic policy in Massachusetts "had more affinity with the iron rule of Calvin's Geneva than with the individualistic tendencies of contemporary English Puritanism." Not market-determined rules of supply and demand, but valorized prices based on the customary or just worth of a commodity or service are said to have governed economic exchange in early Massachusetts. Several generations of scholars have contended that the most distinctive feature of New England's economic culture were the restrictions placed on business profits, pointing in particular to the "terrible" and "black" scandal caused by Keayne's taking 50 percent profits on such humble wares as nails, buttons, and bridles. The abiding assumption here has been that governmental restrictions on profits—along with wage and price controls, import/export bans, interest-rate ceilings, sumptuary codes, and laws protecting debtors—revealed the still essentially "medieval" nature of economic policy in early Massachusetts.[10]

This interpretation of Keayne's 1639 censure rests on the specific meaning imputed to the just price. But surprisingly little attempt has been made to plumb its actual historic usage. The result is considerable confusion. At once an economic doctrine, a legal device, and a moral precept, the just price was the centerpiece to European exchange theory from the twelfth to the sixteenth centuries. Canonists, Roman lawyers, and theologians debated its meanings and applications, with the first two groups usually favoring economic freedom (market-determined prices) and the third advocating regulated prices. In part because of the growing influence of Roman law principles—which recognized the legality of contracts, the freedom of bargaining, and the licitness of trade—the theologians' view remained a minority one from the High Middle Ages onward. The complexity of these positions, however, tends to get flattened in modern discourse. While the inflections modern authors give to the just price doctrine are various, they are almost unanimous in following Werner Sombart in declaring what the just price was *not*—a market-determined price governed by the laws of supply and demand.

This view holds that the just price was largely determined by production costs. It consisted of the total of material costs necessary for producing goods, along with a reasonable wage for the craftsman or merchant. It represented, in theory, an objective value which was inherent in the nature of the goods.[11] Labor, expenses, and a *status-maintaining* profit, these were the criteria for setting prices, according to this view, not the laws of supply and demand. Implicit in all and explicit in some of these interpretations is the assumption that colonial Americans accepted the Scholastic understanding of the just price. The belief is that this doctrine reflected a universal and categorical rejection of the justice of market-determined prices during a period that spanned some five centuries.

Most of these scholars use the writings of Aquinas as their benchmark. As spelled out by Aegídius Lessinus, a commentator on Aquinas's *Summa,* the just price for the Schoolmen was "either that which is fixed by public authority in consideration of the common good or that which is determined by the estimation of the community." *(Respondeo, Justum Pretium, censeri quod vel a potestate publica ob bonum commune est taxatum, vel communi hominum aestimatione determinatum.)* The point of most concern here, of course, is the proper definition for "estimation of the community."[12]

Although the genealogy of the just price doctrine observed in seventeenth-century New England indeed extended back to the Scholastics, its meaning was in fact quite different from the one many scholars have imputed to it. Just price doctrine, though indebted to Aristotle's theory of utility fashioned in the fourth century B.C., emerged full bloom in the thirteenth century in the clash between the *lex divina* of the theologians (which maintained the just price) and the *leges humanae* of the legalists (which advocated freedom of bargaining). The theologians demanded that economic dealings be governed by *Justicia,* not *Cupiditas.* Yet even here the justice of the market price was implicitly acknowledged. Aquinas, in the *Secunda-*

secunda portion of the *Summa theologica* (1266–73), gave the clearest statement of the theologians' position. Even for Aquinas, the just price was not primarily based on labor and expenses. It was rather, in the same language used by seventeenth-century New Englanders, the "current price." The current price was the actual price of certain goods at a specific time and place. It included both free competitive prices and such "legal prices" as were regulated by municipal officials. Expressly excluded were prices determined through such unsanctioned personal monopolistic practices as forestalling, engrossing, and regrating.[13]

The notion of the just price derived from the distinction made by Aquinas between distributive justice and commutative justice. This notion was based originally on Aristotle's distinction between Distributive Justice and Corrective Justice in Book Five of the *Nicomachean Ethics.* Distributive justice for Aquinas rested on the inegalitarian principles of the medieval hierarchy, the Great Chain of Being. It was premised on the belief that each member of a hierarchically ranked community was entitled to a share of worldly goods and wealth according to his or her fixed station in life. Commutative justice, by contrast, was based on egalitarian and contractual principles. It rested on individualistic, not organic, premises. It pertained to relations between individuals, not social classes. According to its precepts, justice required an absolute equivalency in exchanges: what was delivered needed to be equivalent to what was received, regardless of the social rank of buyer and seller. The buying and selling of goods, therefore, fell within the province of commutative justice. In the case of New England, it seems clear that land and resources were allocated under the principles of distributive justice. More was given to such "Useful Men" as Springfield merchant-entrepreneur John Pynchon (in the way of house lots, planting ground, or mill sites), and more was expected (in the way of taxes, entrepreneurial initiative, and charitable giving), under these principles.[14] Economic exchanges—unless one of the parties was in need—took place within the realm of commutative justice. The distinction that John Winthrop made in the *Arbella* sermon between the "Way of Justice" and the "Way of Mercy" followed these principles. The former was based on the natural law, the latter on the law of grace. The first applied to contractual dealings between relative equals; the second applied to the moral obligation the well-off owed the needy.[15]

For the Old World Puritans, as for the Schoolmen, economic problems initially were viewed primarily from an ethical and legal perspective. By the time of the founding of New England, utilitarian criteria increasingly were being introduced, primarily through the efforts of the first wave of mercantilist writers. The need for a favorable balance of trade, the advantage of low interest rates, the ways to achieve favorable exchange rates, the benefits and drawbacks of state-granted trading monopolies—these were the issues that English thinkers increasingly devoted themselves to in the lively debates over economic policy during the 1620s. Moral and ethical issues, more and more, were shifted from the public to the private domain, with one's conscience or confessional group—not the officers of kingdom, municipality, or guild—deemed the final arbiter. The conviction that the buying and selling of goods and labor should be regulated by government, municipality, or guild eroded in the face of the new principles of economic freedom. But Christian beliefs continued to permeate all realms of economic dealings, and no place more so than New England. John Winthrop's utterly standard Protestant declaration in the *Arbella* sermon that every man had "to love his neighbor as himself" left no justification for hard dealing or collusion of any kind, particularly with respect to the needy.

The result, however, was *not* a system premised on the distinction between moral economy and market economy. For both the Schoolmen and the Puritans, the essential principle was that economic dealings not take place at the expense of social justice. Cotton Mather, when he demanded that all New Englanders be "fair-dealers" in the marketplace, and exhorted that "the business of the City shall be managed by the *Golden* Rule," was saying nothing that could not have been said by St. Thomas, St. Augustine, the Stoics, or Aristotle in the second book of the *Nicomachean Ethics*. But for Mather, as for the Scholastic and patristic writers, market prices, in normal circumstances, were just.[16]

Communal notions of fairness or inherent worth, in medieval England and the Continent and seventeenth-century New England alike, were set—as common sense suggests they must have been set—by local and regional markets. Despite what Raymond De Roover refers to as the "bewildering variety of answers" that have been given to the question "What is the just price?", its functional interpretation going back as far as the thirteenth century (and before) is clear: "the just price was the one set by common estimation, that is by the free valuation of buyers and sellers, or, in other words, by the interplay of the forces of demand and supply. By some of the Doctors, this price was called the natural price as opposed to the legal price fixed by public authority. In any case, contrary to widespread belief, the just price was not necessarily based on the cost of production."[17]

With the important exception of cases involving emergency (famine, war, etc.) or collusion, public authorities did not normally interfere with market mechanisms for the purpose of maintaining a fair price. And the exceptions invariably involved foodstuffs such as grain, bread, meat, or beer, not the dry goods—nails, buttons, and bridles—involved in the case of Robert Keayne. This is not to argue that a condition of laissez-faire prevailed in medieval trading towns. Far from it. To the extent that prices were controlled in medieval towns, they were set by guilds, and guilds usually had representation of some kind in urban government. But publicly sanctioned, valorized prices were always the exception and not the rule.[18]

Under both Roman law and medieval practice, the just price in ordinary circumstances was established primarily through the forces of supply and demand. The just price was regarded as the natural price, as distinct from the legal price set by government. Goods were "worth as much as they can be sold for, commonly." *(Res tantum valet quantum vendi potest, sed communiter.)* According to Bernardino of Siena, possibly the ablest economist produced by the Middle Ages, the just or natural price was socially determined by *communitas*—by the community in market transactions. The just price was an expression of the community's estimation, as arrived at by the market *(secundum aestimationem fori occurrentis)*.[19] Ethical principles typically entered over consumer information, not the price mechanism. Particular importance was placed on the buyer's full knowledge of existing market conditions, on his or her ability to make an informed decision about the purchase. The just price, declared a fifteenth-century commentator on Aquinas, was "the one which, at a given time, can be gotten from the buyers, assuming common knowledge and in the absence of all fraud and coercion." For Aquinas's teacher Albertus Magnus, as for all of the Schoolmen except Duns Scotus, the just price was literally the worth of goods according to market estimation at the time of sale *(secundum aestimationem)*.[20]

By the mid-sixteenth century, the period during which humanistic reformers were consciously legitimating the pursuit of gain, market competition—always implicit in just price theory—was invoked explicitly. The word "competition," De Roover finds, "never occurs in scholastic treatises until the end of the sixteenth century, when it is used by Luis de Molina." Competition *(concurrentium)* among buyers, not sellers, was declared responsible for secular fluctuations in prices.[21]

The main ethical issue in the economic dealings of medieval Europeans and seventeenth-century Puritans alike related to issues of fraud and market manipulation, not profit margins. A capitulary issued in 884 by Frankish King Carloman, which was eventually incorporated into the canon law by Raymond of Peñafort (1185–1275), enjoined priests to admonish their parishioners not to charge wayfarers more than the going local market price *(quam in mercato vendere possint)*—thus taking unjust advantage of their ignorance. This admonition was made in precisely the terms employed centuries later by John Cotton and John Winthrop. Even by the thirteenth century, canonists and theologians alike recognized that the "natural" price of a commodity was little more than a polite fiction. The equivalence between two goods was, self-evidently, not an intuitive one. Already emerging in such twelfth-century Italian commercial instruments as *commenda, compagnia* was the idea of risk. In the writings of Aquinas such distinctions were recognized by way of the doctrine of *damnum emergens.* In the seventy-eighth Question of the *Summa theologica,* Aquinas accepted the legitimacy of profiting from a loan *if* the lender bore some of the risk. The concept of risk permitted sale of goods at rates different from what the market might set. It too was eventually incorporated into canon law in terms that would have been recognizable to Cotton and Winthrop. From the High Middle Ages until the writing of Gerard de Malynes early in the seventeenth century, both *damnum emergens* (cost of lending) and *lucrum cessans* (lender's forgone profits) had been used to justify borrowing and lending by merchants. The categories of *periculum sortis* (non-usury interest) and *titulus morae* (interest for delay of repayment) suggest the degree of refinement that credit markets had achieved by the High Middle Ages. It was by these ancient, yet anything but unsophisticated, criteria that the distinction between "biting usury" and legitimate interest was established.[22]

* * *

The economic writings of John Cotton (1584–1652), rightly regarded as the architect of the Bay Colony's public policy on the just price, reveal this doctrine to have been the same as it was under the Schoolmen—with the important exception that taking profit on credit sales (earlier sometimes banned as usurious) was now explicitly authorized. The personal connection between Cotton and Robert Keayne was a long and tangled one. Eleven years earlier in London, at the May meeting of the New England Company (predecessor to the Massachusetts Bay Company), the pious Keayne eagerly took notes while Cotton delivered a lecture to the assemblage.[23] Now it was Keayne himself who had become the object lesson. In a public sermon immediately following the import merchant's 1639 censure by the General Court, Cotton took the occasion to deliver a major statement on business ethics. His goal was to "lay open the error of [Keayne's] false principles, and to give some rules of direction in the case." John Winthrop served as scribe and, in quasi-syllogistic fashion, laid out the commercial principles emerging from Cotton's disquisition.

The false principles Cotton imputed to Keayne included the following:

1. That a man might sell as dear as he can, and buy as cheap as he can.
2. If a man lose by casualty of sea, etc., in some of his commodities, he may raise the price of the rest.
3. That he may sell as he bought, though he paid too dear, etc., and though the commodity be fallen, etc.
4. That, as a man may take the advantage of his own skill or ability, so he may [take advantage] of another's ignorance or necessity.
5. Where one gives time for payment, he is to take like recompense of one as of another.

The correct "rules for trading," according to Cotton, were as follows:

1. A man may not sell above the current price, i.e., *such a price as is usual in the time and place,* and as another (who knows the worth of the commodity) would give for it, if he had occasion to use it; as that is called current money, which every man will take, etc.
2. When a man loseth in his commodity for want of skill, etc., he must look at it as his own fault or cross, and therefore must not lay it upon another.
3. Where a man loseth by casualty of sea, or, etc., it is a loss cast upon himself by providence, and he may not ease himself of it by casting it upon another; for so a man should seem to provide against all providences, etc., that he should never lose; *but where there is a scarcity of the commodity, there men may raise their price;* for now it is a hand of God upon the commodity, and not the person. . . .[24]

Where "there is a scarcity of the commodity," declared Cotton, "there men may raise their price." The ethically correct price was, as for Aquinas, the "current price," the price that was "usual in the time and place." Cotton's just price was the going market price of a product—without monopoly, misrepresentation, or coercion, but fully responsive to the fluctuations of supply and demand.[25] Moreover, Cotton's injunctions on prices cut both ways: the merchant who had "paid too dear" when prices were high had to absorb his losses after "the commodity [was] fallen." In each case the current market price was the true price. In 1641 the General Court, in validating this assessment, made reference to "the market or true price" when discussing reforming the Bay Colony's appraisement system.[26]

What was not acceptable was fraud, collusion, or the failure to perform one's contractual obligations. These were offenses against God's Providence, the Protestant notion of communal responsibility, and the common law itself. In an era with imperfect price information, buyers and sellers were warned against taking advantage of their neighbor's ignorance of these prices during economic transactions. They were not, in the language of Cotton Mather, to "*cheat, cozen,* and *oppress,* and wrong other people in [their] dealing with them." But the final basis of the price was the blind, supply/demand-driven unconscionable force of the market. These were the exchange ethics that prevailed both in New England and Pennsylvania, where the Quaker Book of Discipline made no mention of unfair prices or interest rates but sharply condemned the failure to live up to one's contract.[27]

John Winthrop also recorded the objections made by the Assistants on Keayne's behalf during the censure proceedings, remarks that underscore the wide departure the Bay Colonists had made from pre-capitalist business ethics by as early as 1639. The reasons the magistrates would "have been more moderate in their censure" of Keayne included the following:

1. Because there was no law in force to limit or direct men in point of profit in their trade.
2. Because it is the common practice in all countries for men to make use of advantages for raising the prices of their commodities.

3. Because (though [Keayne] were chiefly aimed at, yet) he was not alone in this fault.
4. Because all men through the country, in sale of cattle, corn, labor, etc., were guilty of the like excess of prices.
5. Because a certain rule could not be found out for an equal rate between buyer and seller, though much labor had been bestowed in it, and divers laws had been made which, upon experience, were repealed as being neither safe nor equal.[28]

Governor Winthrop himself, as his marginal notes attest, was clearly of two minds about the proceedings against Keayne. In conceding that "all men through the country" were "guilty of the like excess of prices," Winthrop effectively destroyed the logic of the case against Keayne. Later, in his *History,* the governor recounted an incident illustrating how the Old World principles of a regulated economy had already been abandoned before the Bay Colonists left for America. It was the story of how "one Taylor, of Linne, having a milch cow in the ship as he came over [to Massachusetts], sold the milk to the passengers for 2d. the quart, and being after at a sermon wherein [price] oppression was complained of, etc., he fell distracted." While himself querying whether the price of 2d. for a quart of milk on a trans-Atlantic voyage was in fact extortionate, Winthrop took the occasion to admit that even among the saints, sharp bargaining practices had been normal from the beginning: "This evil was very notorious among all sort of people, it being the common rule that most men walked by in all their commerce, to buy as cheap as they could, and to sell as dear." Although doubtless with regret, the governor thereby discarded John Cotton's first rule of fair dealing. As Winthrop openly conceded, if Robert Keayne was simply doing what everybody else was doing in their business dealings, the rationale for fining him so heavily—or at all—evaporated.[29]

Winthrop, it is clear, regarded the import merchant as conspicuously avaricious; but he believed that the Deputies went too far in their condemnation of Keayne's profiteering. Moral outrage against "Cormorants" was understandable, even desirable, but the public policy choices were less clearcut in an economy based primarily on the principles of economic freedom. The most troubling fact of all to Winthrop was that a "certain rule" could not be established to ensure equity between buyers and sellers, "though much labor had been bestowed in it." Such variables as the cost of labor, materials, and transport, as well as the factor of risk, demonstrated too great a fluctuation, especially in a New World setting.

Here Winthrop's dilemma was emblematic of the larger moral problem posed by the Protestant ethic: how to draw the line between industrious enterprise and self-regarding acquisitiveness. In the *Arbella* sermon, Winthrop had endorsed the need to lay up a surplus in order to provide for one's family and community. The governor had written that "without question . . . he is worse than an Infidell whoe throughe his owne Sloathe and voluptuousness shall neglect to provide for his family." He emphasized the godly's need "to witnesse the improvement of our Tallent," averring that "it is not onely lawfull but necessary to lay upp as Joseph did to have [goods and wealth] ready uppon such occasions, as the Lord (whose stewards wee are of them) shall call for them from us."[30]

For Winthrop, the very existence of social inequality was the mainspring of all human striving and effort:

> to hold conformity with the rest of his workes, [God] being delighted to shewe forth the glory of his wisdome in the variety and differance of the Creatures and the glory of his power, in ordering all these differences for the preservacion and good of the whole, and the glory of his greatness [was] that as it is the glory of princes to have many officers, soe [that] this great King will have many Stewards, *counting himselfe more honoured in dispenceing his gifts to man by man, than if hee did it by his owne immediate hand.*[31]

Revealing the Bay Colonists' indebtedness to the Thomistic distinctions between distributive and commutative justice, Winthrop declared that "There are two rules whereby wee are to walke one towards another: JUSTICE and MERCY." In commercial transactions, these distinctions translated into the "Way of Commerce" and the "Way of Mercy." The first applied to those dealing from a position of financial health in the normal course of business dealings; the second to transactions with those in straitened circumstances or experiencing any form of want. In making this distinction, Winthrop echoed the arguments of Andrew Willet in his tract on usury, *Hexapola* (1608). Willet emphasized the need to give, not lend, to the poor. By the same token, Willet allowed that those among the middling classes who were driven to borrow by necessity should receive their loan without interest. Only loans to the well-off should carry interest payments, he contended, in part because natural law was now interpreted as allowing interest-bearing loans for capitalization.[32]

Puritans, like their medieval forebears, took their injunctions against usury from Exodus 22:25: "If thou lend money to any of my people that is poor by thee, thou shalt not be to him as an usurer, neither shalt thou lay upon him usury." Best crystallized in credit transactions, the separate set of rules to be applied according to the way of commerce and the way of mercy mandated that one "observe whether thy brother has present or probable, or possible meanes of repayeing" the lender. As Winthrop continued:

> thou must give him according to his necessity, rather than lend him as hee requires; if he hath present meanes of repayeing thee, thou art to looke at him, not as an Act of mercy, but by way of Commerce, wherein thou arte to walke by the rule of Justice, but, if his meanes of repayeing thee be only probable or possible, then is hee an object of they mercy [and] thou must lend [money] to him, though there be danger of losing it (Deut: 15.7).[33]

Where Puritan theorists like John Winthrop departed from medieval and Renaissance practice was in their near-total reliance on conscience, not guild or public authority, to regulate the marketplace. That conscience should be the clerk of the marketplace, that commercial dealings among equals should be governed by the rule of justice, that the rule of mercy should apply in dealings with the poor, these were the main organizing principles of the Bay Colony's business ethics. Like the distinctions made by both Captain John Smith and Governor Winthrop between present profit and an honest gain, the assumption was that market dealings were best regulated by the laws of supply and demand and the ethics of the covenant—as interpreted by the individual believer, not public authority, not craft or merchant guild. Pronouncement from the pulpit and policy enactments from the Massachusetts General Court alike reflected a widely shared consensus on these issues throughout the first charter period (1630–86). The old Christian principles of distributive and commutative justice, reaching back through the Scholastics and St. Augustine to the Sermon on the Mount, were to set the standards of ethical business dealings, including all commercial and credit transactions. But, as the settlers recognized within six months of the founding of Massachusetts Bay Colony, governmental regulations of wages and prices proved in practice to be "neither safe nor equal."

* * *

Even before the proceedings against Robert Keayne in 1639, the doctrine of economic freedom—at least with respect to wage and price controls—had emerged dominant in Massachusetts. The explanation for this development is in part sociological. The laboring poor—the main constituency for edicts governing price regulation, the maintenance of commons rights, and restrictions on free markets—did not migrate to New England in significant numbers. Nor, at least during the colonial period, did New England develop a distinct, permanent laboring class. The issue of economic regulation has always possessed this strong sociological dimension. Those not enjoying economic independence have been, historically, less enthusiastic about free markets and more ready to look to state and municipal regulation on their behalf. Among wage laborers, poor husbandmen, and small craftsmen—the men and women least able to absorb sudden economic shifts—the need for public authority to prevent a world of unchecked competition seemed self-evident. If, as seems likely, one's enthusiasm for economic regulation was inversely proportional to the amount of property one owned, the lack of such enthusiasm among the overwhelmingly propertied settlers of the Bay Colony is not surprising. There is also the issue of the ready availability of land in the New World. Assuming that the remnants of the regulated economy continued to exist in England because of the near impossibility that laborers or husbandmen could realistically aspire to land ownership, a reversal of such attitudes in the Bay Colony seems inevitable. John Smith had readily predicted as much. As Daniel Vickers rightly declares, it was "in the expectation of relative economic freedom . . . that the colonists in Massachusetts Bay set about breaking the land and improving their estates."[34] The issue of wage and price controls, as an illustration, seemed—at least to the Puritan leadership—to accord neither with the law of justice nor the law of mercy.

John Winthrop's observation that statutes setting price controls had invariably proved "neither safe nor equal" went to the heart of the matter. Even as far back as St. Thomas himself, it had been impossible to devise a "certain rule" to ensure equity between buyer and seller in a world of fluctuating costs for foodstuffs, goods, and labor. Characteristically, experiments with price controls tended to lead to black markets, hoarding, scarcity, and market avoidance, not just and predictable dealings between merchants and consumers. Public officials, even at the local level, simply lacked the information—or incentive—to obey the signals of the marketplace as quickly as profit-conscious buyers and sellers could. Moreover, producers, not to mention merchants, would have been ruined if the (regulated) market price fell permanently below cost.[35] Not surprisingly, since the thirteenth century, attempts by municipalities and guilds to eliminate the evils of unrestrained competition have more often than not proved counterproductive. So too in the Bay Colony.[36]

Although Massachusetts Bay has been characterized as the "happy hunting ground for paternalistic controls over religion, morals, and business," a colony in which "the most significant experiment in wage and price controls" in British North America took place, the social reality was considerably more complex.[37] Peacetime wage and price controls in fact were in effect for a *total* of forty-three months during the period from 1630 to 1684. In August and September of 1630, the Court of Assistants established wage maximums for construction workers (carpenters, sawyers, joiners, masons, bricklayers, thatchers) and common laborers. By the terms of the September decree, the former group was prohibited from selling their labor for above 16d. per diem and the latter 12d. per diem, if food and drink were supplied by the employer.[38] But in an environment in which land was abundant, laborers scarce, and settlement laws (tying an indigent laborer to his or her own parish) nonexistent, such controls proved unenforceable. Moved as much by pragmatism as by principle, the magistrates in short order shifted to a policy of economic liberty and contractualism. In March 1631 the Court of Assistants announced that the wages of carpenters, joiners, and other "artificers and workemen" henceforth would "be lefte free and att libertie as men shall reasonably agree."[39]

Two years later, Bay Colony lawmakers repeated the process of passing and then repealing wage controls. This time, prices as well as wages fell briefly under the hand of government regulation. In the fall of 1633 the General Court had reduced the wages of workmen to a "certainety," because of the "greate extortion used by dyvers persons of little conscience," leading to the "vaine and idle waste of much precious tyme, and expense of those immoderate gaynes in wyne, stronge water, and other superfluities." Evidently embarrassed by the naked class discrimination displayed by regulating wages but not prices, the General Court also placed a 33 percent maximum limit on commodity price mark-ups, "least the honest and conscionable workmen should be wronged or discouraged by excessive prices of those commodities which are necessary for their life and comfort."[40]

Yet even as the magistrates were wielding the regulatory weapon of governmental fiat, they (indirectly) acknowledged that such factors as risk and scarcity rendered such measures problematical. Commodities such as cheese and wine were exempted from the regulations because of the risk of spoilage. By the same logic, items that involved an abnormally low risk were also exempted from state regulation. With regard to "lynnen and other commodities, which [by] regard of their close stowage and small hazard, may be afforded att a cheap rate," the magistrates limited themselves to hortatory pronouncements mixed with vague threats against those who violated the "true intent" of such edicts. All settlers were advised "to be a rule to themselves, in keepeing a good conscience, assuring them that, if any man shall exceede the bounds of moderation, wee shall punish them severely."[41] And, not surprisingly in light of the magistrates' defensive tone, the wage and price control legislation of 1633 was routinely flouted. Even the scholar emphasizing the "paternalistic" nature of the Massachusetts economy concedes that "current wages exceeded the levels laid down by 50 per cent."[42] The few offenders who were brought to justice, such as John Chapman, fined 20 shillings for "selling boards att 8s. per 100, contrary to an order of [the] Court," were likely to have their penalties remitted in favor of voluntary contributions to such public works as the Boston sea fort.[43]

From 1634 through the onset of the depression of 1640, the General Court's confidence in the efficacy of wage and price controls eroded steadily. By the end of the first decade, all New Englanders—those from agricultural Dedham as well as those from commercially oriented Springfield—recognized that in order to import what they needed, they had to sell their products in markets that they could create but not control.[44] Through the series of government decrees on this issue can be discerned the triumph in early Massachusetts of the doctrine of economic freedom. In April 1634, the price of corn was "lefte at liberty to be solde [at such prices] as men can agree [on]."[45] In September of that year, the General Court declared that "noe man shalbe lyeable to pay the forfeit of 5s. for giveing more wages to workemen than the Court hath sett."[46] The next year, in a seminal piece of legislation mandating a wholesale elimination of regulatory controls over the exchange economy, the Court shifted decisively from a quasi-medieval to a liberal stance:

> The lawe that prohibited takeing above 3 1/2d. in the shilling profitt for commodities, and that which restrained workemen's wages to a certainty, [and] also

> that which restrained men [from] goeing aboard shipps [to buy imports, instead of allowing specially designated merchants to do so] . . . are repealed.[47]

When in 1636 John Cotton drew up *Moses His Judicialls* as a code of business ethics, the General Court had already abandoned the principle of centralized regulation of economic transactions. Accordingly, Cotton delegated regulatory responsibilities to selectmen in the individual towns, although asserting the governor's residual power to "appoint a reasonable rate of prices."[48] Giving statutory form to Cotton's recommendations—but mandating enforcement at the town level—in October 1636, the Court ordered the freemen of every town to set the "prices and rates of all workemen, laborers, and servants' wages"; but commodity prices were left unregulated.[49] Additional codes were passed in 1648, 1660, and 1672 authorizing the towns to establish wage maximums for workmen and servants, but—as the quarterly court records make abundantly clear—such edicts were indifferently enforced at best.[50]

Wage and price controls, three years before the censure of Robert Keayne, were honored mostly in the breach. And the leadership knew it. When, in March 1638, the General Court learned of "divers complaints made concerning oppression in wages, in prices of commodities, in smith's worke, in the excessive prices for the worke of draughts and teames," its decision was (in the manner of twentieth-century American presidents) to appoint a blue-ribbon commission to study the problem. But no action was taken.[51] Within a decade of the colony's founding, price controls had been almost totally discredited.[52]

In a journal entry for 1641, John Winthrop laid out the reasoning that led to this development, particularly with respect to restrictions on the price at which workmen sold their labor. The laws of supply and demand, especially in a frontier setting, did not defer to the will of the General Court. As Winthrop ruefully admitted, the magistrates had "found by experience that it would not avail by any law to redress the excessive rates of labourers' and workmen's wages, etc." The explanation for this was the simple one of labor scarcity.

Upon "being restrained," such workmen would "either remove to other places where they might have [higher wages], or else being able to live by planting and other employments of their own, they would not be hired at all." In the Old World, employers and public authorities could restrict the mobility of such workers through guilds and labor settlement laws, aided mightily by the lack of countervailing opportunities elsewhere. But such feudal devices as settlement laws, along with the discipline afforded by land shortage and the 1563 Statute of Artificers, were not available in New England. The results were predictable. Even after enforcement had been placed in the hands of local officials, who "in a voluntary way" employed the "counsel and persuasion of the elders, and [the] example of some who led the way," only a short-lived "moderation" was achieved. Even in the setting of the covenanted community, Winthrop regretfully admitted, "it held not long."[53]

For the remainder of the seventeenth century, the Massachusetts public policy on peacetime wage and price regulation was to use persuasion, not punishment. From the late 1630s onward, the Court employed normative pronouncements, not coercive legislation, in seeking to control secular fluctuations in wages and prices. In June 1641, the magistrates directly invoked covenant principles after the "great abatement in the prices of corne, cattle, and other commodities of the country [made it] impossible that men should be able to give such wages to servants and other laborers and workemen as formerly." The very survival of the infant colony hung in the balance. Many employers thought it "better to lay aside their business and impliments (which would tend to the ruine of the churches and common wealth) than to spend the small remainder of their estates for the maintenance of others in such a way as will not afford [the employer] some equall recompense"—i.e., an honest gain.[54]

Seeking to provide a moral check on the vicissitudes of a market economy, the magistrates invoked the language of Winthrop's *Arbella* sermon. In the most oft-quoted passage of that famous document, the governor had declared that "wee must be knitt together in this worke as one man; wee must entertaine each other in brotherly Affection; wee must be willing to abridge our selves of our superfluities, for the supply of others' necessities." Taking to the bully pulpit in June 1641, the General Court advised workmen, laborers, and servants that they

> should bee content to abate their wages according to the fall [in the prices] of the commodities wherein their labors are bestowed, and that they should bee satisfied with payment in such things as are raised by their labor, or other commodities, which the country affoards, and that they are to bee content to partake now in the present scarcity, as well as they have had their advantage by the plenty of former times.[55]

One choice open to the General Court after wage and price controls had been discredited was to pass tender laws, giving teeth to earlier suggestions on the legality of using goods in payment for services. In October 1641, while ordering that "All sorts of corne [shall be] left at liberty, as concerning the prices . . . any former order to the contrary notwithstanding," the magistrates mandated that servants' and workemen's wages could be paid in corn.[56] Two years later, the tables were turned, as poor harvests drove up corn prices to new heights. Winthrop's elegiac commentary on the farmers' pursuit of their advantage, like that of the workmen during the depression of 1641, suggests the Puritans' extreme discomfiture in adjusting to the full-blown market economy that the application of their own economic principles and the New World setting had produced. "Corn was," Winthrop wrote, "very scarce all over the country, so as by the end of [April 1643], many families in most towns had none to eat, but were forced to live off clams, muscles, cataos, dry fish, and etc." When corn had been plentiful two years earlier, it "was so undervalued [that] it would not pass for any commodity: if one offered a shop keeper corn for any thing, his answer would be, he knew not what to do with it. So [would answer] laborers and artificers." Now, however, "they would have done any work, or parted with any commodity, for corn." As for the farmer, "he now made his advantage, for he would part with no corn, for the most part, but for [cash] or for cattle, at such a price as should be 12d. in the bushel more to him than ready money. And indeed, it was a very sad thing to see how little of a public spirit appeared in the country, but of self-love too much."[57]

Such comments suggest the difficulties with existing explanations of Robert Keayne's censure. Clearly Keayne's punishment was not for the offense of violating a customary just price, something that for centuries before the settlement of the Bay Colony had been equivalent to the current market price. Keayne's censure also was not a consequence of a cultural split between pious farmers and bourgeois merchants. The pronouncements of Governor Winthrop and the General Court, as well as the swift rise of the region's commercial economy, make it clear that market-driven bargaining strategies were well-nigh universal in New England and had been employed to their "advantage" by laborers, artisans, and farmers as well as merchants when the conditions of supply and demand stood in their favor. Robert Keayne could not even justly be accused of violating the legal (as opposed to the natural) price, because price controls were in nearly complete disarray by the mid-1630s and had been effectively repudiated by the General Court by 1639.

There remains the possibility that Keayne was singled out for punishment not simply because he was a hard bargainer, but because he was a rich "Cormorant" who preyed on the poor and the weak. The import merchant's fault, Daniel Vickers contends, "lay not in haggling for a high price but in abusing the power he possessed in a thin and easily manipulated market (as Boston was in the 1630s) to extort an even higher one."[58] Such an explanation has the ring of truth, according as it does with the distinction New Englanders made between present profit and an honest gain. It also accords nicely with the corollary distinction Winthrop made between the way of commerce and the way of mercy. But the fact that Robert Keayne was the only merchant singled out for such exemplary punishment still needs to be reckoned with.[59]

The problem, in a nutshell, appears to have been what economists refer to as "blocked development." Too many imports were flowing to too few merchants. And too many of these were living in a single town, Boston. Keayne brought the young colony to an "uproar" not because he was a wealthy merchant per se, but because he was a wealthy Boston merchant, who appeared to many to be taking undue advantage of the country towns' near-complete dependence on New England one major port. It was the dearth, not the surfeit, of markets that produced the social strains leading to the outburst against the import merchant. As Stephen Foster declares:

> Economic backwardness, not economic progress, had caused the Keayne case; it represented no more than an example of inevitable social friction in the early days of a pioneer community, not the first stage of a nascent conflict between a medieval, aristocratic order and a rising class of bourgeois merchants. The cure for the problem lay in more merchants, more markets, better roads, and fewer shortages—in brief, in economic growth.[60]

This explanation of the Keayne censure is surely correct in its overall contours, not least because it accords with the colony's subsequent development. But it fails to take account of what might be dubbed "capitalist shock." The import-driven economy of the 1630s, with its nearly modern levels of price fluctuations and inflation, was a novel experience for most Puritan migrants, even for the Bay Colony's many artisans and town dwellers from the more highly commercialized regions of East Anglia. Describing the speculative ethos resulting from rapidly rising markets, one witness spoke of this period as one in which the inhabitants "Get all they can, sell often, then, and thus old Planters rise. They build to sell, and sell to build, where they find towns are planting."[61] With prices for some commodities during the late 1630s doubling and even tripling in a single year, and with the entire colony dependent for its very livelihood on textiles, metalwares, and even foodstuffs flowing into New England (almost exclusively through Boston), resentment against the major importers was almost inevitable.[62]

Price volatility, particularly during the economic crisis of

1639–40, was extraordinary by early modern standards. When the outbreak of the English Civil War stopped the flow of migrants—and money—into New England, the colony's financial collapse was precipitous.[63] Reflecting how completely the Bay Colony had become dependent on market exchange—and how chimerical were hopes for a market-resistant "moral economy"—prices in 1642 "fell [all] of a suddain in one week from £22 the Cow, to 6, 7, or £8 the Cow, at most."[64] As Governor Winthrop wrote mournfully in a journal entry for October 1640: "The scarcity of money made a great change in all commerce. Merchants would sell no wares but for ready money; men could not pay their debts though they had [sufficient material resources]; prices of lands and cattle fell soon to the one half and less, yea to a third, and after one forth part."[65]

Reflecting the Bay Colony's nearly complete dependence on the price mechanism in the period leading up to the censure of Robert Keayne, Winthrop described the dramatic deflation in commodity prices resulting from the depression of 1641: "[With] few coming to us, all foreign commodities grew scarce, and our own [commodities] of no price. Corn would buy nothing; a cow which cost last year £20 might now be bought for 4 or £5, etc., and many gone out of the country, so as no man could pay his debts, nor the merchants make return into England for their commodities, which occasioned many there to speak evil of us."[66] Everywhere commodity prices collapsed. Wheat fell from 7 shillings per bushel in May to 4 shillings by October. Corn fell from 5 shillings to 3 shillings and, by June 1641, to nothing. Land prices dropped 80 percent. Commerce ground to a halt. John Cotton, minister of Boston's First Church, dubbed these the "times of the Unsettled Humors of many men's spirits to Returne for England."[67]

Robert Keayne, who brought with him to the Bay Colony in 1635 a reputation for hard dealing and cupidity, became—it seems highly likely—a scapegoat for those experiencing capitalist shock. In departing from a familiar economic world, one that included manor stewards, borough councillors, churchwardens, guilds, labor settlement laws, and substantial numbers of citizens still committed to the notions of moral economy, the Bay Colonists were charting new economic terrain. In a colony in which the price of livestock could drop 75 percent in one week—as happened in 1642—it is small wonder that consumers were edgy, or that a man with a reputation for being a "Cormorant" became a lightning rod for their anxieties. One surmises that Robert Keayne appeared, in difficult times, to exemplify the dangers of a world governed by present profit instead of honest gain. The decline of cotton prices in the late nineteenth-century South would provoke similar resentment among farmers against merchants and the railroads.[68] But, as the absence in early New England of any subsequent attempts to prosecute merchants for similar offenses suggests, the line between anti-communal greed and an honest gain was increasingly perceived as beyond the government's capacity to decipher. Equally important, as Winthrop reported with such regret, Keayne was anything but alone in his inclinations toward sharp dealing—a practice that over time would become synonymous with the Yankee merchant. The problem was not that Robert Keayne's aggressive business behavior was atypical in the Bay Colony, but that it was not.

There was, however, one way that Robert Keayne did appear different. What apparently set Keayne apart from his fellow merchants, and thus invited public opprobrium, was the precocious level of rationally calculating behavior he exhibited. If Keayne was an avatar of a new ethic, it was the rational calculating ethic, not the acquisitive ethic, that he most embodied. Bernard Bailyn, after editing the import merchant's 50,000-word apologia, was moved to remark that "The word that expresses best the most basic activity of Keayne's mind is *calculation.* The veil through which he saw the world was not so much colored as calibrated. It was *quantity* that engaged his imagination."[69] Indeed, Bailyn goes so far as to say that "Keayne displays an interest in records and accounts—witnesses of 'economic rationalism'—so intense as to appear at times pathological."[70] And so must it have seemed to Keayne's fellow settlers.

Most striking in this regard was Keayne's annual "casting up" of his net worth—precisely the kind of assessment of yearly profits and losses that Max Weber regarded as the touchstone of the capitalist ethic. So finely calibrated was Keayne's annual accounting process that in 1653 he could declare confidently that "I have not cleared near £100 a year above my expenses since I came [from England], which is not [above] 5 . . . per cent clear gains."[71] In his apologia, Keayne declared that "by casting up my estate, which commonly I do once every year, I can see what [amount] I am increased in my estate. . . ."[72] No detail escaped his notice. In one of his many inventory books, Keayne had

> set down the particulars of my estate in housing, lands, rents, debts, cattle of all sorts, farms, with some plate, jewels . . . with a particular [inventory] of all the wares and commodities and corn, either in my closet, warehouses, cellars, garret, corn-lofts both at Boston and at my farm or anywhere else, that I had to sell at the time of my casting up, with the names, quantities, prices, and sorts of them all.

Again underscoring the need to take an annual accounting of his profits and losses, Keayne stated that this inventory book also contained "a particular [calculation] of the charges that I have been at yearly in building, housekeeping, apparel, servants, and workmen's wages both at my farm and at Boston, and [also] whether I gained or lost by my estate that year and how much."[73]

The paper trail involved in the import merchant's accounting system was truly prodigious. It included day books, shop books, debt books, general account books, inventory books, farm account books, ironworks account books, a "book of creditor and debitor," an "account of my adventures [investments] by shipping with their returns," and an "account of what debts I owe and how they are discharged." For present purposes, the most significant of these record books was "a long paper book bound in white parchment which I call my inventory book." In commenting on the use of this book, Keayne provides as clear an expression of the Protestant ethic as one could wish to find: In it, "I do yearly (commonly) cast up my whole estate. It is a breviate of my whole estate from year to year and shows how the Lord is pleased either to increase or decrease my estate from year to year."[74]

Indeed, his overall fidelity to the tenets of the Protestant ethic was the principal leitmotif running through Keayne's apologia. He intended that the pronouncements of his last will and testament "will testify to the world on my behalf that I have not lived an idle, lazy, or dronish life, nor spent my time wantonly, fruitlessly or in company-keeping as some have been too ready to asperse me, or that I have had in my whole time either in Old England or New many spare hours to spend unprofitably away or to refresh myself with recreations. . . ."[75]

Keayne claimed, one suspects correctly, that his had been a life of constant striving for both worldly and spiritual success. Such dogged, relentless, grim-visaged effort was what set the Protestant merchants apart from their medieval and Renaissance predecessors.[76] The critical difference between Keayne's world and that of those who preceded him was that the earlier merchant classes did not generate a calculating gospel of hard work. Work days were partially filled, interruptions were many, leisure highly prized and frequently enjoyed.[77]

In the Old World, likewise, the virtues of gentility and nobility—neither of which took prominent root in New England—produced an upper-class suspicion of commerce and acquisitiveness that did not develop in North America until the generation of Henry Adams. In the early modern era, and in the New World as well as the Old, those societies that possessed a traditional aristocracy, with a hereditary or quasi-hereditary landowning class, almost always produced an anti-work ethic. The contrasts between the northern colonies and the southern and West Indian colonies come to mind. Where there was a landed aristocracy based on slavery, as in Brazil or the ante-bellum American South, an anti-work ethic ideology became common. Where status came through ascription, anyone possessing a work ethic was debarred from status.[78] New England merchants, by contrast, were anything but social outcasts in the seventeenth-century Bay Colony. Indeed, that was part of the problem. Everyone, to some degree, was a rational calculator. Weber himself declared that "without doubt, [in Massachusetts] the spirit of capitalism (in the sense we have attached to it) was present before the capitalistic order. There were complaints of a peculiarly calculating sort of profit-seeking in New England, as distinguished from other parts of America, as early as 1632."[79]

Throughout his business career, Robert Keayne encapsulated the rationally calculating tendencies that Weber used to differentiate "patrimonial capitalism" from "rational capitalism." Everything was done "in terms of balances": an initial balance at the outset of any enterprise, ongoing attempts to assess its probable profitableness, and "at the end a final balance to ascertain how much profit has been made."[80] For Weber, the capitalist age was primarily distinguished from that which preceded it by the rationally calculating pursuit of profit. For the early inhabitants of Massachusetts Bay, Robert Keayne's embodiment of this new rationally calculating ethic—along with his self-righteous and hectoring personality—was not likely to make him well beloved, especially in a time of economic uncertainty.

Keayne's career testified to the extreme ambivalence many New Englanders felt about their economic bent (and their eventual material success). Keayne, it seems possible, was *too* emblematic of a cast of mind that all the Bay Colonists—to a greater or lesser degree—shared. The import merchant, born into the humble circumstances of a butcher's son, died in 1656 among the richest men in Massachusetts Bay Colony. His personality as revealed in his last will and testament displays the classic traits of the *arriviste,* even the *parvenu.* Obsessive, self-righteous, unforgiving, steeled to see the world in probational terms, Keayne could never rest easy in his success, one suspects, for both spiritual and psychological reasons. His penchant for rational calculation, his long-established reputation as a hard bargainer, and his conspicuous prosperity in an inflationary decade, may have been too much for his neighbors to bear. Such men have not been uncommon in materialist America, as Tocqueville, Sinclair Lewis, Sherwood Anderson, and many others have noted.

But Keayne's humiliation in 1639 was a personal, not a philosophical rebuke. The crabbed figure of Robert Keayne, not the legitimacy of a market economy, was rebuffed in 1639. Moral economy, not market economy, suffered defeat in the late 1630s. Government regulation of the economy for the purposes of maintaining a just price and a fair wage was increasingly seen as unjust, unfair, and—most important—simply unworkable. Despite the import merchant's personal defeat, the economic philosophy he embraced—and to an exaggerated degree, embodied—had triumphed in the first decade of the Bay Colony's settlement.[81]

But this triumph of market economics took place in a Puritan colony. That meant that a person's wealth had to be shared. The double effect of the Protestant ethic needs to be kept in mind when assessing both the trajectory of Robert Keayne's career and the larger economic culture of New England. Even as the Protestant ethic rationalized the urge to accumulate worldly goods, it generated "counter-forces that checked and controlled their free play in behalf of social ideals more medieval than modern."[82] Surplus wealth was to be used to help the poor, and commercial success was to be measured by the good it conferred on the community as much as by the wealth it brought to the individual himself.

Robert Keayne's philanthropic largesse in his last will and testament shows these convictions in operation. Keayne's piety was apparently as strong—and as relentless—as was his calculating ethic. Indeed, as I have emphasized above, the two were inextricably linked in Puritan New England. In his will, the import merchant bequeathed to his son a treatise on the sacrament of the Lord's Supper. In emphasizing the superiority of heavenly to earthly treasure, Keayne described the volume as a "thin little book bound in leather, all written with my own hand, which I esteem more precious than gold, and which I have read over I think 100 and 100 [more] times. . . ." And such piety was translated into deeds. The Protestant ethic's demand that surplus wealth be devoted to socially benevolent or charitable purposes is reflected on virtually every page of Keayne's testament. Here again, the importance of New England's distinct, town-based institutional culture needs to be underscored. While universal benevolence had always been a central ideal of Christian ethical doctrine, Puritan ministers, magistrates, and mothers and fathers hammered home these ethical teachings within the specific context of the covenanted community. One owed a range of concrete communal obligations to the men and women resident in one's town, obligations that did not apply with equal force to those living beyond the community's borders. Viewed positively as mutual obligation within, or negatively as exclusivity (or worse) without, covenant ideology restrained the destructive capacity of a market-oriented regime. Within the community, the godly were enjoined to pursue wealth in order to "make the overflow of their cup serviceable" to their neighbors. This Robert Keayne did with the same single-minded determination that characterized all his actions. The import merchant, long before his death, had decided to bequeath one third of his property for the use of his town and colony. Despite the humiliations he had received at the hands of his fellow settlers, Keayne left funds for a number of eminently practical public works in the town of Boston. These included £300 for the construction of Boston's first townhouse (or townhall), to consist of a marketplace, courtroom, granary, and a library.[83] Keayne also left a bequest for a cistern to provide the town with water for fighting fires. He provided an endowment for Harvard College. He left funds to train militia recruits for the artillery company as well as for a "free school . . . for the training up of the Indians' children in learning and some English scholars to learn the Indian tongue." Only after the town, colony, college, and native inhabitants had been attended to did Keayne's testament turn to the task of bequeathing property to his family.

In his running commentary on his bequests, Keayne emphasized that he intended his benevolence to be "very necessary and useful."[84] Such hopes appear to have been fulfilled. The first Boston townhouse was built with Keayne's bequest in 1658 and remained in continuous use until 1711. Standing as an appropriate symbol of the import merchant's contribution to his community, Keayne's townhouse became the very hub of the Bay Colony's increasingly far-flung commercial network. Whether those availing themselves of its facilities were aware of the irony of the town's using the censured man's money to erect a more spacious and efficient marketplace is not recorded. But this was not the only irony of the Keayne bequest. Within the upper chambers of the townhouse, the members of the Massachusetts General Court worked to continue a process, begun with the onset of the depression of 1640, of fashioning a public policy in accordance with the Protestant ethic.

5

"That Ancient Republican Independent Spirit": Civil Society and Economic Development in the Winthrop Era

It was against the background and experience of prerogative government in the 1620s and 1630s that the Bay Colonists created the civic and legal underpinnings for communal capitalism.[1] During its first two decades of existence, the Massachusetts General Court enacted a series of progressive legislative decrees that secured property rights—including the right to sell one's labor freely—and minimized arbitrary or confiscatory actions by the government. As a result of the General Court's decrees, the acts of buying and selling land, labor, and goods were, in ordinary circumstances, "lefte at liberty to be solde [at such prices] as men can agree [on]."[2] Large-scale trading monopolies, along with merchant and craft guilds, were likewise deemed against "the public goode and the liberty of free men. . . ."[3]

After experimenting with various paternalistic edicts during the 1630s—wage and price controls, class-based sumptuary laws, import monopolies, regulated market days—the General Court opted during the 1640s for a program based more closely on the principles of economic freedom. Breaking new ground, the Bay Colony's leaders used the state to promote economic performance by both legitimizing certain enterprises and demanding specific behavior from individuals. Fifteenth-century Venice had done the first without the second. Calvin's Holy Commonwealth had required the second but not provided the first. In early Massachusetts, the developmental ethic of the mercantilist state was conjoined to the pious industry of the Protestant ethic. This combination provided the institutional backdrop to the other changes I have been describing—the Protestant elevation of secular callings over asceticism and clericalism, the legitimization (even celebration) of trade over agriculture, the striving ethic, conscience-based individualism, a new consciousness of time, and the sacralization of the workplace.

Undergirding all of these was the cardinal principle of English liberty that the Parliamentary forces fought for in the English Civil War: security of property, and indeed all rights, could be guaranteed only by a government in which power was checked and controlled by the people's representatives in Parliament.[4] Charles I went to his death in 1649 proclaiming that while he had endeavored to protect the people's "liberty and freedom as much as anybody whomsoever," this liberty included only the preservation of their lives and property, not their "having a share in government. . . ."[5] The bases of civil society secured by the Civil War—the rule of law, representative forms, and taxation based on consent—during the same period became permanent features of the Bay Colony in America.

Neither capitalism nor civil society could emerge in the absence of some legal/juridical separation between the political realm and the economic realm.[6] The expansion of early modern capitalist enterprise required limits on state intervention if private contracts and markets were to predominate in the overall economy. Only if there was judicially enforced protection of private undertakings against state expropriation, confiscation, interference with contract, and capricious taxation and regulation, could capitalist forms fully take root.[7] Capitalism and civil society required one another. The rise of capitalism, as Karl Marx and many others have noted, both promoted and depended upon the creation of a civil society to mediate between the individual and the state.[8] Only after the elimination of the quasi-feudal organization of society into estates, corporations, guilds, and ascriptively privileged groups could a truly public sphere peopled by autonomous individuals be created. Only after a law-governed regime was established could private actors begin to behave in a rationally calculating fashion.[9]

This brings us to the newly emerging theories of contract law reflected in the voluntaryism of the federal covenant. Governor Winthrop's "Modell of Christian Charity" opens with the organic principles of a hierarchical society—men are born and remain high or low—but the contractualism of a mechanistic and non-hierarchical world permeates the remainder of the document. Drawing apparently on the law of commissions and charters, Winthrop's lay sermon is replete with references to special warrants, commissions, and charters. The conditionality of a "will theory" of contract (which viewed contracts as mutual obligations voluntarily created) rather than the inflexible "Action of covenant" (a sealed promise that cannot be broken) is in evidence.[10] "Wee are," declared the governor, "entered into Covenant with [God] for this worke; wee have taken out a Commission, the Lord hath given us leave to drawe [up] our owne Articles [and] we have professed to enterprise these Actions upon these. . . ." Winthrop's sermon, almost certainly delivered in Southampton Harbor before the migrants left British shores, presents the federal covenant to the Almighty in the legal form of offer and acceptance: "Now, if the Lord shall please to heare us, *and bring us in peace to the place wee desire,* then hee hath ratified this Covenant and sealed our Commission. . . ."[11]

Covenant theology, with its emphasis on human agency and reciprocity, proved compatible with the new legal practices, as well as the new political economic theories, with their descriptions of society as "a joint stock company of shareholders bound together by economic self interest."[12] Contracts had become the foundation of the natural law school of jurisprudence during the revival of natural law theory in the late sixteenth and early seventeenth century. During the seventeenth century, contracts were extended by such jurists and political theorists as Grotius, Pufendorf, Hobbes, and Locke to explain such phenomena as the origins of all social bonds, the source of the ruler's legitimacy, and the relations among nations.[13] It was Grotius who, in his defense of the interests of the Dutch East India Company, did much to create the modern natural law vocabulary. His *De Jure Belli ac Pacis Libri Tres* (1625) attempted to base natural law on rational axioms that could be understood and accepted by all, high-born and low-born, Protestant and Catholic, alike.[14] Grotius, like Cicero before him, declared that natural law was a "dictate of right reason."[15] The doctrine of the people's right to resist unjust rulers was hammered out in the new political context brought by the Reformation and rise of political absolutism in both early Stuart England and on the Continent.[16] The very idea of contract—or, in Puritan lexicon, covenant—was increasingly seen as the primary basis of both political authority and the social order. In the *Leviathan* (1651), Thomas Hobbes had made one of his three "Laws of Nature" the principle that "men performe their Covenants made." Where the Puritans differed from Hobbes and Grotius was in their insistence that in contractual dealings—as indeed in all interpersonal transactions—scrupulousness be tempered with charity. William Ames declared that even though, "in all contracts, we should proceed according to right and good, not the letter or extreme rigour of the law, in which often times the most extreme injury is found," the law of charity should prevail.[17]

What Perry Miller calls the "special tenets of English Puritanism," rule by fundamental law and the social compact, were early features of the Bay Colony.[18] As the self-described New Israel, the Bay Colonists drew on biblical precedent as well as English common law traditions in fashioning their legal and political system. The *Book of General Lawes and Libertyes* (1648) stated that "So soon as God had set up Political Government among his people Israel, he gave them a body of Lawes for judgement both in civil and criminal cases. These were brief and fundamental principles."[19] The author of *A Discourse About Civil Government in a New Plantation Whose Design is Religion* (1663) declared that "the people that have the power of chusing their Governours [must be those] in Covenant with God."[20] Such criteria for civil society as the rule of law and a wide franchise were not to be taken for granted in either pre–Civil War England or its North American colonies. The early inhabitants of Massachusetts and Connecticut had only to look across their borders to New Haven or (later) New York to find governments that failed to provide common law rule, jury trials, and a relatively wide franchise. While the Chesapeake and West Indian colonies were much more deeply enmeshed in the commercial matrix of the British imperial system (particularly with respect to credit, factorage, and marine insurance), the absence of a strong civil society in these plantation settlements helped produce a highly stratified and more nakedly exploitative form of "bastard capitalism."[21]

The Massachusetts Bay leaders, although not without their own arbitrary tendencies, brought to the New World an abiding distaste for prerogative rule and a commitment to the rule of law. Undergirding the Bay Colony's constitutionalism, as we shall see throughout this chapter, was both the cultural memory of the settler generation and the ecclesiastical structure of Congregationalism. The struggle between Stuart despotism and Parliamentary liberty, like the contest between Arminian ceremonialism and Calvinist covenantalism, shaped Bay Colony institutions from the very beginning. The actions of the English Parliament during the Civil War era to define the property rights of individuals and create institutions to secure them from royal usurpation or arbitrary taxation were continued and in some cases accelerated in the Bay Colony. The early seventeenth-century trend toward absolutist rule in such varied locales as England, Prussia, and Wűrttemberg shaped the political principles of Jacobean and Caroline Puritans.[22] The Puritans' conflicts with the Stuart monarchs drove the saints into an alliance with the common law and extreme contractualism and forced them to provide arguments that would justify constitutional resistance to the King.[23] In defending the ancient constitution against the heightened claims of divine right monarchy to engage in non-Parliamentary taxation and religious innovation, the saints adumbrated notions of natural rights constitutionalism, democracy, and equality. Following the lead of Chief Justice Sir Edward Coke

(1552–1634), they set the rule of common law against prerogative decree.[24]

Debates during the 1620s over non-Parliamentary taxation, censorship, imprisonment without trial, and the use of the prerogative—all reflected in the 1628 Petition of Right—were reflected in the Bay Colonists' constitutionalism. In 1629, when King Charles's use of extra-Parliamentary prerogative measures climaxed in the decision for personal rule, the Massachusetts Company leadership made its final decision to emigrate to the New World. Constitutional forms and the rule of law, the English gentry's principal weapons against prerogative governance, not surprisingly, became main concerns of the migrants once in Massachusetts.[25]

The Bay Colony's constitutionalism also drew sustenance from the recent battles in English jurisprudence fought by Sir Edward Coke and his Parliamentary allies against the summary and discretionary justice of the courts of Chancery and Star Chamber. In seeking to rationalize and adopt English law to a more commercialized society, these prerogative courts had attempted to formulate law through magisterial authority with minimal precedential limitations. Such rationalization had not only broken "the cake of centuries of custom crystallized in many doctrines of the common law," but also awakened longstanding English fears of arbitrary authority. Coke declared in *The Second Part of the Institutes* (1642) that "The Common law hath so admeasured the prerogatives of the king that they should not take away nor prejudice the inheritance of any [subject]; and the best inheritance that the subject hath is the law of the realm." During its deliberations over codifying the colony's first law code, the 1641 *Body of Liberties,* the Massachusetts General Court authorized funds for the purchase of copies of *Coke on Littleton, Coke on Magna Carta,* and *Coke's Reports.* These volumes were ordered "To the end that [the Bay Colonists] may have better light for making and proceeding about laws."[26]

The saints received the very opportunity to establish their covenanted society as a result of the distractions of the

English Civil War. From the outbreak of the first Bishop's War in Scotland in 1639 until the time of the Restoration of the Stuart throne in 1660, the Bay Colonists enjoyed almost complete autonomy from serious imperial control.[27] Even during the early 1630s the Privy Council's Committee on Trade and Foreign Plantations failed to regulate the colonies effectively, and the collapse of the monarchical state in 1640 ended these vestigial controls. The most radical decisions that would be made by the Bay Colonists—declaring their colony a republic and Boston a free port, flying their own flag, eliminating the King's name from the oath of allegiance, issuing land without recognition of the Crown's right to it, and banning judicial appeals to the Privy Council—were all made possible by the Civil War. Throughout the 1640s, the religious and political radicalism of that extraordinary decade reinforced one another.[28]

As a Covenant People, the Bay Colonists rejected even the authority of Parliament itself during its epic struggles with the King.[29] In 1641, John Winthrop declared that "if we [in Massachusetts] should put ourselves under the protection of the parliament, we must then be subject to all such laws as they should make, or at least such as they might impose upon us; in which course though they should intend our good, yet it might prove very prejudicial to us."[30] In 1645, the year that the Battle of Naseby and the Parliamentary recapture of Bristol ensured the Royalists' defeat, the New Englanders announced candidly that they considered Massachusetts to be a self-governing republic: "ours is [a] *perfecta respublica*" (perfect commonwealth), subject to "no other power but among ourselves."[31] Elaborating on the sources of this authority in 1646, the Massachusetts government declared that "The highest authoritie here is in the general court, both by our charter and by our owne positive lawes."[32] In the same year, when those favoring Presbyterian forms accused the Bay Colony of behaving "rather [as] a free state than a colonie or corporation of England," the Massachusetts leadership admitted as much.[33] The General Court forthrightly proclaimed the conditional nature of its allegiance to England: "Our allegiance binds us not to the laws of England any longer than while we live in England, for the laws of [the] parliament of England reach no further [than English shores], nor do the king's writs under the great seal [reach to America]."[34] The Bay Colonists also embraced the principle of free trade, not publicly claimed as a natural right in America until Jefferson's *Summary View of the Rights of British-America* (1774). On May 14, 1645, Massachusetts, although nominally part of the British mercantilist system, declared itself a free port: "It is ordered, by the authority of the Court, that all ships that come for trading onely from other parts, shall have free accesse into our harbors, and quiet riding there, and free leave to depart without any molestation by us, they paying all such duties and charges required by law in the country as others do."[35]

Such pronouncements and actions continued even after the Restoration of the monarchy in 1660. In one of the most categorical denials of Parliament's right to rule the colonies issued before the First Continental Congress's *Declaration of Colonial Rights and Grievances* in 1774, the Massachusetts General Court in 1678 declared that "the lawes of England are bounded within the four seas and doe not reach America." Advancing the principles that would eventually spark the American Revolution, the General Court declared that because the colonists were "not represented in Parliament, so we have not looked at ourselves to be impeded in our trade by them." For taxation purposes, the Massachusetts General Court was a miniature—and equally sovereign—House of Parliament. Only if the colonists' own representatives had voted on taxation or trade regulations could they be regarded as legitimate. Parliamentary edicts could not be obeyed in Massachusetts "without invading the liberties and propperties of the subject, untill the Generall Court made provission therein by a law. . . ."[36] As Captain Thomas Breedon had informed the Council for Foreign Plantations in 1661, the New Englanders continued to "looke on themselves as a Free State."[37] The Bay Colony illegally operated a mint, created—again illegally—a provincial navy office for the supervision of local shipping, and attempted to establish ports of entry, a power vested exclusively in the English Lord High Treasurer.

Like Virginia, Massachusetts overvalued its currency (relative to sterling) in an effort to attract and keep metal coin circulating in the colony. Chronically short of currency, like every British colony, in 1690 Massachusetts became the first colony to experiment with paper money when it emitted twenty-shilling bills of public credit.[38] Throughout the first charter period, the Bay Colonists made few attempts to disguise their "great discontent at the Acts of Trade and Navigation," a discontent that was often translated into action. Edward Randolph, in his 1677 "Representations" against New England, laid out Whitehall's bill of indictment against the recalcitrant colony. The Massachusetts colonists, Randolph declared, had illegally "formed themselves into a Common Wealth," "Coine[d] money with their owne Impress," and—most galling of all for a British mercantilist—"ingrossed the greatest part of the West India Trade, whereby his Majestre is damaged in his Customs above £100,000 yearly."[39]

In declaring that obedience to God meant resistance to tyrants, the saints—in England and America—obtained a powerful rationale for repudiating the *ancien régime.* The saints' resistance to a tyrannical government was explicitly justified by such older doctrines as the *salus populi suprema lex* favored by Roman law and the newer imperatives brought by covenant theology.[40] The overthrow of Governor-General Sir Edmund Andros in 1689, in what proved to be a dress rehearsal for 1776, was justified on the grounds that the Dominion government (1686–89) had abridged the New Englanders' long-established rights to representation. When the 1629 charter was revoked by a writ of *scire facias* in 1684, all land titles granted under the charter were called into question. In petitioning the Crown following the *quo warranto* proceedings by the Committee on Trade and Plantations in June 1683 against the Massachusetts charter, the colonists embraced what was soon to emerge as the Lockean labor theory of property: title to land—and hence right to representation—belongs to those whose labors subdue and improve it. This was especially true, as the colonists had steadfastly maintained, in "a wilderness and hard country." On 24 July 1685 the colonists petitioned the King

> on behalfe of ourselves, inasmuch as our fathers, and some of us with them, left their native land, with all their pleasant and desirable things therein, embarking themselves and familyes, and came over the vast ocean, and, through divine conduct, arrived heere in a vast howling wilderness, a considerable part whereof, after they had purchased the natives' right, with sore labour and indefattigable industry, at their owne charges, have subdued and made fitt for habitation.[41]

Cognizant of such traditions, Loyalist Jonathan Sewall offered an interpretation of American resistance during the Revolutionary crisis that linked such behavior directly to the Puritan founding. In writing to General Frederick Haldimand in May 1775, Sewall laid the blame squarely on the seditious attitudes carried to Massachusetts by the first settlers and subsequently nurtured by their civic institutions. He located the origins of the imperial crises in "that ancient republican independent Spirit, which the first Emigrants to America brought out with them; and which the Forms of Government, unhappily given to the New England Colonies, instead of checking, have served to cherish and keep alive."[42]

* * *

The Bay Colonists' fear of prerogative government shaped internal political development as well. The civil society of the New England colonies rested on a popularly based determination to uphold rule by fundamental law, a determination that sometimes clashed with the "discretionary" principles of the magistrates. In a highly appropriate metaphor for a maritime society, the Massachusetts *Book of General Lawes and Libertyes* declared that "a Common-wealth without lawes is like a Ship without rigging and steeredge." Because for the New England Puritans the most important liberty of all was the liberty to "raise up a pure church," there was before 1692 a selective nature to the application of the rule of law, a practice that earned Massachusetts colonists a reputation for persecution even among their fellow saints in England. But while Bay

Colonists were bitterly intolerant (and in the case of Indians and Quakers, worse) toward all outsiders, those deemed within the Puritan community enjoyed a wide variety of legal protections against arbitrary treatment.[43]

The Bay Colonists' constitutionalism reflected the anti-authoritarianism and egalitarianism latent in the Puritan mission, or indeed in Reformed Protestantism itself. Protestantism, especially in its Calvinist manifestations, undercut the traditional conception of religion as propitiation. By building its entire doctrine on the distinction between the states of grace and reprobation, ascetic Puritanism subverted existing notions of social hierarchy. According to its dictates, the status of the equality of individuals rested ultimately on their individual responsibility to God.[44] When Puritan intellectuals like John Winthrop declared that the law of nature had been superseded by the law of grace, they fractured the centuries-old alliance between natural law doctrines and existing social hierarchies. In anticipation of its eventually explosive potential, even the boundaries of race and gender could be breached by the sovereignty of grace. Winthrop recorded in 1641 that "A negro maid, servant to Mr. Stoughton of Dorchester, being well approved by divers years' experience, for sound knowledge and true godliness, was received into the church and baptized."[45]

The teaching that the Protestant believer is subject to no sanction by any external spiritual authority but only to the inner sanctions of his or her own conscience—what Perry Miller refers to as the "irrepressibly democratic dynamic in Protestant theology"—had real social and political consequences.[46] This was so not least because Puritanism was, in both England and America, predominantly the religion of ordinary people. While colonial Massachusetts always possessed a number of communities like Springfield, Marblehead, and Lynn where Puritan religiosity ran shallow, the hegemony in both elite and popular culture generally of Calvinist linguistic codes was remarkable. More than a century after Massachusetts' founding, these codes continued to permeate popular discourse. While traveling through New England in 1744, Dr. Alexander Hamilton of Maryland noted acerbicly that even "the lower class" of men and women in

New England talked of nothing but "justification, sanctification, adoption, regeneration, repentance, free grace, reprobation, original sin, and a thousand other such pritty, chimerical knick-knacks, as if they had done nothing but studied divinity all their life time." Which, of course, most had. In arming themselves with the Word of God, ordinary New England men and women both mastered the daunting theological lexicon of Puritan divinity and learned to think—and eventually act—according to the dictates of conscience.[47]

Not only did Protestantism strengthen such virtues as responsibility, self-control, and spiritual independence among all its adherents—of whatever social status, age, or gender—but it hardened and annealed the believer to live in a hostile world unaided by paternal clerical intermediaries. Ascetic Puritans took to a new level the ancient Christian doctrine of the particularism of grace.[48] John Milton, in his defense of individual liberties during the 1640s, voiced his conviction that "all men naturally were born free, being the image . . . of God himself." In Massachusetts Bay the saints repeatedly demonstrated the power of conversion to make religion a real force in one's life instead of mere form. The newly converted felt themselves empowered to rebuff old hierarchies and old authorities and to rely on the moral legitimacy of self-initiated action.[49] (It was for many of these reasons that Max Weber's friend and fellow Heidelberg professor, Georg Jellinek, declared in 1895 that seventeenth-century pious dissenters—not Enlightenment *philosophes*—played the greatest role in creating civil society by promoting civil, religious, and domestic rights.)[50]

At base, the saints' conception of civil society rested on their radical elevation of conscience. Conscience, for the Calvinist reformers, was everything, quite literally the voice of God. In *Cases of Conscience* (1613), William Perkins declared that "The naturall condition or properties of every man's conscience is this; that in regard of authoritie and power, it is placed in the middle between man and God, so it is under God, and yet above man." Leaving little doubt of the anti-authoritarian dimension of this proposition, Perkins wrote that "no man's commaundment or law, can of itselfe, and by its owne soveraigne power, binde conscience." In the *Areopagitica,* Milton eloquently demanded that Parliament allow Englishmen "the liberty to know, to utter, and to argue freely according to conscience, above all liberties." He said that "when God gave man reason, he gave him freedom to choose, for reason is but choosing. . . ." It was conscience, rather than priest, bishop, Pope, or intercessory saint, that stood between the Puritan and his or her God.[51]

This reliance on conscience helped give many Calvinists an "incurably republican spirit." As early as 1613, members of the Puritan-dominated Cambridge University openly debated whether governmental succession should be accomplished through royal succession or election.[52] In 1637 Charles I's chief adviser, Sir Thomas Wentworth, averred that "the very genius of that nation of people [the Puritans] leads them always to oppose . . . authority." Archbishop William Laud—who, like Wentworth, eventually ended up on the executioner's block as a result of the saints' implacable opposition—described Puritan lecturers as but "the people's creatures [who] blew the bellows of their sedition." In charging Lincolnshire's Thomas Shepard to "neither preach, read, marry, bury, or exercise any ministerial function in any part of my diocese," an enraged Laud accused the Puritan divine of having already "made me a company of seditious Bedlams. . . ."[53] Puritan lecturers in Caroline England were routinely castigated by royal officials as "Seditious Preachers" who "poyson the people with their Antimonarchical Principles."[54] For some Royalist officers during the Civil War, the saints' single-minded and rebellious behavior put them beyond the pale of normal civility. After massacring the Puritan defenders of Nantwich in January 1644, Lord Byron reported to the Earl of Newcastle, without regret, that "I put them all to the sword . . . which I find is the best way to deal with those kind of people, for mercy to them is cruelty."[55]

The anti-monarchical tendencies in Puritan theology were reflected, and amplified, in Massachusetts' civil society. The traditional English distrust of arbitrary government, in tandem with the voluntaristic dimension of ascetic Puritanism, made accountability a central issue from the earliest years of the Bay Colony. The decentralized and democratic nature of Congregationalism itself followed the logic of the federal covenant. As elsewhere, an exclusive theology—the attempt to purge the unregenerate from church and civil society alike—produced democratic results. To the discomfort of many English saints, federal covenant theology in fact elevated the congregation over the state, grounding civil rights in testified regenerate membership. This policy, at once radically exclusive and potentially tyrannical, in practice resulted in levels of popular participation that always threatened hierarchical stability. This was true even before the test for church membership was dropped during the 1690s. After three years in the infant Bay Colony, the lawyer Thomas Lechford, although an orthodox Puritan, returned to England complaining about both the excessively democratic character of church government in Massachusetts and its likely social and political consequences: "If the people may make Ministers, or any Ministers make others without an Apostolicall Bishop, what confusion will there be?" Lechford had reason for these sentiments. In few ecclesiastical systems in the early modern world could so democratic and decentralized a system of church organization be found. In 1640, the Puritan colonizer of Providence Island, William Fiennes, first Viscount Saye and Sele, upbraided New Englanders for elevating the authority of the congregation above that of the state and for the excessively democratic political culture that resulted. Lord Saye declared that "noe wise man should be soe foolish as to live where every man is a master, and masters must not correct theyr servants; where wise men profounde and fooles determine, as it was sayde of the Citties of Greece."[56]

The Calvinist vision of a community of individuals under God's dominion redefined the rights to representation, to property, and to autonomy.[57] The adoption of the principle of testified regenerate membership as the basis of Non-separating Congregationalism, coupled with the General Court's decision in the early 1630s to base the franchise on church membership, gave ordinary people a greater voice in their government than they would have had in England. In 1630, the Massachusetts General Court transformed freemanship from membership in a joint stock company into a franchise to vote and hold office in a commonwealth. In 1631, freemanship was restricted to church members. In one of Puritanism's apparently inexhaustible supply of ironies, the division of humankind between a spiritual aristocracy of those who were saved and the remainder who were not produced unintended democratic consequences. By shifting the basis of one's status from birth to the possession of grace, the Puritan leadership unwittingly fostered a political inclusiveness that was the very opposite of its initial intentions.[58]

The constitutional underpinnings of the Holy Commonwealth were found in the Massachusetts corporate charter of 1629, which the King—astonishingly—permitted the settlers to bring to the New World. Although Charles I had issued the charter with the explicit proviso that all laws passed by the Massachusetts General Court be "not contrairie to the Lawes of this Realm of England," the settlers wasted little time in repudiating the King's will in matters both large and small. Like its Virginia counterpart, the Massachusetts Bay Colony began as a trading corporation. Its patent was originally a commercial charter offering concessions of powers by the Crown to enterprisers willing to assume the risk of exploration and settlement. The new ventures created in Tudor-Stuart England for colonizing and trading with distant lands—beginning first with the Russia Company in 1553 and followed by the East India Company, the Levant Company, the Plymouth Company, and the Massachusetts Bay Company—broke new ground in commercial practice by initiating techniques now associated with the modern corporation. These included the crucial concept of limited liability for the majority of the stockholders, as well as the use of perpetual stock, management committees, and dividend payments.[59] And, as in Virginia, a commercial charter metamorphosed into the frame of government for a state.[60]

Company meetings in Boston became the basis of a representative government in which virtually all heads of families were offered the chance to become freeholders. Unlike that other Puritan colony founded in 1630, on Providence Island in the West Indies, the first Bay Colonists would receive the rights to both representative government and private property.[61] They also escaped the centralized, overmanaged control that characterized the Providence Island government (in its efforts to avoid the chaos experienced by early Virginia). John Winthrop took the lead in using the 1629 charter to create a representative government, although he later would have cause to regret unleashing democratizing forces that ultimately led to his impeachment by the House of Deputies in 1645. Most consequential was Winthrop's decision to allow the redefining of "freemen" from stockholders in a commercial venture to citizens of a state. Between 1630 and 1634, Massachusetts freemen were transformed from members of a limited business venture to representatives in a public government. At its 19 October 1630 meeting, the General Court—acting in clear violation of the charter—transformed itself from a trading company into a commonwealth. The twelve ruling Assistants (magistrates) were given the power to select the Governor and Deputy-Governor from among themselves and to make laws and select officials to carry them out.

Massachusetts' ecclesiastical policy of testified regenerate membership would form the basis of the civil polity. In 1631, Winthrop and the Assistants expanded the franchise to include all male church members. On 18 May of that year, to "the end [that] the body of commons may be preserved by honest and good men," the General Court ordered that "noe man shalbe admitted to the freedome of this body polliticke, but such as are members of some of the churches within the lymitts of the same."[62] Church members were admitted into the ranks of freemen, thereby giving them more of a stake in society and—presumably—making governing easier. In 1632, the leadership mandated that all civil officers would be elected by the freemen.[63] In effect making Massachusetts a republican government in everything but name, every adult male church member received the power to vote for Governor, Deputy-Governor, and Assistants. That same year, when the residents of Watertown balked at being taxed by the General Court without their consent, Winthrop assured them that "this government was rather in the nature of a parliament. . . ."[64]

The Massachusetts General Court thereby was transformed from an executive council of a commercial company into a legislative government. This transformation reflected the saints' political convictions that the commonwealth should be divided into two ranks, gentlemen and freeholders, and each should be given a veto over the decisions of the other. Most of the university-trained leaders of the Bay Colony accepted the Platonic and Renaissance postulate that only the very few possessed a talent for governing.[65] In the spring of 1634, the freemen appointed two Deputies from each town to consider what issues should be brought before the General Court's May meeting. By this action, and within four years of its creation, Massachusetts Bay became a representative government.[66] In 1644 the General Court became a full-fledged bicameral legislature, with the Deputies and Assistants sitting separately. The magistrates represented the gentlemen, the Deputies the freeholders. Highly unusual in seventeenth-century America (by 1692 bicameralism had been established only in Massachusetts, Virginia, and Maryland), bicameral government fostered both judicial independence and the authority of the lower house generally.[67] Seventeenth-century Massachusetts Bay was not—nor was it intended to be—a democracy; but two of the principal ideological bulwarks of Old World government, the feudal and the hereditary, were conspicuous by their absence. In rejecting a sacerdotal order ruled by ministers, while seeking to establish a pure social order based on testified regenerate membership, the Bay Colonists created one of the early modern world's first civil societies.[68]

In its transformation from a trading corporation into a commonwealth between 1630 and 1634, the Massachusetts Bay government took upon itself the full sovereign powers to legislate, tax, and erect a court system with full—and final—powers of adjudication. Appeals to the Privy Council were consistently barred throughout the first charter period. The decision to endow civil courts in the Puritan colonies with an undisputed monopoly of judicial power—in contrast to England, where ecclesiastical courts still handled probate—was likewise a conscious public policy choice. In 1643, the three inferior quarterly courts in Massachusetts with jurisdiction over lesser civil and criminal cases became the county courts of Essex, Suffolk, and Middlesex; Norfolk was added in 1648. In basing the franchise on church membership instead of property ownership or corporate rights, the Bay Colony subverted English practices, but at considerable gain. The federal covenant fostered a robust public sphere at the local as well as provincial level, as a chain of covenants joining family, church, town, and commonwealth created the distinctive civic ecology of Puritan New England. With localism prevailing from the outset, towns were given the overall responsibilities to allocate land, keep the peace, raise and spend taxes, and supervise economic improvement.[69]

Sovereignty in the Bay Colony ultimately rested on civil, not clerical, authority. Although Massachusetts was established, as Edward Johnson put it, so "that our Lord Christ may raigne over us, both in Churches and Commonwealth," real barriers were erected between ecclesiastical and civil authority.[70] While both church and state were saturated with religion (and the latter was founded upon the former), Massachusetts vested political power exclusively in elected officials throughout the first charter period. New England ministers enjoyed unrivaled social prestige during the seventeenth century, but they were explicitly barred from wielding civil power. In response to Lord Saye and Sele's intimation that Massachusetts Bay was a theocracy, John Cotton assured the viscount in 1636 that in the Bay Colony, "magistrates are neyther chosen to office in the church, nor doe [they] govern by directions from the church, but by civill lawes, and those enacted in generall corts, and executed in corts of justice, by the governors and assistants."[71] While magistrates and ministers were both charged with the transcendent task of fostering godly behavior, the line between church and state in the Bay Colony was drawn as sharply as any place in the early modern world. In addition to the fact that ministers in Massachusetts were barred from holding civil office, such important Old World clerical powers as administering the sacrament of marriage became civil responsibilities in the Bay Colony. In England or on the Continent, excommunication carried heavy civil disabilities; in Massachusetts, it did not. A number of activities supervised by the church in England became state functions in Massachusetts: the dispositions of estates; marriage and divorce; and the recording of vital statistics.[72]

John Winthrop's "discretionary" view of magisterial authority was also subverted in relatively short order. From the 1630s onward, the loudest demands for political accountability and the rule of law came from below. From the calls in the early 1630s for town representation in the General Court through the demands by the "popular faction" in 1689 for a restoration of the suspended first charter, Bay Colony rulers faced consistent pressure from the towns for a more accountable government. In 1632 Governor Winthrop informed his fellow magistrates that "he had heard that the people intended, at the next general court, to desire that the assistants might be chosen anew every year." It was the Deputies (town-based representatives), not the Assistants (the twelve elected magistrates), who took the lead in agitating for the creation of the *Body of Liberties* in 1641. In the Deputies' view, the colony could not long abide the "want of positive laws." The Deputies cited historical precedent as justification for their actions against the Assistants, going back as far as Parliament's attempt in 1542 to limit such concentrations of power in a small group of corporate leaders.[73]

Reluctantly acknowledging the rejection of his form of benevolent paternalism, John Winthrop described the process that led to the creation of the *Body of Liberties*. Even (or perhaps especially) in the covenanted communities of Puritan Massachusetts, rulers of Englishmen were not to regard themselves as above the law. "The people," Winthrop admitted in November 1639, "had long desired a body of laws, and [they] thought their condition very unsafe, while so much power rested in the discretion of the magistrates." Responding to the Deputies' protests in 1635, the magistrates had ordered that "a body of grounds of laws, in resemblance to a Magna Charta . . . should be received for fundamental laws."[74] The first effort in this direction, in 1636, John Cotton's heavily biblicized *Moses His Judicialls*, was not accepted by the General Court, leading lawyer Nathaniel Ward to draw up what became the *Body of Liberties* that the Court approved in 1641.[75] In 1643, during a debate on whether the magistrates should hold veto power over the actions of the deputies, Winthrop would concede that "originally and vertually" the "greatest power is in the people," although he continued to maintain that magistrates held discretionary power once elected.[76] It was in accord with such popular sovereignty logic that the Deputies and freemen explicitly voted to give their endorsement to the *Body of Liberties.* At the December 1641 meeting of the General Court, John Winthrop attested that "the bodye of lawes formerly sent forth amonge the Freemen, etc, was voted to stand in force."[77]

The 1641 *Body of Liberties* reflected the background of the English Puritans' experience of prerogative government in the 1620s and 1630s. It guaranteed the rights to representative government, trial by jury, due process of law, and protection against double jeopardy. Reflecting the like-minded trends in England during the Civil War period, the *Body of Liberties* attempted to curtail prerogative government, ensure due process, and guarantee natural rights.[78] A decade and a half of contending with Charles I over un-Parliamentary taxation, illegal arrest, censorship of speech, and garrison rule led Puritans on both sides of the Atlantic to take steps during the 1640s to place legal restrictions on prerogative government once they were in a position to do so. The same year, 1641, that Nathaniel Ward wrote his draft of the *Body of Liberties,* the Long Parliament struck down the prerogative courts of Star Chamber and High Commission and passed the "Grand Remonstrance" against the constitutional usurpations of Charles I. The Stuarts' increased use of Star Chamber, which combined legislative, executive, and judicial powers, had been a key to circumventing common law and Parliamentary rule.[79]

The 1641 *Body of Liberties* began with a paraphrase of Magna Charta (1215) and stated the entire legal system in terms of the "liberties" of various groups—of freemen, women, children, foreigners, even "brute creatures." The Eighteenth Liberty provided that "no man should strike his wife," a practice that remained legal in England itself as late as the mid-nineteenth century. The preamble to the *Body of Liberties* declared that the vitality of both church and commonwealth rested on the preservation of due process and the rule of law. It rooted the Bay Colony's civic ecology in the preservation of humanity, civility, and Christianity, asserting that

> The free fruition of such liberties, Immunities, and priveleges as humanitie, Civilitie, and Christianitie call for as due to every man in his place and proportion without impeachment and Infringement, hath ever bene and ever will be the tranquillitie and Stabilitie of Churches and Commonwealths. And the deniall or deprivall thereof [brings] the disturbance, if not the ruine, of both.[80]

Reflecting a desire to protect due process and personal liberty from arbitrary governmental action, the first provision of the *Body of Liberties* proclaimed:

> No man's life shall be taken away, no man's honour or good name shall be stayned, no man's person shall be arested, restrayned, banished, dismembered, nor any wayes punished, no man shall be deprived of his wife or children, no man's goods or estaite shall be taken away from him, nor any way indammaged under colour of law or Countenance of Authoritie, unless it be by vertue or equitie of some expresse law of the Country waranting the same, established by a generall Court and sufficiently published. . . .[81]

Property rights and basic political liberties were inextricably linked in the Bay Colony. For the middling-rank settlers of New England, the foundation of liberty rested on land ownership, and the opportunity to work for one's own family.[82] The Puritan commonwealth was to rest on private property, with security of tenure. The cautionary tales provided by the failure of several years of communal ownership in both Virginia and Plymouth—a failure that was simultaneously being demonstrated in the Providence Island colony—only strengthened such sentiments among Massachusetts' founders. A system that severed the link between work and land ownership, according to Plymouth Governor William Bradford, was doomed to failure, even among the saints. Bradford's description of Plymouth plantation's three-year experiment with communal property distills some of the major imperatives of the Protestant ethic—and this includes its application to young and old, male and female, alike:

> The experience that was had in this common course and condition, tried sundry years and that amongst godly and sober men, may well evince the vanity of that conceit of Plato's and other ancients applauded by some of later times; that the taking away of property and bringing in community into a commonwealth would make them happy and flourishing; as if they were wiser than God. For this community [of property] (so far as it was) was found to breed much confusion and discontent and retard much employment that would have been to their benefit and comfort. For the young men, that were most able and fit for labour and service, did repine that they should spend their time and strength to work for other men's wives and children without any recompense. The strong . . . had no more in division of victuals and clothes than he that was weak and not able to do a quarter [that] the other could; this was thought injustice. The aged and graver men, to be ranked and equalized in labours and victuals, clothes, etc., with the meaner and younger sort, thought it some indignity and disrespect unto them. And for men's wives to be commanded to do service for other men, as dressing their meat, washing their clothes, etc., they deemed it a kind of slavery. . . .[83]

The Protestant dimension of English attitudes toward land, property, and inheritance bears emphasis here. The Catholic Church had not accepted the legitimacy of private property until the twelfth century, and canonists and theologians thereafter continued to display an extreme wariness regarding its potentially corrupting influence. English Protestants during the Elizabethan period were the first Western Christians openly to challenge the ancient, communally based system of land ownership—the notion that "the earth is the Lord's and the fulness thereof, and its fruits belong to all His creatures in common." The Thirty-Eighth Article of Religion of the Church of England, promulgated in 1563, openly legitimated private property. It declared that "The Riches and Goods of Christians are not common, as touching the right, title, and possession of the same, as certain Anabaptists do falsely boast." Such rhetoric often explicitly yoked the work ethic to the principle of private property. The Puritan magnate Nathaniel Rich, in leading the County of Essex's vigorous resistance to Charles I's Forced Loan in 1628, linked security of property to both personal industry and national security: "If no propriety there will be no industry, and then nothing will follow but beggary, and if no propriety there will follow no valor."[84]

New England could not become a capitalist society unless land, its principal form of wealth, could be used as a liquid economic commodity. Nor was a choice in this direction a foregone conclusion. Forms of tenancy had prevailed in the early years of Virginia, Plymouth, Bermuda, and Providence Island. Moreover, many English colonists expected American land to be parceled out in huge baronies, after the fashion of the Irish example a generation earlier.[85] In an unambiguous signal of the Massachusetts leadership's views on this issue, Article 10 of the *Body of Liberties* disposed of the feudal element from land conveyance altogether:

> All our lands and heritages shall be free from all [entry] fines and licenses upon Alienations, and from all hariotts, wardships, Liveries, Primerseisins, yeare day and wast, Escheates, and forfeitures, upon the deaths of parents or ancestors [be] they naturall, casuall, or Juditiall.[86]

The landholding system that emerged in accordance with these principles allowed land to be alienable, inheritable, and devisable *without* fines, fees, or the use of legal fictions. It represented a philosophical move away from the older notion of land tenure as a bundle of rights and obligations, and toward the modern concept of absolute control. Only upon the acceptance of such legal doctrine could real property be seen and used as a commodity of exchange.[87] Free socage tenure was in effect an early version of fee simple tenure (which conveyed absolute dominion).

The key feature of free socage tenure was the ease of alienating land through sale or inheritance.[88] In the *Wealth of Nations,* Adam Smith took note of the progressive implications of this transformation for British Americans in contending that "in all the English colonies the tenure of the lands, which all held by free socage, facilitates alienation." Socage tenure provided Massachusetts, throughout the colonial period, with a notion of exclusive, private, hereditary property in land. Socage tenure allowed the owner full rights to exploit both surface and subsurface resources in any manner he saw fit. Rapid alienation meant "selling, buying, and settling land as fast as men and women were willing to take up new territories." The manner in which the colonists owned (and exploited) landed resources helped fix how the economy grew. Attempting to foster the process of development in 1634, the Massachusetts General Court made "improvement" the price of possession. "Any man," the Court decreed, "that hath any greate quan[tity] of land graunted him, and doth not builde upon it or imp[rove] it within three years," would forfeit ownership. Under the Massachusetts system of land proprietorships within the township, land could be acquired and sold quicker and more easily than in any other colony. The Bay Colony's land system, as Governor Sir Edmund Andros discovered to his dismay during the Dominion period, was "particularly naked of standard and legitimate English encumbrances."[89]

In addition to abolishing feudal land tenure, the *Body of Liberties* liberalized existing English inheritance practices. It provided a double portion for eldest sons of intestates and equal portions to all others. Although Massachusetts, like Virginia, failed to abolish primogeniture for lands held in fee tail instead of fee simple, in neither colony did primogeniture and entail prove to be common means of holding and devising lands.[90] The Bay Colony's inheritance practices were ratified by the new constitutional regime after 1691 and, along with those of the colony of Connecticut, served as models for the men who drew up the Northwest Ordinance legislation during the 1780s.[91]

By providing for a system that validated private property, as well as ensuring that it be recorded, transacted, and devised in a relatively efficient court system, the Bay Colony founders provided the institutional infrastructure for the market-oriented instincts of the colonists. The creation of a quarterly court system by the 1640s allowed real estate transactions to be entered into the public record for the purpose of protecting a mobile and land-hungry populace from fraudulent conveyances. Massachusetts Bay, unlike Virginia, Plymouth, and Providence Island, was established firmly on a system of private property from its very beginning.[92] But a commitment to private property did not connote a privatistic society.

Because of covenant theology, the public sphere in Massachusetts was an extensive one at both the local and provincial levels. The Protestant ethic's injunction that the colonists "improve their labor" through time-consciousness and enterprising zeal was reflected in General Court statutes and town bylaws alike.[93] The General Court organized the Great Migration, supervised the establishment of towns, offered—along with individual communities—incentives for the building of bridges, roads, mills, smithies, and wharves, as well as providing for the setting up of courts and public schools.[94] The Massachusetts government attempted to promote the development of textiles and ironwares; prohibited the export of certain raw materials, bullion, and money; levied tonnage duties; established ports of entry; and promoted a favorable balance of trade. The General Court's activist philosophy is also found in later seventeenth-century governmental actions such as minting and printing money and making loans.[95] Public authority also regulated the weight of bread loaves, ferry tolls, and the business hours of taverns, as well as imports and exports generally. It told people where they could sell their mares and ewe lambs and in what form leather products could be exported. It prescribed the weights of nails and set price ceilings for locally produced iron.[96] It imposed the culture of discipline on "idlers" and "night walkers" six days of the week and banned all productive activity on the seventh.[97]

In seventeenth-century New England, policy choices made at the provincial level with respect to property and resource allocation were implemented at the local level. The New England town was both the core institution in the Bay Colony's civil society and the main arena for economic and human development. It was an arena in which individual interest and the general good could be mediated. Its basis was found in covenant ideology, with its strong emphasis on the "publique good." It was within the external (or collective) covenant that the management for the public good of all material possessions largely fell in seventeenth-century New England.[98] Through the activities of the May and October meetings of the Massachusetts General Court, the fiction of the Chosen People was briefly given institutional expression in representative forms. But the real action was at the town level—New England's equivalents of Blackstone's "little republics." The importance of the civic sphere in the orthodox colonies of Massachusetts and Connecticut is best illustrated by the promotive activities and resource allocation of individual communities. Some of these bore fruit and others did not, but all revealed the colonists' confidence that the individual township could successfully synthesize the public and private good, communal concerns and individual rights.[99]

The federal nature of the Holy Commonwealth meant that promotive efforts, carried out at both the local and provincial levels, produced a synergistic "multiplier effect." While the General Court offered land grants, limited franchise monopolies, tax relief, or release from militia duty to entrepreneurs or artisans in favored industries such as shipbuilding, metalworking, or fishing, individual towns supplemented such offers with their own array of inducements of land grants, shop sites, mill sites, home lots, or labor allotments. Rare was the seventeenth-century town that did not offer land grants, building sites, or water rights to prospective smiths, millers, or tanners. Individual town meetings were charged with responsibility for allocating resources and setting tax assessments in accordance with the freemen's will. The General Court established the larger legal and institutional infrastructure, but individual towns took the actual initiatives needed to stimulate the construction of sawmills, gristmills, smithies, tanneries, or shipyards. Likewise, the General Court mandated that towns with sufficient numbers of families establish free schools, but the towns themselves voted to allocate the resources necessary for building the school, hiring and paying the schoolmaster, and purchasing firewood to heat the schoolhouse. Massachusetts was not the only settlement to call itself a "commonwealth," but in the Bay Colony town-based covenantalism gave institutional substance to such declarations.[100]

Indeed, nowhere in British America was the public promotion of mixed enterprise pursued so aggressively.[101] Individual towns and the General Court conferred land grants and special privileges and immunities on artisans, entrepreneurs, and larger combines like the Hammersmith Ironworks to promote economic development. Massachusetts policymakers plumbed the arts of promotive legislation, fiscal management, debt creation, and taxation to fulfill what they saw as their overriding task—the creation and maintenance of the commonwealth.

To the time-honored public tasks of regulation and protection, the Puritan theorists added promotion. During the decade of the 1640s, the General Court took vigorous and sustained public action to make Massachusetts into something that no imperial planner could countenance: a clone of England. In 1650, the town of Pequot (New London), Connecticut, offered John Winthrop, Jr., a wide array of inducements in its ultimately successful attempt to persuade the influential merchant-entrepreneur to settle there. These included: a stone quarry, the town ferry, mill sites, water rights, timber rights, and tax exemptions for all Winthrop's landholdings. Winthrop received special land grants on which to locate his saltpeter and glass-manufacturing operations, and he built the town's first gristmill and sawmill.[102] The Springfield town meeting in 1659, having satisfied itself on the quality of John Stewart's smithy work, voted that "The

Smith's shop [shall be] given to John Stewart as his own forever."[103] During the 1660s, in its attempts to persuade the merchant-entrepreneur John Pynchon to erect a sawmill on the town stream, the Springfield town meeting voted to award Pynchon 150 acres, the "free use of the said Stream," and "free Liberty for felling and Sawing what trees he shal please that are upon the Comons. . . ."[104] In 1684, the town's inhabitants voted to give the tanner Thomas Sweatman a generous land grant "because they would accommodate themselves with such a tradesman as he is (viz., a dresser of leather)."[105]

The complexity and diversity of the Bay Colony's town-based economy rested, somewhat paradoxically, on the doctrine of "inseparable interests" that lay at the heart of the Puritan commonwealth. It was this doctrine that validated the efforts of both town and provincial governments to create an institutional environment favorable to enterprise by creating a large and vigorous public sphere. Indeed, J. A. W. Gunn maintains that the "very expression 'public interest' was familiar by the middle of the seventeenth century, gradually replacing the 'common good' of scholastic philosophy and the '*salus populi*' favoured by Roman law."[106] Massachusetts' description of itself in 1645 as a *perfecta respublica* showed an awareness of such developments. The Bay Colony's configuration of intermediate public institutions was varied and robust: town meetings, county courts, boards of selectmen, ad hoc committees, and provincial governments. Moreover, legal devices such as joint stock companies, joint partnerships, land proprietorships, share-system land corporations, tender laws, negotiable instruments, and special franchise monopolies rested on the existence of such a public zone—and the governmental expenditures required to create and uphold its legal existence.

The public sphere in Puritan Massachusetts, present at the town, county, and provincial levels, shaped the colony's distinctive pattern of economic development. New England's federal system of government made possible the use of nonmilitary land tenure such as free and common socage, the amortization of instruments of credit, and the development of (reasonably egalitarian) laws for the alienation and descent of land. The Hammersmith Ironworks could not have been established without such innovative quasi-corporate forms as share capital, continuity, delegation, and transferability, all of which required an appropriate legal framework established by the state and enforced by county courts. Hammersmith in particular represented a business form that in everything but name was a corporation. It offered partial investment, part-time interest, and limited liability (rather than the liability *in solido* found in a simple partnership). These legal devices, along with the punctilious arrangement of deeds, contracts, sales, and leases, provided investors the predictability and rationality essential for the functioning of a capitalist economy. Without such devices, and in the absence of a staple crop like tobacco, New England almost certainly would have remained an economic backwater.[107]

* * *

New England's civic ecology was also distinguished by the absence of several Old World institutions, notably merchant and craft guilds. Here again, the Bay Colonists were distilling and crystallizing recent trends in England itself. The progressive disintegration of the guilds had led the Tudor-Stuart realm to assume the responsibility for maintaining an equitable correlation between the earnings and expenses of workers. Moreover, as part of the process of state building under Queen Elizabeth, England had created in the 1563 Statute of Artificers, an elaborate code which turned local law into national law. The statute extended the scope of ancient principles of wage assessment, apprenticeship, and poor relief from the locality to the nation. The result was to sharply reduce the power of municipalities, boroughs, and especially merchant and craft guilds by transferring their responsibilities to state authority. The municipal government of Coventry, for example, had heretofore restricted entry into various crafts by mandates that "no person of the Craft [shall] teache [any] poyntes of the Craft to [any] person save to his prentice and his wife," on pain of a 100s. fine, to be divided between the mayor and the craft.[108]

The curbing of merchant and craft guilds was for Adam Smith one of the key benchmarks that separated the feudal-mercantilist from the liberal-capitalist society. Smith described guilds ("oppressive monopolies") as among the principal "Inequalities occasioned by the Policy of Europe."[109] These town- and borough-based corporations, whose rules were nationalized by the statute of 1563, required a strict seven-year apprenticeship. Indeed, under the provisions of the Statute of Artificers, no worker could perform *any* craft without a seven-year apprenticeship indenture that defined the mutual obligations of master and servant. By thus restricting craft entry, declared Smith, the corporations were "obstructing the free circulation of labour and stock, both from employment to employment and from place to place." For Smith, it was the worker himself who suffered most from these restrictions on free competition. Espousing the Locke-Petty labor theory of property, he declared that

> The property which every man has in his own labour, as it is the original foundation of all other property, so it is the most sacred and inviolable. The patrimony of a poor man lies in the strength and dexterity of his hands; and to hinder him from employing this strength and dexterity in what manner he thinks proper without injury to his neighbor is a plain violation of this most sacred property. It is a manifest encroachment upon the just liberty both of the workman and of those who might be disposed to employ him.[110]

Smith believed that the real purpose of the customary seven-year term of apprenticeship was to restrict competition, not ensure quality workmanship. "Long apprenticeships," he concluded, "are altogether unnecessary." Directly echoing Captain John Smith, he declared that even such recondite trades as clockmaking and watchmaking "contain no such mystery as to require a long course of instruction." Virtually all crafts, Smith declared, "cannot well require more than the lessons of a few weeks; perhaps those of a few days might be sufficient. In the common mechanic trades, those of a few days might certainly be sufficient." Although Smith doubtless was exaggerating for rhetorical effect—one cannot become a tailor, goldsmith, or glover from the "lessons of a few weeks"—his views suggest why guilds failed to take root in the New World. Even the mercantilist writers Smith was so fond of castigating had drawn similar conclusions a century earlier. Sir Josiah Child identified as among "our old mistaken principles" the notions that "none shall use any manual occupation except he has been apprentice to the same," or that "to suffer artificers to have as many apprentices as they [wish] is to destroy trade."[111]

The Massachusetts General Court took less than four years' experience with guildlike corporations to determine they were superfluous. Merchant and craft guilds, especially in a labor-short New World setting, violated both developmental logic and the rights of individual craftsmen. The impetus to establish the guild corporations in the first place came from coopers and shoemakers in Boston and Charlestown, allegedly for the purposes of ensuring product quality control. On 18 October 1648, upon petition of Boston and Charlestown coopers, and "upon consideration of many complaints made of the grate damage the country hath sustained by occasion of defective and insufficient casks," the General Court awarded a charter to the coopers, modeled on British guilds.[112] The corporation was to have a full complement of officers: master, wardens, gaugers, sealers, packers, and searchers. Its main purpose was to improve quality control by the use of inspection laws for the economically vital fish, pork, and brewing industries.

Apparently not fully trusting the coopers to keep their own regulatory house in order, the Court appended an extraordinarily detailed set of guidelines—ones that anticipated the eventual state and federal roles in providing consumer protection rather than relying on guilds for this function. The magistrates asserted that "we goe by London Rule, for [London coopers] never cut out the sape out of beere and water Cask: but for wine and oyle they doe because wine and oyle ly long in a cask and they [leach] more the caske than bere and water doe: and when we say 5-sape staves, we mene not falty staves but they must be sound and good timber and the sap sound." Following the custom of "England at yermouth," the magistrates ruled that no "fisherman was to pack his fish for the marchant: they pakt them at sea to save them, but when they com to be packt for the marchant or for a market: then were coopers sworne for that service: and non were acounted marchentable but such as [the coopers] pack."[113]

By 1652, however, the economic policymakers at the General Court had concluded that the state should take over the entire responsibility for regulating the quality of export goods. The petitions by the cooper and shoemaker corporations for charter renewal were not approved. In part, the Court was responding to free trade petitions from country-based artisans, bridling under the hegemony of Boston and Charlestown craftsmen. As with the outlying towns' animosity toward Boston import merchants like Robert Keayne, the issue for country-based craftsmen was not one of principle but one of access. The Boston corporation's monopoly over shoes sold in that town's market led the country artisans to petition the General Court in 1648 not to allow their "Brethren in Boston" to "have power put into their hands to hinder a free trade." Embracing a quasi-Smithian system of natural liberty logic, the petitioners declared that "Keeping out Country shoomakers from Coming into the Market . . . will be a great dammage unto the Country" because it would "weaken the hands of the Country shoomakers from using their trade," or force them to move to Boston.[114]

The Boston coopers sought guild privileges again in 1668, but their petition was rejected.[115] Viewers and gaugers, appointed by the General Court, were stationed at Boston, Charlestown, Salem, and Ipswich to ensure that casks of "beefe, porke, mackerell, [and] fish" were packed "full gage," of "true and full assize and gage," on pain of a ten-shilling per cask fine for violators. Pipestaves, fish, meat, and ships, New England's principal exports, were all subsequently regulated by the use of government-licensed officials rather than by merchant and craft guilds. In like manner, colonial governments assumed regulatory responsibilities over trades throughout British North America.[116]

And it did not take long before urban artisans became outraged at this loss of their Old World authority. The 1668 petition by the Boston coopers seeking a second Act of Incorporation reflected precisely the kind of exclusivist, protectionist sentiments that so exercised Adam Smith. The coopers' main complaint was that parents were paying enterprising (or, if you will, avaricious) renegade craftsmen to teach their children the "mystery" of cooperage as quickly as possible. This reliance on the free market, the petitioning coopers declared, had produced "frequent and gross abuses caused by the great indulgent affection of many Parents too Eagerly Desiring the Advancement of theire Children to such a calling and to be masters . . . before they attaine to sufficient yeares and discretion to receive and obtaine the full mistery thereof." The older assumpsit-based argument that all crafts needed to be regulated for the public good was also invoked. The masters averred that these callow youths were more "fitt to bee taught than to teach others or well governe themselves." Most important, they lacked the "ability to manage the same to [the] Publique good."[117]

Following exactly the procedure Adam Smith later endorsed, the aspiring craftsmen chose

> to give a peece of money to such [coopers] who are necessitous and Covetous, who for theire private advantage are willing to engage, to teach such theire full Art in a yeare or two, which they are not able to perform under seven yeares time, unless they meete with choyce witts, which is rare, breaking all the Laudable Customs and Experiences of our nation that have judged seaven yeares time little enough to learn well such a mistery, and soe such raw-workemen are swarming and increasing . . . and those that have served theire Apprenticeships for it are endangered to be greatly injured if not ruined.[118]

Despite the "Laudable Customs and Experiences" of the seven-year apprenticeship, having young craftsmen swarming and increasing was just the point. It was, self-evidently, the most efficient way to service an export-led economy. So the General Court, characteristically choosing pragmatism over custom, rejected the coopers' petition to reincorporate.

Guilds, like encumbered real property or patrimonial economic intervention, did not transfer to the New World, with major consequences for the development of communal capitalism. Their failure to take root in early America illustrates the larger process of institutional simplification by which many economically outmoded institutions of the old corporatist world failed to transfer. The colonists did not so much intentionally jettison this paternalist detritus as discover from experience that these institutions had no *raison d'être* in the New World. Surviving apprenticeship indentures tell the story. In a typical indenture made in 1679 between the hornbreaker Robert Cooke and young Luke Perkins, the craftsman promised to teach Perkins the trade of comb making in just four months for the fee of £20. In a proviso that was a remnant of the guildlike preservation of the "mystery" of a craft from outsiders, Perkins was enjoined not to teach the trade to anyone except his own children, on pain of a £40 forfeiture.[119]

Parallel developments during the French Revolution highlight the importance of the failure of merchant and craft guilds to take hold in Massachusetts (and in British America generally). One of the principal reasons that the French Revolution is still often described as the real "birth of free enterprise" is the benchmark brought by the dissolution of the guilds by the Constituent Assembly in 1791. The decisive decrees on trade introduced that year by deputies Pierre d'Allarde, Isaac Le Chapelier, and Pierre Goudard were designed to abolish guilds, state corporations, and centralized management of the economy. The famous Article 7 of the d'Allarde decree banning guilds mandated that "Any person will be free to choose the trade, profession, art or occupation he wants."[120] In England itself, it was not until 1814 that the provisions relating to apprenticeship in the Statute of Artificers were formally repealed in the name of "the true principles of trade." By 1652, the leaders of Massachusetts Bay had reached the same conclusion: guildlike corporations and personal liberty were incompatible.[121]

One consequence of the failure of guilds to take root in New England was a significant augmentation of state power to regulate product quality. Without either a professional bureaucracy or a strong tax base, such regulatory efforts were accomplished through inspection laws and licensed professional viewers. These efforts were, of course, powerfully reinforced culturally within the population by the Calvinist conviction that all work was done to glorify God and must be done in His image. Poor workmanshop was a routine preoccupation of clerical jeremiads. Whenever it seemed to the ministers that the "Spirit of Over-Trading and Over-doing" threatened the quality of Massachusetts products, denunciations were sure to follow. In one such jeremiad by Cotton Mather, virtually every important New England commodity was taken account of—and found wanting:

> The fish is naught; the Tar has undue mixtures; there is Dirt and Stone instead of Turpentine; there are thick Layers of Salt instead of other things that should be there; the Cheese is not made as tis affirmed to be; the Liquor is not for Quantity or Quality such as was agreed for; the Wood is not of the Dimensions that are promised unto the Purchaser; or perhaps there was a Trespass in the place of cutting it; the Hay does not hold out weight by abundance; the Lumber has a false Number upon it; or, the Bundles are not as Good Within as they are Without.

Public authority could not hope to ensure quality workmanship in colonial Massachusetts without the rhetoric of obligation supplied weekly by clergymen and daily by mothers and fathers.[122]

The fishing, pipestave, and packing industries were the earliest and most closely regulated enterprises, not least because of their central importance in the West Indies trade. In 1642, the year that the Bay Colony's commerce with the West Indies and Atlantic Wine Islands began in earnest, the General Court ordered that all "vessels of caske used for any liquor, fish, or other commodities to be put to sale shalbe of London assize." The magistrates relied on information provided by merchants about the reputation of the Bay Colony's products in foreign markets. When in 1646 the Court heard reports "from diverse forrain parts of the insufficiency of our pipe staves [from excessive wormholes], whereby the commodity is like[ly] to be prohibited in those parts, to the great damage of the country," the magistrates took immediate action. They ordered selectmen in Boston and Charlestown to appoint viewers "skilfull in that commodity" to "search all such pipestaves as are to be transported to any parts of Spain or Portingall." In 1652, because "much damage hath formerly arisen to market tradeing, by bad makeing of fish, and the credite of [the colony's] trade [in overseas markets] hath much suffered, tending to the prejudice of our commerce with other nations," the Court ordered that fish viewers judge as unmerchantable all "sunne burnt, salt burnt, and dry fish that hath been first pickled."[123]

Massachusetts public policy reflected the Christian doctrine of stewardship in its attempts to conserve as well as develop existing resources. The Massachusetts General Court took action after midcentury to preserve the region's economically essential stocks of fish. Acting under commonwealth doctrine to restrict the rights of one group for the good of the whole—and of future generations—the Court took steps against those who overfished, fished during spawning season, or polluted the fishing grounds. In 1668, the magistrates ordered that "no man shall henceforth kill any codfish, hake, haddock, or pollucke, to be dried for sale, in the month of December or January, because of their spawning time, nor [are] any mackerell to be barrell[ed] up in the months of May or June." Fines were also to be assessed on "any fishermen [who] cast[s] the garbage of the fish they catch overboard at or neere the ledges or grounds where they take the fish."[124] It was through such decrees that the New World state took over from the Old World guild the responsibility to ensure product quality, protect consumers, and preserve natural resources. Whether or not the elimination of the guilds in fact signaled what Karl Marx called the triumph of "movable" over "natural" capital, an important shift in regulatory authority had taken place.

Labor, as well as capital, became more mobile in the New World as a result of government action and changing law.[125] Here, as with merchant and craft guilds, the colonists innovated by simply not receiving the considerably more rigid institutions and doctrines of the mother country. In the area of colonial labor practices, in particular, there were fewer direct carryovers from English law than in most other fields of law.[126] The contrast between the Law of Master and Servant as embodied in the 1563 Statute of Artificers and colonial practices as they evolved during the early years of Massachusetts Bay helps make this point.

Free labor in the modern sense was a rather late development in the West's economic history. Such basic rights as the freedom to choose one's employment, to quit without being imprisoned for breach of contract, and not be beaten by an employer were routinely denied to laboring men and women during the early modern era. Although in seventeenth-century England—unlike Poland and the German principalities—no laborers were actually tied to the land, it was not until 1875 that the relationship between master and servant became fully contractual.[127]

The legal basis for the abridgment of these rights in England extended as far back as the Statute of Labourers of 1351, which was passed primarily to limit demands for wages. It was reinforced by the statute of 1388, but proved very difficult to enforce. From the time of the Black Death (1347–48) until the Statute of Apprentices of 1563, the English propertied classes, through their representatives in Parliament, adopted various strategems to deal with the scarcity and high cost of labor. This meant, in effect, using state apparatus to coerce laboring men and women to do the bidding of the landed classes. The 1563 Statute of Apprentices provided for maximum wage rates, compulsory service for those without visible means of support, and prohibitions against departure from service before the end of an agreed term (typically six months or a year) with criminal, not civil, punishments mandated for violations. Those identified by the statute as compellable to serve in husbandry (as well as some thirty nonagricultural occupations) included all unmarried laborers as well as married laborers under the age of thirty without a specific minimum of land and physical capital. The "conservation of work" philosophy underpinning such policies extended to most trades. Employers were typically required to hire labor by the year, not by the day. To allow market-driven hiring by the day, according to one Essex justice, would lead to "the great depauperization of other labourers." The mobility of English laborers was also curtailed by the settlement provisions of the 1601 Poor Law and the Settlement Law of 1662. Under the provisions of these laws, any recent migrants into a parish who appeared likely to end up on public relief could be sent back to their last parish of settlement by the overseer of the poor rate.[128]

In England those among the laboring poor who refused to work could be arrested as a vagrant and whipped as a criminal, but in Massachusetts Bay all attempts to replicate the full apparatus of the mother country's Master-Servant legislation were evident failures by 1660. The reasons for these failures had less to do with the rise of a free trade–free labor ideology in British America than with the simple fact of countervailing opportunities. Workers who were "restrained" from taking higher wages, as John Winthrop lamented, would either refuse to work altogether, or—more likely—move to Rhode Island, New Hampshire, or Maine. Recreating the ordered and hierarchical world of guilds and labor settlement laws proved impossible in the fluid and opportunity-rich colonial setting. While indentured servitude and slavery both existed (albeit in marginal form) in early Massachusetts, non-bonded laborers achieved at least a formal freedom that would not become available to their British counterparts for two centuries.

Also absent from the civic ecology of Massachusetts were large-scale government-granted trade and manufacturing patents, dubbed "monopolies" by their critics.[129] These were discarded in favor of what was known as the short-term limited franchise monopoly. Monopolies, detested by Adam Smith as the very embodiment of the mercantilist-patrimonial society, were chartered corporations licensed by the Crown. Monopoly patents had two main purposes: to promote and protect the invention of new processes; and to serve as instruments of economic nationalism, in England's case largely for the purpose of penetrating the Low Country–dominated textile trade. Government-licensed monopolies and chartered trading companies of both the regulated and joint-stock variety had been the linchpins of Tudor-Stuart economic control. They originated as a form of public works to meet some pressing social need, usually the delivery of goods or services. In Tudor-Stuart England, there were four general types of monopolies. These included: (1) an exemption to a particular individual or firm from an existing mercantile law (typically this would be a patent to import or export some restricted commodity); (2) large-scale trade monopolies given to particular companies (the Levant Company, or the Merchant Adventurers, for examples); (3) grants of the rights to monopolize the selling of products that otherwise would be exposed to free competition; and (4) monopolies to exploit such things as minerals or the resources of a particular New World colony.[130]

Granting exclusive public control of a product, trade, or service, patents became a source of rising protest in Tudor-Stuart England, largely because an instrument designed for start-up purposes had too often become an entrenched form of special privilege.[131] By the beginning of the seventeenth century, many English merchants and jurists believed that private enterprise could accomplish these goals more efficiently—and more equitably. Far from being a public benefit, monopolies were increasingly regarded as a corrupt form of special privilege. The so-called "scandalous age of patents" extended in England from the 1590s to the 1630s, with the peak of controversy occurring between 1601 and 1624. During Elizabeth I's reign, as the monopolies multiplied, the basis of the award appeared to many critics to be less the novelty and public utility of the product than the private connections of the patentee. Monopolies in trade were believed to be increasingly falling into the hands of courtiers and parasites, not genuine entrepreneurs.[132]

The patents issued to England's burgeoning numbers of projectors, granting exclusive rights of manufacture of a product "according to the particular methods of which they were the true pioneers and inventors," were especially controversial. The large state-chartered trading companies such as the Merchant Adventurers, Russia Company, Eastland Company, Levant Company, and East India Company came under increasingly strident attack.[133] The monopolies ostensibly were granted out of the government's desire to reward "diligent travail" and to provide "encouragement to others."

Their defenders retorted that "A well-governed trafficke practised in a Kingdome, by judicious and expert Merchants, to foraine and remote countries will easily bee granted, and confessed to bee both honourable, and of singular reputation, both to the Soveraigne in his particular, and to the nation in generall."[134] But more and more such self-serving rhetoric fell on deaf ears, as patents became popularly regarded as a form of unjust special privilege.[135]

By 1601, public protest reached such a crescendo that many of the lesser monopolies were canceled outright. In that year, the common law courts handed down the "Case of Monopolies," declaring the Crown's use of monopolies illegal at common law.[136] But, with a depleted royal treasury, James I found the granting of monopolies an especially inviting way of increasing his income. Charles I, with a still greater appetite for augmenting non-Parliamentary revenues, followed suit. By the eve of the Puritan migration, "all items except the staples of life such as meat and bread were organized and licensed as monopolies, which ran the alphabetical gamut from belts, butter, and buttons to tar, timber, and tobacco, and from beer sold in monopoly barrels and distributed in licensed alehouses to soap manufactured in government factories." The typical Englishman lived "in a house built with monopoly bricks . . . heated by monopoly coal. . . . His clothes were held up by monopoly belts, monopoly buttons, monopoly pins. . . . He ate monopoly butter, monopoly currants, monopoly red herrings, monopoly salmon, [and] monopoly lobsters." During the early years of the reign of Charles I, the licensing of monopolies producd nearly £100,000 in royal revenues annually.[137]

The royal prodigality in granting monopolies was especially unpopular among two groups heavily represented in the Puritan migration: artisans and merchants. For both groups, monopoly symbolized the royal absolutism and prerogative to which dissenters grew increasingly hostile during the reign of Charles I. During the 1630s and early 1640s, London artisans bitterly complained over what seemed an arbitrary and capricious monopoly-granting policy. In a petition from 1640, one group asserted that "No Freemen of London, after he hath served his yeares, and set up his Trade, can be sure long to [enjoy] the Liberty of his Trade, but whether he is forbidden to use it, or is forced at length with the rest of his trade to purchase it as a Monopolie, at a deare rate, which they and all the Kingdome pay for." John Pym (1584–1643), in his opening speech to the Short Parliament in April 1640, decried the effects of monopolies as well as un-Parliamentary taxation. Both made subjects uncertain whether they would reap the fruit of their labor and enterprise, which for Pym was the "Condition of slaves." East Anglian Puritan merchants took especial umbrage at the monopoly grant to the Merchant Adventurers for the Flemish cloth trade. It was precisely this kind of royal monopoly that rankled Puritan merchants and artisans forced either to remain out of the lucrative trading companies or make substantial payments for the privilege of joining. (There was, it should also be noted, a specifically Protestant dimension to hostility toward monopolies, dating back to the very beginning of the Reformation. At the Diet of Worms, Luther's demands for ecclesiastical reform were accompanied by pleas for imperial legislation to curtail monopolies and business cartels such as those employed by the Fugger trading and banking house.)[138]

The debate in England between the monopolists and the free traders came to a head in the 1620s. Opponents of monopoly rights found support for their position in the provision in Magna Charta that merchants should have the right to "move about as well by land as by water, for buying and selling by ancient and right customs, quit from all evil tolls." In 1621 a bill against monopoly, largely the creation of Sir Edward Coke, was unsuccessfully presented to the House of Commons. Coke's views on monopolies were made clear in the *Institutes.* They were against the liberty and freedom of the subject and therefore against the common law of the realm.[139] Coke's bill was eventually passed by Parliament in 1624 as the Statute of Monopolies. The most effective and influential patent law of the seventeenth century, the Statute of Monopolies signaled a shift toward the modern law of patent. In truly sweeping fashion, the statute voided "all monopolies and all commissions, grants, licenses, charters and letters patent heretofore made or granted to any person or persons, bodies politick or corporate whatsoever, of or for the sole buying, selling, making, working, or using of anything. . . ."[140]

Fully steeped in the Cokean objections to the older forms of monopoly, the Bay Colony leaders initially forbade the licensing of any monopoly in Massachusetts, except for short-term grants for labor-saving inventions. Barriers to economic development in the Old World, monopolies—in dramatically scaled-down form—were designed to achieve the opposite purpose in the New. In 1641 the General Court declared that "no monopolies shall be allowed or granted among us, but of such new Inventions that are profitable to the Countrie, and that for a short time." Writing in his journal three years later, Governor Winthrop confirmed that the General Court was "very unwilling to grant any monopoly."[141] So determined was Springfield magnate William Pynchon in 1638 not to accept Connecticut's imposition of a fur monopoly on him—a trade he already effectively controlled—that he engineered his town's secession from the Hartford government over the issue. He declared that it was against "the public goode and the liberty of free men to make a monopoly of trade."[142] As a result of Connecticut's determination to issue monopolies for the fur trade and for the corn trade, on 14 February 1639 the inhabitants of Springfield declared that "by Gode's providence [they had] fallen into the line of the Massachusetts Jurisdiction."[143]

With the onset of the severe 1640 depression, however, the Massachusetts General Court decided to use a modified form of monopoly grant in order to help socialize the start-up costs of economic development. Technically known as a short-term limited franchise monopoly, this charter—like subventions, bounties, and tax abatements—was regarded as a temporary expedient, appropriate to the early stages of a community's growth but not thereafter. By the first half of the seventeenth century, mercantilist writers were beginning to conceptualize economic expansion in a primitive "stages of development" fashion. According to a pamphlet published in London in 1645 entitled *A Discourse . . . For the Enlargement and Freedome of Trade,* "Those immunities which were granted in the infancy of trade, to incite people to the increase and improvement of it, are not so proper for these times, when the trade is come to that height of perfection, and that the mystery of it is so well known. . . ."[144]

Long-term, state-subsidized corporations on the Continental model, however, found no place in the Bay Colony. There were to be no French-style Tax Farmers in Puritan New England. Necessity alone justified the violation of the Puritans' anti-monopolist principles. As John Winthrop conceded when explaining why the General Court had issued a twenty-one-year fur-trading monopoly to a group of Boston merchants seeking "to discover the great lake," without such a monopoly, "they would not proceed. . . ."[145] Only when there was a clear developmental goal would the General Court grant a monopoly of local markets, and then usually for terms limited to three, fourteen, or twenty-one years. The Court also transformed monopoly rights into something similar to the modern law of patent, providing protection for what today would be described as intellectual property. Labor-saving inventions or schemes to extract scarce commodities such as salt or graphite were the typical targets of such General Court licensing. In the spring of 1641, merchant Samuel Winslow believed that he had discovered an improved method for processing salt and he asked the General Court for monopoly rights for his invention. The magistrates were informed that Winslow "hath made a proposition to this Court to furnish the country with salt at more easy rates than otherwise can bee had, and to make it by a meanes and way which hitherto hath not been discovered." Anxious to encourage Winslow but also alert to the need not to cut off alternative supplies of a product so essential to the fishing industry, the Court granted him a ten-year exclusive patent on the method. But the magistrates did not ban imported salt or alternative methods of saltmaking. Strict performance provisions were also attached. The Court ordered that only if Winslow "shall, within the space of one yeare, set upon the said worke," shall he "enjoy the same, to him and his associats, for the space of 10 yeares, so as it shall not bee lawfull [for] any other person to make salt after the same way during the said yeares."[146]

In that same 1641 session, as we shall see in the next chapter, the Massachusetts General Court offered monopoly rights for the promotion of the eagerly anticipated New England ironworks. For "incuragment of such [inhabitants] as will adventure for the discovery of [iron ore] mines," the Court promised to those who discovered and developed such mines, the rights to the minerals for twenty-one years, as well as the right to purchase the land from the Indians.[147] Three years later, eager to tap the fur-rich interior regions of the Northeast, the General Court granted the twenty-one-year trade monopoly to the consortium of Boston merchants seeking to locate the reputed "great lakes."[148]

Inevitably, the General Court attached strict conditions, accompanied by a timetable, to the grant of monopoly rights. In 1645, in granting a twenty-one-year monopoly of local markets to the ironworks Undertakers, the General Court mandated that the investors build a technologically advanced indirect-process ironworks rather than the traditional one-hearth bloomery forge. The Court specified that the Undertakers, within ten years, should establish "an iron furnace [and] forge in each of the [proposed] places [Braintree and Lynn], and not a blomery [furnace] onely."[149]

Inventors of labor-saving devices received special priority among monopoly privileges granted during the 1640s. Playing the role of a modern patent office, the General Court took pains to provide protection for the intellectual property of the inventors, usually for terms of seven or fourteen years. Joseph Jencks, the most enterprising of the Bay Colony's mechanicians, received a patent in 1646 for an improved watermill "engine." The General Court, considering the "necessity of raising such manufactures of engines of mils to go by water, for speedy dispatch of much worke with few hands, and being sufficiently informed of the ability of the petitioner to performe such workes, grant[ed] his petition (that no other person shall set up or use any such invention or trade for fourteene yeares, without the licence of him, the said Joseph Jenckes)." While offering short-term monopoly rights to the inventor, the Court also retained control over the disposition and price of the final product. It asserted its right to "restraine the exportation of such manufactures, and the prices of them, to moderation, if occasion so require."[150] A decade later, Jencks received a seven-year monopoly for a mowing machine. Jencks and his assignees received liberty to "make that engine the said Jenkes hath proposed to this Court for the more speedy cutting of grass, for seven years." Anyone wishing to use the device was required to obtain a license from the inventor.[151] In 1656 the Court mandated that consumers pay the subsidy directly to the inventor. John Clarke was to receive 10 shillings from "every family that should make use of his invention for saveinge of fire-wood and warminge of howses." Clarke's patent was originally issued for three years, but the Court subsequently extended the term to the duration of the inventor's life.[152]

By 1650, New England's town-based institutional culture had been substantially transformed from that of 1640. As a result of federal covenant theology, a civic society had been created. Towns had been established, land tenure had been defeudalized, the rule of law instituted, labor formally freed, and guilds and monopolies curbed. This had been done partly as a response to the conditions of a shortage of both capital and labor, and during a period in which the mother country was distracted by the cataclysms of civil war and regicide. It was during the settlement period itself that Massachusetts—although dominated by Puritan gentlemen such as John Winthrop, Sr., Thomas Dudley, and John Endecott—established the civic ecology and tradition of mixed enterprise necessary for communal capitalism. It was also during this period that Massachusetts built what was for a time the New World's most sophisticated ironworks factory.

6

The Puritan Ironworks

In the opening chapter of the *Wealth of Nations,* Adam Smith illustrated the principle of division of labor by the fabrication of a shepherd's shears. The array of skills needed to manufacture this humble device was more than a little daunting. It included: "The miner, the builder of the furnace for smelting the ore, the seller of the timber, the burner of the charcoal to be made use of in the smelting-house, the brick-maker, the brick-layer, the workmen who attend the furnace, the mill-wright, the forger, the smith, [who] must all of them join their different arts in order to produce [the shears]." Smith's use of ironmaking to illustrate his revolutionary principle of economic life was quite sensible. Ironworking, then as now, symbolized the new industrial order—Smith's "progressive" society—and helped set it off from the older pre-industrial "stationary" society. What is noteworthy, for our purposes, is that such an advanced example of industrial workers "join[-ing] their different arts in order to produce" finished iron-wares could be found in the howling wilderness of early

Massachusetts Bay. The same complex array of workers—miners, smelters, forgers, colliers, carpenters, millwrights, masons, sawyers, and smiths—was represented among the men assembled at ironworks established in the towns of Braintree and Lynn during the 1640s. Moreover, the Massachusetts ironworks employed the newly invented continuous-smelting process, by which iron ore and fuel were added to the furnace for the duration of the "blow," producing a constant stream of pig iron. When Edward Johnson visited the town of Lynn during his midcentury canvass of Bay Colony settlements, he found "an Iron Mill in constant use."[1]

The Hammersmith (Saugus) and Braintree ironworks founded during the 1640s spawned additional units. Many of the more localized New England ironworks continued in production throughout much of the colonial period, manufacturing in some cases in excess of 30 tons each of wrought iron annually. By 1700, eight ironworks had been built to help supply New England's iron needs: North Saugus, Concord, Rowley, Westvale, Groton, Braintree, Taunton, and Pawtucket Falls.[2] A number of these units would continue in operation until the nineteenth century, one until 1876. Producing much-needed ironwares for New England's commercializing society—anchors, weights, edge tools, harpoons, ox shoes, nails, pots, pans, firebacks—these locally owned ironworks played a significant role in the region's economic expansion, not least because they fostered what developmental economists refer to as "backward" and "forward" manufacturing linkages.[3]

The original Hammersmith factory, however ambitiously conceived, passed into receivership during the mid-1650s, less than a decade after it began operation in 1648. New England's chronic developmental barriers—scarce capital and high labor costs—proved insuperable for an enterprise organized on such a scale and, until 1654, largely under absentee ownership. Throughout the seventeenth century, it was cheaper in most cases to import English ironwares rather than purchase the locally manufactured product.[4] During the bulk of the first charter period, New England's productive sector rested on a firm triad of fish, livestock, and wood products. Textile goods as well as metalwares—overwhelmingly—

were imported from Britain, not manufactured locally. But this did not keep local entrepreneurs from trying.

The English background in ironmaking, as in all areas of colonial economic development, needs to be taken into account. The commercial transformation that had been reshaping England's economy since the dissolution of the monasteries in the 1530s included dramatic advances in metallurgy and mining, no less so than in textile production, shipbuilding, long-distance trade, legal reform, and political economy. Indeed, one might as easily locate the origins of the Industrial Revolution in the exploits of the coal-mining regions of the Tyne Valley during the sixteenth and seventeenth century as in innovations in the Lancashire textile industry during the 1780s. The increase in the volume of coal exports was, by any measure, quite remarkable. Coal exports from the Tyne Valley passing through the port of Newcastle, bound primarily for the London market, rose from 32,951 tons for the year 1563–64 to 452,625 tons for the year 1633–34.[5] Much of the coastal trade between Newcastle and London was dominated by this one commodity.

The same pattern obtained in the ironmaking industry. During the period between the introduction of the blast furnace in 1540 and the departure of the Puritan migration in 1630, iron production in England increased fourfold. Blast furnaces, the principal technological innovation, could produce from between five to ten times more iron than could the more primitive, one-step "bloomeries." The annual output of iron during the decade of the 1550s had been 5,000 tons. By the 1650s this figure had risen to nearly 24,000 tons, although England still found it necessary to import substantial quantities of the higher-grade Swedish bar iron. The two principal ironworking regions were the Andred Weald of Kent-Sussex in the southeast and the Forest of Dean across the River Severn along the Welsh border. By the beginning of the seventeenth century, the center of the English iron industry was shifting toward the Forest of Dean, West Midlands, and South Yorkshire, where ore of a higher grade than in the Wealden regions was found.[6]

By the 1570s, three quarters of England's seventy blast furnaces still were found in the Weald—the prime recruiting ground for Massachusetts ironworkers.[7] During the 1630s, some 150 blast furnaces each capable of producing between 100 to 500 tons of cast iron annually were operating in England, Scotland, and Wales. Nearly three hundred large finery and chafery forges existed for hammering the cast iron into bars fit for sale to smiths and merchants. Glassmaking also was concentrated in the Andred Weald, making it one of the leading industrial regions in Britain. The invention in 1612 of the coal-fired reverbatory furnace for glassmaking gave English glassmakers their first real comparative advantage over their Italian and French rivals. By 1620, England was the West's most rapidly industrializing nation, particularly in the areas of coal mining, iron manufacture, and shipbuilding. It was during these years that England became a genuine maritime giant. In 1560, the nation possessed some 50,000 tons of merchant shipping and was by no means a maritime power. In 1572, it could only claim fourteen ships of 200 tons or more; by 1629, however, total merchant tonnage had grown to 115,000 and included over 145 ships of 200 tons or more. The enormous 1500-ton *Sovereign of the Seas,* launched for the Royal Navy in 1637, announced that a new era of maritime development was at hand. The English fishing industry—including both the east coast herring fleets and the Newfoundland fisheries—rose from insignificance in the mid-sixteenth century to a position in 1618 where it employed nearly 250 ships and 2,000 men on a full- or part-time basis. That year it earned gross recipts of £135,000 sterling. The English fishery at Newfoundland alone, which had included thirty ships in 1574, reached between three hundred and five hundred craft by 1630.[8]

After relying for much of the sixteenth century on imported ironwares from Sweden as well as from its great geopolitical rival Spain, England achieved sufficiency and then surplus production by the beginning of the eighteenth century.[9] Like the Dutch, the English concentrated on producing utilitarian manufactures rather than—in the manner of the French or Italians—on splendor and beauty. Also like the Dutch, the English placed a very high premium on technological innovation. As its name suggests, the Walloon process blast furnace utilized at Hammersmith was invented in the Low Countries. With both labor and raw materials in shorter supply in England and the Low Countries than in Spain, France, or the German states, the English and Dutch found technological innovation a virtual necessity.

The Derbyshire lead industry is a case in point. By 1600, the lead-mining and -smelting industry was producing Britain's second most valuable export good (after textiles). Technological advances during the late sixteenth century, especially the development of the ore hearth smelting mill, raised the output of refined ore no less than tenfold between 1570 and 1600.[10] Although still predominantly a rural-based industry, lead refining was now concentrated in the hands of projectors drawn from the gentry and nobility, supplanting the old "brenners" or small-scale mine owners who could not meet the level of capital investment required by the new mills. Enclosure-related dispossession of cottagers provided the manpower to run these much more overtly capitalist enterprises. During the century after 1540, outputs in lead—along with coal, iron, glass, salt, and ships—increased dramatically.[11]

The fact that England, unlike the United Provinces, possessed rich supplies of lead ore, iron ore, and coal was critical. As the eventual fate of England's great commercial rival, the Dutch Republic, revealed, the absence of such raw materials kept the West's first commercial revolution from turning into its first industrial revolution. In Holland, the principal sources of energy were peat, windpower, and horsepower. Indeed, it is likely that the Industrial Revolution did not take place in the Dutch Republic precisely because of the absence of iron ore and coal.[12]

Iron products helped fuel what has been called the West's first "consumer revolution," a revolution that had its impact on the material culture of Massachusetts Bay from the very beginning. By the early seventeenth century, for the first time, wares that previously had been available only to the well-off were coming within the reach of middling- and lower-class men and women. The English increasingly became leaders in manufacturing cheap but serviceable ironwares: kettles, skillets, pots, nails, pins, trivets, andirons, wool combs and cards, axletrees, bits, stirrup irons, spurs, grates, locks, and keys. These ironwares for household and farm, along with newly available glasswares and textiles, helped raise the standard of living for the families of gentlemen, yeomen, and even craftsmen. By the early seventeenth century, the inventories of yeomen, craftsmen, and merchants reveal a proliferation of glass windows, chimneys, linen, spare beds, and household utensils.[13] These were all amenities that the migrants to Massachusetts Bay expected to continue to enjoy in their new homes. Such a goal, along with plans for a domestic shipbuilding industry, would require a large-scale ironworks in the colony.

Not only was the Massachusetts ironworks intended to further the expansion of English ironmaking, but it would also help remedy Britain's increasingly acute timber shortage. Industrial progress, in what would prove to be a familiar story in the West, could be achieved only at the cost of substantial environmental rapine. Even before the turn of the seventeenth century, the voracious demand for charcoal and building timber was denuding England and Scotland of thousands of acres of hardwood forest annually. In addition to the proliferation of charcoal-demanding furnace industries, forests had been depleted by the "great rebuilding" of rural areas during the late sixteenth and early seventeenth centuries. Both the gentry and the yeomanry rebuilt and refurnished their houses, adding parlors, kitchens, halls, chambers, or even whole stories. Such massive construction came at great cost to England's available stands of timber.[14] The same was true for England's critical shipbuilding industry during the age of the Armada. A single large warship could require over two thousand oak trees, many between one hundred and one hundred and fifty years old. As early as the 1580s, cries that the realm was growing short of timber were being heard. For an industrializing, maritime nation, such a situation was potentially catastrophic. By the late sixteenth century many Englishmen believed they were facing a timber crisis at precisely the time the need for wood for the shipbuilding and smelting industries was expanding so significantly. The shortage of wood brought inconvenience to many and outright suffering to more than a few. Firewood prices doubled between the 1540s and 1570s, and tripled again by the 1630s, an increase "almost without precedent in the history of Western Civilization."[15]

With reason, many Englishmen blamed ironmongers for the timber crisis. William Vaughan's *The Golden Fleece* (1626) lamented that England's forests had been "lately wasted by the covetousnesse of a few Ironmasters."[16] After the publication in 1664 of John Evelyn's *Sylva . . . A Discourse of Forest Trees,* a highly regarded report on the timber crisis for the Royal Society, Parliament ordered that the depleted wastes of the Forest of Dean be replanted with 11,000 acres of oak. Other voices were added to Evelyn's, calling for a "universal plantation of all sorts of trees." If this were not done, critics warned, the proliferation of charcoal industries would eventually leave the British Isles virtually treeless.[17]

Indeed, the quantities of wood needed to make the ironworks' charcoal were, by early modern standards, truly staggering. While limeburners required about four loads of wood to produce a ton of lime and a glasshouse burned about seven hundred cords of wood annually, a typical ironworks needed thirty-five cords of wood to produce a single ton of cast iron and hammer it into wrought iron. In 1588, the blast furnace at Cannock Chase, Staffordshire, consumed 24.5 cords of wood to produce each 1.5 tons of cast iron. The workers at the forge required an additional 17.5 cords to hammer each ton of cast iron into wrought iron. A single ironworks might consume no less than 22,000 cords (128 cubic feet) of wood annually. Moreover, the general conversion from wood fire to coal fire in England served to increase, not reduce, the demand for wood. As the demand for coal grew sevenfold in the century after 1530, colliers required much larger timbers to sink mine shafts to ever greater depths.[18] By the 1630s the shortage of timber reserves for charcoal led English ironmongers to look abroad for additional wood supplies, first to Ireland and then to North America.[19]

The possibility of building ironworks in timber-rich North America had gripped the imaginations of the earliest colonial promoters—New England's included. Captain John Smith, after his exploratory voyage in 1614, contended that the region possessed "Iron ore none better." In his influential tract *Of Plantations* (1625), Sir Francis Bacon recommended to prospective colonizers that "If there be iron ore [in the new settlement], and streams whereupon to set the mills, iron is a brave commodity where wood aboundeth." Unlike the mother country, New England was richly endowed with hardwood forests, to go along with its plentiful supplies of iron ore, water power, and land. This was especially true for the oak-chestnut region of southeastern New England.[20] The Bay Colony was also known to possess large deposits of limonite (called bog or rock ore, and usually found in swamps, bogs, and low-lying areas). Limonite ore, which had been the mainstay of the ironworks in the Weald of Kent-Sussex, was among the most common minerals found in Massachusetts.[21] Moreover, New England was also blessed with an ample supply of fluxing agents such as gabbro rock. Gabbro, found most abundantly on the Nahant peninsula south of Cape Ann, contained the calcium carbonate needed to separate the iron from the earthy parts of the ore.[22] New England's fields and forests would also provide food and shelter for the nearly two hundred full- and part-time workers needed to staff a large-scale ironworks. Captain Smith flatly predicted that the availability and lower cost of materials in New England would give its ironworks a decisive comparative advantage over British factories: "Who will undertake the rectifying of an Iron forge, if those that buy meate, drinke, coals, ore, and all necessarie [materials] at a dear rate [in England] . . . ; where [in New England] all these things are to be had for the taking up," he declared, "cannot lose."[23]

The early promoters of New England were virtually unanimous in supporting an ironworks. The Reverend John White singled out iron as one of the products that New England would most profitably yield. Puritan nemesis Thomas Morton did likewise in *New-English Canaan* (1634–35).[24] Governor John Winthrop himself, on the eve of his departure from England, enthused over the opportunities for "makeing of Iron, [and] what other mines there are we know nott." In 1632, Winthrop's friend and trading partner Richard Saltonstall expressed confidence that "iron as we hope" would be among those products from which "we shall raise good profit."[25] After the initial explorations during the 1630s and 1640s, the millennialist Edward Johnson chose to interpret the rise of New England's ironworks in providential terms: "The Land affording very good iron stone, divers persons of good rank and quality in England were stirred up by the provident hand of the Lord to venture their estates upon an iron work."[26]

Determined as they were to maintain an English "middling" standard of living, the Bay Colonists could not subsist without plentiful amounts of edge tools, plowshares, nails, anchors, weights, ox shoes, and kitchen utensils. The material culture of Caroline England—a world created by oxen and plows, ironworks and smithies, mines and shipyards, looms and mills—meant that efforts to establish a locally based ironworks (as well as textile manufacturing) were virtually inevitable. Indeed, many New Englanders believed that they could not prosper (or even subsist) in the absence of domestic iron and cloth industries. While no one imagined that New England could free itself entirely from dependence on imported iron goods, the advantages of a native ironworks were self-evident—particularly to those who looked to the development of a domestic shipbuilding industry.[27]

Accordingly, during the founding decades, the ironworks venture received strong legislative support from the General Court. Even before the Winthrop fleet set sail in April 1630, the Massachusetts Bay Company took steps to investigate New England's potential for ironmaking. John Malbon, "having skyll in Iron works," was dispatched to Salem in 1629 to assess the feasibility of building an ironworks on Cape Ann.[28] Thomas Graves, similarly experienced in ironmaking (as well as saltmaking and fortifications), was sent to Salem with the same mission.[29] In 1641, after the Hammersmith operation had begun to get off the ground, John Winthrop wrote in his journal that the ironworks venture was "well approved by the [General] court, as a thing much conducing to the good of the country." By May 1645 things had progressed to the point that the Court was confident that there was "sufficient proof that the iron worke is very successfull, (both in the richnes of the ore and the goodnes of the iron), and like to be of great benefit to the whole country." In the Court's estimation, it seemed clear that "such an oportunity for so great [an] advantage to the common wealth [must] not be let slip."[30]

Nor did it. The Court's own aggressively promotive ordinances following the onset of the depression of 1640 saw to that. The near collapse of the Massachusetts economy resulting from the end of the "artificial prosperity" brought by the Great Migration was the catalyst to the ironworks effort. John Winthrop, Jr., in particular, believed that a native ironworks would go a long way toward restoring the settlers' prosperity.[31] In 1641, the General Court passed legislation for "encouragement to discovery of [iron ore] mines." By this special franchise monopoly, as we saw in Chapter 5, any entrepreneur who discovered ore or mineral deposits in Massachusetts received exclusive rights to them for twenty-one years. The entrepreneurs were allowed to purchase lands from the Indians and to secure rights from existing English owners to develop mines on their lands. The ironworks and its employees were to be exempt from all taxes for ten years. The Undertakers committed themselves to making "sufficient" quantities for the colony's needs within two years, and they agreed to permit local settlers to buy shares in the company the following year. The Undertakers were also authorized to establish ironworks on six additional sites under these arrangements.[32]

Supplemental legislation was passed in November 1644 and October 1645 after the London-based Iron Works Company had been organized and construction of Hammersmith begun along the Saugus River in Lynn. The Company was granted extensive tracts of land and timber, along with water-power rights, tax exemptions, relief from militia duty for its workers, and their exemption from church attendance. In its most important concession, in October 1645 the Court granted the Company a twenty-one-year monopoly for the manufacture of iron in the Bay Colony. In exchange for these extensive privileges, the Court specifically mandated that a fully integrated indirect-process ironworks—containing a blast furnace, forge, and refinery—be set up no later than 1647. Bar iron was ordered to be sold locally at a maximum price of £20 per ton.[33] The provincial-local "multiplier effect" discussed in Chapter 5 was also in evidence. The General

Court offered a special franchise monopoly, but it was the town of Boston that offered 3,000 acres to attract the ironworks venture to that town's landholdings in Braintree. In the absence of such public promotion of enterprise, as both the General Court and Boston town meeting recognized, sufficient venture capital to finance the start-up of an ironworks was unlikely to be forthcoming.[34]

With the Bay government's imprimatur, John Winthrop, Jr., sailed for England in the summer of 1641, carrying copies of the General Court's ordinance, iron ore samples, and preliminary site assessments. During the next eighteen months—as the monarchical state crumbled and the King opened the Civil War by raising his standard at Nottingham (on 22 August 1642)—the younger Winthrop organized a business corporation with the title of the "Company of Undertakers of the Iron Works in New England." Some two dozen investors, almost all of them Puritan merchants, bought shares in the enterprise. By 1642 the Iron Works Company, now capitalized at a substantial £15,000, came under the control of a small group of English ironmongers led by Gloucestershire furnace owner John Becx and Lionel Copley, both among Britain's leading iron manufacturers.[35]

Throughout these efforts, there was no split in the Massachusetts General Court between pro- and anti-developmental forces. Indeed, to a striking degree, there was *no* genuine dissent on the decision actively to promote a major ironworks venture for the Bay Colony.[36] It was the very same Puritan country gentlemen who established the colony that took the lead in establishing and promoting the Hammersmith Ironworks. Governor Winthrop, as we have seen, secured General Court sponsorship, and it was his son and namesake—New England's leading scientist, metallurgist, and industrialist—who oversaw the building of the factory, recruitment of its workforce, and initial supervision of its day-to-day operation.[37]

No faction within the New England leadership saw fit to oppose the ironworks. Even so stern a Puritan as John Endecott, future fourteen-term Governor of Massachusetts and so uncompromising in his religious views that he risked hanging for treason by effacing the "popish" St. George's Cross from the colony's flag in 1634, championed the venture. In 1643, the year John Winthrop, Jr., succeeded in establishing the first ironworks at Braintree, Endecott wrote to the senior Winthrop to affirm that "I rejoice much to heare of your sonne's Iron and steele. If the Country will not be incouraged by so usefull a designe, to inlarge themselves for the advancing of it, I know not what will." Himself an active investor in copper mine ventures, Endecott viewed the ironworks as worthy of aggressive public promotion.[38] The radically devout colonists of New Haven, easily the most uncompromising Puritans in British America, eagerly established an ironworks in 1655, in the belief that it would serve to stimulate economic development. New Haven leader Stephen Goodyear predicted that if "an Iron Mill might be set up here, it would be a great advantage to the Towne." New Haven's men volunteered some one hundred twenty days of their labor for the construction of the ironworks' hydraulic system. New Haven guaranteed the ironworks' operators water rights, as well as liberty to gather iron ore, wood for charcoal, lime, and "what else is necessary for that work." Individual ironworkers were offered land, provided that they agreed to stay in New Haven for a minimum of three years.[39]

Throughout New England, as Samuel Eliot Morison has wryly observed, "Smelting even received the blessing of the clergy: Thomas Shepard conceded that it was not a profanation of the Sabbath, to keep the fires going in the [blast] furnaces!" Other clergymen, like Concord's Peter Bulkeley, offered material as well as spiritual support for ironmaking in the Bay Colony by themselves becoming investors. In a codicil to his last will and testament, added on 13 January 1658, Bulkeley bequeathed to his wife his "sixteenth part in the Iron Works which is now in framing."[40]

Equally important, the factory that New England chose to build was the most technologically advanced model then available: a Walloon indirect-process blast furnace. In granting monopolies for ore supplies and local markets to the ironworks investors, as we have seen, the Court had specifically directed that the investors erect "an iron furnace [and] forge in each of the places [Braintree and Lynn] and not a blomery [furnace] only." Under the older single-hearth bloomery method then in use of most of the West, the iron never became liquefied, passing instead in one direct step from ore into wrought iron.[41] Under the Walloon indirect process, smelting and refining were separate procedures. A blast furnace smelted the ore to produce iron and hollow ware (pots, skillets, firebacks, etc.). The intense heat of the blast furnace created a liquid iron which was then cast into long bars called sows. In the second step of the process, the cast-iron sows were converted into wrought iron in a series of complex heating and hammering operations in a two-hearth forge. At these two hearths, called respectively the finery and chafery, craftsmen worked the cast iron into wrought iron with the aid of a huge water-powered trip-hammer. In the finery and chafery hearths, the sow iron was melted down, decarburized by oxidation, and reheated into semi-finished wrought iron. In a third procedure, approximately one out of every twelve merchant bars produced in the forge was converted into flats and nail rods in the rolling and slitting mill. The merchant bars were reheated yet again, then passed through a set of rollers (to create the flat) and cutting discs (to produce the nail rods). The *pièce de résistance* of the Hammersmith works, the rolling and slitting mill was one of only some dozen such units in the world.[42]

Interestingly in light of the famous description of pinmaking that opens Smith's *Wealth of Nations,* Hammersmith also possessed the capacity to mass-produce sewing pins. The forge of edge toolmaker Joseph Jencks (which shared the ironworks' water supply) manufactured three sizes of mass-produced sewing pins. Mass-producing pins, as Adam Smith famously showed, was anything but simple. The amount of equipment needed seemed to be inversely proportionate to the simplicity of the final product. Pinmakers utilized drawing benches to fashion wire, hammers, and such sophisticated instruments as cutting mills, pointing mills, and heading mills. All of these instruments were found in Jencks's forge, along with the papering mills needed to manufacture the paper in which the pins were wrapped for sale.[43]

Hammersmith as an enterprise, from its Walloon-type blast

furnace to its sewing-pin manufactory, was nothing if not ambitious. Akin to building a nuclear accelerator in the Amazonian wilderness today, it called for the transfer across 3,000 miles of ocean of some of the most sophisticated machines and technology then available in the West. Once in Massachusetts, the company needed to build a great stone furnace with a water-driven bellows to fire it, a three-hearth forge powered by no less than four waterwheels, and a state-of-the-art slitting mill powered by an additional two waterwheels. The Saugus River had to be dammed and a complex hydraulic system erected and maintained. A large and specialized labor force—precisely the one Adam Smith listed for making shears—needed to be assembled: foundry workers, fillers, and potters to work the furnace; finers and chafers to man the forge; miners and carters to provide the ore and fluxing agents; sawyers and colliers to cut and prepare the charcoal.[44]

* * *

It was in assembling and controlling this labor force that the Saugus entrepreneurs experienced their greatest headaches. The ironworkers, along with the laborers in New England's other major industrial enterprise, the cod fishery, put the culture of discipline to its greatest test. Profane, rowdy, often violent, and laboring in a difficult and dangerous trade, both groups of workers proved to be, in Puritan lexicon, "very chargeable and forward." The very epitome of industrial labor in the early modern world, ironworking was difficult and dangerous labor that tended to attract—and produce—semi-brutalized workers. Bernard Bailyn's graphic description of conditions in the ironworks of eighteenth-century America suggests why such an enterprise seems so anomalous in the Bible commonwealth:

> Work in the mines and quarries, in the charcoal pits, furnaces, and forges, was repellent—hot, filthy, at times dangerous. Mining was the worst: "the most laborious employment allotted to worthless servants," William Eddis wrote from Maryland in 1770. . . . There were very few satisfactions for any of the workers. Isolated in forest

> encampments dominated by smoldering wood, hot, smoky furnaces, and clanging forge hammers, the work gangs found relief, commonly, in drunken brawls and brutal disorder. As early as 1726 and then again in 1736 Pennsylvania had prohibited the sale of liquor at or near the furnaces, and in 1773 the colony tried to ban fairs in towns that the ironworkers frequented because of the "debauchery, idleness, and drunkenness" that resulted from their visits.[45]

Daniel Vickers's parallel description of the Bay Colony's cod fishermen could be applied virtually *in toto* to the ironworkers: "As a community, they drank more heavily, cursed more lustily, and resorted to their fists more readily than rural New Englanders ever did. Coping with life at sea and in port was a hard, even brutalizing, experience, and decades of it bred a peculiar toughness into maritime society. . . . A cultural gulf did divide seaward from landward society in colonial New England." Emblematic of Marblehead's tough and anti-Puritanical fishermen was George Harding, a man who in 1649 was ordered to pay a fine or be whipped for "saying that next year he intended to be a [church] member and would then have his dog christened." While Puritanism fostered economic development in the realms of public policy and personal behavior, its very demand for "godly conversation" brought acute contradictions as well. Nowhere was this more evident than in the fisheries and the ironworks.[46]

It did not take the General Court long to discover that building an ironworks was much easier than staffing it. Mandating an up-to-date iron factory was one thing; finding willing, able, and sober workers capable of meeting the Bay Colony's standards of testified regenerate membership was quite another. Massachusetts policymakers were fully aware that their colony's commitment to ironmaking meant the introduction of often unruly ironworkers into the Puritan commonwealth. The Hammersmith plant would literally embody the tension between two apparently irreconcilable goals: industrial development and the culture of discipline. The disciplined probity that both John Smith and John Winthrop expected of the New England labor force was not likely to be found among either ironworkers or fishermen.[47]

Ironworkers in the British Isles had a long, and apparently well-earned, reputation for stout-hearted truculence and profane living. English miners and colliers were regularly described by contemporaries in such terms as "lewd persons, the Scums and dreggs of many countries, from whence they have been driven." Indeed, these industrial workers appeared to represent the mirror-opposite of the culture of discipline: "lewd, vagrent, and wandering persons who waste their goods in the most lewd and viscious manner, as well in tippoling and [boozing] there upon the sabbath and holy days at the time of divine service, as at and on the other days and times when they should be at their work."[48] The world of the ironworkers—like that of the fishermen—was tumultous, superstitious, and violent, punctuated by frequent bouts of heavy drinking, hard fighting, and profanity.[49] Rejoicing to be away from the sulfurous language used by such groups, one early settler declared after arriving in New England that "Here . . . our ears are not beaten nor the air filled with oaths, swearers, nor railers, nor our eyes and ears vexed with the unclean conversation of the wicked."[50]

In one of many such ironies associated with Hammersmith, it fell to the governor's own son, John Winthrop, Jr., to recruit these ungodly professional workers. The Hammersmith unit would require a minimum of thirty-five highly specialized workers. With a shortage of skilled ironworkers in England itself and with both the Civil War and Irish Rebellion disrupting life in the British Isles, Winthrop's labor recruitment task was a formidable one. The fact that virtually all of Ireland's many ironworkers had been killed in the ferocious rebellion of 1641 posed an especially formidable barrier. The Irish regarded the ironworks that had been built in Ireland since 1635 as a particularly naked example of English oppression, not least because of the extensive deforestation caused by charcoal production. As a result, during the rebellion of 1641 almost all the ironworks were destroyed. An observer visiting the island several years afterwards found that the Irish had "broke down and quite demolished all . . . the Iron-works."[51]

In 1643, the London ironmonger and Hammersmith investor Joshua Foote ascribed much of his difficulty in recruiting ironworkers for New England to the Irish Rebellion: "I have inquired and sought out For to gete a blomrie man [foundry worker] and can hear of none. I was with Sir John Clattworthie about [getting] blomrie men [and] he tells me that times are so in Ireland that he thinks they are killed or dead, for he can hear of none." The ironmonger's advice to Winthrop was to retool blacksmiths into foundry workers, a complicated and time-consuming but not impossible task: "you must Joyne all your workmans' hedes togather and see to breed up blomries; a smith after a lettell teaching will make a blomer man."[52] It was on this kind of Smithian ingenuity and pragmatic willingness to make do with what was available that British America's first industrial workforce would be fashioned.

Earlier in 1643 Foote's recruitment efforts had yielded a mere three workmen and one of their sons. Although Foote had given the workers a daily allowance for food and board, they became agitated over delays in shipping to New England which meant that the bogs and swamps would be frozen and unworkable upon their arrival. The "3 workemen and the Founder's sonn . . . much grombell because that they have layne so longe here and have lost ther labor and have had but bare 12d. a day for their diete and loging which they say thay have spent all and more." Foote was especially anxious that the workers should be placated as "all the other 3 men are Runawaye."[53] A month later another investor, the scientist and future Remonstrant Robert Child, promised Winthrop that "Ile do my [best] indeavor to get a bloomer, and to get those knaves that ran way punished," confessing that "these times put me at my wits End." Although discouraged by the difficulty in finding skilled workers, Child believed that the eventual success of the ironworks would justify all their efforts, concluding his letter with the observation that "if our Iron business goe on, all is well."[54]

The younger Winthrop's vivid description of the perilous trans-Atlantic voyage he undertook with a group of ironworkers in 1643 suggests the magnitude of the problems encountered by colonial labor recruiters, not to mention the dangers and discomforts faced by the workers themselves. Confronted by the disruptions of civil war, obdurate (and possibly corrupt) naval officials, contrary winds, seasickness, fevers, and grumbling workers, Winthrop was pushed to the point of despair. In seeking no less than £1,000 in damages from Parliament for these discomforts, Winthrop described the star-crossed journey:

> The said ship *[Anne-Cleve]* was againe when she was setting saile stopped and hindered by one Robinson an officer at Gravesend . . . [and the ship being so stopped, and hindered, was afterward kept in port by an easterly wind]; your petitioner, having beene unjustly deprived of this opportunity was afterward in the said ship kept above six weeks upon the coast of England, and by reason thereof was above 14 weekes before he could attaine port in New England [in the less favorable winds] and forced to be at sea all the heat of the summer, to the danger of the lives of your petitioner and all his workmen and servants, being all of us dangerously sick of feavors in the latter part of our voyage, and so weakened that his said servants and workmen were not fitt for any labor or imployment when they came ashore, and it being neere winter before [they] arrived, he is hindered from proceeding in the said Iron workes, and is forced to keepe his workmen and servants at great wages and charges without imployment.[55]

Compounding the problems in recruiting skilled furnace and forge hands was the fact that many of those who did travel to Massachusetts were anything but visible saints. No sooner had the ironworkers begun to arrive in New England than their reputation for drunkenness and brawling began to grow apace. Indeed, even before one shipload of ironworkers left the British Isles, Company officials were writing to warn the Winthrops that trouble was on the way.

Their reasoning in imposing such types on the Holy Commonwealth is illuminating, particularly for the confidence it displays that the unruly workmen could be reformed. Ironworkers, the Undertakers apparently believed, could be turned into respectable folk through the culture of discipline. "Every new undertaking hath its difficulty," the investors' letter began. These included "Casuall accidents [which] have cost us very deare," as well as "want of experience in the Minerals in most of our workmen," which "hath bin loss and charge to us." But the most intractable problem was the rowdy character of the workers themselves. Already, the "worse qualities in some of [the workers] have beene a trouble to you," the Undertakers admitted. They proceeded, however, to express sentiments that seem deeply at odds with the Manichaean moral culture we associate with Calvinist New England:

> It is our earnest desire, and we have endeavored all we can to be furnished with better men than some of them are: But notwithstanding all our care, we have bin necessitated to send some for whose civilitie we cannot undertake [to guarantee], who yet we hope by the good example, and discipline of your Country, with your good assistance may in time be cured of their distempers.[56]

This "reformation of manners" justification was regularly used by some of New England's labor merchants and company investors. In particular, the hope that the Puritans' culture of discipline would "cure" workers of their "distempers" was a characteristic sentiment of labor recruiters. Thomas Weston, in warning Governor William Bradford that nearly sixty "rude fellows" were en route to early Plymouth, expressed the hope "not only to be able to reclaim them from that profaneness that may scandalize the voyage, but by degrees draw them to God."[57] In a predestinarian society, based firmly on the theological concept of limited atonement, such sentiments seem to undermine the very foundations of the social order, conflating as they do justification and sanctification—the condition of grace and the condition of outwardly civil behavior.[58]

Although, to most observers, it is axiomatic that Puritans did not believe that the reprobate could be "reclaimed" for God, their labor recruiters for the ironworks and fisheries proceeded from the opposite premise. As with their labor force generally, the Puritans' recruitment of ironworkers revealed the socially radical dimension of early capitalism.

The goal of having a pious and quiescent workforce, like the notion of fixed social hierarchy, could not be reconciled with the reality of New World economic development. In both cases, economic growth had the potential severely to undermine the original ideological basis of the Puritan commonwealth.

The investors' confidence that the refractory ironworkers could be "cured of their distempers" was quickly put to the test. Truculent and quarrelsome on board ship, the ironworkers continued such behavior both during and after their residence at Hammersmith. The Essex County quarterly court records are littered with accusations against ironworkers—for murder, assault, battery, rape, arson, larceny, lewdness, contempt of authority, and drunkenness. The formidable task of imposing the culture of discipline on such a conspicuously unsaintlike group of workers fell for the most part to the magistrates of the quarterly courts. How they went about their task is revealed by the career of one singularly misnamed collier, Richard Pray.

Pray arrived at Hammersmith with his wife Mary sometime before 1648. As a collier (charcoal maker), Pray had one of the most remunerative tasks at the Saugus works. At a time when English day laborers earned approximately £15 per year, colliers could make that amount in a single month. One Hammersmith collier's pay ledger for 1653 credited him with £104 for making 520 loads of charcoal. Another received £64 12s. for "Coallinge of 235 Loades of Coales at 5s. 6d. per Loade." A third took £51 10s. for "Coaling 206 Loads."[59]

Colliers like Pray received such high wages because charcoal making was as physically taxing and mentally demanding as any work at Hammersmith. Typically, a burning involved over a solid week's work, five days of which comprised virtually round-the-clock labor. At Hammersmith, the months for charcoal burning extended from May to October. Colliers needed to produce prodigious amounts of charcoal during these five months. Every ton of wrought iron required the burning of some 265 bushels of charcoal along with 3 tons of bog ore. With Hammersmith's weekly production goal set at 20 tons, nearly 5,300 bushels of charcoal and 60 tons of bog ore would be consumed each week.[60]

To make charcoal, the black porous form of carbon created by slowly burning wood, required the construction of large "pits"—mounds of wood containing up to thirty cords of hewn timber. Usually between 10 and 14 feet high and 30 to 40 feet in diameter, the pits were covered by a layer of leaves, turf, and dirt before being ignited. The stacking and chinking of the wood demanded the greatest care, lest the pile burn unevenly or cave in during tending. Once the pile was ignited, the collier took off to enjoy his last good night's sleep for as long as a week. If everything went according to plan, the pit could be left unwatched for the first twelve hours or so. Thereafter, "it had to be tended night and day, with the skilled craftsman snatching as much sleep as he could in the nearby cabin in which he lived." According to the ironworks historian E. N. Hartley's compelling description of the charring process,

> The collier's enemy was fire, the "live" fire which would consume and undo all the efforts to secure the "dead" or charring fire. Flames might break through the covering and destroy the whole pile. A gas explosion might blow off the cover. Strong winds might do the same, or cause uneven charring, however carefully selected had been the site, however well protected with "hurdles," or wind screens, the pit itself. Soft spots could also easily develop. These the collier had to find by the rather dangerous expedient of jumping up and down on the pile, and then reinforce them by readjusting the wood layers or replacing really bad areas with new wood, leaves, and dust. When charring was not proceeding evenly, the collier had to discover the weak areas with a long stake, or probing rod, and correct the difficulty by cutting draft holes. Too much draft, on the other hand, meant too rapid burning. Keeping everything in balance, achieving the blue smoke and the even setting of the pile that indicated that all was going well, took experience and almost constant attention.[61]

Such demanding, unrelenting work was as common at an ironworks as it was uncommon in the early modern world generally. And the unusual psychological strain imposed by such labor seems to have taken a toll on ironworkers—and their families. In a syndrome that has not been confined to the early modern period, this frustration often took the form of violence against women. A number of ironworkers' wives, such as Richard Pray's wife Mary, appear to have been what now would be regarded as battered women. In March 1648, in the first of many such occasions, the Essex quarterly court fined Richard Pray a total of £4 for an array of offenses: beating his wife; cursing; swearing; and contempt of court. The defendant was given a choice to pay the fines or "to be whipped at the Iron works." Jabish Hackett, an iron ore miner who had lived with the Prays for a time, provided a pungent description of relations between Richard and Mary. Some of Hackett's testimony suggests that the Prays had conflicting allegiances over the Civil War. He deposed that he "often heard Pray call his wife jade and roundhead, and curse her, wishing a plague and a pox on her, and especially after Richard Pray came home from meeting last Lord's day, having beaten her that day." Suggesting the existence of a power struggle within the Pray household, Hackett continued:

> He had heard Pray say he would beat her twenty times a day before she should be his master, and that on the Monday following the Lord's day, [as] Pray's wife [was] going to put on her waistcoat, [she] stripped up the sleeve of her shift and said, "Here are the marks of the blowes" that her husband had given her, which were two great places black and blue. Also that Pray said he had heard it reported . . . that he stayed at home cursing and swearing at his wife. . . . Pray took up a long stick about the size of the great end of a bedstaff and said to her, "Did I sweare, I'le tell you whether I did or noe," and with that struck at his wife, but the deponent being present stepped in and warded off the blows with his arm. Pray, seeing this, gave his wife a kick, and kicked her against the wall.[62]

Although no match for her husband, Mary Pray—like many ironworkers' wives—attempted to give as good as she got. An ongoing source of tension in the Pray household was

Mary's mistreatment of Richard's mother, which featured intense verbal (and occasionally physical) violence. In February 1650, Mary was convicted by the quarterly court for saying "to her mother in lawe, get you [home], you old Hogge, get you [home] and withal threw stones at her. . . ." When her husband took away "a letter [Mary] had gotten wrighten for England, shee at supp[er] threw a trencher at him, and also a bone. . . ."[63]

The authorities' manner of dealing with the domestic chaos in the Pray household reveals the culture of discipline in operation. As an ironworker, Richard Pray was exempt from the colony's church-attendance requirement, so ecclesiastical discipline was not available. Nor, given the Prays' exceedingly truculent cast of mind, was it likely to have been effective. Hammersmith's separate incorporated status within Lynn also rendered problematic the town's authority to bring the Prays to heel. So with the three main institutions in New England's civic apparatus (family, church, and town) dysfunctional or unavailable, the task of upholding the culture of discipline was left to the magistrates of the Essex quarterly court. Theirs was the unenviable task of "taming" such a "stout-hearted" man as Richard Pray.

The local populace expected the court to play this role. According to Jabish Hackett's continuing testimony on Pray's abuse of his wife:

> being at supper one evening, one Thomas Wiggins spoke to Pray about cursing and swearing upon a Lord's day when he and his wife stayed at home from the meeting. Pray answered that it was a lie, and his wife reminded him of his previous actions, Pray took his porrige dish and threw it at her, hitting her upon the hand and wrist, so that she feared her arm was broken.

When "some one present told Pray that the court would not allow him to abuse his wife so," he was all defiance. He declared that he "did not care for the court and if the court hanged him for it, he would do it [anyway]." Pray then was warned that "the court would make him care, for they had tamed as stout a heart as his." Uncowed, at least initially, by this admonition, Pray proceeded to make additional threats against his wife. If the justices gave him "trouble about abusing his wife," Pray vowed in a sadistic assertion of male dominance, he "would cripple her and make her sit on a stool, and there he would keep her."[64] The court eventually did "make him care," and by means of fines and the threats of whipping, Richard Pray learned to behave at least civilly enough toward his wife to stay out of court. Though a change of heart appears unlikely, a reformation of manners apparently was achieved.

Forge worker Nicholas Pinion was another stout-hearted man—and wife abuser—who was eventually tamed by the Essex quarterly court. A forge carpenter as well as a skilled forge hand, Pinion was one of the most versatile members of Hammersmith's core of professional employees. In payment ledgers from the early 1640s, Pinion was credited for "6 months carpentor's Work at the forge," "dressing 2 of [the] bellows," "making of furnace pipes," "markeing Several gudgins for [the] furnace, forge, and slitting Mill and other Tooles," as well as "Coarding of 1114 Coard woode 5 foote [long]."[65]

The daily work conditions that Pinion experienced in the forge itself were often harrowing: "With three fires in use, four waterwheels turning, and the great hammer pounding on its anvil, the forge was the busiest of the three ironworks buildings. . . . The workers were constantly exposed to suffocating heat, flying streams of hot metal shooting out from under the blows of the hammer, deafening noise, and exhaustion from the back-breaking work."[66] Whether charring wood, tending the blast furnace, working the forge, or cutting nail rods, ironworkers (like fishermen) faced a level of danger and stress that took a toll on them, their families, and their neighbors. Working long hours in dangerous circumstances amid Puritan neighbors who made few attempts to hide their contempt, the ironworkers exhibited what have become the classic signs of industrial stress. Women and children often bore the brunt of the resulting tension. As in the case of Richard Pray, the female members of Nicholas Pinion's family lived under the most precarious—and sometimes deadly—circumstances.

Like the Prays, no sooner had Nicholas and Ester Pinion arrived at Hammersmith than they were being called into court to answer for their violent misbehavior. The array of charges has a similar ring. During the winter of 1647–48, in addition to several complaints for "common swearing" and "swearing by God's blood," Nicholas Pinion was accused in court of "beating his wife," and later of "Beating his wife and causing a miscarriage." To these serious charges was appended the more appalling accusation of "killing five children, as his wife says, one of them being a year old."[67]

Given the stormy state of the Pinions' marriage, one doesn't quite know what to make of these horrifying charges. Ester Pinion had established—apparently quite openly—a sexual liaison with another ironworker, Nicholas Russell, a sometime drinking companion of her husband. In February 1648, Russell was fined for "remaining in Nicholas Penyon's house after he had ordered him to keep away," Pinion "being jealous of his wife." Ester Pinion had responded with the assertion that "if Nicholas Russell departed the house, she would depart also." The matter was further complicated by the fact that the court also punished Russell "for spending a great part of one Lord's day with Nicholas Penyon, at [the] house of Joseph Armitage . . . and drinking strong water, delivered to them by Armitage, and then return[ing] home, spending the remainder of the day drinking strong water and cursing and swearing."[68]

Despite the court's intervention, things did not improve for the Pinions. A month later, Ester Pinion was presented for "fighting three times with [her] husband"—this after being bound by the court to ensure her future good behavior. Not one to keep her hands to herself, Goodwife Pinion was later fined for striking the wife of Charles Phillips. And, along with her husband, she disdained to attend the church meeting or abide by the colony's sumptuary laws. Nicholas himself was sometimes victim as well as victimizer when it came to physical violence. In 1649, in one of several such instances, Quinton Pray was fined for "striking Nicholas Penion with a staff, having an iron two feet long on the end of it and breaking his head."[69]

Despite this rich record of anti-social behavior, Nicholas

Pinion continued to be a fully employed member of the Hammersmith workforce until the Company's financial failure in 1653. At that point, Pinion became one of several former Hammersmith workers who were recruited by John Winthrop, Jr., for the ironworks Winthrop was establishing in New Haven Colony. E. N. Hartley's description of life at the New Haven works suggests more than a few parallels with Hammersmith:

> The record of [the New Haven ironworkers'] sins and shortcomings is as extended as it is pungent. Now there is a case of an ironworks clerk accused of trying to violate the chastity of [Nicholas] Pinnion's daughter, now one in which a Pinnion son is found guilty of contemptuous speeches against the authorities, now one involving breaking and entering [ironmaster Thomas] Clarke's house and making off with merchandise *and* the book in which the workers' debts were carried, and early and often, incidents of drunkenness, Sabbath-breaking, assault and battery, swearing, slander, and defamation. Even amidst Puritans who considered their Massachusetts coreligionists lax, the men who made iron, and their womenfolk, were clearly refractory in the extreme.[70]

Disorder at New Haven's ironworks eventually reached the point where the town was forced to hire a special constable to police the works. In 1665, New Haven officially instructed its chief magistrate to "write Captain Clarke about those disorderly persons that were at the iron-works; and upon consideration of so much trouble that arises to the town by means of disorderly persons coming thither." The officials also ordered that no further ironworkers be admitted to the town without "a certificate from some Persons of known reputation."[71]

Nicholas Pinion apparently returned to Massachusetts when the New Haven ironworks failed in the late 1660s. At Hammersmith alone, he had been accused of murder, infanticide, wife beating, assault, battery, drunkenness, contempt of authority, and chronic profanity. At New Haven, he evidently continued along the same course. Yet Pinion does not appear to have been whipped, let alone jailed, for his many offenses, and it was John Winthrop, Jr., who personally selected him to help get the New Haven ironworks established. In some ways Pinion simply seems to represent an extreme example of the prevailing dictum that hardpressed employers in New England hired "what they could" when they could not get "what they would." Yet more is involved here than brute necessity. New England authorities, while anything but eager to have refractory workers in their midst, displayed surprising confidence that the culture of discipline eventually would bring such types to heel. And, like Richard Pray, Nicholas Pinion displayed a sharp decline in both criminal and civil misconduct during his later years in Massachusetts. It was not likely, one suspects, that Pinion ever truly behaved like a Puritan; but, like Pray, his stout heart was sufficiently "tamed" to enable him to live at peace with his wife and neighbors.

The same pattern of reformation describes the fortunes of New England's premier ironworking family: the Leonards. During the seventeenth century, the Leonards were known for two things, ironworking and troublemaking. More than any other ironworking family, the Leonards illustrate the gulf between the culture of discipline and the culture of the hearth.[72] The Leonards may have been recruited from kinsman Richard Lennard's furnace in Brede, Sussex (in the Weald). Soon after their arrival at Hammersmith during the mid-1640s, the family—in fact an extended clan—established a reputation as the leading group of ironworkers in New England. "Where you find iron-works," ran a local saying, "there you will find a Leonard."[73] The constancy with which the Leonards stuck to ironworking over successive generations was extraordinary. For over seven generations—from the 1640s until the 1780s—the Leonards manned the furnaces and forges of New England's increasingly dispersed ironworks industry. From the Hammersmith works the Leonards spread out across Massachusetts, Plymouth, New Haven, and New Jersey to set up furnaces and forges, fineries and chaferies. The Leonards labored at, and in some cases built and owned, ironworks in Lynn, Topsfield, New Haven,

Taunton, and Raynam during this period, leaving their stamp on units with such names as Hammersmith, Bromigum Forge, Two Mile River, Whittenton Forge, Chartley Forge, King's Furnace, and Brummagem Forge. Some of these enterprises were short-lived, but most lasted much longer—in some cases astonishingly so. The Whittenton Forge in Taunton, established in the late 1660s, remained in the possession of Leonards until 1807.[74] Nearby Chartley Forge, founded in the 1690s by third-generation members of the family, continued in operation until the 1790s. In the early eighteenth century, the Two Mile unit in Raynam was already being described as the "Ancient Iron Works which begatt most of the Ironworks of this Province." It would continue in operation until 1876.[75]

Indeed, the Leonard-controlled Taunton ironworks exemplify the fate of the many later plants after Hammersmith. In the fall of 1652 Henry Leonard and his brother James, along with forge worker Ralph Russell, received an official invitation from the town of Taunton (then in Plymouth Colony) for the purpose of erecting a "bloomary work on the Two Mile River."[76] While all three men received offers of land grants as inducements, only James Leonard actually took up residence in Taunton. He managed to set up a furnace there and a forge in nearby Raynam, and eventually became the "sire of a mighty clan."[77]

Taunton, in a policy similar to that adopted by other towns, went to some lengths to help James Leonard get started. Bog ore and timber were provided from the town's common lands. Two Mile River was dammed for the purpose of providing water power for the furnace. The Raynam forge was a double-hearth bloomery, a prototype of the many plants established in the wake of Hammersmith's bankruptcy. The two hearths, the "East" and the "West," were apparently finery and chafery hearths. The roughing-out operations were performed at the finery hearth, the finishing operations at the chafery (with the two heating units working sequentially rather than simultaneously.) Fully operational by 1656, the Two Mile ironworks produced between 20 and 30 tons of iron annually, worth—depending on price levels—between £400 and £675.[78]

Organized on a smaller scale than Hammersmith, the Two Mile ironworks was also based on local (not English) investors. But local investment did not mean unsophisticated financing; even here in the remote reaches of Plymouth Colony, sophisticated forms of capital investment flourished. Typical of how ironworks were capitalized in the post-Hammersmith era, Two Mile was a dividend-paying company owned by local inhabitants of reasonably modest means. Twenty-two men joined the original partnership. A full share cost £20; the first stock offering, in 1656, brought in just under £300, subscribed in amounts between £5 and £20.[79]

Two Mile ironworks proved to be a financial success for the stockholders as well as the Leonards themselves. It returned a consistent (although modest) profit to the investors and provided Plymouth Colony with badly needed ironwares. Over fifty-seven years, from 1656 to 1713, the furnace returned dividends of approximately 12 percent per annum. During the next thirty years, this figure rose to 15 percent. Holders of shares originally valued at £20 received dividends of £3 6s. each in 1683. In 1688, this figure had risen to £4 8s. And, as was intended with Hammersmith, the entire region benefited as well. In addition to providing agricultural tools and shipbuilding supplies, iron bars found use as a medium of exchange.[80]

As the success of the Taunton ironworks reveals, the Leonards eventually achieved both prosperity and respectability in New England. Indeed, according to Hartley, the Leonards became the "very epitome of the American success story."[81] James Leonard, patriarch of the (more respectable) Taunton Leonards, established Whittenton Forge on Mill River during the 1660s and used profits from the ironworks to become a wealthy and influential landowner. His son Thomas, part-owner of the Three Mile ironworks, left an estate valued at £2,500 when he died in 1717. Thomas took up land speculation as well as ironworking, and on a large scale. Two of the sixth generation of Leonards, Jonathan and Eliphalet, were sufficiently successful and enterprising to have petitioned the Massachusetts General Court in 1788 for a special franchise monopoly and protective tariff for their invention of a new method of blistering steel. Between 1787 and 1808 they successfully established several steel furnaces and a nailery that eventually became the highly successful Ames enterprise.[82] Such a record has prompted Samuel Eliot Morison to declare that "if the history of all the local ironworks and tool factories established in New England before 1800 were followed up, it would probably be found that most of them could be traced through [Joseph] Jencks and the Leonards to the old Hammersmith plant in Saugus."[83] Morison may exaggerate somewhat, but there can be little doubt that the Leonards played a large role in helping establish British North America's cast- and wrought-iron industry.

There can also be little doubt that this success came at a considerable cost to social peace. Surely among the most unlikely migrants to the Bible commonwealth, the Leonards—particularly those on Henry Leonard's side of the family in Essex County—made it clear from the beginning that they were no Puritans. During the middle decades of the seventeenth century, the some half-dozen males among the Essex County Leonards were accused at various times of armed robbery, rape, arson, assault, battery, lewdness, profanity, and chronic drunkenness. The Leonard females, not to be outdone, were cited for fistfighting, indecent exposure, singing bawdy songs, and that ubiquitous Leonard offense, contempt of authority.[84]

Although sheer contrariness rather than the brutal misogyny of Richard Pray or Nicholas Pinion marked the Leonards' style, for over thirty years they were arguably the most troublesome family in Essex County. Earthy, high-spirited, and contumacious, the Essex Leonards showed their contempt for Puritan sensibilities at every turn: running naked footraces by the millpond, drunkenly accosting local women, singing ribald songs (often under the leadership of Mary Leonard, the family matriarch), and, as one scandalized neighbor testified, using "very bad words, as Divell and Damn thee and many words which [the deponent had] been ashamed to heare, which wicked Expressions have been very Frequent with them." When reproached for "talking so vilely," one Leonard male replied that "he would not care if he were in hell a fortnight, and he did not care if the devil plucked the soul out of him, and a pox take him, he did not care."[85] In virtually every way possible, the Leonards made it clear that they "did not care."

As with Richard Pray and Nicholas Pinion, the Leonards were also brought to court for abuse of women. Hannah Downing, a maidservant in the household of Nicholas Leonard, sued her master and his sons Samuel and Thomas in 1674 for their "lascivious carriages" and physical abuse. Downing testified that "the Leonards had on many occasions annoyed her when she was in bed, kicked her and struck her several times until she thought they would kill her." Another deponent informed the court that she "saw the Leonards abuse said Hannah and pull off her head-cloth, etc." Downing testified that "she told [the Leonards'] father and mother and they would not believe it. . . ." Macam Downing, Hannah's father, declared that he "came to [the Leonards'] to see his daughter when her master and dame were not at home." He discovered "Samuel [Leonard] in the girl's room and went and told him 'I did not like such doing': and so I lodged in that bed my selfe and Samuell lodged in the Chamber." Hannah also accused Samuel of attempting "uncleanness with her and with Elesabeth Looke." She believed that, in the absence of intervention by the civil authorities, her very life was in danger. She testified that she was "afraid that they would kille me if the authority does not take some course with them."[86]

Yet despite their many violations of both the law and the religious sensibilities of their neighbors, the Leonards were not harried out of the land. Indeed, quite the opposite.[87] As Hartley declares: "The Leonards rose in the world. They took on offices in government, militia, and church. In many, indeed most cases, they acquired more and more property and became 'first families' of the towns to which their work carried them." When in 1813 John Adams wished to illustrate to Thomas Jefferson that reverence for old families was as strong in Massachusetts as in Virginia, he declared: "Our Winthrops, Winslows, Bradfords, Saltonstalls, Quincys, Chandlers, Leonards, Hutchinsons, Olivers, Sewells, etc are precisely in the Situation of your Randolphs, Carters and Burwells, and Harrisons . . . [being preferred] to all others."[88] Even the Essex Leonards eventually earned a measure of acceptance from their orthodox Puritan neighbors. There are signs that some family members experienced a Puritan-like change of heart. In June 1679 we find several members of the erstwhile renegade family engaged in the quintessentially Puritan act of calling a minister to their community. Henry Leonard and two of his sons pledged sums of up to £5 for the purpose of luring Amesbury's minister to the town of Topsfield.[89] Although one wonders, as with Richard Pray and Nicholas Pinion, at the depth of the personal reformation implied by the Leonards' subscription, the past had given little prologue for this symbolic act.

The Leonards' careers also reveal the multiplier effect achieved through local promotion in New England's federally based civil society. In the aftermath of Hammersmith's first insolvency in the mid-1650s, local initiative from the towns took over from centralized direction by the General Court. With the expiration of Hammersmith's monopoly privileges, local officials and entrepreneurs were free to make their initiatives. In October 1657, "in answer to the petition of Concord, Lancaster, and etc., the [General] Court, taking into consideration the great necessitie of a constant supply of iron to carry on the occasions of the countrie" after the failure of Hammersmith, granted the petitioners "liberty to erect one or more iron works within the limit of their owne towne bounds." Well before the Leonard-owned Taunton-Raynam ironworks came under Massachusetts jurisdiction under the second charter (1691–1774), the Bay Colony to a considerable degree had achieved the goals of the original creators of Hammersmith.

Several New England communities in the post-Hammersmith period responded enthusiastically to the possibilities inherent in iron production by offering land grants, labor requisitions, wood-cutting privileges, and relief from taxation and militia service. The town of Andover voted in 1689 to promote the establishment of an ironworks, so long as it did not "damnifye" the other mills on Shawsheen River. The towns of Concord and Lancaster made similar decisions. When in 1696 the Springfield magnate John Pynchon and his partner Joseph Parsons "made some proposals in order to the setting up and carrying on [of] an Iron Mill," the townspeople acknowledged "the great benefitt [the ironworks] will bee to this place." The town granted the two entrepreneurs monopoly rights to all iron ore within the township, following this up a month later with the grant of an 80-acre site on which to build the ironworks. The Springfield ironworks evidently were up and running two years later, as in October 1698 Pynchon "Agreed with Sam Ely for Twenty Load of good Coale [charcoal] for the Iron workes . . . for which I am to pay him £12 in Money."[90] During the seventeenth century, almost a dozen New England towns took steps to establish local ironworks.[91] In part, such local efforts were made possible by the failure of the original Hammersmith unit.

Although competition from iron ore-rich Pennsylvania and Maryland during the eighteenth century eventually marginalized less well endowed New England, the legacy left by workers like the Prays, Pinions, and Leonards was a substantial one. For the remainder of the colonial period, New England would represent a small but significant sector of a burgeoning American industry that by 1775 would include 82 charcoal-fed blast furnaces and 175 forges (many of them refinery forges). These forges, concentrated most heavily in Pennsylvania and Maryland, produced some 30,000 tons of ironwares annually (one seventh of the world's yearly iron production). Pennsylvania, with sixty-four ironworks, produced the most iron of any one colony. Although in New England iron was eventually outstripped by commodities in which the Puritan colonies had a much clearer comparative advantage—fish, livestock, lumber, ships—ironworks remained a permanent and vital feature of the region's economic life.[92]

Even more important is the question of human capital. Ironworkers helped set the tone for what eventually became known as Yankee ingenuity. Their skills in metalworking and mechanical engineering spread and ramified throughout the province. In the region's growing number of iron-fabrication shops, hammer mills, and smithies, men with the names of Leonard, Pinion, and Pray passed on to others the mystery of their craft. In so doing they helped provide the Massachusetts economy with one of its most notable features: its complex and diversified human and material infrastructure. It was this infrastructure, within the context of the Bay Colony's civic ecology, that made possible the rise of maritime New England—source of Massachusetts' ultimate economic salvation.

7

The Making of Maritime New England

In 1711, in a shipyard not far from James Leonard's Whittenton forge, two of the largest vessels ever built in British North America, the 600-ton *Thomas and Elizabeth* and the 400-ton *Sea Nymph,* were launched onto the Taunton River. The two leviathans, each owned by a consortium of some forty-three investors, had been constructed under the direction of the noted London shipwright Thomas Coram. Coram had established his shipyard at Dighton, the highest navigable point on the Taunton River, in 1697; plentiful natural resources and access to iron were his reasons for selecting this location instead of competing sites at Kittery and Newbury. Coram afterward recalled that it was the "convenience of the vast great planks of oak and fir timber, and iron oar which I found abounding at a place call'd Taunton [that] encouraged me to take some of my English shipwrights from Boston."[1] Coram's reasoning, and his very presence in the Bay Colony, reveal much that was distinctive in the region's swift economic rise. Captain John Smith had predicted that shipbuilding would be the "chief engine wee are to use" in building New England's productive economy. And he was right.

By the early eighteenth century, Massachusetts was second only to London as a center of shipbuilding in the English-speaking world. During the years between 1674 and 1714, over 1,200 ships totaling in excess of 75,000 tons were launched from New England shipyards.[2] Of these, 437 vessels totaling some 30,000 tons were built in Boston alone. Despite the need to import all building materials into the peninsula, Boston's rise to shipbuilding preeminence came in remarkably short order. Largely because of the presence of capital and craftsmen in ample amounts—as well as a town and colonial government policy favoring the shipbuilding industry—the capital town could boast fifteen shipyards by 1700. An early eighteenth-century estimate of the aggregate tonnage of English merchant shipping placed Boston third in the British Empire in the number of registered ships, behind only London and Bristol.[3] Massachusetts Royal Governor Lord Bellomont (1636–1701) declared categorically in 1700 that "There are more good vessels belonging to the town of Boston than to all Scotland and Ireland."[4] On the eve of the depression of the mid-1730s, Boston was reported to "often [have] had thirty or forty Vessels on the Stocks." Although eventually rivaled by New York and Philadelphia as a shipbuilding center, throughout its first century Boston was producing more ships than most of the rest of the British North American colonies combined. Massachusetts launched over 80 percent of the colonial tonnage recorded between 1674 and 1696, and over 90 percent from 1697 until 1714. The entire colony of Virginia, although almost as populous as Massachusetts, possessed a total of twenty-seven vessels in the 1698 estimate of its governor, Sir Edmund Andros; South Carolina registered between ten and twelve vessels during the seventeenth century.[5]

By 1660 Samuel Maverick, a crusty non-Puritan whose arrival in New England had antedated the coming of the saints, marveled:

> It is wonderful to see the many Vessels belonging to the Country [of Massachusetts] of all sorts and sizes, fromm

> Shipps of some reasonable burthen to Skiffes and Cannoes, many other Shipps of Burthen from 350 Tunns to 150 have been built there, and many more in time may be. And I am confident there hath not in any place out of so small a number of People been raised so many able Seamen and Commanders as there hath been [there].[6]

Two imperial reports from 1676, one provided by Edward Randolph, reveal the extent to which the Bay Colony's shipbuilding trade had grown by as early as the third quarter of the seventeenth century. Indicating that the colony had a clear comparative advantage because its ships were built "very cheap," the first report listed some 730 Massachusetts-built and owned vessels. The tonnage distribution was broken down as follows:

300 vessels between 6 and 30 tons
200 vessels between 30 and 50 tons
200 vessels between 50 and 100 tons
30 vessels between 100 and 250 tons.

The second report (Randolph's) indicated how the Bay Colony's progressive integration into the British Empire after the 1660s stimulated the Massachusetts shipbuilding industry (this even before the radical increase in the demand for ships brought by the French Wars of 1689–1713). Underscoring the importance of the infusion of British merchant capital, Randolph's report declared that the Massachusetts colonists "have launched 20 ships [annually], some of 100 tons, and this year 30 were ordered to be set on the stocks by the merchants in England."[7]

By the beginning of the eighteenth century, the pace of ship construction had increased, and dramatically so, with some seventy ships annually clearing Massachusetts wharves. As Bernard and Lotte Bailyn's analysis of the shipping register for Massachusetts during the years 1697 to 1714 reveals, the Bay Colony—and especially its capital city—had become the unchallenged center of shipbuilding in the western hemisphere. The numbers tell the story:

> From January 1699 to October 1714, Massachusetts added to its fleet 1,113 vessels totaling over 58,980 tons—an average yearly addition of 69.6 vessels and at least 3,686.2 tons. Of these new acquisitions, Boston held the overwhelming proportion; 83.8 per cent of the vessels and 89.7 per cent of the tonnage. If these new entries had represented net increases—if there had been no compensating sales and losses—the Massachusetts fleet of 1698 would have been doubled in two years and five months; it would have been wholly reproduced six and one-half times in terms of numbers of vessels and about seven times in tonnage during the subsequent sixteen years.[8]

The colony's governor told imperial officials that by 1712 Massachusetts was producing seventy vessels annually for sale in Britain and the West Indies alone. An official survey from 1721 estimated that Massachusetts shipbuilders had "annually launched 140 to 160 vessels, of all sorts," with a yearly production of 6,000 tons.[9] The rise of maritime New England was a source of pride even for the clergy. Preaching to his congregation in the centennial year of the Bay Colony's founding, the Reverend Joseph Sewall (1688–1769) reminded his auditors that during the preceding century, "God has been pleased to smile on our Merchandize and Navigation, Trade and Business."[10]

By the time of the Revolution, the Massachusetts-dominated American shipbuilding industry ranked fifth in value among exports from the continental colonies, just behind New England's other major export, fish. Indeed, as we will see below, from the earliest years of settlement, the two industries—along with the domestic livestock trade—fed off each other. It has been estimated that shipbuilding in the thirteen colonies during the years between 1763 and 1775 totaled some 40,000 tons annually (worth £300,000 sterling), almost half of which was sold abroad.[11] By the end of the colonial period, one quarter to one third of all British-owned vessels were of American manufacture. Their importance for the overall balance of trade was substantial. The combined earnings derived from shipbuilding and freight transport by colonial-owned vessels rivaled the earnings produced by North America's principal export, tobacco.[12]

Shipbuilding was big business in the early modern world, the signature of a capitalist economy. In searching for an adequate description of what connoted a capitalist good during the early modern period, Fernand Braudel declares that "A ship was one *ipso facto*."[13] During the colonial period, the presence of shipbuilding was the demarcation point between extractive enterprises such as lumbering, fur trapping, and fishing and large-scale colonial manufacturing. Shipbuilding was important not only for its demonstrable value in providing exports and carrying capacity, but for the role it played in fostering "linked" manufacturing development. Shipyards were invariably nodes of economic development in British America, attracting the wide array of ropeworks, canvasworks, smithies, ironworks, and other enterprises required to adequately outfit an oceangoing vessel during the early modern period.[14] Boston physician William Douglass, writing in the mid-eighteenth century, estimated that fully one third of the total cost of a New England–built vessel represented ironwork, rigging, canvas, and small stores imported from England.[15]

The symbiotic relationship between shipyards, ironworks, and sawmills was particularly strong, a point many colonial promoters stressed. John White, John Winthrop, and the Reverend Hugh Peter joined Captain Smith in underscoring the favorable developmental prospects shipbuilding offered New England. In *The Planter's Plea* (1630), White wrote, "How serviceable [New England] must needs be for provisions for shipping is sufficiently known already." The Puritan promoter was confident that the region would yield sufficient "planks, masts, oars, pitch, tar, and iron, and hereafter, by the aptness of the soil for hemp, [and] if the colony increase, soils and cordage" as well.[16] In addition to the abundant stands of oak and pine—two thousand trees per large vessel—needed to build shipframes, masts, and spars, and provide the resin, turpentine, and tar used for caulking and repairing oceangoing craft, shipyards also required ironworks, smithies, and sawmills to fashion the necessary ironwares and planking. Iron was needed not only for the superstructure of a vessel, but also for its bolts, rudder braces, and anchors. Each 100-ton vessel used approximately 1 ton of ironwork. Between them, the Coram-built *Thomas and Elizabeth* and the *Sea Nymph* (1,000 total measured tons) required a total of 10 tons of iron fittings. Moreover, the ironwork for each ship had to be custom-fitted on the spot rather than being imported from England in standardized sizes. The decision of the Massachusetts General Court to promote both shipbuilding and ironworking as part of its economic program of 1641 reflected an awareness of this symbiotic relationship.[17]

Along with sawmills and the cod fishery, New England shipyards afforded the region with a rich network of backward (production) and forward (consumption) linkages.[18] Profits derived from shipbuilding, along with those from fishing and merchandising, allowed local capitalists to invest in sawmills in Maine and New Hampshire as well as the gristmills constructed in virtually every town of consequence. The shipbuilding and timber industries grew in tandem and decisions over resource allocation became focal points of townsmen's policymaking. Selectmen in coastal towns such as Gloucester, which early and aggressively promoted shipbuilding, found themselves contending by the 1690s with increased requests for masts and other building material from the town common lands. In 1711, one Gloucester sawmill owner shipped five hundred cords of wood to Boston in less than a month. Local initiatives to foster the maritime trades also brought improvements such as wharves and docks, especially after midcentury. In 1655, the town of Newbury granted land to Paul White for the purpose of building what proved to be the first wharf, dock, and warehouse on the Merrimack River. When colonial traveler John Josselyn visited Boston in 1663, he found that "the houses are for the most part raised on the Seabanks and wharfed out with great industry and cost, many of them standing upon piles, close together on each side [of] the streets as in London and furnished with many fair shops, their materials are Brick, Stone, Lime, handsomely contrived."[19]

It was the symbiotic connection between New England's

shipyards and cod fisheries that first sparked the mercantilist fears of Sir Josiah Child. His warning to imperial officials was explicit on this score, particularly about the link between shipbuilding and human capital in the New England colonies:

> Of all the American Plantations his Majesty has, none are so apt for the building of Shipping as New-England, nor none more comparably so qualified for the breeding of Seamen, not only by reason of the natural industry of that people, but principally by reason of their Cod and Mackeral Fisheries: and in my poor opinion, there is nothing more prejudicial, and in prospect more dangerous to any Mother-Kingdom, than the increase of Shipping in her Colonies, Plantations, or Provinces.[20]

Linked development, as Child's comments suggest, played a major role in the rise of maritime New England. Profits resulting from the shipbuilding and fishing industries remained within the Massachusetts economy to ramify into new enterprises. London capitalists, local merchants and shipwrights, and Bay Colony fishermen contributed their resources and labor power to create a dynamic network of credit and production. Writing in 1648—six years after the vital West Indian trade network was established—the author of *Good News from New-England* offered a concrete estimate of the higher returns from investment brought by the maturing of the region's maritime infrastructure: "I dare assure [the reader] that one hundred pounds will doe that which five hundred could not doe at [the] first planting of this little Common-wealth, which was the reason [so] many [at that time declined] in their estates." Investing in New England became increasingly attractive, particularly to those London merchant-entrepreneurs with Puritan sympathies. By the mid-seventeenth century, the New England fishing industry was being capitalized by a combination of Puritan-minded merchants from London, Massachusetts investors and shipwrights, and New Hampshire timber dealers.[21]

As foreseen by both John Smith and John Winthrop, the Bay Colony's mixed farming-fishing-timber economy, with its prominent emphasis on shipbuilding, was the fruit of a distinctive institutional culture. It was a reflection both of conscious public policy choices and the nature of the colony's mixed agricultural economy. Nor should we underestimate the importance of raw need. Lacking a tropical staple and chronically short on credit during the founding decades, Massachusetts had every incentive to develop a domestic shipbuilding industry. The colony of Virginia, blessed (or cursed) with a lucrative crop that attracted both credit and vessels to its shores in plentiful amounts, lacked the incentive to do likewise. Despite the presence of some modest shipbuilding activity on its Eastern Shore and the passage of an act by the House of Burgesses in 1662 offering 50 pounds of tobacco per ton built for the "encouragement of building vessels," Virginia failed to develop a shipbuilding industry of any consequence during the seventeenth century. Governor William Berkeley attributed this failure, like the colony's larger failure to economically diversify and urbanize, to the "vicious, ruinous plant of Tobacco."[22]

New England's mixed-grain-livestock economy demanded—and fostered—infrastructural development. Despite energetic recent efforts to portray the seventeenth-century Chesapeake as more reflective of English society than New England, the material culture of the mother country—a domain created by oxen and plows, smithies and ironworks, shipyards and waterwheels—found much clearer expression in the northern than the southern colonies.[23] Unlike the monocultural plantation colonies, where laborers broke up the land with a hoe, not a plow, and local milling and processing facilities could be minimal, New England's exports required a broad range of productive enterprises and financial services. Grain-based agriculture required plows, gristmills, smithies, oxcarts, and a multitude of skilled artisans to build and service them. Grain-producing regions demanded the presence of millwrights, blacksmiths, cartwrights, and wheelwrights, as well as ever valuable woodworkers such as carpenters and joiners. Gristmills quickly became a virtual necessity in the Bay Colony. So dependent were Springfield's inhabitants on their town's gristmill that its destruction during King Philip's War threatened the town's future. John Pynchon wrote to Governor John Leverett in the fall of 1675 that "our People are under great discouragement, Talke of Leaving the Place," for the "Want of a Mill is difficult." Springfield, as a major meat exporter, still had "flesh enough," Pynchon emphasized; yet, he predicted that having "noe Mill will drive many of [the town's] Inhabitants away. . . ."[24]

The Massachusetts fishing industry also necessitated shipyards, ironworks, ropewalks, and joineries as well as a complex array of institutions for credit, factorage, and marine insurance. The need for farmers to get their grains, livestock, and pipestaves to market meant that local and provincial officials had to take action to promote the construction of roads and bridges of sufficient width and sturdiness to accommodate carts as well as horses. The founding agreement of Springfield in 1636 made provision for "all highways that shall be thought necessary."[25] In 1648, because of the "great perill which men, horses, teames, and other cattell are exposed to, by reason of defective bridges and high wayes between Boston and Salem, and elsewhere in this jurisdiction," the Massachusetts General Court mandated a £100 fine for each loss of life caused by a town's defective roads or bridges. The West Indian–oriented export trade kept entire communities (especially port towns such as Boston, Charlestown, and Salem) occupied in servicing it: merchant capitalists who financed the voyages and linked the colony to the Atlantic trading system; fishermen—often in client relationships with these same merchants—who caught and packed the cod and mackerel; shipwrights, sailmakers, carpenters, joiners, and ironworkers who fashioned the vessels; outfitters who oversaw the provisioning of merchant ships and fishing craft alike; butchers who turned cattle and hogs into preserved meat; tanners who cured hides; sawyers who felled and mauled trees; innkeeping women who provided bed and board for the mariners; and ordinary farmers and artisans who spent their free time shaving shingles and making pipestaves. All these found themselves increasingly by the late 1640s "look[ing] to the West Indies for a trade. . . ."[26]

New England's early—indeed, almost instantaneous—creation of a thriving local market in cattle and swine served as the foundation for the colony's first West Indian links. That so many of the vessels dropping anchor in Boston Harbor each summer during the twelve years of the Great Migration carried in their holds cattle, pigs, sheep, goats, and horses proved of inestimable benefit to the early settlers. It was the domestic trade in cattle and pigs, in particular, that kept New England's economy afloat during the 1630s and that offered a sure commodity for the West Indian trade when it began to develop in the early 1640s. With so many of Massachusetts' inhabitants hailing from the cattle- and sheep-dominated wood-pasture regions of England, the early prominence of livestock husbandry in the Bay Colony is not surprising. And the reasons so many of these migrants paid substantial sums to bring livestock with them to Massachusetts are not hard to find. While productive energies could be divided relatively equally between cattle and grain husbandry in England, in labor-scarce Massachusetts the balance would be tipped strongly in favor of the more easily raised livestock.[27] Early promoters and colonizers displayed striking unanimity in proclaiming that, while New England offered few prospects for staple crop production, livestock husbandry could be expected to flourish there. In 1621, Edward Winslow wrote home from Plymouth that "if we have once but kine [cattle], horses, and sheep, I make no question, but men might live as contented here as any part of the world." In 1629, Salem's Francis Higginson informed his friends in Leicester that "It is scarce to be believed how kine and goats, horses and hoggs do thrive and prosper here." Plymouth Governor William Bradford estimated that "there is grass enough to keep a hundredfold the cattle" that the English raised. Pigs, more difficult to raise in England because of the shortage of forest mast, were found to double their numbers every eighteen months in normally acorn-rich New England. As early as 1631 pigs were being described as the Bay Colony's "best cattle for profit."[28]

In 1633, John Winthrop went so far as to say that the domestic cattle trade—fueled by the new consumers pouring into Boston's docks—had saved the Massachusetts economy from ruin. The commonwealth, Winthrop declared, "by reason of so many foreign commodities expended, could not have subsisted to this time, [except] that it was supplied by the cattle and corn, which were sold to new comers at very dear rates." Cows were selling at the almost extortionate price of between £20 and £26 per head. Mares cost the newcomers £35 and live goats between £3 and £4. With demand so high, local livestock herds were being supplemented by the "many cattle [that] were every year brought out of England and some from Virginia." In one of the first cattle drives in British America, one hundred oxen were taken from Piscataqua to Boston in 1638, garnering prices of £25 per head. Plymouth cattle farmers also prospered through the Massachusetts trade. To the Bay Colony authorities, the most alarming feature of the economic collapse of 1640 was the fact that "cattle and all commodities grew very cheap." Although the bonanza prices of the mid-1630s were gone for good, the development of the West Indian trade after 1642 provided a reliable market for New England livestock.[29]

Not only did New England possess abundant pastureland and meadow for cattle and an apparently inexhaustible supply of mast (especially acorns) for swine, but the towns and colonial government used creative policymaking to allow such resources to be effectively deployed. By the summer of 1633 it had become clear to Bay Colony leaders that the commitment to a mixed livestock-tillage economy necessitated policy shifts. An unusual shortage of acorns that year brought a serious threat to Massachusetts' food supply. John Winthrop reported that "There was [a] great scarcity of corn, by reason of the spoil our hogs had made at harvest, and the great quantity they had [eaten during] the winter (there being no acorns)." In 1634 and again in 1651 the General Court voted, in effect, to reverse the laws of trespass in lawsuits involving livestock. The Bay Colonists were ordered to fence *in* their crops and fence *out* their livestock, the opposite of English practice. The 1651 edict ordered that "all fences agaynst cornefeild, meddow ground, gardens, orchardes or pastures which are made of stones, pales, rayls, rivers, or creeks . . . [shall] be sufficient agaynst greate cattle, [and] all swine. . . ." The authorities also refused to allow farmers to sue a livestock owner for crop damage caused by cattle or swine.[30]

The reliance of livestock farmers on the New England

town's civic sphere is illustrated in matters large and small. Land-use decisions usually were the most consequential ones, particularly the initial demarcation of a township into home lots, planting lots, wood lots, pastures, and meadows. Such decisions in effect imposed a template over the development of all community resources during the succeeding decades. It was at these points that a community's path toward economic specialization could be set. Many interior towns such as Sudbury were founded with the express purpose of specializing in cattle; local decision making reflected that orientation.[31] Communal cooperation was especially vital for livestock husbandry. In communities like Deerfield, for example, where the common field system prevailed, the entire town needed to reach agreement on the precise date after the fall harvest when the citizens' livestock were to be allowed into the cornfields and meadows.[32] By the same token, the appointment of fence viewers (to ensure that livestock were kept away from the crops during growing season) and blacksmiths to "ring the swine" (insert iron rings in the animal's nose to impede the rooting up of crops) were communally based decisions that all citizens participated in—and profited by. The town of Springfield, where pork exports were a major enterprise, paid the blacksmith John Stewart threepence per hog for going through the community twice a week from March to November for the purpose of ringing any unrung swine. Many settlements, including communities as remote as Deerfield, elected "packers" of pork and beef for the purpose of ensuring quality control for the town's meat products. Major port towns such as Boston, Charlestown, Salem, and Ipswich were mandated by the General Court to provide such officials.[33]

Town meetings and boards of selectmen made choices to accommodate their communities to livestock husbandry. The early inhabitants of Springfield recognized that the Connecticut Valley's extensive pasturage and superb water-transport system meant that beef, pork, and horses could profitably be raised for export. Springfield's original incorporation agreement, accordingly, allotted two acres of new mowing land for each head of neat cattle and twice that for each horse, "because estate is like[ly] to be improved in cattle, and such ground is aptest for theyr use."[34] In 1654 the Springfield voters granted John Pynchon 21 acres of the town's most valuable land on condition that he purchase "40 sheepe within the space of Sixe months." For his part, Pynchon agreed to "use his best endevoure to bring [the sheep] into Towne and there to dispose of them as hee shall see cause."[35] Again in 1660, Pynchon and two partners were granted 40 acres of land "according as they carry on theire designe of keeping swine there."[36] When the Springfield town meeting voted to establish a "cow pasture" and "sheep pasture" out of the common land on the village's outskirts, it offered further evidence of the residents' long-term commitment to making their town one of the principal livestock-exporting centers in western Massachusetts.[37]

Town meetings voted to hire at public expense one or two men (or boys) to act as keepers of the inhabitants' herds of cattle during the growing season, freeing everyone else for the myriad tasks of farming. Towns possessing substantial herds of livestock maintained a registry of cattle and horse earmarks (or brands). Because colonial New Englanders allowed their swine (and, when necessary, cattle and horses) free range during the months from November to March, a record of each family's distinctive earmark was required to identify the beasts owned by each inhabitant.

A cattle economy also demanded high levels of social discipline and material infrastructure, strong suits both in the Bay Colony. By 1640 there were an estimated twelve thousand cattle (along with three thousand sheep) that needed to be cared for in Massachusetts. Cattle required spring feeding, summer grass, and winter fodder (considerably more of this last than in the more temperate mother country). Cattle kept in barns needed nightly feeding; milch cows had to be milked each morning. New England women, in addition to their varied tasks of preparing food, looking after children, and domestic manufacturing, assumed responsibility for the care of livestock not kept in the outer fields. Even so wealthy a woman as Anna Pynchon, wife of Springfield's founder William Pynchon, inspected the family's herds on a daily basis. During the difficult winter of 1637–38, William reported that "My wife, walking more amongst my Cattle . . . professed that

It was her dayly grief to see them in that poore starveing condition."[38] New England's fierce winters required not only the provision of winter fodder for livestock but, for those settlers who could afford it, the construction of barns with dimensions of between 20 and 50 feet. In 1657, William Pynchon's son John "Agreed with Thomas Barber to Build me a Barne over the great [Connecticut] River [of] 50 foote long and 24 feete wide, with a leantoe all along the back side" to be completed before the next harvest, at a cost of £21.[39] Following the Indian attack on Springfield during King Philip's War, Pynchon contracted with Increase and Victory Sikes to build a barn of 52 by 24 feet, for a fee of £14.[40] Despite such relatively modest labor costs, fully completed and stocked barns represented substantial capital investments. When Newport's William Coddington lost "A larg Corne Barne" to fire in 1644, he estimated its value at £150.[41]

Livestock husbandry shaped New England society in myriad ways. When the rapid expansion of cattle herds led to a land shortage by the mid-1630s, the General Court—albeit grudgingly—permitted expansion of settlement to the Connecticut Valley. Communal *decline* was not a problem in seventeenth-century New England, but community *fragmentation* was, and the need to find pasturage was behind much of it. A cattle economy demanded extensive acreage. One eighteenth-century colonist estimated that it took as many as 3 1/4 acres to sustain each cow for a year.[42] In beginning the "great reshuffling" of Massachusetts Bay's population in the mid-1630s, the residents of Newtown (Cambridge) "complained of straitness for want of land, especially meadow [for cattle] and desired leave to look out either for enlargement or removal" to the west. Moralizing over the preference for cattle over crops in early Massachusetts, Edward Johnson said of the migrants that "seeing that Tillage went but little on [in Newtown], [the settlers] Resolved to remove, and breed up store of Cattell, which were then at [£28] a Cow." To Johnson, it was a manifest spiritual failure that the migrants preferred livestock husbandry to producing "their bread with the toile of hand and [hoe]." In describing the town of Haverhill,

Johnson declared that its people "are wholly bent to improve their labour in tilling the earth, and keeping of cattel, whose yearly increase incourages them to spend their days in those remote parts." The people, he wrote, were "laborious in the gaining [of] the goods of this life. . . ." Yet, he nervously added, they were "not unmindful also of the chief end of their coming hither, namely to be made partakers of the blessed Ordinances of Christ. . . ." John Winthrop found by 1635 that Watertown, Roxbury, and indeed "all towns in the bay," began "to be much strained by their nearness to one another, and their cattle being much increased."[43] So abundant were the livestock owned by Dorchester's residents that when they "removed their cattle to Connecticut before the winter," losses in transit were estimated by Winthrop to be no less than £2,000. Bewailing the cattle-related fragmentation of community in 1642, John Cotton accused his fellow settlers of believing that "If [only] we could have large elbow-roome enough, and meddow enough, though we had no [church] Ordinances, we can then go and live like lambs in a large place."[44]

Governor William Bradford, in assessing why his townsmen so quickly scattered throughout the Plymouth Bay area, pointed to the Pilgrims' "all striving to increase their stocks [of cattle]." Indeed, the most elegiac rendering of the role of livestock husbandry in fracturing the New England community is found in Bradford's *Of Plymouth Plantation.* During the 1630s, Bradford wrote, "the people of the Plantation began to grow in their outward estates, by reason of the flowing of many people into the country, especially into the Bay of the Massachusetts." As a result of the heightened demand in Massachusetts, "corn and cattle rose to a great price, by which many were much enriched and commodities grew plentiful." In a comment that distills the essence of the Protestant dilemma—how the right thing became the wrong thing—Bradford maintained that "in other regards this benefit turned to [the colonists'] hurt, and this accession of strength, to their weakness":

> For now, as their stocks increased and their increase [grew] vendible, there was no longer any holding them

> together; but now they must of necessity go to their great lots. They could not otherwise keep their cattle, and having oxen grown they must have land for plowing and tillage. And no man now thought he could live except he had cattle and a great deal of ground to keep them [upon], all striving to increase their stocks. By which means, [the Plymouth colonists] were scattered all over the Bay quickly; and the town in which they [had] lived compactly till now was left very thin and, in a short time, almost desolate.

Although, as we have seen, elsewhere in *Of Plymouth Plantation* Governor Bradford offers one of the most eloquent defenses of private property to be found in the Puritan canon, his laments over the social and spiritual costs of everyone "striving to increase their stocks" struck the opposite note. Cattle-driven community fragmentation, Bradford predicted, would be "the ruin of New England, at least of the churches of God there, and will provoke the Lord's displeasure against them."[45]

Such laments notwithstanding, livestock husbandry emerged as the principal form of surplus production for New England farmers. Only after the expansion of the fishing, shipbuilding, and wood-products industries during the 1640s did the Bay Colonists become less exclusively reliant on the cattle trade. Despite his misgivings over the relatively labor-free nature of animal husbandry, Edward Johnson admitted that it was preeminent during Massachusetts' first two decades. The cattle trade brought prosperity to many in the Connecticut Valley and Narragansett region. Livestock husbandry helped turn Ipswich into the Bay Colony's second wealthiest town by midcentury, with "many hundred quarters [of meat] to spare yearly and feed, at the latter end of Summer, the Towne of Boston." In New England generally, as Johnson declared, it was "the common practice of those that had any store of Cattel to sell every year a Cow or two, which cloathed their backs, fil'd their bellies with more varieties [of goods] than the Country of it selfe afforded, and put gold and silver in their purses beside." By the late 1640s, cattle had become so central to the Bay Colony's ship-outfitting and export economy that Boston petitioned the General Court for a separate fair "for Cattle to make provisions both for our selves and [for] shipping."[46]

Financing the building of the ships that would carry these cattle (along with fish and lumber) to the West Indies proved to be, in John Winthrop's words, a "work [that] was hard to accomplish." Even the most primitive shipyard required a building slip or two, docks, storehouses, and large reserves of seasoned timber. Both the labor and capital necessary for such enterprises were at a premium, particularly during the Bay Colony's founding period when the construction of houses, barns, roads, fortifications, and fencing all laid pressing claims on the settlers' resources of time and money. As John Winthrop, Jr., catalogued the myriad tasks facing the settlers: "Plantations in their beginnings have worke enough, and find difficulties sufficient to settle a comfortable way of subsistence, there beinge buildings, fencings, clearinge, and breakinge up of ground, lands to be attended, orchards to be planted, highways and bridges and fortifications to be made, and all things to doe, as in the beginninge of the world."[47]

Still, it took scarcely more than a year after the founding of Massachusetts for the settlers to launch their first coasting craft and a little more than two years after that to build their first trans-Atlantic vessel. In helping to fulfill his—and Captain John Smith's—vision of New England's maritime future, John Winthrop financed the first ship built in the Bay Colony. During his second summer in New England, Winthrop recorded in his journal that "The governour's bark, called the *Blessing of the Bay,* being of thirty tons, went to sea." By the fall of 1631 the coasting trade as far north as the Kennebec River had already been established. Winthrop noted that "Mr. [William] Pynchon's boat, coming from Sagadahock [Kennebec], was cast away at Cape Ann, but the men and chief goods saved, and the boat recovered."[48] In 1633, the Bay Colonists launched from Medford the 60-ton *Rebecca,* the first vessel with trans-Atlantic capabilities constructed in British America. In 1636, shipwrights at Marblehead launched the 120-ton *Desire,* a large craft even by London shipyard standards. Employing a creative means to reduce the financial risks of capitalizing large oceangoing vessels, investors divided up the cost of a vessel into shares: quarters, eighths, and sixteenths. Well before the depression of 1640, or even the full flowering of the cod-fishing industry, Massachusetts had committed itself to establishing a major domestic shipbuilding industry.[49]

But, as with the Bay Colony's economic development generally, it was the depression of 1640 that catalyzed public efforts to both promote shipbuilding and initiate commercial ties with the West Indies. "These straits," declared Winthrop, "set our people on work to provide fish, clapboards, planks, etc. . . . and to look to the West Indies for a trade." A West Indian trade, the magistrates recognized, would require the creation of a major domestic shipbuilding industry. The General Court in 1639 had taken some measures in this direction by exempting ship carpenters, along with fishermen and millers, from militia training. As Winthrop noted in his journal, the Bay Colonists had discovered that they could not live without imported goods: "The general fear of want of foreign commodities, now [that] our money was gone . . . set us on to work to provide shipping of our own. . . ." The Reverend Hugh Peter, future chaplin to Oliver Cromwell and martyr to the Parliamentary cause—and a man already pushing strongly for a domestic fishing industry—took the initiative. "[B]eing a man of very public spirit and singular activity for all occasions, [Peter] procured some [shipwrights and investors] to join for building a ship at Salem of 300 tons, and the inhabitants of Boston, stirred up by his example, set upon the building [of] another at Boston of 150 tons."[50]

Shipwright Richard Hollingsworth, as well as other Bay Colony shipbuilders during those straitened times, followed the spirit of Winthrop's *Arbella* sermon by "abridging" themselves in favor of the public good. As circulating cash was in exceedingly short supply, Hollingsworth agreed to "be content with such pay as the country could make." With the help of similar sacrifices, the 300-ton *Mary Ann* was launched from Salem in June 1641. By the end of 1643 two more 300-ton ships were launched in Boston, and between 1642 and 1646 a total of six vessels were constructed by Boston shipwrights. When one of Nehemiah Bourne's vessels, the 160-ton *Trial,* was launched in August 1642, the Reverend John Cotton was asked "to preach aboard her, but upon consideration that the audience would be too great for the ship, the sermon was held at the meeting house." That same year Governor Winthrop reported with pride that "This summer five ships more were built, three at Boston, and one at Dorchester, and one at Salem."[51]

A letter from Hugh Peter and Emmanuel Downing to John Winthrop in January 1641 illustrates the federally based civil society in action. Peter and Downing entreated Winthrop's help in "the supressing [of] pipe stave [makers] and clapboards [makers] in our towne [of Salem]; because we have 2 or 3 ships building." In order to avoid competition for wood from settlers seeking to fashion pipestaves and clapboards for what was becoming a vigorous export trade in both commodities, Peter and Downing sought public regulation of the resource. The two men notified Winthrop that "wee desire that within 2 or 3 miles neere any river they may not fell great tymber [that can be used] for shipping, for they may as well cut [trees for pipestaves and clapboards] further of[f], it being so portable, and ship-timber being so heavy." The pipestave makers, moreover, offended against the Puritan doctrine of stewardship because they "cut downe but halfe of the tree for their use, and the rest lyes rotting and spoyles our Comons, with many more inconveniencyes than we can name."[52] But even before the General Court could act, as John Endecott reported to Winthrop, local initiatives prevailed. Salem voted on its own to preserve all timber within a two-mile radius for shipbuilding:

> I called our towne together before your Lettre came, seeing the spoile of timber which might serve for many good uses. And the towne agreed not to cutt any great tymber which is fitt for shipping planckes or knees, etc., nor any for clapboard within two miles of the towne every way, nor to fell any other timber but for their owne private use.[53]

As this correspondence reveals, if the General Court failed to take remedial measures, towns were capable of acting on their own to safeguard their interest. Town meetings acted to promote selected products and to ensure local control over them. In 1639 the townsmen of Springfield, a community heavily dependent on the canoes needed to transport its pork, beef, and fur exports down to Enfield Falls, voted that "it shall be lawfull for any inhabitant to fell any Cannoe trees [growing on the common] and make them for his owne use or for the use of any inhabitant . . . but not to sell or any ways pass away any Cannoe out of the Plantation [town] untill it be five years old."[54] Similarly, in 1702 the Gloucester town meeting banned the non-local sale of any shipbuilding material and required shipwrights using wood from the town's commons to post a bond that the ship would not be sold out of town for six years.[55] Towns also took action to attract and keep skilled shipwrights in their midst. One of the Bay Colony's leading shipwrights, Nehemiah Bourne, received a lucrative land grant from the town of Boston, and after 1641 Boston, Salem, and Charlestown vied with one another to attract shipwrights to their flourishing shipyards. Gloucester rose to shipbuilding prominence in part by offering special privileges in the form of land grants and timber rights to prospective shipwrights. Competition for such craftsmen forced other towns to do likewise if they hoped to establish a local shipyard.

The towns set resource-use policies at the local level, but the General Court established provincewide inspection standards. The centerpiece of the General Court's shipbuilding program was an inspection act passed in October 1641. Without guilds (although a guildlike corporation was unsuccessfully introduced in 1644), the provincial government was left with the task of ensuring quality control. But the hand of governmental regulation was to be a light one, as the Court left the bulk of policing responsibility to the shipowners themselves. Noting that "the country is nowe in hand with the building of ships, which is a business of great importance for the common good, and therefore sutable care is to bee taken that it bee well performed, according to the commendable course of England," the Court ordered that

> when any ship is to bee built within this jurisdiction, it shalbee lawfull for the owners to appoint and put in some able man to survey the worke and workemen from time to time, as is usuall in England; and the same so appointed shall have such liberty and power as belongs to his office, and if the shipcarpenters shall not, upon his advice, reforme and amende any thing which hee shall find to be amisse [viewers will be appointed to rectify it].

And in 1667, when the General Court learned that "divers unskilfull persons, pretending to be shipwrights, [were] build[ing] shipps and other vessells in severall parts of the country, which are very defective, both for matter and forme," it appointed a committee to rectify the problem.[56]

The human capital responsible for the shipbuilding boom was substantial. Up to two hundred workers could be required for the construction of a 100- to 300-ton vessel, virtually all of whom in Massachusetts were independent specialist artisans or suppliers who worked on subcontracts from the master builder. Notable among the extraordinarily talented assemblage of shipwrights that the Bay Colony managed to attract to its shores during the founding decades were Salem's Hollingsworth, Boston's Bourne, and Thomas Hawkins (builder of the 400-ton *Seafort* in 1645), and—especially—William Stephens, who worked for most of his Massachusetts career in shipyards in Salem and Gloucester. Emmanuel Downing, while staying in London and inquiring "what shipcarpenters Mr. Winthrop the Governor had with him in New England," learned from the Lord Keeper of the Seal's brother-in-law that

> the Governor hath with him one William Stephens, a shipwright; soe able a man, as they believe there is hardly such an other to be found in this kingdom. . . . This Stephens hath built here [in London] many ships of great burthen: he made the *Royal Merchant,* a ship of 600 tons. This man they enformed me, had more regard to his substantiall performance [as a shipwright] than the wages he was to receive, and soe grew to poverty: whereupon he was preparing to goe for Spayne, where he knew he

> should have wages answerable to his paynes, had not some friends persuaded him to [go] to N[ew] England, where he now lives with great content.

Downing concluded his comments with the mercantilist observation that "Had the state of Spayne obteyned [Stephens], he should have be'n as a pretious Jewell to them."[57]

By the mid-seventeenth century, the town of Boston was turning out an impressive array of full-rigged ships, ketches, pinnaces, and yawls. Second in importance was the town of Salem, with four shipyards and a dozen shipwrights. Specializing in ketches for the offshore fishing industry, Salem shipyards launched the remarkable total of thirty-two of these oceangoing craft between 1697 and 1702. Dorchester, Milton, the Merrimack Valley towns, and Scituate and Taunton in Plymouth Colony also numbered substantial numbers of professional shipwrights in their midst throughout the seventeenth century.[58]

But Boston always remained predominant. A French visitor to the town in 1687 found that "there are here craftsmen of every kind, and particularly carpenters for the building of ships." In 1724, master shipwrights of the River Thames in London petitioned the Board of Trade for restrictions on American shipbuilding, claiming in support of their request that half of Britain's shipwrights had left for the colonies since 1710, a large percentage of them bound for the Massachusetts Bay capital. Occupational statistics for Boston during the 1750s reveal that some 80 percent of the town's adult white males were independent skilled or specialist workers, the majority with either direct or indirect ties to the shipbuilding industry.[59]

The shipwrights' work was the only genuinely labor-intensive activity in New England. In the larger context of the colonial economy, shipbuilding was the only industry in which the relatively low cost of raw materials was not decisively offset by North America's much higher labor costs.[60] Productivity rates, however, made an important difference, even in such a relatively undeveloped economic setting. By the turn of the century, New England shipwrights were able to build vessels at costs substantially lower than those achieved by shipyards anywhere else in the Anglo-American world. Estimates for the price of a ship of 200 measured tons built in 1784 suggest the substantial comparative advantage that New England shipbuilders enjoyed:

Price per ton of a ship of 200 tons

Colony	*Price range per ton*	*Mean*
New England	£3 18s.–£5 9s.	£4 13s.
New York, Philadelphia	£6 8s.–£7 19s.	£7 4s.
London	£8 8s.–£9 9s.	£8 19s.

Others estimate the price of a vessel fitted for sea during the Revolutionary era as £6 19s. per ton for New England shipyards as compared to a rate of £10 13s. per ton elsewhere in British North America. Similar rate differentials obtained throughout the eighteenth century. In 1700 New York's governor reported that, overall, Bostonians could build merchant vessels at a cost 40 percent lower than similar vessels cost in England.[61]

In addition to a clear comparative advantage, Massachusetts shipbuilders benefited from a highly democratic pool of investors. Substantial infusions of capital from London helped finance the founding and expansion of the Massachusetts fleet, and throughout the colonial period Bay Colonists remained dependent on these sources. Yet the New Englanders supplemented these resources through creative investment practices. They helped to finance shipbuilding by the same method used for other local capital improvements such as sawmills, gristmills, and ironworks—by relying on a large pool of small investors. In their analysis of the shipping register of 1697–1714, Bernard and Lotte Bailyn regard as the "most remarkable piece of information" the fact that 544 of the some 1,800 adult males in Boston were part-owners of at least one oceangoing vessel.[62] With nearly one third of the town's freemen serving as investors in one or more ships, the cross-section of the investing population was necessarily a wide one. The pool of owners would have brought delight to Captain John Smith. It included

> not only merchants but people claiming a variety of humbler occupations. No fewer than 154 of the Boston investors who stated their occupations called themselves mariners; nine claimed to be shipwrights; five, blacksmiths; five, coopers; four, shopkeepers; two, traders; two, carpenters; two, sailmakers; one, baker; and one, ropemaker. Nor was the participation restricted to the male part of the population: nine of the owners from Boston were women; four of these listed themselves as widows.[63]

A similar pattern of reliance on the capital of small investors was found in the Cape Ann fishing industry. Because the capital resources in towns like Gloucester and Marblehead were not sufficiently concentrated to allow a small number of men to assume all the risks of financing fishing voyages, as many as twenty-five investors might venture a few pounds or more for each trip to the fishing grounds. As with such locally based enterprises as sawmills, gristmills, and ironworks, the practice of spreading the risk through the use of multiple investors—owning one fourth, one eighth, one sixteenth, or one thirty-second of an enterprise—both generated sufficient capital for such endeavors to get off the ground and afforded protection for the part-owners thereafter.[64]

Small investors in New England's maritime trades also enjoyed the support of General Court policy. Recognizing that, in the absence of substantial numbers of small investors willing to venture their capital, maritime expansion would suffer, the Court took measures to protect the interests of such petty capitalists. In 1668 the Court took note of the fact that "through the blessing of God upon this jurisdiction, the navigation and maritime affaires thereof is growne to a considerable interest [and] the well management whereof is of great concernment to the publick weale." Because disputes among owners over the proportioning of ship cargoes threatened to impede the continued expanion of such traffic, the lawmakers acted to safeguard the interests of the smaller owners. Observing that "there is many times differences between owners of shipps, ketches, barques, and other vessels in setting forth their severall parts, whereby damage doth accrew to the particular concernment of owners," the magistrates took action in order to prevent "a great obstruction of trade." The Court mandated that "Where there are severall owners concerned" in "trafficque, commerce, fishing, logs, board, timber, wood, or stone [during] carriage upon salt or fresh waters, all such owners of lesser part shall be concluded for the setting forth of his part by the major part of the whole concerned."[65]

Maritime New England started to come into its own in the mid-1640s. During this time, the Bay Colonists began exporting substantial quantities of pipestaves, fish, and meat to the British West Indies and Spanish and Portuguese Wine Islands (Madeira, the Canary Islands) in Massachusetts-built and -owned vessels. Beginning in earnest in 1641, when the Boston merchants George Story and Samuel Maverick were informed of the existence of markets for wood products and foodstuffs in Spain and the Atlantic islands, the first shipments to the Azores and Canaries were quickly followed by voyages to Barbados and the Leeward Islands. Shifting abruptly from a policy of banning to a policy of promoting the export of wood products, the General Court in 1640 declared that "The order that restrained pipe staves, plank, and other wrought timber from being transported [overseas] is repealed." Along with fish and preserved meat, wood products immediately became a mainstay of the West Indies trade. In July 1644, Winthrop noted that "Two new ships, one of 250 [tons] built at Cambridge, the other of 200 [tons], built at Boston, set sail towards the Canaries laden with pipe staves, fish, etc." In 1645 alone some 20,000 bushels of wheat, worth £4,000 in Boston prices, were exported from Massachusetts.[66]

The link between the fishing, pipestaves, and shipping industries had been made painfully clear to the governor during the period before the shipbuilding boom of 1642–46. In the absence of markets among the sugarcane growers for their surplus lumber, fish, and meat, the Bay Colonists faced a grim future of economic stagnation. In the depression era of the early 1640s, the arrival of a single ship could make a critical difference to the young colony. In September 1642, Winthrop reported that "There arrived another ship with salt which was [exchanged] for pipe staves, etc., so by an unexpected providence [we] were supplied of salt to go on with our fishing, and of ships to take off our pipe staves, which lay upon men's hands." Of the six ships that departed from Massachusetts that autumn "laden with pipe staves and other commodities," four had been "built in the country this year." Thus, Winthrop declared gratefully, "God provided for us beyond expectation." Edward Johnson ascribed the prosperity that local coopers eventually achieved to their having, "by reason of trade with forraign parts, [an] abundance of work." In 1643 alone, eleven New England vessels set sail for the Sugar Islands with cargoes of lumber.[67]

New England's trade with the West Indies, Wine Islands, and the Iberian peninsula proved its economic salvation. By the mid-1640s, the shipments of pipestaves, preserved meat, grains, and fish to the West Indies had assumed the lion's share of the Bay Colony's exports. The economically symbiotic relationship between Massachusetts and Barbados, in particular, played a critical role in the initial survival—and eventual prosperity—of the two colonies. Barbadians dearly needed what the Bay Colonists had to export and were prepared to pay high prices to get it. As Governor Winthrop was informed in 1647, the Barbadians were "so intent upon planting sugar that they had rather buy foode at very deare rates than produce it by labour, soe infinite is the profitt of sugar workes. . . ." A severe drought in Barbados in 1647 made that island still more reliant on New England foodstuffs. By 1648, as Winthrop noted in his journal, Massachusetts was experiencing a scarcity of corn for domestic consumption because so much had been exported to the West Indies and the Azores. Admiral William Penn wrote from Barbados in 1655 that "What provisions they [New England] have to spare are usually sent to this island for sale, where the inhabitants give excessive rates for all they bring." It was largely to take advantage of the lucrative Sugar Island and Wine Island markets that the Bay Colonists developed a thriving export economy in wood products, fish, cattle, and horses, as well as sufficient merchant tonnage for shipping them.[68] When royalist uprisings in the Sugar Islands led Parliament in October 1650 to impose a ban on trade with Barbados, Antigua, Bermuda, and Virginia, Massachusetts petitioned the Admiralty for exemption for its commerce with these colonies.[69]

The author of *Good News from New-England* included among those who would "reape benefit" from migrating to New England "merchants skilled in commerce with forraigne nations lying near the Indies." By the 1670s, New England merchants like Boston's pious John Hull were routinely building their commercial plans around the West Indian connection. In 1677 Hull wrote to Benedict Arnold, fellow partner in a horse farm on Point Judith Neck in Narragansett Sound, to propose raising "a very choice breed of coach-horses, some for the saddle, some for the draught, [so that] in a few years [the partners] might draw off considerable numbers and ship them [to] Barbadoes, Nevis, or such parts of the Indies where they would vend." By the 1680s, over three hundred horses were being shipped out of Boston annually, worth in excess of £4,000.[70] During the remainder of the colonial period, more than 70 percent of New England's exports were shipped to the slave plantations of the British West Indies. In addition, some two thirds of the region's "invisibles" (earnings from the carrying trade) derived from West Indian commerce. More dependent on the West Indian trade than the other mainland colonies, New England sent £303,000 in exports annually to the Caribbean as late as 1768–72, comprising nearly 64 percent of the region's exports during those years.[71]

Commercial survival in the New World produced strange bedfellows and, for a Puritan society, moral dilemmas. Just as the fishing and ironmaking industries demanded a reliance on visibly "ungodly" laborers, the West Indies trade linked the very survival of the Holy Commonwealth to the growth of a slave-based plantation society. Moreover, once the codfish and mackerel export industry was established by the mid-seventeenth century, the bulk of fish exports to Southern Europe were ending up on the tables of Roman Catholics—people most Bay Colonists still regarded as minions of the

Antichrist. But in the absence of trade with the West Indies or Southern Europe, New England's economic prospects were decidedly unpromising. And for the remainder of the colonial period, the vitality of Massachusetts Bay's most lucrative exports—salted fish and seagoing vessels—would depend on the West Indian connection. During his visit to Massachusetts in 1760, the Reverend Andrew Burnaby declared categorically that "a great part of the opulence and power of America depends upon her fisheries, and her commerce with the West Indies; she cannot subsist without them." Burnaby described Massachusetts as "a rich, populous, and well-cultivated province," in large part as a consequence of its exports of "salt fish and vessels," the latter of which the Bay Colonists "build annually a great number, and send them [abroad] laden with cargoes of the former. . . ."[72]

It is this connection between the shipbuilding and fishing industries that affords the most telling example of manufactural linkage in early New England. Captain John Smith, as we recall, had declared of the Dutch that "Herring, Cod, and Ling, is that triplicate that makes [the Hollanders] wealthy and shippings multiplicities. . . ." Puritan promoter William Wood agreed that "Codfish hath been the enrichment of other nations and is likely to prove no small commodity to the planters."[73] The Reverend John White predicted that the fisheries would become the heart of the Massachusetts economy.

By 1660, these prophecies had been fulfilled. Fishermen, whether working in small coasting boats such as shallops, or from larger vessels such as ketches and barks, produced New England's most valuable export commodity outside of ships. New Englanders shipped salted first-quality cod and mackerel to Catholic Europe, while lower-quality "refuse" fish went to feed the slaves of Barbados, Jamaica, Nevis, and Antigua. A leading sector in the Bay Colony's economic development from the mid-seventeenth century onward, the fishing industry stimulated the West Indies and Newfoundland trade routes, the ship- and boatbuilding industries, and coastal and trans-Atlantic commerce generally.

Governor Winthrop took an eager personal interest in the rise of the native fishery, chronicling all major developments in his journal. In September 1639, he reported that there was "such store of exceeding large and fat mackerel upon our coast this season [bringing] a great benefit to all our plantations." One three-man boat, the governor marveled, "would take in a week ten hogsheads [of fish] which was sold at Connecticut for £3 12s. the hogshead." In September 1641 he declared, "This year men followed the fishing so well, that there was about 300,000 dry fish [6,000 quintals] sent to market."[74] This catch, which was worth some £6,750, swelled to over 500,000 four years later, with an export value of £10,000.[75] Between the years 1645 and 1675 the total output of the New England fisheries increased at an annual rate of over 5 percent, from some 12,000 to 60,000 quintals per year. By the mid-1670s there were reported to be four hundred boats and some one thousand men working the coastal fisheries between Boston and Maine.[76]

After establishing initial contacts with the Portuguese and Spanish Wine Islands in the early 1640s, the Bay Colonists progressively expanded their fish exports to Barbados and Southern Europe. By 1660, the New Englanders not only controlled their own fishery but also possessed a fleet of locally owned vessels working the trade routes of the southeastern Atlantic.[77] Moving after 1670 from a shore fishery worked by shallops to a deep-sea fishery worked by barks and ketches, and eventually sloops and schooners, New England's fisheries remained a lucrative export industry for the rest of the colonial era. So important were fish to the health of the Massachusetts economy that in November 1675, when the General Court banned the export of all foodstuffs from the commonwealth because of the threat of famine brought by King Philip's War, cod and mackerel alone were exempted.[78]

In some instances, entire settlements in the Bay Colony were given over to fishing and shipbuilding. The sparsely populated town of Medford, originally known as "Cradock's Plantation," by the beginning of the eighteenth century was one of the wealthiest communities in the colony, richer than such prominent settlements as Newbury, Ipswich, Hingham, and Weymouth. Medford boasted flourishing fishing and shipbuilding industries that were owned by one man, Matthew Cradock, among the most prominent London merchants to invest in seventeenth-century New England. Tiny Scituate, which became part of Massachusetts when Plymouth was incorporated into the commonwealth in 1692, produced 159 vessels of 7,621 total tons during the years between 1674 and 1714. Capitalized by Boston merchants, Scituate—along with Salem, Charlestown, and Boston itself—was one of the major centers of shipbuilding by 1700, and remained so until the exhaustion of the local stores of timber and iron ore drove it into decline thereafter.[79]

Fish and ships were largely responsible for keeping New England's export economy robust until the Revolution. During the years between 1675 and 1775 (allowing for major downturns during the years of war with France and Spain), the Massachusetts fishing fleets' annual catch rose from some 60,000 quintals to some 350,000 quintals.[80] These were also, not coincidentally, the years in which the shipbuilding industry expanded so dramatically. On the eve of the American Revolution, New England merchants were exporting an annual catch of fish worth in excess of £160,000 pounds sterling. Exports of fish from Massachusetts to Southern Europe alone averaged £81,500 sterling annually during 1768 to 1772.[81] Boston merchants reported in 1769 that "Four hundred Vessels are constantly employed in the Fishery, and the Annual Profits of their Labour amounted to upwards of one hundred and sixty thousand pounds Sterling."[82] By the end of the colonial period, over 10 percent of the Massachusetts labor force derived the bulk of its income from work in the fisheries. While we often think of the colonists in terms of northern farmers and southern planters, contemporaries more typically saw a threefold division. In his *Letters from a farmer in Pennsylvania* (1767–68), John Dickinson described the North American continent as "a country of planters, farmers, and fishermen. . . ."[83]

* * *

The third major element in the New England maritime triad was sawmill-produced lumber. With processed lumber the major component in ship construction and with wood products comprising over half of seventeenth-century Massachusetts' export tonnage, sawmills played a vital role in the region's process of linked development. A surprisingly high proportion of the sugar mills, slave cabins, and warehouses on Barbados, the Leeward Islands, and Jamaica were fashioned from New England lumber. Along with refuse fish for feeding the slaves and Narragansett horses for powering the sugar mills, wood products were a mainstay of the West Indian trade for the duration of the colonial period. In the year of 1671 alone, Portsmouth merchants exported some 20,000 tons of boards and pipestaves and 10,000 quintals of fish (apparently mostly to the Leeward Islands), and received in return 300 tons of wine and brandy and 2,000 tons of salt.[84]

Although the resistance of English and Dutch sawyers delayed the introduction of the sawmill in those otherwise commercially progressive nations until the end of the seventeenth century, New England (including Maine and New Hampshire) was in possession of several hundred of these mini-industrial enterprises by the 1670s. Water-powered mills represented the most technologically advanced form of mechanical power available in the seventeenth-century world. A reciprocating saw powered by a waterwheel was capable of producing between 500 and 1,000 feet of one-inch boards daily, over ten times the output of a team of hand sawyers. Sawmills operating in northern New England by 1675 are estimated to have produced between 4.5 and 9 million feet annually, with the total value of between £6,750 and £13,500 at the mill sites and double that in the West Indies.[85] We have the testimony of a millhand who worked at William Paine's sawmill in Exeter that "in the year 1650 and part of 1651 . . . there was sawed at that mill in boards and some planks about [80] thousand [board feet] for three-fourths of the mill and about 60,000 [board feet] in 1652 and 1653." The millhand also asserted that "if the mill had been furnished as it ought to have been . . . that it would have cut much more." By 1665 there were in excess of twenty sawmills in the Piscataqua region alone. In the 1670s two merchant-entrepreneurs, Edward and Elisha Hutchinson, held control of no less than nineteen sawmills on the Great Works River in New Hampshire.[86]

Timber, while never as valuable a commodity as fish, was an important element in the triangular trade between New England, the West Indies, and England. Wood products accounted for well over half the annual export tonnage from the region. Local specialization occurred relatively early in the Bay Colony's development. As we have seen, by the mid-seventeenth century, Hingham had already begun to specialize in lumbering, its residents having "much profited themselves by transporting Timber, Planke and Mast for Shipping to the Town of Boston, as also Ceder and Pine-board to supply the wants of other Townes, and also to remote parts, even as far as Barbadoes." In a visit to Hingham in the 1660s, John Josselyn found that "here is great store of Timber, deal-boards, masts for ships, white-Ceder, and fish is here to be had." Describing the linked development impact of the timber trade on the town of Gloucester, Christine Heyrman observes that "by establishing closer commercial connections with Boston, by stimulating the growth of local shipbuilding, by encouraging the conversion from joint to private land ownership, and by eliminating public constraints on private enterprise, the timber economy wrought fundamental changes in the structure of Gloucester's economic life."[87] The same could be said of towns throughout the upper Merrimack Valley, in New Hampshire, and along the coast of Maine.

Even before they left England, the Puritan leaders were planning to introduce in Massachusetts the most sophisticated mill technology available. Declaring "*Et soli deo gloria,*" John Winthrop, Jr., depicted for his father his prototype of a horizontal windmill, which he believed would "equall if not to exceed the ordinary vertical motion of the windmill sailes, both in swiftness, and force. . . ." The inventor conceived that it "may be aplied to many laborious uses as any kind of milles, Corne milles, saw milles, etc. . . ." Moreover, young Winthrop was confident that his creation would be cheaper to build than existing "saw milles, oyle milles, etc., which are not made eyther for wind or water without great cost." Once in Massachusetts, the elder Winthrop took the initiative for procuring millstones for a windmill to be built in 1634. The governor wrote to his shipmaster Thomas Graves, praying him to "bring me a pair of mill stones, peak stones, seven foot broad and of thickness answerable."[88]

Plymouth Colony waited thirteen years to establish its first gristmill and thirty-six years to build its first sawmill; Massachusetts had built functioning versions of both within four years of landfall. The General Court offered prospective entrepreneurs mill sites, land grants, grinding toll proceeds, and alewive franchises as inducements to lay out the £400 to £750 it took to build a gristmill or sawmill in early New England. In April 1634 the Court declared that Israel Stoughton "hath liberty graunted him to builde a myll, a weir, and a bridge over Naponsett Ryver, and [he] is to sell the alewyves hee takes there att 5s. the thousand."[89] The next year, deferring to the need for local control, the Court awarded investors planning to build a mill in Newbury "such previlidges of ground and tymber as is expressed in an agreement betwixte them and the towne."[90] Typical of the conditional nature of such arrangements was the General Court's grant in 1651 to wealthy merchant-entrepreneur and magistrate Samuel Symonds: "Mr Samuell Symonds, uppon his request, hath three hundred acres of land graunted him, with the timber thereupon, beyond the River Merrimacke [provided that] he or his assignes set up a saw mill within the space of seven yeares."[91] As early as 1636, Governor Winthrop could report with pride that "Another windmill was erected at Boston, and one at Charlestown and a watermill at Salem, and another at Ipswich, and another at Newbury." By the end of the 1630s, one or more mills had been constructed in Boston, Charlestown, Lynn, Watertown, Dorchester, Newbury, Ipswich, Concord, and Salem. The town of Salem alone, by the end of the 1630s, had a water-powered gristmill, a windmill, and a tidemill. Rare was the substantial seventeenth-century Bay Colony town without one or more gristmills and sawmills. Dedham was reported to have built no less than eleven mills during the seventeenth century, mostly for the purpose of processing locally produced grains and lumber for export.[92]

Although the efforts of the General Court were instrumental in establishing the Bay Colony's earliest mills, by the 1640s the responsibility for establishing local gristmills and sawmills had passed to the towns. Land grants, short-term monopolies, release of millers from militia duty, and a regulated proportion of the processed grain or lumber were the inducements towns typically offered to prospective mill developers. In 1658 merchant-entrepreneur John Prescott declared that he "would by the help of God set up a sawmill" in Lancaster. The town offered him a land grant, exemption from taxation, and rights to timber on the town commons. When the town of Springfield wanted John Pynchon to build a new sawmill, the inhabitants voted that "Captain Pynchon shall have 50 acres of Upland and 30 acres of Meddow . . . Provided that he build a Saw Mill . . . within three yeeres from this tyme." In Plymouth Colony, the town of Duxbury offered prospective mill builders land grants and protection from future competition until such time as the first gristmill could no longer meet the town's needs. Scituate and Marshfield, both rising centers of shipbuilding, voted to grant land and a £20 subsidy to those who would undertake such projects. With other towns pursuing similar strategies, sawmills, as well as gristmills, became a familiar feature of New England's material culture by the second generation of settlement.[93]

The construction of a Salem sawmill on joint partnership principles highlights many of the distinctive features of the Bay Colony's economic culture: linkage, innovative financing, contractualism, and the wide diffusion of capital investment. Since each New England sawmill cost as much as £750 to build, the need to spread both capital and risk was apparent. Shipwright Bartholomew Gedney agreed in October 1688 with

> Thomas Guld, Joshua Buffum, [and] John Nurse that they . . . do hereby enter into a Joint partnershepe in building a dam and saw mill at beaver dam nere to mr. Clarke's farm upon that land of the said Guld, each parties to bare one quarter of the hole charge of the dam mill and Irone work and all other things necessary to the fiting and casing [for] said worke fit for service in sawing all sortes of timber as shall be brought for that end; and

> the said Johsua Buffum is to manege and carry on the billding of the mill in the behalf of the Company and John Nurse to manage and carry on the making [of] the dam [by] the last day of next october; the above said Josua Buffum and John Nurse is to manege and performe said work for the best advantage they can and give an accounte thereof to the Company, and payment [is] to be made to each partner or quarter partner of what it amounts unto. . . .[94]

Thomas Gould was also a major investor in the consortium of eight investors who owned the ironworks run by Henry Leonard in Rowley village during the early 1670s. At the Rowley works, ship anchors were among the most highly demanded products of the Leonards' forge. These supplied the Salem shipyards that were the only real rival to Boston in the world of Massachusetts shipbuilding. As we have seen, Salem shipyards produced no less than thirty-two ketches (between 30 and 50 tons) in the years from 1697 to 1702. Although Salem and its environs during the late seventeenth century are more typically associated with the atavistic witchcraft hysteria, the region—like maritime New England generally—had its feet firmly planted in the world of rationality, innovation, and capitalist development.

Tax legislation passed by the Massachusetts General Court in 1647 suggests how quickly the lineaments of the maritime economy emerged in the Bay Colony. Few diagnostics are more revealing than the way in which a given society taxes its productive resources. The list of productive enterprises taxed during Massachusetts' second decade is a fascinating one. In addition to ratable "polls" and real estate, the General Court authorized taxation on the income of "mils, ships and all smaller vesels, marchantable goods, cranes, wharfes, and all sorts of cattell and all other visible estates."[95] Although true economic development in Massachusetts, based on the industrialization of cotton-textile and machine-tool manufacture, would await the nineteenth century, its origins may be located in Puritan New England—in the diversified and symbiotically linked human and material infrastructure of the maritime economy.

* * *

Crèvecoeur believed that North America's prosperity was a product of institutions as much as its natural resources. There are reasons to think that he was right.[96] It was the locally based nature of New England institutions—and indeed, the Bay Colony's federally organized government generally—that allowed for a multiplier effect from public policy initiatives. Most seventeenth-century towns attempted to provide their residents with basic services—grazing fields, gristmills, sawmills, smithies, and sometimes shipyards and tanneries. Although the overall institutional structure of the Bay Colony was set by General Court legislation, along with the larger corpus of English common law, all of these acts were implemented by selectmen and town meetings at the local level. Moreover, the early strength of bicameral, representative government in Massachusetts meant that the towns' Deputies articulated local views at the May and October meetings of the General Court.[97]

Much of what was distinctive about the Bay Colony's civic ecology derives from the nature of the New England township. The town was among the more intentionally innovative structures created by the Massachusetts settlers. It combined elements of the English borough, parish, and feudal manor. Virtually all New England men and women, whether land proprietors or not, possessed a stake in their local government, and conducted their economic affairs and political deliberations accordingly. The towns, moreover, had the resources—particularly with respect to land—to stimulate economic development. In England the basic unit of local government, the ecclesiastical parish, typically averaged about five square miles; New England towns such as Dedham during the seventeenth century, on the other hand, could include as many as 200 square miles. The early settlers of Windsor, Connecticut, claimed almost 600 square miles, an area that eventually would contain six towns. By 1640, Windsor's inhabitants had distributed among themselves over

16,000 acres. Even by the 1760s, the average Massachusetts town included 45 square miles. And it was the land grants from such holdings that proved to be the biggest spurs to development.[98]

Alexis de Tocqueville, in commenting on the potent but carefully circumscribed nature of local civic power in the American North during the 1830s, used the New England township as his leading example. Waxing enthusiastic, he pointed to the federal dimension of the region's government—one that had existed since the Puritan era: "The township of New England possesses two advantages which strongly excite the interest of mankind—namely, independence and authority. Its sphere is limited, indeed; but within that sphere, its action is unrestrained. This independence alone gives it a real importance, which its extent and population would not insure." In New England, Tocqueville declared, "political life had its origin in the townships; and it may almost be said that each of them originally formed an independent nation."[99]

Conclusion

Massachusetts succeeded by freeing its economy of anachronistic restraints and by recognizing the link between land ownership and productive labor. Labor, a painful necessity in the Old World, became a source of increased productivity in this portion of the New.[1] In contrast to the patrimonial mercantilism that prevailed in early Virginia, Bermuda, and in the Puritan experiment on Providence Island (where tenancy, not freehold tenure, had prevailed), the Bay Colonists recognized that successful New World colonization would necessitate a shift from paternalism to reciprocal obligations.[2] Instead of deferring to the will of kings, nobles, and prelates, local initiative and responsibility were to be the hallmarks of the covenant-based society of the Bay Colony. To a striking degree by early modern standards, social, political, and religious networks were organized horizontally, not hierarchically. New England's communally based individualism—grounded in the concept of the grace-bearing individual—produced the fundamental basis of civil society.[3]

New England also succeeded because its leaders and people used their newfound autonomy and freedom to pursue "honest gaine" instead of "present profit." The Protestant ethic and the culture of discipline fostered an ethos of production—with high value given to work, enterprise, sacrifice, and deferred gratification.[4] Capitalism, in the early modern period no less than the present, required countervailing institutions if its destructive capacities were to be kept in check. It required a measure of local control over economic policy and resources—what is now called "devolution of control." It demanded civic protection against what Puritans decried as "cruelty and unmercifulness to the poor."[5] It required not only the preservation of individual rights, contracts, and due process of law but also a vibrant civil society capable of promoting social justice and mutual responsibility in the face of capitalism's tendency to undermine both. Most important, for our purposes, was the fact that civil society fostered the creation of social capital—networks, norms, and the trust that facilitates mutual cooperation.

Social capital, along with physical capital and human capital (tools and training), increases a society's capacity for economic development and shared prosperity. The link between a society's store of social capital and its rate of economic prosperity is a formidable one (not least because social capital, unlike physical capital, is a resource that expands rather than contracts from use). According to Robert D. Putnam: "social capital is coming to be seen as a vital ingredient in economic development around the world. Scores of studies of rural development have shown that a vigorous network of indigenous grassroots asociations can be as essential to growth as physical investment, appropriate technology, or (that nostrum of neoclassical economics) 'getting prices right.' " In his study of economic development in the twenty new regional governments established in Italy in 1970, Putnam found that the best predictor of economic development "is one that Alexis de Tocqueville might have expected. Strong traditions of civic engagement—voter turnout, newspaper readership, membership in choral societies and literary circles, Lions Clubs, and soccer clubs—are the hallmarks of a successful region."[6] Social capital fosters, in the words of a recent papal encyclical, "the ability to perceive the needs of others and to satisfy them."[7] Such an ability rests—the example of Puritan New England suggests—on a connection between capitalism, community, and civil society.

The Puritan covenant provided an essential counterweight to capitalist development, a measure of social solidarity and trust.[8] The federal covenant fostered what became New England's considerable store of social capital. For colonial New England, the civic ideals of social justice and mutual responsibility were provided by Puritan covenantalism, by the mandate that some abridge themselves of their superfluities in order to provide for the necessities of others. The belief that surplus wealth should be put to socially benevolent purposes—shared with the community and the church—helped restrain the Protestant ethic from turning into the spirit of capitalism. Mothers, fathers, preachers, and civil leaders alike took responsibility for inculcating covenantal ethics in succeeding generations of young New Englanders. The Reverend John Preston enjoined the faithful to "exercise the duties of our particular callings, not for our own good, but for the good of others." Profit seeking was fine—indeed, it was morally imperative—so long as it was grounded in communal necessity. Sin entered not through acquisitiveness but through *self-regarding* acquisitiveness. Preston explicitly condemned those who "have such an eye to their own profit, and not to the profit of others, whom they deal with, that they have such an eye to their own credit, and advantage, and not to others' good."[9] It was by such means that Puritanism fostered the two cultural traits shared by most successful capitalist countries: deferred gratification and a link between individual and collective well-being. The covenant held out a vision of social solidarity that was expressed in the gathered church. The economic dynamism that was produced by the Protestant ethic was to be channeled and restrained by the ethical obligation to succor one's neighbors and the less fortunate.

Puritan communities incorporated the distinction Tocqueville later made between "self-interest properly understood"—which acknowledged the need for collective action and restraint—and raw individualism. From his vantage point in the 1830s, Tocqueville feared that the current tendencies would eventually result in the dissolution of the ties of civil society in America. In contrasting age-old selfishness to the new American creation of individualism ("a mature and calm feeling which disposes each member of the community to sever himself from the mass of his fellows"), Tocqueville declared,

> Selfishness blights the germ of all virtue: individualism, at first, only saps the virtues of public life; but, in the long run, it attacks and destroys all others, and is at length absorbed in downright selfishness. Selfishness is a vice as old as the world, which does not belong to one form of society more than another: [but] individualism is of democratic origin, and threatens to spread in the same ratio as the equality of condition.[10]

In addition to their covenant-based civic ecology, New Englanders succeeded economically because of their self-created myth as a Covenant People. Their peculiar confessionally based experience simultaneously bound New Englanders together and set them apart from the larger mainstream of British North America. Their doctrine of Providence connected outward success with inward conviction of being right with God. As with typology, it served to establish a series of correspondences between sacred history and daily events.[11] The belief that they were acting according to providential design, revealed in the books of Daniel and Revelation, gave New Englanders their identity and much of their sense of purpose. The Bay Colonists' distinctive economic culture—what Max Weber called the Protestant ethic—is incomprehensible unless grounded in such providentialism.

In their belief that God had a plan for His saints, to be acted out according to the dictates of both sacred and secular time, New England's men and women took measures that created a distinctive work culture. In their determination to glorify an inscrutable God by all their actions, Puritans helped usher in the new world of striving behavior and enterprise. In part because they refused to accept the distinction between everyday labor and meritorious practices, between daily labor and "good works," New Englanders ended up creating a work regime that was truly historically aberrant. Whereas those free settlers who labored in the more Arminian-inclined Chesapeake colonies were driven primarily by the labor-intensive imperatives of tobacco cultivation, Bay Colonists responded to the powerful cultural imperative to "improve every bright and shining moment." Puritanism fostered economic development by promoting time methodization, striving behavior, and literacy; through its civic and communal institutions and shared sense of identity, it served to mitigate some of the socially destructive consequences of this development.

The Congregational clergy's sermons have too often been interpreted in descriptive rather than typologic terms, yet they bore witness to a social process that was something quite different from secularization.[12] While it is going too far to say, as some have, that New England was founded in order that it might decline, the Puritans' special devotion to the first half of the Book of Jeremiah and to the typology of the Sinai Covenant made self-accusation the central trope of New England literature. As far back as the eighth century B.C., Old Testament prophets had railed against the hegemony of commercial values, a sign both of the potency of such values in Israelite society and the moral leaders' conviction of the need to set their face against them. So too in Puritan New England—and for the same reasons. The same religious precepts and civil institutions that systematized and amplified the virtues likely to produce commercial success checked their free play on behalf of the common good. Clergymen never tired of reminding their charges that selfishness and self-indulgence, like hard dealing and poor workmanship, were not reconcilable with a properly formed Christian conscience.[13] If, as Henry Adams later opined, "resistance to something" is the defining New England trait, its sources likely lie in the early colonists' tortured attempts to prevent the Protestant ethic from turning into the spirit of capitalism.

It was the conviction that they were armed with a covenant with God to build a "New Sion," and that this covenant would be abrogated through "backsliding," that helped fuel the potent Puritan work ethic. If the New England jeremiad can indeed be seen as a mode of public exhortation designed to "join social criticism to spiritual renewal, public to private identity," then the Puritan clergy's continuous admonitions to their congregations to return to the purported moral rectitude of the founding generation both reaffirmed civic identity and reanimated the colonists' work ethic.[14] It was by such means that what would become the enduring myth of New England's origins and decline was both fashioned and perpetuated. As Perry Miller observed, only "by remaining ascetic in the midst of prosperity" could the saints "abide their covenant."[15] No other British colony was so self-consciously engaged in the ongoing task of fashioning and refashioning what Abraham Lincoln—himself a descendant of Puritans—would later describe as the "mystic chords of memory." Prominent among these chords was the trope of self-accusation. In no other colony could the most industrious women and men, who throughout their lifetimes had striven to "improve [their] Time and Talents for God's glory," daily lacerate themselves with accusations of "selfishness, sensuality, unbeleef, inordinate love to creatures, etc." and the overwhelming conviction that they were—"and ever have been"—the most "unproffitable" of the Lord's servants.[16]

Notes

Introduction

1. Colonies employing tenancy or communal ownership, such as Providence Island and Virginia and Plymouth in the early years, failed largely because they severed the link between hard work and landowning prospects. See Karen Ordahl Kupperman, "Errand to the Indies: Puritan Colonization from Providence Island Through the Western Design," *William and Mary Quarterly,* 3d Ser., 45 (1988), 80; *idem., Providence Island, 1630–1641: The Other Puritan Colony* (Cambridge, Engl., 1993).
2. Although the explicit focus of this book is on Massachusetts Bay Colony during the period of the first provincial charter (1630–86), many of its general findings apply to the orthodox Puritan colonies of Connecticut and New Haven as well, and—to a lesser degree—Plymouth and New Hampshire. New Haven was absorbed by Connecticut in 1662; Plymouth became part of Massachusetts in 1691.
3. John J. McCusker and Russell R. Menard, *The Economy of British America, 1607–1789* (Chapel Hill, 1985), 92.
4. In *The Philosophy of Rights* (1821), G. W. F. Hegel declared that "The creation of civil society is the achievement of the modern world."
5. See Adam B. Seligman, *The Idea of Civil Society* (New York, 1992), 1–91; John Keane, "Despotism and Democracy: The Origins and Development of the Distinction Between Civil Society and the State, 1750–1850," in Keane, ed., *Civil Society and the State: New European Perspectives*

(London, 1988), 35–71; Michael Walzer, "The Idea of Civil Society," *Dissent* (Spring 1991), 293; and Edward Shils, "The Virtue of Civil Society," *Government and Opposition,* 26 (1991), 3–4. In contemporary parlance, civil society is the sphere animated by the principle of subsidiarity—the belief that social tasks should be performed in the smallest available unit, from the family through the church, town government, to the central state. Shelley G. Burtt, *Virtue Transformed: Political Argument in England, 1688–1740* (New York, 1992), chap. 1; Allan Carlson, "Forward to the Past: Rebuilding Family Life in Post-Socialist Sweden," *The Family in America,* 6 (1992), 4; Michael Novak, *The Catholic Ethic and the Spirit of Capitalism* (New York, 1993), 80–81, 260.

6. Harry S. Stout, *The New England Soul: Preaching and Religious Culture in Colonial New England* (New York, 1986), 22; John Demos, *A Little Commonwealth: Family Life in Plymouth Colony* (New York, 1970), 61–125; Edmund S. Morgan, *The Puritan Family: Religion and Domestic Relations in Seventeenth-Century New England* (New York, 1966, [orig. 1944]), 133–160.
7. John Cotton, *A Briefe Exposition . . . upon the Whole Book of Ecclesiastes* (London, 1654), 81.
8. Morgan, *The Puritan Family,* 7; Carole Pateman, "The Fraternal Social Contract," in Keane, ed., *Civil Society and the State,* 102–103. I derive the term "culture of discipline" from William Hunt, *The Puritan Moment: The Coming of Revolution in an English County* (Cambridge, Mass., 1983), 79–84, 198.
9. Novak, *Catholic Ethic,* xiv.
10. Charles H. Reynolds and Ralph V. Norman, eds., *Community in America: The Challenge of "Habits of the Heart"* (Berkeley, 1988), 43. I am grateful to Professor Karen Ordahl Kupperman for her assistance in helping me clarify these relationships.
11. Shepard quoted in Stout, *New England Soul,* 21–22.
12. Emile Durkheim, "The Dualism of Human Nature and Its Social Condition," in Robert Bellah, ed., *Emile Durkheim on Morality and Society* (Chicago, 1973), 149–168; Seligman, *Idea of Civil Society,* 29.
13. Robert D. Putnam, *Making Democracy Work: Civic Traditions in Modern Italy* (Princeton, 1993), 83–120, 163–185; Putnam, "The Prosperous Community: Social Capital and Public Life," *The American Prospect,* 13 (1993), 35–36.
14. John Winthrop, "A Modell Of Christian Charity" (1630), in Samuel Eliot Morison, et al., eds., *The Winthrop Papers, 1498–1654,* 6 vols. to date (Boston 1927–92), 2:282–295, quotation at 295; Scott Michaelsen, "John Winthrop's 'Modell' Covenant and the Company Way," *Early American Literature,* 27 (1992), 91–92.
15. John White, *The Planter's Plea* (1630), in *Massachusetts Historical Society Proceedings,* 62 (1929), 391. At the time of the Massachusetts colonization, White was Rector of the Church of the Holy Trinity in Dorchester, England.
16. [Edward] *Johnson's Wonder-Working Providence, 1628–1651* (1654), J. Franklin Jameson, ed. (New York, 1910; cited hereafter as *Johnson's Wonder-Working Providence), 21; Lord Saye and Sele to John Winthrop, 9 July 1640, Winthrop Papers,* 4:265; Anonymous letter, 1637, in Everett Emerson, ed., *Letters from New England: The Massachusetts Bay Colony, 1629–1638* (Amherst, Mass., 1976), 214–215; Roger Williams to John

Winthrop, Jr., 15 February 1654, *Massachusetts Historical Society Collections,* 4th Ser., 6 (1863), 291 (Cromwell quotation).

17. The quotations are from James A. Henretta and Gary B. Nash: James A. Henretta, *The Origins of American Capitalism: Collected Essays* (Boston, 1991), 58; and Nash, "Social Development," in Jack P. Greene and J. R. Pole, eds., *Colonial British America: Essays in the New History of the Early Modern Era* (Baltimore, 1984), 236. In general, scholarship since the 1970s has tended toward a somewhat stereotypical portrayal of early New England as an economic and agricultural wasteland. The recent work of Virginia Anderson, Christine Heyrman, Daniel Vickers, and John Frederick Martin has offered a more market-oriented view of early New England. Still, one of the most impressive of the new generation of town histories, Richard I. Melvoin's study of colonial Deerfield, includes references to "the late medieval, subsistence-farming world of seventeenth-century New England,"—Melvoin, *New England Outpost: War and Society in Colonial Deerfield* (New York, 1989), 148. For the more market-oriented interpretations, see Virginia D. Anderson, *New England's Generation: The Great Migration and the Formation of Society and Culture in the Seventeenth Century* (Cambridge, Engl., 1991); Christine Leigh Heyrman, *Commerce and Culture: The Maritime Communities of Colonial Massachusetts, 1690–1750* (New York, 1984); Daniel Vickers, *Farmers and Fishermen: Two Centuries of Work in Essex County, Massachusetts, 1630–1850* (Chapel Hill, 1994); John Frederick Martin, *Profits in the Wilderness: Entrepreneurship and the Founding of New England Towns in the Seventeenth Century* (Chapel Hill, 1991); and Stephen Innes, *Labor in a New Land: Economy and Society in Seventeenth-Century Springfield* (Princeton, 1983).
18. Darrett B. Rutman, "Governor Winthrop's Garden Crop: The Significance of Agriculture in the Early Commerce of Massachusetts Bay," *William and Mary Quarterly,* 3d Ser., 20 (1963), 396–415; Rutman, *Small Worlds, Large Questions: Explorations in Early American Social History, 1600–1850* (Charlottesville, Va., 1994), 287–304.
19. Putnam, "The Prosperous Community," 36.
20. Winthrop, "Modell of Christian Charity," *Winthrop Papers,* 2: 283.
21. Max Weber, *The Protestant Ethic and the Spirit of Capitalism,* Talcott Parsons, trans. (New York, 1958; cited hereafter as *Protestant Ethic*), 60; Adam Smith, *Wealth of Nations,* Andrew Skinner, ed. (Middlesex, Engl., 1980; cited hereafter as *Wealth of Nations*), 120; italics added.
22. Ralph Waldo Emerson, "Nature," in Stephen Whicher, ed., *Selections from Ralph Waldo Emerson* (Boston, 1957), 26; Faulkner quoted in Studs Terkel, *Working* (New York, 1972), xi; Richard Lignon, *A True and Exact History of the Island of Barbadoes* (London, 1673), 43–47. In economists' parlance, cultural attributes are known as the "residual"—that part of growth not accounted for by such conventional categories as capital, labor, resources, and the like. But such a humble term should not imply a lack of potency. The developmental economist Evsey Domar discovered the residual as recently as the 1950s after realizing that conventional factors did not explain the dramatically divergent growth rates among non-Western countries. As David Landes has pointed out, still more surprising (even astonishing) was "the size of the unexplained category: on the basis of statistics drawn from national accounts (in itself a new branch of economics), *the residual appeared to represent half or*

more of the growth of advanced economies in the modern period." David Landes, "Rich Country, Poor Country," *The New Republic* (20 November 1989), 25; italics added. See also Evsey D. Domar, et al., "Economic Growth and Productivity in the United States, Canada, United Kingdom, Germany and Japan in the Post-war Period," *Review of Economics and Statistics,* 46 (1964), 33–40; Evsey D. Domar, *Capitalism, Socialism, and Serfdom* (Cambridge, Engl., 1989), 49–50, 54–69, 105–106; and Albert O. Hirschman, *The Strategy of Economic Development* (New Haven, 1958), 119–120.

23. Alexis de Tocqueville, *Democracy in America,* Phillips Bradley, ed., 2 vols. (New York, 1945; cited hereafter as *Democracy in America*), 1:377; Roger Boesche, "Why Did Tocqueville Fear Abundance? Or the Tension Between Commerce and Citizenship," *History of European Ideas,* 9 (1988), 25–45. Work always possesses a cultural dimension. For modern Spaniards, as Jenny Mazur points out, "work maintains life rather than gives meaning to it, and whenever possible they devote time and energy to leisure, not work." Mazur emphasizes that work is never viewed neutrally, but "is seen as joyous, degrading, boring, or meritorious, depending on the culture's ideology of work." She underscores the difficulty of defining an analytical notion of work as either paid labor, subsistence activity, or production without making reference to cultural notions. Mazur, "Women's Work in Rural Andalusia," *Ethnology,* 23 (1984), 25.

    The increased attention to ethnicity, gender, community, and household by many recent scholars has led to a renewed interest in the cultural dimensions of economic behavior. One such approach involves a reformulation of market theory to take account of what is termed "social economics," a partial analogue to the "social capital" discussed above. Social economics is based on a recognition that production is shaped by cultural factors—institutions and values—growing out of particular historical conjunctures. Undergirding these new approaches is the assumption central to my book: that economic analysis has something to contribute to substantive ethics in the world in which we live. Patrick Joyce, "The Historical Meanings of Work," in Joyce, ed., *The Historical Meanings of Work* (Cambridge, Engl., 1987), 3; Jeanne Boydston, *Home and Work: Housework, Wages, and the Ideology of Labor in the Early Republic* (New York, 1990), 120–141; Amartya Sen, "Individual Freedom as a Social Commitment," *New York Review of Books* (14 June 1990), 49. See also George E. Marcus and Michael M. J. Fischer, *Anthropology as Cultural Critique: An Experimental Moment in the Human Sciences* (Chicago, 1986), 77–110; Barbara Karsky and Elise Marienstras, eds., *Travail et Loisir dans les Sociétés Pré-Industrielles* (Nancy, France, 1991); Carol Smith, "Commodity Economies," *Peasant Studies,* 11 (1984), 60; and Maurice Godelier, "Work and Its Representations: A Research Proposal," *History Workshop,* 10 (1980), 164–174.

24. This is John Keane's gloss on Hegel. "Despotism and Democracy," 50–51.

25. Stephen Foster, *Their Solitary Way: The Puritan Social Ethic in the First Century of Settlement in New England* (New Haven, 1971), 99. The literature on the Weber thesis is mammoth. Among the works most useful to me were S. N. Eisenstadt, ed., *The Protestant Ethic and Modernization: A Comparative View* (New York, 1968); Wilhelm Hennis, *Max Weber: Essays in Reconstruction,* Keith Tribe, trans. (London, 1988), especially 21–61;

M. J. Kitch, *Capitalism and the Reformation* (London, 1967); Gordon Marshall, *In Search of the Spirit of Capitalism: An Essay on Max Weber's Protestant Ethic Thesis* (New York, 1982); Gordon Marshall, *Presbyteries and Profits: Calvinism and the Development of Capitalism in Scotland, 1560–1707* (Oxford, 1980); Randall Collins, "Weber's Last Theory of Capitalism: A Systematization," *American Sociological Review,* 45 (1980), 925–942; Daniel Chirot, "The Rise of the West," *American Sociological Review,* 50 (1985), 181–195; Novak, *Catholic Ethic,* 1–9; and Rex A. Lucas, "A Specification of the Weber Thesis: Plymouth Colony," *History and Theory,* 10 (1971), 318–346. I am indebted to Professor Virginia DeJohn Anderson for her help in formulating these issues.

26. Perry Miller, *The New England Mind: From Colony to Province* (Boston, 1961 [orig. 1953]), 52, 41.
27. Bernard Bailyn, *The New England Merchants in the Seventeenth Century* (New York, 1964 [orig. 1955]), 19–23; Adam Seligman, "Inner-worldly Individualism and the Institutionalization of Puritanism in Late Seventeenth-Century New England," *British Journal of Sociology,* 41 (1990), 538.
28. Foster, *Their Solitary Way,* 108.
29. Amanda Porterfield, *Female Piety in Puritan New England: The Emergence of Religious Humanism* (New York, 1992), 3; Rutman, *Small Worlds,* 188–208.
30. Quoted in Charles H. and Katherine George, *The Protestant Mind of the English Reformation, 1570–1640* (Princeton, 1961), 132–133.
31. Stout, *New England Soul,* 312–316; Stephen Carl Arch, *Authorizing the Past: The Rhetoric of History in Seventeenth-Century New England,* (Dekalb, Ill., 1994).
32. "Modell of Christian Charity," *Winthrop Papers,* 2:295.
33. John P. Diggins, "Comrades and Citizens: New Mythologies in American Historiography," *American Historical Review,* 90 (1985), 623.
34. Miller, *New England Mind,* 40–41.
35. Last will and testament of a seventeenth-century Virginian, quoted in Rutman, *Small Worlds,* 189.
36. David D. Hall, "On Common Ground: The Coherence of American Puritan Studies," *William and Mary Quarterly,* 3d Ser., 44 (1987), 198–199; John M. Murrin, personal communication; Edmund S. Morgan, *American Slavery-American Freedom: The Ordeal of Colonial Virginia* (New York, 1975), 295–296; Samuel Eliot Morison, *Builders of the Bay Colony* (Boston, 1958 [orig. 1930]), 166.
37. James Deetz, *Flowerdew Hundred: The Archaeology of a Virginia Plantation, 1619–1864* (Charlottesville, Va., 1993), 36. In contrast to the New England practice of building framed houses on a stone (or brick) foundation, in Virginia the more impermanent "earthfast" (post-in-ground) houses were constructed well into the eighteenth century, considerably after the end of the tobacco boom in the 1660s. According to James Deetz, "Recent reassessments of surviving seventeenth-century buildings in Virginia and Maryland leave us with but a scant half dozen in the entire Chesapeake, and these mostly date to the very end of the century. Only one is a hole-set structure. By contrast, New England can boast seventy-one buildings surviving from the same period, with ten predating 1660. Here archaeology has produced the critical evidence to account in part for the difference. The basic reason is quite simple; in the Chesapeake, earthfast buildings were almost universal; they were

employed even by the wealthiest people in the region." Deetz points to the labor-intensive nature of tobacco cultivation as the main explanation for the contrast between Chesapeake and New England building techniques. Earthfast construction, he writes, "not only makes sense in terms of spending priorities in a situation where most investment must be committed to raising tobacco; it also provides the assurance that one's equipment will be maintained without any significant cash outlay for the service." *Ibid.,* 52, 55. For the pioneering work on this issue, see Cary Carson, et al., "Impermanent Architecture in the Southern American Colonies," *Winterthur Portfolio,* 16 (1981), 135–196.

38. The Rev. Francis Higginson to his friends at Leicester, July 1629, in Emerson, ed., *Letters from New England,* 27.
39. J. T. Main, in "Forum: Toward a History of the Standard of Living in British North America," *William and Mary Quarterly,* 3d Ser., 45 (1988), 116–170, quotation at 161.
40. John M. Murrin, "The Irrelevance and Relevance of Colonial New England," *Reviews in American History,* 18 (1990), 181; Stout, *New England Soul,* 3.
41. Darrett B. Rutman, *American Puritanism* (New York, 1977 [orig. 1970]), 49–51.
42. Stout, *New England Soul,* 57.
43. *Johnson's Wonder-Working Providence,* 247; Rutman, "Governor Winthrop's Garden Crop." 406.
44. *Johnson's Wonder-Working Providence,* 246–247, 209; Anderson, *New England's Generation,* 203.
45. *Johnson's Wonder-Working Providence,* 179.
46. *Johnson's Wonder-Working Providence,* 247.
47. Winthrop quoted in Percy Wells Bidwell and John I. Falconer, *History of Agriculture in the Northern United States, 1620–1860* (Washington, D.C., 1925), 43.
48. Samuel Maverick, "A Brief Description of New England and the Severall Townes therein, together with the Present Government thereof," in *Massachusetts Historical Society Proceedings,* 2d Ser., 1 (1884–85), 247; K. G. Davies, *The North Atlantic World in the Seventeenth Century* (Minneapolis, 1974), 165–166.
49. Randolph quoted in Bidwell and Falconer, *History of Agriculture,* 42.
50. Josiah Child, *A New Discourse of Trade* (London, 1693), 207, repr. in *Sir Josiah Child: Selected Works, 1668–1697* (Farnborough, Engl., 1968).
51. Andros quoted in Curtis P. Nettels, *The Money Supply in the American Colonies Before 1720* (Madison, 1934), 99–100.
52. David Richardson, "Slavery, Trade, and Economic Growth in Eighteenth-Century New England," in Barbara L. Solow, ed., *Slavery and the Rise of the Atlantic System* (Cambridge, Engl., 1991), 244.
53. Heyrman, *Commerce and Culture,* 52.
54. Gloria L. and Jackson T. Main, "Economic Growth and the Standard of Living in Southern New England, 1640–1774," *Journal of Economic History,* 48 (1988), 37. As the Mains point out, "Many of Connecticut's exports went through New York, losing their identity, and swelling the statistics of this middle colony at the expense of New England's and obscuring the extent of Connecticut's economic prosperity." *Ibid.,* 37n.
55. F. R. Harris, *The Life of Edward Mountagu, K.G. First Earl of Sandwich, 1625–1672,* 2 vols. (London, 1912), vol. 2, Appendix K.
56. T. L. Anderson, *The Economic Growth of Seventeenth-Century New England*

(New York, 1975); W. I. Davisson, "Essex County Wealth Trends: Wealth and Economic Growth in 17th Century Massachusetts," *Essex Institute Historical Collections,* 103 (1967), 291–342; Richardson, "Slavery, Trade, and Economic Growth in Eighteenth-Century New England," in Solow, ed., *Slavery and the Rise of the Atlantic System,* 238–239; T. L. Anderson, "Economic Growth in Colonial New England: 'Statistical Renaissance,' " *Journal of Economic History,* 39 (1979), 243–258. Marc Engal estimates that, for the thirteen continental colonies as a whole during the period 1720–75, the rate of growth in per capita income was as low as 0.5 percent. "The Economic Development of the Thirteen Continental Colonies, 1720 to 1775," *William and Mary Quarterly,* 3d Ser., 32 (1975), 191–222. The most persuasive account of the development of the Massachusetts economy during the century after 1750 is found in Winifred Barr Rothenberg, *From Market-Places to a Market Economy: The Transformation of Rural Massachusetts, 1750–1850* (Chicago, 1992), 214–240.

57. Gerald F. Moran and Maris A. Vinovskis, *Religion, Family, and the Life Course: Explorations in the Social History of Early America* (Ann Arbor, 1992), 1.
58. Russell R. Menard, "Immigrants and Their Increase: The Process of Population Growth in Early Colonial Maryland," in Aubrey C. Land, Lois Green Carr, and Edward C. Papenfuse, eds., *Law, Society, and Politics in Early Maryland* (Baltimore, 1977), 88–110; Lois G. Carr and Lorena S. Walsh, "The Planter's Wife: The Experience of White Women in Seventeenth-Century Maryland," *William and Mary Quarterly,* 3d Ser., 34 (1977), 542.
59. James Axtell, *Beyond 1492: Encounters in Colonial North America* (New York, 1992), 227–228; R. C. Simmons, *The American Colonies: From Settlement to Independence* (New York, 1976), 24, 175, 178.
60. Axtell, *Beyond 1492,* 227–228; Jim Potter, "Demographic Development and Family Structure," in Greene and Pole, eds., *Colonial British America,* 123–156.
61. Potter, "Demographic Development," 148 (quotation). Philip Greven calculates a life expectancy mean in seventeenth-century Andover at 71.8 years for the thirty men who settled in the town before 1660; the average age of 138 second-generation men at the time of their deaths was 65.2 years. The average age at death for 66 second-generation women was 64.0. The first-generation Andover families produced 8.5 children each, of which 7.2 are known to have reached the age of 21. Greven, "Family Structure in Seventeenth-Century Andover, Massachusetts," *William and Mary Quarterly,* 3d Ser., 23 (1966), 234–256. Robert Blair St. George finds the same patterns among craftsmen in the woodworking trades during the seventeenth century that Greven discovered among Andover's farmers. First-generation woodworkers had a mean life expectancy of 69.8 years, second-generation workers a mean of 62.0 years. As Gary Nash points out, "New Englanders in the second half of the seventeenth century were mostly the children and grandchildren of healthy, fertile founding immigrants; in the same period Marylanders and Virginians were mostly newly arrived immigrants replacing the sickly and infertile settlers of earlier years." St. George, "Fathers, Sons, and Identity: Woodworking Artisans in Southeastern New England, 1620–1700," in Ian M. G. Quimby, ed., *The Craftsman in Early America* (New York, 1984), 98–100; Nash, "Social

Development," in Greene and Pole, eds., *Colonial British America,* 243–244.

For New Englanders' diet, see Sarah F. McMahon, "Provisions Laid Up for the Family: Toward a History of Diet in New England, 1650–1850," *Historical Methods,* 14 (1981), 4–21; McMahon, "A Comfortable Subsistence: The Changing Composition of Diet in Rural New England, 1620–1840," *William and Mary Quarterly,* 3d Ser., 42 (1985), 26–65.

62. Rutman, *Small Worlds,* 193.
63. Lois Green Carr, Russell R. Menard, and Lorena S. Walsh, *Robert Cole's World: Agriculture and Society in Early Maryland* (Chapel Hill, 1991), xviii, 17–18; Menard, "Immigrants and Their Increase," 95; Carr and Walsh, "The Planter's Wife," 542.
64. Rutman, *Small Worlds,* 192–195.
65. Potter, "Demographic Development," 134–136; Murrin, "Relevance of New England," 181.
66. Jackson T. Main, *Society and Economy in Colonial Connecticut* (Princeton, 1985), 68–69, 233–234; Eric G. Nellis, "Work and Social Stability in Pre-Revolutionary Massachusetts," *Canadian Historical Association Historical Papers* (1981), 85; Main and Main, "Standard of Living in Southern New England," 27–46, especially 35; Lois Green Carr and Lorena S. Walsh, "The Standard of Living in the Colonial Chesapeake," *William and Mary Quarterly,* 3d Ser., 45 (1988), 135–159; Carole Shammas, *The Pre-Industrial Consumer in England and America* (New York, 1990).
67. Murrin, "Relevance of New England," 183.
68. Richard R. Johnson, *Adjustment to Empire: The New England Colonies, 1675–1715* (New Brunswick, N.J., 1981), 26.
69. Miller, *New England Mind,* 49.
70. Foster, *Their Solitary Way,* 103; Isaac Kramnick, *Republicanism and Bourgeois Radicalism: Political Ideology in Late Eighteenth-Century England and America* (Ithaca, N.Y., 1990), 214. I am grateful to L. Bruce Coffey, Jr., for his assistance in these formulations.
71. Cotton Mather, *Magnalia Christi Americana,* 2 vols. (Boston, 1853), 1:63; Wesley quoted in Gertrude Himmelfarb, *The Idea of Poverty: England in the Early Industrial Age* (New York, 1984), 31; John Adams to Thomas Jefferson, 21 December 1819, in Lester J. Cappon, ed., *The Adams-Jefferson Letters: The Complete Correspondence Between Thomas Jefferson and Abigail and John Adams,* 2 vols. (Chapel Hill, 1959), 2:551; Joseph Schumpeter, *Capitalism, Socialism, and Democracy* (New York, 1950), 81–86; Fred Hirsch, *Social Limits to Growth* (Cambridge, Mass., 1976), 117–118; Daniel Bell, *The Cultural Contradictions of Capitalism* (New York, 1970); Reinhold Niebuhr, *The Irony of American History* (New York, 1952).
72. Miller, *New England Mind,* 49, 40, 51.
73. *Ibid.,* 51, 40.
74. *Ibid.,* 40.
75. Nathaniel Bradstreet Schurtleff, ed., *Records of the Governor and Company of the Massachusetts Bay in New England, 1628–1686,* 5 vols. in 6 (1853–54; cited hereafter as *Mass. Recs.*), 3:287–288.
76. John Oxenbridge, *New-England's Freeman Warned and Warmed* (Cambridge, Mass., 1673), 41.
77. Gordon Wood, "Struggle Over the Puritans," *New York Review of Books* (9 November 1989), 29.

78. Benjamin Nelson, "Conscience and the Making of Early Modern Cultures: *The Protestant Ethic* Beyond Max Weber," *Social Research,* 36 (1969), 15; Theodore Bozeman, "*To Live Ancient Lives*": *The Primitivist Dimension of New England Puritanism* (Chapel Hill, 1988).
79. Seligman, "Inner-worldly Individualism," 538–539.
80. Clarke E. Cochran, "The Thin Theory of Community: The Communitarians and Their Critics," *Political Studies,* 32 (1989), 422–423.
81. Seligman, "Inner-worldly Individualism," 537–557.
82. Sacvan Bercovitch, *The American Jeremiad* (Madison, 1978), xi.
83. Dod and Cleaver quoted in Christopher Hill, "Protestantism and the Rise of Capitalism," in F. J. Fisher, ed., *Essays in the Economic and Social History of Tudor and Stuart England* (Cambridge, Engl., 1961), 33; Perkins, *Works,* I.
84. Richard Mather, *Farewell Sermon* (Boston, 1657).
85. Cotton Mather, *Theopolis Americana* (Boston, 1710), 5, 13–14.
86. Cotton Mather, *Bonifacius: An Essay upon the Good* (1710), David Levin, ed. (Cambridge, Mass., 1966), xxii.
87. Laurel Thatcher Ulrich, *Good Wives: Image and Reality in the Lives of Women in Northern New England, 1650–1750* (New York, 1982), 14. As Amanda Porterfield writes of Anglo-American Puritanism: "In fundamental ways, mothers were guardians, interpreters, and inculcators of Puritan culture. They were essential members of the Puritan family, which was an arena of religious experience and social reform more extensive than church life, and at least as much cherished. Mothers were especially influential in New England, where Puritanism was institutionally established and where Puritan commitment to the authority of the family had the full support of civil officers and established ministers. As primary supervisors of children and servants, mothers had primary responsibility for shaping religious experience and for implementing the domestic discipline and affection that lay at the heart of Puritan strategies for world renewal. Mothers explained God to their children and servants, if not as leaders of family worship sessions, then in the context of their surveillance of household activities. On a daily basis, Puritan mothers made the challenges of ordinary household life opportunities for inculcating lessons in Puritan theology." Porterfield. *Female Piety,* 94.
88. Cotton quoted in Morgan, *Puritan Family,* 42.
89. Porterfield, *Female Piety,* vii. During the mid-1630s the Antinomian musings of midwife Anne Hutchinson almost brought the Bay Colony leadership to its knees before Hutchinson's eleventh-hour claims to immediate revelation provided the rationale for crushing her movement. In attacking the "preparationist" doctrines of those she dubbed "legal" preachers (those allegedly believing in a covenant of works rather than a covenant of grace), Hutchinson attracted a wide following among men as well as women. She spread, according to one of her opponents, "the venome of these [anti-preparationalist] opinions into the very veines and vitalls of the People in the Country." While conceding that Hutchinson was a "woman of a ready wit and a bold spirit," John Winthrop informed her that the magistrates "do not mean to discourse with those of your sex. . . ." Hutchinson, during her civil trial in 1637 for holding weekly Scripture discussions among between sixty and eighty women and men at her Boston home, declared that her learning qualified her to instruct men as well as women. She quoted in her

defense Acts 18:26, in which Priscilla and Aquila "tooke upon them[-selves] to instruct Apollo more perfectly, [although] he was a man of good parts" because even Priscilla, "being better instructed, might teach him." Thomas Weld, "The Preface" to John Winthrop's "Short Story," in David D. Hall, ed., *The Antinomian Controversy, 1636–1638: A Documentary History* (Middletown, Conn., 1968), 207; Lyle Koehler, "The Case of the American Jezebels: Anne Hutchinson and Female Agitation during the Years of Antinomian Turmoil, 1636–1640," *William and Mary Quarterly,* 3d Ser., 31 (1974), 55–78; Edmund S. Morgan, *The Puritan Dilemma: The Story of John Winthrop* (Boston, 1958), 149; *The Works of Anne Bradstreet,* John Howard Ellis, ed. (Gloucester, Mass., 1962), 220.

90. Patrick Collinson, *The Elizabethan Puritan Movement* (Oxford, 1990), 82; Porterfield, *Female Piety,* 84, 89.
91. Cited in Christopher Hibbert, *Cavaliers and Roundheads: The English at War, 1642–1649* (London, 1993), 102.
92. M. G. Hall, ed., "The Autobiography of Increase Mather," *American Antiquarian Society Proceedings,* 71 (1961), 328, 331, 336, 341; Johnson, *Adjustment to Empire,* 178.
93. Moran and Vinovskis, *Religion, Family, and the Life Course,* 87, 130–131.
94. Charles E. Hambrick-Stowe, *The Practice of Piety: Puritan Devotional Disciplines in Seventeenth-Century New England* (Chapel Hill, 1982), 47–48; Emory Elliott, *Power and the Pulpit in Puritan New England* (Princeton, 1975), 56–58; Robert G. Pope, *The Half-Way Covenant: Church Membership in Puritan New England* (Princeton, 1969), 213–214, 217–218; Cotton Mather, *El Shaddai* (Boston, 1725), 21; Ulrich, *Good Wives,* 182. Nor was women's influence confined to spiritual affairs. Increasingly, with the Court's permission, New England women were allowed to own property and conduct the family business in their husband's absence. Considerably more literate than their Old World sisters, Bay Colony women also engaged in intellectual pursuits that went beyond schoolteaching. At midcentury, the poet Anne Bradstreet, described by one critic as "the founder of the literature of English America," responded to those who "says my hand a needle better fits" by publishing *The Tenth Muse Lately Sprung up in AMERICA* (1650). Elliott, *Power and the Pulpit,* 56–57; Ulrich, *Good Wives,* 35–50; A. Owen Aldridge, *Early American Literature: A Comparatist Approach* (Princeton, 1982), 25–26, 29.

Puritanism's tendency to elevate the status of women was reflected by the appearance in the Boston book market in the 1680s of tracts bearing such titles as *Her and His, or The Feminine Gender more worthy than the Masculine* and *Wonders of the Female World.* Expected to be literate and industrious as well as pious—to read the Bible through once a year and take notes during ministers' sermons—Massachusetts women were well equipped to be custodians of the culture of discipline. Although New England society was patriarchal and ministers were expected to be "faithful shepards" of their flocks, the clergy—lacking an ecclesiastical hierarchy—were dependent on the support and religious beliefs of their female-dominated congregations. Barred from the deacon's bench, the franchise, and attendance at Harvard or Yale, New England women were aptly described by Cotton Mather as the "Hidden ones." But there is little question that they played an instrumental role in molding the Puritan conscience. Laurel Thatcher Ulrich has found that "For the years between 1668 and 1735, Evans' *American Bibliography* lists

55 elegies, memorials, and funeral sermons for females plus 15 other works of practical piety addressed wholly or in part to women." Ulrich, "Vertuous Women Found: New England Ministerial Literature, 1688–1735," in Alden T. Vaughan and Francis J. Bremer, eds., *Puritan New England: Essays on Religion, Society, and Culture* (New York, 1977), 68.

When Alexis de Tocqueville came to America in 1831, he discovered that while men employed the rhetoric of political and economic freedom, women spoke a second language of community. With characteristic pertinacity, Tocqueville declared that "the Americans are at the same time a puritanical people and a commercial nation; their religious opinions as well as their trading habits consequently lead them to require much abnegation on the part of woman and a constant sacrifice of her pleasures to her duties, which is seldom demanded of her in Europe." In posing the question "to what the singular prosperity and growing strength of [the American people] ought mainly to be attributed," Tocqueville answered, "To the superiority of their women." *Democracy in America,* 2:209–225, quotations at 212, 225; Robert Booth Fowler, *The Dance with Community: The Contemporary Debate in American Political Thought* (Lawrence, Kan., 1991), 36.

95. J. E. Crowley, *This Sheba, Self: The Conceptualization of Economic Life in Eighteenth-Century America* (Baltimore, 1974), 52; Hambrick-Stowe, *The Practice of Piety,* 47–48; Ulrich, "Martha Ballard and Her Girls," in Stephen Innes, ed., *Work and Labor in Early America* (Chapel Hill, 1988), 81–82; Laurel Thatcher Ulrich, *A Midwife's Tale: The Life of Martha Ballard Based on Her Diary, 1785–1812* (New York, 1990), 84–87; Ulrich, "Vertuous Women Found," 215–231.
96. "Modell of Christian Charity," *Winthrop Papers,* 2:294.
97. Karen Ordahl Kupperman, "Definitions of Liberty on the Eve of Civil War: Lord Saye and Sele, Lord Brooke, and the American Puritan Colonies," *Historical Journal,* 32 (1989), 26.
98. "Miantonomo's Call for Indian Unity, 1642," in Karen Ordahl Kupperman, ed., *Major Problems in American Colonial History: Documents and Essays* (Lexington, Mass., 1993), 135. Puritan imperialism was not limited to Native Americans. Declares Richard Johnson: "in terms of the imposition of government and ideology upon other European colonists, the Bay Colony was the most aggressive and successful expansionist power on the American continent in the seventeenth century." *Adjustment to Empire,* 19.
99. Ursula Brumm, *American Thought and Religious Typology,* John Hooglund, trans. (New Brunswick, N.J., 1970); Rutman, *American Puritanism,* 31.
100. Stout, *New England Soul,* 3–4; Lucas, "The Weber Thesis and Plymouth Colony," 322, 327.
101. *Johnson's Wonder-Working Providence,* 33.
102. Anderson, *New England's Generation,* 219; Hall, "On Common Ground," 229; Bercovitch, *American Jeremiad,* 28.
103. Stout, *New England Soul,* 3–4, 282–316.
104. Charles L. Cohen, *God's Caress: The Psychology of Puritan Religious Experience* (New York, 1986), 47–72; Hambrick-Stowe, *The Practice of Piety,* 197–241.
105. Winthrop, "Modell of Christian Charity," *Winthrop Papers,* 2:294. The New Englanders' sense of distinctiveness, as with the seventeenth-century Dutch, was always bound up in their identity as a Covenant People.

The typology of chosenness in New England was rooted in God's covenant with the Jews at Mount Sinai during the Exodus. The rise of monotheism—the belief in "Yahweh alone" among the Israelite tribes exiled in Babylon—provided the core of a communal identity that would embrace Old Testament Jews and seventeenth-century Calvinists alike. Covenant and Election, the core of Jewish identity for nearly three thousand years, served a similar function for Calvinist New Englanders. Simon Schama, *The Embarrassment of Riches: An Interpretation of Dutch Culture in the Golden Age* (New York, 1987), 600.

106. Increase Mather, "Epistle Dedicatory" to Cotton Mather, *Magnalia Christi Americana* (London, 1702), Bk.4:161.
107. Stout, *New England Soul,* 3–4, 282–316.
108. David Harris Sacks, *The Widening Gate: Bristol and the Atlantic Economy, 1450–1700* (Berkeley, 1991), 361.
109. Stout, *New England Soul,* 7; D. Hall, "On Common Ground," 209; Paul Boyer and Stephen Nissenbaum, *Salem Possessed: The Social Origins of Witchcraft* (Cambridge, Mass., 1974), 170.

CHAPTER 1: Puritanism, Capitalism, and the "Human Capital" Question

1. After an extended survey of historians' use of the term, Fernand Braudel wrote that "The word is never, the reader will have noticed, used in a friendly sense." Braudel, *Civilization and Capitalism, 15th–18th Century,* Siân Reynolds, trans., 2 vols. (New York, 1979), vol. 2, *The Wheels of Commerce* (cited hereafter as *Wheels of Commerce*), 236.
2. Peter L. Berger, *The Capitalist Revolution: Fifty Propositions About Prosperity, Equality, and Liberty* (New York, 1986), 15–31.
3. Weber, *Protestant Ethic,* 174; Mary Douglas and Baron Isherwood, *The World of Goods* (New York, 1979), 27–28.
4. Michael Walzer, "Puritanism as a Revolutionary Ideology," *History and Theory,* 3 (1964), 70.
5. Weber, *Protestant Ethic,* 172; David Little, *Religion, Order, and Law: A Study in Pre-Revolutionary England* (New York, 1969), 1.
6. Gertrude Himmelfarb, *The Idea of Poverty: England in the Early Industrial Age* (New York, 1984), 23–24; David Ormrod, "R. H. Tawney and the Origins of Capitalism," *History Workshop,* 18 (1984), 138–159; Gordon Marshall, *In Search of the Spirit of Capitalism: An Essay on Max Weber's Protestant Ethic Thesis* (New York, 1982), 9–16, 69–96; Michael Walzer, *The Revolution of the Saints* (Cambridge, Mass., 1965).
7. Kenneth A. Lockridge, *A New England Town: The First Hundred Years, Dedham, Massachusetts, 1636–1736* (New York, 1970); Richard L. Bushman, *From Puritan to Yankee: Character and the Social Order in Connecticut, 1690–1765* (Cambridge, Mass., 1967); Philip J. Greven, Jr., *Four Generations: Population, Land, and Family in Colonial Andover, Massachusetts* (Ithaca, 1970); Christopher M. Jedrey, *The World of John Cleaveland: Family and Community in Eighteenth-Century New England* (New York, 1979); James Henretta, "Families and Farms: Mentalité in Pre-industrial America," *William and Mary Quarterly,* 3d Ser., 35 (1978), 3–32; Michael Merrill, "Cash Is Good to Eat: Self-sufficiency and Exchange in the Rural Economy of the United States," *Radical History Review,* 4 (1977), 42–72. The quotation is from Lockridge, *New England Town,* 76.

8. James Truslow Adams, *The Founding of New England* (Boston, 1921); Bercovitch, *The American Jeremiad,* xi–30; David Harlan, "A People Blinded from Birth: American History According to Sacvan Bercovitch," *Journal of American History,* 78 (1991), 949–971; William Cronon, *Changes in the Land: Indians, Colonists, and the Ecology of New England* (New York, 1983).
9. David T. Konig, *Law and Society in Puritan Massachusetts: Essex County, 1629–1692* (Chapel Hill, 1979), 126.
10. Bruce H. Mann, *Neighbors and Strangers: Law and Community in Early Connecticut* (Chapel Hill, 1987), 1–136. The inland bill of exchange was the main financial instrument in seventeenth-century England. It was an unconditional order signed and addressed by one firm or person to another requiring the addressee to pay on demand, or at a specified time, a sum of money to (or to the order of) a specified person or the bearer. Eric Kerridge, *Trade and Banking in Early Modern England* (Manchester, Engl., 1988), 57.

    As David Konig points out, "the promissory notes common in Massachusetts might continue in circulation long after having been paid by the original maker, which would render the note worthless." Fully negotiable bills of exchange, by contrast, "passed free of any [legal] defenses that the original promisor might plead, and he remained liable for the full face value." For these reasons, Konig describes bills of exchange as "a hallmark of the modern economy." David Thomas Konig, "The Virgin and the Virgin's Sister: Virginia, Massachusetts, and the Contested Legacy of Colonial Law," in Russell K. Osgood, ed., *The History of the Law in Massachusetts: The Supreme Judicial Court, 1692–1992* (Boston, 1992), 99.
11. Winifred Barr Rothenberg, *From Market-Places to a Market Economy: The Transformation of Rural Massachusetts, 1750–1850* (Chicago, 1992), xiv, 214–244.
12. Alexander Young, ed., *Chronicles of the First Planters of the Colony of Massachusetts Bay, 1623–1636* (New York, 1970), 111.
13. Harry S. Stout, *The New England Soul: Preaching and Religious Culture in Colonial New England* (New York, 1986), 45.
14. Alan Heimert and Andrew Delbanco have recently gone so far as to assert that the General Court's 1639 censure of merchant Robert Keayne for profiteering "was perhaps the last time in American history that there existed a governmental authority as well as a private conscience to hold every individual accountable for what we believe to be the 'natural' thing—the desire, as our jargon puts it, to maximize profit." Heimert and Delbanco, *The Puritans in America: A Narrative Anthology* (Cambridge, Mass., 1985), 187; *Winthrop Papers,* 2:295; J. E. Crowley, *This Sheba, Self: The Conceptualization of Economic Life in Eighteenth-Century America* (Baltimore, 1974), 52.
15. Perry Miller, *The New England Mind: From Colony to Province* (Boston, 1961 [orig. 1953]), 40. The emphasis during the past twenty years on the "traditional" nature of New England society has gone too far in the (necessary) task of modifying the old stereotypes. We also need to avoid the problems of ahistoricism and distortion that result from the frequent use of "upstream" comparisons (comparing English settlers to modern individualists rather than their demonstrably more traditional contemporaries elsewhere in the early modern world).
16. [Nathaniel Ward], *The Simple Cobler of Aggawam in America,* 5th edn,

repr. in Peter Force, comp., *Tracts and Other Papers* (Gloucester, Mass., 1963 [orig. 1844]), 3, nos. 8, 6.

17. John M. Murrin, "Magistrates, Sinners, and a Precarious Liberty: Trial by Jury in Seventeenth-Century New England," in David D. Hall, John M. Murrin, and Thad W. Tate, eds., *Saints and Revolutionaries: Essays on Early American History* (New York, 1984), 152–206.
18. James K. Hosmer, ed., *Winthrop's Journal, "History of New England," 1630–1649,* 2 vols. (New York, 1908; cited hereafter as *Winthrop's Journal*), 2:17.
19. Berger, *Capitalist Revolution,* 16. R. H. Hartwell declares that "There is no agreed definition of capitalism, no agreed dating, no agreed causes, and no agreed theory of the development of capitalism." Fernand Braudel has called attention to the temporal dimension of some of this confusion: "Ambiguous, hardly scientific, and usually indiscriminately applied, [capitalism] is—above all—a word that cannot be used of the ages before the industrial period without being accused of anachronism." As Braudel suggests, what one chooses to include—and exclude—from a definition of capitalism goes a long way toward predetermining the analytical result. R. M. Hartwell, "The Origins of Capitalism: A Methodological Essay," in Svetazar Pejovich, ed., *Philosophical and Economic Foundations of Capitalism* (Lexington, Mass., 1983), 11, 20; Braudel, *Wheels of Commerce,* 231.

    Capitalism likewise is almost always defined in value-laden terms. Pro-capitalist and anti-capitalist critics alike set up what amounts to a selective definitional schema, which then has the effect of predetermining the analytical result. Thus, those drawing on a Smithian-Weberian interpretation speak of the avid pursuit of an improved standard of living through market exchange. Neo-Marxians, by contrast, speak of a system of social relations of production in which most people are compelled to sell their labor for monetary wages to the capitalists who own the means of production. Or, in the more pungent words of Robert L. Heilbroner, "Capitalism is the regime of capital, the form of rulership we find when power takes the remarkable aspect of the domination, by those who control access to the means of production, of the great majority who must gain 'employment'—the capitalist substitute for the traditional entitlement of the peasant to consume some portion of his own crop." Heilbroner, *The Nature and Logic of Capitalism* (New York, 1985), 52; Berger, *Capitalist Revolution,* 15–31. Drawing on Weber's definition of a "rational capitalistic enterprise," Winifred B. Rothenberg has proposed to document the emergence of capitalist agriculture by tracing "the appearance in farmers' account books of genuine double-entry bookkeeping, that is of the striking of a balance between assets and liabilities plus equity, with Profit and Loss annually accounted as such." Rothenberg, "The Market and Massachusetts Farmers: Reply," *Journal of Economic History,* 43 (1983), 480.

20. Berger, *Capitalist Revolution,* 16; Albert O. Hirschman, *Rival Views of Market Society* (New York, 1986), 105–141. Addressing the First International in 1864, Karl Marx declared that "the economical subjection of the man of labour to the monopolizer of the means of labour, that is, the sources of life, lies at the bottom of servitude in all its forms, of all social misery, mental degradation, and political dependence." Karl Marx, "Inaugural Address and Provisional Rules of the International Working Men's Association," in Eugene Kamenka, ed., *The Portable Karl Marx* (New York, 1983), 365.

21. Braudel, *Wheels of Commerce,* 238. Christopher Clark, in his study of the "roots of rural capitalism" in western Massachusetts between 1780 and 1860, argues that "rural society was not . . . 'capitalist' at the end of the colonial period but that it had become so by the time of the Civil War." Clark, *The Roots of Rural Capitalism: Western Massachusetts, 1780–1860* (Ithaca, 1990), 14.
22. G. E. M. de Ste Croix, "Greek and Roman Accounting," in A. C. Littleton and B. S. Yamey, eds., *Studies in the History of Accounting* (Homewood, Ill., 1956), 14, 21; Kerridge, *Trade and Banking in Early Modern England,* 1; Francis MacDonald Cornford, trans., *The Republic of Plato* (New York, 1945), 281; Elizabeth A. Meyer, *Belief, Practice, and Law: Documents in the World of Roman Justice* (forthcoming); Pejovich, ed., *Philosophical and Economic Foundations of Capitalism,* 1; Michael Novak, *The Catholic Ethic and the Spirit of Capitalism* (New York, 1993), 11.
23. John A. Hall, *Powers and Liberties: The Causes and Consequences of the Rise of the West* (Harmondsworth, Engl., 1986), 115, 123; Novak, *Catholic Ethic, 11;* Braudel, *Wheels of Commerce,* 233.
24. Terence W. Hutchison, *Before Adam Smith: The Emergence of Political Economy, 1662–1776* (Oxford, 1988), 255–260; Raymond De Roover, "Scholastic Economics: Survival and Lasting Influence from the Sixteenth Century to Adam Smith," *Quarterly Journal of Economics,* 69 (1955), 164.
25. Braudel, *Wheels of Commerce,* 234. The word "profit" itself emerged in the High Middle Ages, originally derived from *profectus,* meaning a person who had advanced or made progress. It first came into general use in France during the early twelfth century. The word "gain," derived from the Old French *bénéfice,* appeared in the late twelfth century, meaning privilege or advantage. In Adam Smith's *Wealth of Nations,* profit achieved a specifically capitalist meaning as "that derived from stock, by the person who manages or employes it." Maurice Godelier, "Work and Its Representations: A Research Proposal," *History Workshop,* 10, (1980), 165; Smith, *Wealth of Nations,* 190–202.
26. Robert Brenner, "Bourgeois Revolution and the Transition to Capitalism," in A. L. Beier, David Cannadine, and James M. Rosenheim, eds., *The First Modern Society: Essays in English History in Honour of Lawrence Stone* (Cambridge, Engl., 1989), 271–304. To a considerable extent, Brenner's pathbreaking essay was the inspiration for much of the present chapter. See also Himmelfarb, *The Idea of Poverty,* 42–44.
27. Brenner, "Bourgeois Revolution," 274–285; Smith, *Wealth of Nations,* 109–126. Karl Marx, in his early writings—the *German Ideology,* the *Poverty of Philosophy,* and the *Communist Manifesto*—updated and refined Adam Smith's division of labor thesis in light of the Industrial Revolution. Then, in his later works, especially *Grundrisse* and Volume I of *Capital,* Marx elaborated his master principle: the mode of production. This model of transition from feudalism to capitalism postulated that a class of peasant producers with access to the means of subsistence were dispossessed by a class of landlords and aristocrats who "reproduced themselves" by extracting a surplus from the peasants through "extra-economic compulsion." What Marx called "primitive accumulation" (in contrast to Smith's emphasis on the initial amassing of investment funds) was made possible by the transformation of social property relations resulting from the peasants' separation from the means of subsistence. Smith's benign and progressively self-regulating "system of

natural liberty" envisioned market forces as socially egalitarian, acting as solvents on existing systems of privilege and economic hierarchy. Marx, writing from the other side of the Industrial Revolution, found such optimism fatuous, believing that the declining rate of profit would lead inevitably to growing exploitation and misery for the propertyless classes. Smith's vision of the social benefit brought by the "improving" landlord (which did acknowledge the horrors visited on such groups as the Scottish crofters) was transmogrified by Marx into the heedless encroachment of landlord property and the spread of agrarian capitalism. After production by machinery superseded the heretofore dominant manufacturing stage, the final maturation of capitalism for Marx came with the emergence of a two-class society: industrial capitalist managers exploiting deskilled factory proletarians. Brenner, "Bourgeois Revolution," 273; Leszek Kolakawski, *Main Currents of Marxism,* 3 vols. (Oxford, 1978), 1:237; Marx, *Capital,* I, Part VIII.

The first, and older, of the "transition-to-capitalism" theories found the main catalyst of change in the so-called "bourgeois revolution," with the main focus again placed on seventeenth-century England. Marx, in his writings during the 1840s, declared that during the early modern period, the bourgeoisie and "absolute monarchy" entered into an alliance to destroy their common enemy, the "parasitic feudal nobility." The subsequent triumph of the bourgeoisie, principally through the efforts of the improving gentry, eventually brought the old nobility and absolute monarchy into a desperate rearguard coalition against the rising middle classes. The defeat of these reactionary forces in the English Civil War was considered the first successful bourgeois revolution.

The second—and currently dominant—transition-to-capitalism theory rejected the "bourgeois revolution" thesis. The later Marx, and more recent work by such scholars as Lawrence Stone, J. H. Hexter, and Robert Brenner, portrayed the transition to capitalism as taking place *within* the aristocratic landlord classes. Rather than being undone by a combination of customary rents, the price revolution, and an inability to innovate, the nobility, according to these scholars, eventually turned the general crisis to its benefit. The aristocracy adopted the new commercial values rather than being overwhelmed by them. By the mid-twentieth century the Civil War—although instigated by religious dissenters—had come to be interpreted almost exclusively in materialist terms. Christopher Hill offered a Marxian version of the war as a conflict between a bourgeois Parliament controlled by progressive-minded Puritans on the one hand and a feudal monarchy on the other. R. H. Tawney and Lawrence Stone rejoined that the Civil War was not a class conflict but rather a conflict between a rising gentry and a declining aristocracy (or, in Hugh Trevor-Roper's terms, between rising and declining members of the gentry). All parties to this debate, even Hill (whose book focuses mainly on the Puritans) radically devalued religion. Virtually all authors expressed the conviction that the various political and religious beliefs of the contending parties were largely projections of their material interests. See Karl Marx and Friedrich Engels, *The German Ideology* (1845–46), in Kamenka, ed., *Portable Karl Marx,* 191; Brenner, "Bourgeois Revolution," 277–278; Marx and Engels, "Manifesto of the Communist Party" (1848), in Kamenka, ed., *Portable Karl Marx,* 201–241; Christopher Hill, *The World Turned Upside Down: Radical Ideas During the English Revolution* (New York, 1975), 151–183;

R. H. Tawney, "The Rise of the Gentry, 1558–1640," *Economic History Review,* 11 (1941), 1–38; Lawrence Stone, "The Anatomy of the Elizabethan Aristocracy," *Economic History Review,* 18 (1948), 1–53; Lawrence Stone, *The Crisis of the Aristocracy, 1558–1641* (London, 1967), 135–267; Lawrence Stone, *The Causes of the English Civil War, 1559–1642* (London, 1972); J. H. Hexter, "Storm Over the Gentry," in *Reappraisals in History: New Views on History and Society in Early Modern Europe* (New York, 1961), 117–162; and Blair Worden, "Revising the Revolution," *New York Review of Books* (17 January 1991), 38.

28. Charles Petit-Dutailles, *The Feudal Monarchy in France and England: From the Tenth to the Thirteenth Century,* E. D. Hunt, trans. (New York, 1964), 126–140, quotation at 137. According to Petit-Dutailles, "The characteristic of royal justice in England [by the late twelfth century] was that it held local custom as of little account and that through its system of assizes and writs it established a procedure and a jurisprudence of general application which was, on the whole, favourable to a free middle class and hostile to the seignorial spirit." *Ibid.,* 137. I would like to thank Professors Martin J. Havran and Everett U. Crosby of the Corcoran Department of History, University of Virginia, for their assistance in these formulations.
29. Kathleen Biddick, "Medieval English Peasants and Market Involvement," *Journal of Economic History,* 45 (1985), 823–831. For a consideration of peasant ownership of property in medieval England, see Biddick, "Missing Links: Taxable Wealth, Markets, and Stratification Among English Peasants," *Journal of Interdisciplinary History,* 18 (1987), 277–298.
30. Michael M. Postan, "Medieval Agrarian Society in Its Prime," *Cambridge Economic History of Europe,* 3 vols. (Cambridge, Engl., 1966), 1:618–620; Biddick, "Missing Links," 277; Biddick, "Medieval English Peasants and Market Involvement," 823–825.
31. Postan, "Medieval Agrarian Society," 618–620; R. J. Faith, "Peasant Families and Inheritance Customs in Medieval England," *Agricultural History Review,* 14 (1966), 77–95.
32. Berger, *Capitalist Revolution,* 17. For Max Weber, even large-scale demesne farming during the medieval era was not capitalist because it lacked an "estimate beforehand of the chances of profit from a transaction." Weber defined modern occidental capitalism as "the rational capitalistic organization of (formally) free labor." For Weber, a capitalistic action was "one which rests on the expectation of profit by the utilization of opportunities for exchange, that is on (formally) peaceful chances of profit." The most important fact is always that "a calculation of capital in terms of money is made, whether by modern book-keeping methods or in any other way, however primitive and crude. Everything is done in terms of balances: at the beginning of the enterprise an initial balance, before every individual decision a calculation to ascertain its probable profitableness, and at the end a final balance to ascertain how much profit has been made."

Weber believed it was critical that the historically discrete phenomenon of capitalism not be equated with simple cupidity. The "impulse to acquisition, pursuit of gain, of money, of the greatest possible amount of money," he declared famously, "has in itself nothing to do with capitalism." This impulse, he emphasized, "exists and has existed among waiters, physicians, coachmen, artists, prostitutes, dishonest officials, soldiers, nobles, crusaders, gamblers, and beggars . . . [among] all sorts and conditions of men at all times and in all countries of the earth. . . ." Of the six preconditions of capitalism listed in Weber's *General Economic History* (1922), three relate directly to this rational calculating cast of mind. These were rational capital accounting, rational technology, and calculable law. The other three criteria were freedom of the market, free labor, and the commercialization of economic life. These six criteria allowed Weber to discriminate between commercial and capitalistic behavior. Weber, *Protestant Ethic,* 17–18, 21–22; Weber, *General Economic History,* Frank H. Knight, ed. (New York, 1961), 53; Alan Macfarlane, *The Culture of Capitalism* (Oxford, 1987), 223–227.

33. H. R. Trevor-Roper, "The Reformation and Economic Change," in M. J. Kitch, ed., *Capitalism and the Reformation* (London, 1967), 24–36.
34. Barbara L. Solow, ed., *Slavery and the Rise of the Atlantic System* (Cambridge, Engl., 1991), 1; Berger, *Capitalist Revolution,* 17.
35. Thomas K. McCraw, "The Trouble with Adam Smith," *American Scholar,* 61 (1992), 359.
36. Fernand Braudel, *Civilization and Capitalism, 15th–18th Century,* Siân Reynolds, trans., 2 vols. (New York, 1979), vol. 1, *The Structures of Everyday Life: The Limits of the Possible,* 74; Andrew B. Appleby, "Grain Prices and Subsistence Crises in England and France, 1590–1740," *Journal of Economic History,* 39 (1979), 865–887.
37. C. B. A. Behrens, *Society, Government, and the Enlightenment: The Experiences of Eighteenth-Century France and Prussia* (New York, 1985); Robert Darnton, *The Great Cat Massacre, and Other Episodes in French Cultural History* (New York, 1984), 23–27. The English inheritance system, particularly in its treatment of the stem family, was based on more individualistic principles than prevailed on the Continent. Hermann Rebel, "Peasant Stem Families in Early Modern Austria: Life Plans, Status Tactics, and the Grid of Inheritance," *Social Science History,* 2 (1978), 284–285.
38. Randall Collins, "Weber's Last Theory of Capitalism: A Systematization," *American Sociological Review,* 45 (1980), 928–932; Weber, *General Economic History,* 54; Weber, *Protestant Ethic,* 22; Rex A. Lucas, "A Specification of the Weber Thesis: Plymouth Colony," *History and Theory,* 10 (1971), 331; Macfarlane, *Culture of Capitalism,* 178; Berger, *Capitalist Revolution,* 213; John A. Hall, *Liberalism: Politics, Ideology, and the Market* (Chapel Hill, 1987), 52; Aristide R. Zolberg, "How Many Exceptionalisms?" in Ira Katznelson and Zolberg, eds., *Working-Class Formation: Nineteenth-Century Patterns in Western Europe and the United States* (Princeton, 1986), 397–455; Kolakowski, *Main Currents of Marxism,* 1:120–131; Michael Mann, "The Autonomous Power of the State: Its Origins, Mechanisms and Results," in J. A. Hall, ed., *States in History* (Oxford, 1986), 109–136; Hirschman, *Rival Views of Market Society,* 105–141; Patrick Joyce, "The Historical Meanings of Work," in Joyce, ed., *The Historical Meanings of Work* (Cambridge, Engl., 1987), 1–30; I. Hont and Michael Ignatieff, eds., *Wealth and Virtue: The Shaping of Political Economy in the Scottish Enlightenment* (Cambridge, Engl., 1983), 1–44; Rothenberg, *From Market-Places to a Market Economy,* 242.
39. Weber, *General Economic History,* 258; Little, *Religion, Order, and Law,* 17–18; Brenner, "Bourgeois Revolution," 271–304. Montesquieu proclaimed by the mid-eighteenth century that the English had "progressed the farthest of all peoples of the world in three important

things: in piety, in commerce, and in freedom," characteristics that he regarded as mutually reinforcing and productive of a distinctive, rationalized society. Moreover, while other nations had "made the interests of commerce yield to those of politics, the English, on the contrary, have ever made their political interests give way to those of commerce." Montesquieu, *The Spirit of Laws,* Thomas Nugent, trans., 2 vols. (New York, 1899), 1:321; Macfarlane, *Culture of Capitalism,* 174.

40. Brenner, "Bourgois Revolution," 271–304; Kerridge, *Trade and Banking,* 1; Lawrence Stone, "England's Financial Revolution," *New York Review of Books* (15 March 1990), 50; Gordon S. Wood, *The Radicalism of the American Revolution* (New York, 1992), 95–109; Hall, *Liberalism,* 53; C. Warren Hollister, *The Making of England, 55 B.C. to 1399* (Lexington, Mass., 1988), 46–48.
41. Brenner, "Bourgeois Revolution," 303.
42. J. H. Hexter, "Parliament, Liberty, and Freedom of Elections," in Hexter, ed., *Parliament and Liberty: From the Reign of Elizabeth to the English Civil War* (Stanford, 1992), 54; see also Robert Zaller, "Parliament and the Crisis of European Liberty," *ibid.,* 201–224.
43. Lacey Baldwin Smith, *This Realm of England, 1399–1688* (Lexington, Mass., 1988), 176; Adam B. Seligman, *The Idea of Civil Society* (New York, 1992), 15–58.
44. Brenner, "Bourgois Revolution," 303; Joyce O. Appleby, *Economic Thought and Ideology in Seventeenth-Century England* (Princeton, 1978), 242–279.
45. Robert McCrum, William Cran, and Robert MacNeill, *The Story of English* (Boston, 1986), 93; Elizabeth Eisenstein, *The Printing Press as an Agent of Change: Communications and Cultural Transformations in Early Modern Europe,* 2 vols. (Cambridge, Engl., 1979), 1:378–403; John Morgan, *Godly Learning: Puritan Attitudes Towards Reason, Learning and Education, 1560–1640* (Cambridge, Engl., 1986), 309; David Cressy, *Literacy and the Social Order: Reading and Writing in Tudor and Stuart England* (New York, 1980), chap. 2; Gloria L. Main, "An Inquiry into When and Why Women Learned to Write in Colonial New England," *Journal of Social History,* 24 (1991), 579–580; Gerald F. Moran and Maris A. Vinovskis, *Religion, the Family, and the Life Course: Explorations in the Social History of Early America* (Ann Arbor, 1992), 123–134; David D. Hall, *Worlds of Wonder, Days of Judgment: Popular Religious Belief in Early New England* (Cambridge, Mass., 1990), 23; C. John Sommerville, "The Distribution of Religious and Occult Literature in Seventeenth-Century England," *The Library,* 5th Ser., 29 (1974), 222–224.
46. Eisenstein, *Printing Press,* 1:378–403; J. A. Leo Lemay, *The American Dream of Captain John Smith* (Charlottesville, Va., 1991), 186; C. John Sommerville, *The Discovery of Childhood in Puritan England* (Athens, Ga., 1992), 21–40, quotation at 23.
47. Ste. Croix, "Greek and Roman Accounting," 65; Raymond De Roover, "Double-Entry Book-Keeping," in Kitch, ed., *Capitalism and the Reformation,* 75–77; Eisenstein, *Printing Press,* 1:384–386, 407; S. H. Steinberg, *Five Hundred Years of Printing* (Bristol, Engl., 1961), 194.
48. E. A. J. Johnson, *Predecessors of Adam Smith: The Growth of British Economic Thought* (New York, 1937), 77–82; Hutchison, *Before Adam Smith,* 21–24, 178.
49. Rothenberg, *Market-Places to a Market Economy,* 17–18.
50. Thomas Mun, *England's Treasure by Forraign Trade: Or The Ballance of*

our Forraign Trade is The Rule of our Treasure (New York, 1895 [orig. 1664]), 44, 104, 112;, Appleby, *Economic Thought,* 118–119; Misselden, *Free Trade,* 25.

51. Norman Jones, *God and the Moneylenders: Usury and Law in Early Modern England* (Oxford, 1989), 5–6. The concept of political economy was principally introduced into England by Sir William Petty, also the author of England's first labor theory of value (labor as "the chiefest, most fundamental and precious commodity"). E. Lipson, *The Economic History of England,* vol. 2, *The Age of Mercantilism* (London, 1956), cxxvi; E. Strauss, *Sir William Petty: Portrait of a Genius* (Glencoe, Ill, 1954), 214.
52. Hutchison, *Before Adam Smith,* 5; Smith, *Wealth of Nations,* Book 1, chap. 6.
53. Thomas L. Pangle, *The Spirit of Modern Republicanism: The Moral Vision of the American Founders and the Philosophy of Locke* (Chicago, 1988), 19; Appleby, *Economic Thought,* 115.
54. Misselden, *Circle of Commerce,* 17; Johnson, *Predecessors of Adam Smith,* 69; Appleby, *Economic Thought,* 115; Richard Wrightman Fox, "The Liberal Ethic and the Spirit of Protestantism," in Charles H. Reynolds and Ralph V. Norman, eds., *Community in America: The Challenge of "Habits of the Heart"* (Berkeley, 1988), 245.

    The apotheosis of this ideal came in the celebrated chapter V, "Of Property," in Locke's *Second Treatise of Civil Government* (1690). In this work, Locke attempted to demonstrate that unlimited private acquisition, for centuries subject to scathing religious and philosophic criticism, was justifiable according to both ethical and utilitarian criteria. Locke understood, as did Adam Smith after him, that the increased accumulation resulting from such acquisitive behavior would expand the yield for everyone, especially for those farthest down on the social scale. Both theorists also focused on the psychological link between work habits and material expectations (Smith's main justification for higher wages for laborers). In his *Essay Concerning Human Understanding* (1690), Locke located the motivation to all work and enterprise in emulative-driven "uneasiness"—the desire to augment one's possessions—which provided the psychological basis for striving behavior. The older objections to the profit motive, based on the principles of Adam Smith's stationary (or zero-sum) society—that unlimited acquisition would impoverish others or waste goods that could be available to the community—were now turned on their head. Heilbroner, *Nature and Logic of Capitalism,* 112–113; John Locke, *An Essay Concerning Human Understanding,* Alexander Campbell Fraser, ed., 2 vols. (Oxford, 1894), 1:304.
55. Clark, *Roots of Rural Capitalism,* 322; Michael Van Cleave Alexander, *The Growth of English Education, 1348–1648* (New York, 1990), 233–246; Joel Mokyr, *The Lever of Riches: Technological Creativity and Economic Progress* (New York, 1990), 58.
56. Joyce Appleby, "Consumption in Early Modern Social Thought," Clark Library Lecture (21 October 1988), 3.
57. William Hunt, *The Puritan Moment: The Coming of Revolution in an English County* (Cambridge, Mass., 1983), 24–25.
58. During the seventeenth century, according to Joyce Appleby, "the English moved beyond the threat of famine. . . . In the future there would be food shortages, skyrocketing grain prices, distress and dearth, but never again would elevated grain prices go hand in hand with rising mortality rates. Agricultural productivity, combined with the purchas-

ing power to bring food from other places in time of shortage, had eliminated one of the four horses of the apocalypse from England's shores. A powerful reason for maintaining strict social order had unobtrusively disappeared, leaving behind a set of social prescriptions whose obsolecence had to be discovered one by one in the course of the next two centuries." Appleby, "Consumption," 2–3.

59. Appleby, *Economic Thought,* 85.
60. Mark Bond-Webster, "John Winthrop's 'Christian Charity,'" unpublished paper; Scott Michaelsen, "John Winthrop's 'Modell' Covenant and the Company Way," *Early American Literature,* 27 (1992), 85–100.
61. Herbert Butterfield, *The Origins of Modern Science, 1300–1800* (New York, 1957), 67–88; De Roover, "Scholastic Economics," 172; Keith Thomas, *Religion and the Decline of Magic* (New York, 1971), 643.
62. Raymond De Roover, "Monopoly Theory Prior to Adam Smith: A Revision," *Quarterly Journal of Economics,* 65 (1951), 495; Johnson, *Predecessors of Adam Smith,* 69; Misselden, *Circle of Commerce,* 17.
63. John M. Murrin, personal communication.
64. Stephen Foster, *Their Solitary Way: The Puritan Social Ethic in the First Century of Settlement in New England* (New Haven, 1971), 110.
65. Winslow, *Good News from New England* (1624).
66. Jeremy Dyke, *A Counterpoison against Coveteousness* (London, 1619), 41.
67. John Downame, *The Plea of the Poore, or a Treatise of Benifice and Almes-Deeds* (London, 1616), 23; Appleby, *Economic Thought,* 62, 71, 94; John Preston, "Eighteen Sermons," in John Davenport and Richard Sibbes, eds., *The Breastplate of Faith and Love* (London, 1630), 189.
68. Quoted in Weber, *Protestant Ethic,* 162.
69. By the end of the seventeenth century, the calculating pursuit of gain was being defended by some as a positive virtue. Far from being a sign of the natural incapacity of ordinary men and women to lead lives unsupervised by social elites, the profit motive was redefined by these thinkers into a cure for idleness and a regulator of commerce. In his astonishingly modern *Discourses upon Trade* (1691), Sir Dudley North (1602–1677) declared that the main spur to trade and industry was "the exorbitant appetites of men." Were men and women to "content themselves with bare necessaries," Dudley averred, "we should have a poor world." In 1699 the Cambridge Association of Ministers in Massachusetts asserted that "Humane Society, as now circumstanced, would sink if all Usury were Impractable." In France during the second half of the seventeenth century, the Jansenist Pierre Nicole built his economic philosophy on the foundation of enlightened self-interest. Nicole, although an ethical rigorist, openly endorsed an economy in which "Cupidity . . . takes the place of charity for the meeting of our needs. . . ." The infamous assertion of Bernard de Mandeville in *The Fable of the Bees* (1714) that private vices produced public benefits was the logical—if hotly contested—culmination of this line of reasoning. By such ideological shifts was the way prepared for Adam Smith's dictum that "Man's self-love is God's providence." Smith declared that the wage laborer would enjoy a higher standard of living than even the property-owning citizen of the classical polis because the division of labor allowed modern economies to break out of the seemingly inexorable cycle of luxury, corruption, and decline. (It fell to Marx and Engels, of course, to pillory—and caricature—the tradition in one of the most memorable passages in the *Communist Manifesto:* "The bourgeoisie, wherever it got

the upper hand, put an end to all feudal, patriarchal, idyllic relations, and pitilessly tore asunder the motley feudal ties that bound man to his 'natural superiors,' and left remaining no other bound between man and man than naked self-interest and callous cash payment." Kamenka, ed., *Karl Marx,* 206). Albert O. Hirschman, *The Passions and the Interests: Political Arguments for Capitalism Before Its Triumph* (Princeton, 1977), 39–40; Joan Thirsk, *Economic Policy and Projects: The Development of a Consumer Society in Early Modern England* (Oxford, 1978) 3, 18; Appleby, "Consumption"; Johnson, *Predecessors of Adam Smith,* 69; Lipson, *Economic History of England,* 2:lxxiv; Miller, *New England Mind,* 40, 309; Hutchison, *Before Adam Smith,* 80, 101; and Keith Thomas, review essay, *New York Review of Books* (27 February 1986), 38. On the relationship between "vaulting ambitions" and economic growth, see J. Appleby, "Ideology and Theory: The Tension between Political and Economic Liberalism in Seventeenth-Century England," *American Historical Review,* 81 (1976), 500–505.

Summing up the consequences of these developments, Joyce Appleby observes that "In the seventeenth-century analysis, the whole elaborate construction of the natural rates of interest and exchange, the automatic pricing mechanism, the interchangeability of investments rested upon the presumed dependability of human beings to seek actively to maximize gain in the market. Because self-interest was construed as dependable and constructive, economics had acquired that rationality which, as William Petty put it, made it worthwhile for a man 'to imploy his thoughts about.' " *Economic Thought,* 247–248.

70. Marx and Engels, *The German Ideology,* in Kamenka, ed., *Karl Marx,* 191; italics added.
71. Virginia D. Anderson, *New England's Generation: The Great Migration and the Formation of Society and Culture in the Seventeenth Century* (Cambridge, Engl., 1991), 28–29; Phillip Benedict, *Rouen During the Age of the Wars of Religion* (Cambridge, Engl., 1981), 16; Douglas R. McManis, *Colonial New England: A Historical Geography* (New York, 1975), 107. Roger Thompson has also found a disproportionate share of artisans and urban dwellers in his sample of over two thousand East Anglian migrants. Thompson, *Mobility and Migration: East Anglian Founders of New England, 1629–1640* (Amherst, Mass., 1994), 14–113.
72. Darrett B. Rutman, *Small Worlds, Large Questions: Explorations in Early American Social History, 1600–1850* (Charlottesville, Va., 1994), 297.
73. Virginia DeJohn Anderson, *William and Mary Quarterly* "Forum" (1991), 234; Hunt, *Puritan Moment,* 81–82.
74. Thompson, *Mobility and Migration.* The Neolithic flint mines of Grimes Groves were, according to Richard Muir, "England's first factory." During the medieval period, Muir avers, "East Anglia was far and away England's most dynamic region." John Hadfield, *English Villages* (London, 1980), 113.
75. Joseph H. Smith and Thomas G. Barnes, *The English Legal System: Carryover to the Colonies* (Los Angeles, 1975), 78–79; Virginia DeJohn Anderson, "Migrants and Motives: Religion and the Settlement of New England, 1630–1640," in Stanley N. Katz, John M. Murrin, and Douglas Greenberg, eds., *Colonial America: Essays in Politics and Social Development* (New York, 1993), 96, 102.
76. Albert Matthews, "University Alumni Founders of New England," *Colonial Society of Massachusetts Publications,* 25 (1924), 14–23; Anderson,

New England's Generation, 12–88; Anderson, "The Cattle Economy of Seventeenth-Century New England," unpubl. paper.

77. Johnson, *Predecessors of Adam Smith,* 45–46; Foster, *Their Solitary Way,* 99.
78. Wood, *Radicalism of the American Revolution,* 171.

CHAPTER 2: An "Honest Gaine"

1. John Smith, *A Description of New England . . .* (1616), in Philip L. Barbour, ed., *The Complete Works of Captain John Smith (1580–1631),* 3 vols. (Chapel Hill, 1986; cited hereafter as Smith, *Complete Works*), 1:332, 333. Smith's 1616 map of New England included a woodcut of his likeness, with the description: "The Portraictuer of Captayne John Smith, Admirall of New England."
2. Smith, *Complete Works,* 1:343, 332.
3. J. A. Leo Lemay, *The American Dream of Captain John Smith* (Charlottesville, Va., 1991), 198.
4. Christopher Hill, "Pottage for Freeborn Englishmen: Attitudes to Wage-Labour," in Hill, *Change and Continuity in Seventeenth-Century England* (London, 1974), 219–238; Thomas, "Work and Leisure in Pre-Industrial Society," *Past and Present,* 29 (1964), 63.
5. Joan Thirsk and J. P. Cooper, eds., *Seventeenth-Century Economic Documents* (Oxford, 1972), 109; E. A. Wrigley and R. S. Schofield, *The Population History of England, 1541–1871: A Reconstruction* (Cambridge, Mass., 1981); Keith Wrightson, *English Society, 1580–1680* (New Brunswick, N.J., 1982), 121–148; Margaret Spufford, *Contrasting Communities: English Villagers in the Sixteenth and Seventeenth Centuries* (Cambridge, Engl., 1974), 3–167; B. E. Supple, *Commercial Crisis and Change in England, 1600–1642: A Study in the Instability of a Mercantile Economy* (Cambridge, Engl., 1959), 33–51; William Hunt, *The Puritan Moment: The Coming of Revolution in an English County* (Cambridge, Mass., 1983), 25.
6. Hunt, *Puritan Moment,* 35; Robert Brenner, "Bourgeois Revolution and the Transition of Capitalism," in A. L. Beier, David Cannadine, and James M. Rosenheim, eds., *The First Modern Society: Essays in English History in Honour of Lawrence Stone* (Cambridge, Engl., 1989), 299; Joel Mokyr, *The Lever of Riches: Technological Creativity and Economic Progress* (New York, 1990), 58; Norman Jones, *God and the Moneylenders: Usury and Law in Early Modern England* (Oxford, 1989), 175; David G. Hey, *An English Rural Community: Myddle Under the Tudors and Stuarts* (Leicester, Engl., 1974), 142.
7. Andrew B. Appleby, "Grain Prices and Subsistence Crises in England and France, 1590–1740," *Journal of Economic History,* 39 (1979), 865–887.
8. Hunt, *Puritan Moment,* 160; Peter Bowden, "Agricultural Prices, Farm Profits, and Rents," in Joan Thirsk, ed., *The Agrarian History of England and Wales,* vol. 4, *1500–1640* (London, 1967), 621; Spufford, *Contrasting Communities,* 48; D. C. Coleman, "Labour in the English Economy of the Seventeenth Century," *Economic History Review,* 2d Ser., 8 (1956), 283–284; Christopher Hibbert, *Cavaliers and Roundheads: The English at War, 1642–1649* (New York, 1993), 214–215; Maurice Ashley, *The English Civil War* (Dover, N.H., 1993), 143.

9. Michael M. Postan, "Medieval Agrarian Society in Its Prime," *Cambridge Economic History of Europe,* 3 vols. (Cambridge, Engl., 1966), 1:618–620; Joan Thirsk, "Industries in the Countryside," in F. J. Fisher, ed., *Essays in the Economic and Social History of Tudor and Stuart England* (Cambridge, Engl., 1961), 70–88; Joseph Schumpeter, *Capitalism, Socialism, and Democracy* (New York, 1950), 81–86. In his analysis of the extraordinary rise in emigration to America from the British Isles on the eve of the Revolution, Bernard Bailyn makes an argument for the eighteenth century strikingly similar to the one offered here for the seventeenth. He points out that "not only was the demand for labor powerful in the expanding middle colonies and in the Chesapeake region, but the supply was potentially plentiful in the chronically underemployed population of London and in the many areas of the British provinces, north and south of the Scottish border, where 'declivities' in the upward slope of the British economy created the kind of misery and fear that impels people to search for radical solutions." Bailyn, *Voyagers to the West: A Passage in the Peopling of America on the Eve of the Revolution* (New York, 1986), 296.
10. David Underdown, *Revel, Riot, and Rebellion: Popular Politics and Culture in England, 1603–1660* (Oxford, 1987), 18.
11. J. E. Crowley, *This Sheba, Self: The Conceptualization of Economic Life in Eighteenth-Century America* (Baltimore, 1974), 37–38; Joan Thirsk, *Economic Policy and Projects: The Development of a Consumer Society in Early Modern England* (Oxford, 1978), 118 (quotation), 159.
12. The complete (prolix but descriptive) title of Misselden's pamphlet is *The Circle of Commerce, or The Ballance of Trade in defense of free Trade: opposed to Malynes' Little Fish and his Great Whale, and poised against them in the Scale. Wherein also Exchanges in generall are considered: and wherein the whole trade of this Kingdome with forraine countries, is digested into a Ballance of Trade, for the benefite of Publique Necessary for the present and future times* (London, 1623), 132–134; Joyce Oldham Appleby, *Economic Thought and Ideology in Seventeenth-Century England* (Princeton, 1978), 151; E. A. J. Johnson, *Predecessors of Adam Smith: The Growth of British Economic Thought* (New York, 1937), 68–69.
13. [William Wood?], *Good News from New-England* (1648), in *Massachusetts Historical Society Collections,* 4th Ser., 1 (1852), 197.
14. John Winthrop, "The Grounds of Settling a Plantation in New England" (1629), *Winthrop Papers,* 2:146.
15. Winthrop, "Modell of Christian Charity" (1630), *Winthrop Papers,* 2:283.
16. John Winthrop, "Reasons to be Considered, and Objections with Answers" (1629), *Winthrop Papers,* 2:139; Hunt, *Puritan Moment,* 125.
17. John Winthrop, "Reasons to be Considered," *Winthrop Papers,* 2:139.
18. John White, *The Planter's Plea* (1630), in *Massachusetts Historical Society Proceedings,* 62 (1929), 384.
19. Weber, *Protestant Ethic,* 35–46; Charles H. and Katherine George, *The Protestant Mind of the English Reformation, 1570–1640* (Princeton, 1961), 154–155.
20. George and George, *Protestant Mind,* 154–155.
21. Lacey Baldwin Smith, *This Realm of England: 1399 to 1688* (Lexington, Mass., 1988), 176.
22. Andrews quoted in George and George, *Protestant Mind,* 157–158.
23. John Winthrop, "Reasons to be Considered," *Winthrop Papers,* 2:138–139; Edmund S. Morgan, *The Puritan Dilemma: The Story of John Win-*

throp (New York, 1958), 39; The Rev. Francis Higginson to his Friends at Leicester, September, 1629 in Everett Emerson, ed., *Letters from New England: The Massachusetts Bay Colony, 1629–1638* (Amherst, 1976), 36–37.

24. Supple, *Commercial Crisis and Change in England*, 33–51.
25. John Dane, "A Declaration of Remarkable Providences in the Course of My Life" (1670s?), in John Demos, ed., *Remarkable Providences, 1600–1760* (New York, 1972), 85.
26. John Cotton, *God's Promise to His Plantation* (London, 1630), 9, 15, 17–18.
27. John Winthrop to ______, 1629, *Winthrop Papers*, 2:122.
28. Smith, *Description of New-England* (1616), in *Complete Works*, 1:332.
29. Karen Ordahl Kupperman, *Captain John Smith: A Select Edition of His Writings* (Chapel Hill, 1988), 22, 239.
30. Smith, *Description of New-England*, in *Complete Works*, 1:332, 360; Smith, *The Generall Historie of Virginia, New-England, and the Summer Isles* (1624), in *Complete Works*, 2:206–207.
31. Smith, *Advertisements for the Unexperienced Planters of New England, or Any Where* (1631), in *Complete Works*, 3:276–277.
32. George and George, *Protestant Mind*, 147. Weber distinguished the sober, prudent entrepreneurialism of Calvinist merchants from the more swashbuckling style he associated with Renaissance Venice. Weber, *General Economic History*, 351–369.
33. Smith, *Advertisements*, in *Complete Works*, 3:272.
34. *Ibid.*, 273.
35. Smith, *The Proceedings of the English Colonie in Virginia* . . . (1612), in *Complete Works*, 1:264–265. J. A. Leo Lemay points out that II Thessalonians 3:10, with its manifestly anti-aristocratic implications, "was a rallying cry of social unrest during the Interregnum." *American Dream of John Smith*, 186.
36. Smith, *Generall Historie*, in *Complete Works*, 2:213–214.
37. Smith, *Advertisements*, in *Complete Works*, 3:271–272.
38. Smith, *Generall Historie*, in *Complete Works*, 2:157.
39. Edmund S. Morgan, *American Slavery–American Freedom: The Ordeal of Colonial Virginia* (New York, 1975), 71–91.
40. Smith, *Advertisements*, in *Complete Works*, 3:271–272; italics added.
41. *Ibid.*, 272.
42. Karen Ordahl Kupperman, *Providence Island, 1630–1641: The Other Puritan Colony* (Cambridge, Engl., 1993).
43. Edward Winslow, *Good Newes from New England; or a true Relation of things very remarkable at the Plantation of Plimoth in New-England* (London, 1624), repr. in Alexander Young, ed., *Chronicles of the Pilgrim Fathers of the Colony of Plymouth, from 1602 to 1625*, 2d ed (Boston, 1844), 272–273, 370–371; Matthew Cradock to John Winthrop, 27 February 1639/40, *Winthrop Papers*, 4:207–208.
44. Smith, *Advertisements*, in *Complete Works*, 3:287.
45. Thomas Mun, *England's Treasure by Forraign Trade* (New York, 1903 [orig. 1664]), 7–8.
46. William Ames, *Cases of Conscience*, in *Works* (London, 1643), 254–255.
47. Smith, *Complete Works*, 1:346.
48. *Ibid.*, 3:287; *Description of New England*, 1:349.
49. Robert L. Heilbroner, *The Worldly Philosophers: The Lives, Times, and Ideas of the Great Economic Thinkers* (New York, 1980), 18.

50. Smith, *Advertisements,* in *Complete Works,* 3:287.
51. Smith, *Generall Historie,* in *Complete Works,* 2:463; Smith, *Advertisements,* in *Complete Works,* 3:287.
51. Smith, *Advertisements,* 3:300.
52. Smith, *Advertisements,* 3:270.
53. *Winthrop's Journal,* 1:117; Hunt, *Puritan Moment,* 79–81.
54. *Winthrop Papers,* 2:147.
55. George and George, *Protestant Mind,* 142.
56. Lemay, *American Dream of John Smith,* 206.
57. Peter N. Carroll, *Puritanism and the Wilderness: The Intellectual Significance of the New England Frontier, 1629–1700* (London, 1969), 56, 53; White, *Planter's Plea,* 391.
58. [Edward] *Johnson's Wonder-Working Providence,* J. Franklin Jameson, ed. (New York, 1910), 210; Karen Ordahl Kupperman, "Climate and Mastery of the Wilderness in Seventeenth-Century New England," in *Publications of the Colonial Society of Massachusetts,* 63 (1984), *Seventeenth-Century New England,* 4–5.
59. Richard Mather to William Rathband and ________, 25 June 1636, in Emerson, ed., *Letters from New England,* 205; *Johnson's Wonder-Working Providence,* 209–210.
60. John [?] Pond to William Pond, 15 March 1630/31, in Emerson, ed., *Letters from New England,* 64–65.
61. John Winthrop, "Reasons to be Considered," *Winthrop Papers,* 2:144, italics added; *Johnson's Wonder-Working Providence,* 111.
62. *Johnson's Wonder-Working Providence,* 187; "Narrative Concerning the Settlement of New England," in *Massachusetts Historical Society Proceedings,* 5 (1862), 131.
63. Karen Ordahl Kupperman, "Errand to the Indies: Puritan Colonization from Providence Island to the Western Design," *William and Mary Quarterly,* 3d Ser., 45 (1988), 70–99.
64. *Winthrop's Journal,* 1:116, 133; *Johnson's Wonder-Working Providence,* 111.
65. Lemay, *American Dream of John Smith,* 170.
66. Josiah Child, "A Discourse Concerning Plantations," in Trevor R. Reese, ed., *The Most Delightful Country of the Universe: Promotional Literature of the Colony of Georgia, 1717–1734* (Savannah, 1972), 106–107; Whistler quoted in David W. Galenson, *White Servitude in Colonial America: An Economic Analysis* (Cambridge, Engl., 1981), 48 (spelling modernized); Bradford, "Some Observations of God's Merciful Dealing with Us in the Wilderness" (1654), reprinted in David Levin, *Forms of Uncertainty: Essays in Historical Criticism* (Charlottesville, Va., 1992), 15.
67. The equation between a warm climate and a weak work ethic eventually became, of course, a staple of American discourse. Ignoring the radically labor-intensive nature of tobacco cultivation, Robert Beverley took his fellow Virginians to task in 1705 for depending "altogether upon the Liberality of Nature, without endeavouring to improve its Gifts, by Art or Industry." Employing improving rhetoric, Beverley declared of the Virginians: "They spunge upon the Blessings of a warm Sun, and a fruitful Soil, and almost [begrudge] the Pains of gathering in the Bounties of the Earth. I should be ashamed to publish this slothful Indolence of my Countrymen, but I hope it will rouse them out of their Lethargy, and excite them to make the most of all those happy Advantages which Nature has given them." Robert Beverley, *The History and*

Present State of Virginia (1705), Louis B. Wright, ed. (Charlottesville, Va., 1968), 319.

For some Americans, the link between a warm climate and a weak work ethic undergirded the sectional crisis that ultimately led to the Civil War. The key was always the degradation of hard, productive, property-creating toil thought to have been caused by the enervating climes of the plantation colonies. Thomas Jefferson wrote, in linking Virginia's climate to the rise of slavery, that "in a warm climate, no man will labour for himself who can make another labour for him." During the debates over ratification of the Constitution, one of the Anti-Federalists' arguments against the new government was that it conjoined the markedly dissimilar work cultures of the North and South. Sounding strikingly like John Winthrop in his endorsement of the Protestant ethic, "Cato" (probably New York Governor George Clinton) drew a direct correlation between a cold climate and the preservation of liberty. Writing in October 1787, he warned that "The people, who may compose this national legislature from the southern states, in which, from the mildness of the climate, the fertility of the soil, and the value of its [products], wealth is rapidly acquired, and where the same causes naturally lead to luxury, dissipation, and a passion for aristocratic distinctions; where slavery in encouraged, and liberty of course, less respected, and protected; who know not what it is to acquire property by their own toil, nor to oeconomise with the savings of industry—will these men therefore be as tenacious of the liberties and interests of the more northern states, where freedom, independence, industry, equality, and frugality, are natural to the climate and soil. . . ?" For Smith and Winthrop, as for "Cato" and Alexis de Tocqueville, this was self-evidently a rhetorical question. Thomas Jefferson, *Notes on the State of Virginia . . .* (1787), William Peden, ed. (Chapel Hill, 1954), 163; "Cato" III, *New York Journal* (25 October 1787), in John P. Kaminski and Richard Leffler, eds., *Federalists and Antifederalists* (Madison, 1987), 16–17. For additional considerations of the contrast between the northern and southern work ethic, see C. Vann Woodward, "The Southern Ethic in a Puritan World," *William and Mary Quarterly,* 3d Ser., 25 (1968), 343–370; Fred Bertleston, *The Lazy South* (New York, 1967), 104, 244; and Elliott J. Gorn, "Gouge and Bite, Pull Hair and Scratch: The Social Significance of Fighting in the Southern Backcountry," *American Historical Review,* 90 (1985), 18–43.

68. Terence Hutchison, *Before Adam Smith: The Emergence of Political Economy, 1662–1776* (Oxford, 1988), 35–41.
69. Crowley, *Sheba, Self,* 155–156; E. A. J. Johnson, "Economic Ideas of John Winthrop," *New England Quarterly,* 3 (1930), 235–237, 246; Lemay, *American Dream of John Smith,* 217.
70. Winthrop, "Reasons to be Considered," *Winthrop Papers,* 2:138–139. I would like to acknowledge L. Bruce Coffey's assistance in these formulations.
71. John Winthrop to [John Wheelwright?], [ca. March 1638/39], *Winthrop Papers,* 4:102.
72. *Winthrop's Journal,* 1:144; Winthrop, "Reasons to be Considered," *Winthrop Papers,* 2:143–144; Darrett Rutman, "God's Bridge Falling Down," *William and Mary Quarterly,* 3d Ser., 19 (1962), 410–412.
73. Johnson, "Economic Ideas of Winthrop," 235–236.
74. *Winthrop Papers,* 2:282–295.

75. Winthrop, "Modell of Christian Charity," *Winthrop Papers,* 2:285.
76. Roy P. Basler, ed., *Abraham Lincoln: His Speeches and Writings* (New York, 1962), 394–395, 792–793.
77. Marion H. Gottfried, "The First Depression in Massachusetts," *New England Quarterly,* 9 (1936), 655; William Cronon, *Changes in the Land: Indians, Colonists, and the Ecology of New England* (New York, 1983), 108–126.
78. Kenneth Silverman, *The Life and Times of Cotton Mather* (New York, 1984), 280.
79. Perry Miller, *The New England Mind: From Colony to Province* (Boston, 1961 [orig. 1953]), 44.
80. Appleby, *Economic Thought,* 73; Jan deVries, "On the Modernity of the Dutch Republic," *Journal of Economic History,* 33 (1973), 191–202.
81. Simon Schama, *Embarrassment of Riches: An Interpretation of Dutch Culture in the Golden Age* (New York, 1987), chaps. 1–3.
82. Hutchison, *Before Adam Smith,* 38–41; Appleby, *Economic Thought,* 79.
83. Appleby, *Economic Thought,* 97; deVries, "On the Modernity of the Dutch Republic," 200.
84. Smith, *Description of New-England,* in *Complete Works,* 1:330–331.
85. *Ibid.,* 1:326, 323, 330.
86. Smith, *Advertisements,* in *Complete Works,* 3:289.
87. Thomas Paine, *Common Sense,* Isaac Kramnick, ed. (Middlesex, Engl., 1976), 25–57; Isaac Kramnick, *Republicanism and Bourgeois Radicalism: Political Ideology in Late Eighteenth-Century England and America* (Ithaca, 1990), 133–160.
88. Richard Saltonstall to Emmanuel Downing, 4 February 1631/32, in Emerson, ed., *Letters from New England,* 92.
89. Winthrop, "The Grounds of Settling a Plantation in New England," *Winthrop Papers,* 2:146–147; John Winthrop to Thomas Hooker [ca. March 1638/39], *ibid.,* 4:99–100.
90. Winthrop, "The Grounds of Settling a Plantation in New England," *Winthrop Papers,* 2:147.
91. William Wood, *New England's Prospect* (1634), Alden T. Vaughan, ed. (Amherst, Mass., 1977), 72–73.
92. Michael Zuckerman, "The Fabrication of Identity in Early America," *William and Mary Quarterly,* 3d Ser., 34 (1977), 194; Frederick B. Tolles, *Meeting House and Counting House: The Quaker Merchants of Colonial Philadelphia, 1682–1763* (New York, 1963), 206.
93. Perry Miller and Thomas H. Johnson, eds., *The Puritans: A Sourcebook of Their Writings,* 2 vols. (New York, 1963), 1:7.
94. Bond-Webster, "Christian Charitie." It was in the seventeenth century, writes Joyce Appleby, that began "that stream of improvement tracts that has never ceased to flow from Western presses—descriptions of how to reclaim wastelands, link up rivers with canals, thresh wheat and, yes, build better mousetraps." Appleby, *Capitalism and a New Social Order: The Republican Vision of the 1790s* (New York, 1984), 35.

    As Keith Thomas summarizes this English enlightenment, it was primarily an intellectual and cultural transformation: "The change which occurred in the seventeenth century was . . . not so much technical as mental. In many different spheres of life the period saw the emergence of a new faith in the potentialities of human initiative. The energetic if unsuccessful Tudor efforts to control poverty and eliminate vagabondage were continued and extended. Agricultural writers campaigned against what they called the pattern of ancient ignorance, just as politicans rejected the appeal to precedent. It was a sustained period of innovation, of experiment with ley farming, fen drainage, and new crops: fertilisers in place of fertility rites. 'If one experiment fail,' wrote John Norden in 1607, 'try a second, a third, and many.' In industry there were innovations of many kinds, and the prolonged experiment with ways of using coal in the manufacture of iron reached the eve of successful completion. Equally notable faith in the potentialities of activism and experiment were displayed by the radical groups of the Interregnum, who proposed to remodel the whole of society by legislative action. Their hopes were dashed by the Restoration, but the notion that political remedies could be found for social and economic discontents was less easily checked." Thomas, *Religion and the Decline of Magic,* 661.

95. The saints, as I have been emphasizing, attempted to channel and control the industriousness their own ethic inspired. The General Court, although with some initial reluctance, loosened government's regulatory hand on the acts of buying and selling goods and labor, but it was New England's rich array of local institutions—families, churches, and schools—that worked to try to ensure that this new freedom would be exercised in an ethical and socially responsible fashion. While New England's public culture was contractual, its private was communal. "If thy brother be in want," Winthrop declared in the *Arbella* sermon, "and thou canst help him, thou needst not make doubt what thou shouldst doe; if thou lovest God, thou must help him." Winthrop, "Modell of Christian Charity," *Winthrop Papers,* 2:286.
96. Erasmus, *Ten Colloquies,* Craig R. Thompson, trans. (New York, 1986), 56–91.
97. Dugald Stewart, *Biographical Memoirs of Adam Smith* (Edinburgh, 1811), 100.
98. Johnson, *Predecessors of Adam Smith,* 45–46; Foster, *Their Solitary Way,* 99.
99. *Mass. Recs.,* 1:111.
100. *Ibid.,* 1:126.
101. *Ibid.,* 1:253.
102. *Ibid.,* 3:243.
103. *Ibid.,* 3:243; 4 (pt. 2):41–42; Miller, *New England Mind,* 312. As late as 1786 the General Court was still using such grievances to proclaim the need for a general "reformation of manners" (morals) in Massachusetts if there was to be any "hope to prosper in our public and private concerns." Notable by its absence in the now republican Bay State, however, was the tendency to blame everything on the "Ordinary sort." Amidst the tumult of Shays' Rebellion, the Court forged an appeal that combined elements of Puritanism, republicanism, and liberalism: "That virtue, which is necessary to support a Republic, has declined; and as a people, we are now in the precise channel, in which the liberty of States has generally been swallowed up. But still our case is not desperate; by recurring to the principles of integrity and public spirit, and the practice of industry, sobriety, economy, and fidelity in contracts, and by acquiescing in laws necessary for the public good, the impending ruin may be averted, and we [may] become respectable and happy." "An Address from the General Court, to the People of the Commonwealth of Massachusetts" (1786), in Richard D. Brown, ed., *Major Problems in*

the Era of the American Revolution, 1760–1791 (Lexington, Mass., 1992), 431.

104. John Eliot to Sir Simonds D'Ewes, 18 September 1633, in Emerson, ed., *Letters from New England,* 107–108.
105. *Winthrop's Journal,* 2:228.
106. This realization eventually became a staple of political economic discourse in British America. In explaining the depopulation of the Hudson Valley patroonships during the pre-Revolutionary era, New York's Cadwallader Colden wrote in the spirit of John Smith when he declared that "every year the Young people go from this Province and Purchase Land in the Neighboring Colonies, while much better and every way more convenient Lands [in New York itself] lie useless to the King and Country. The reason for this is that the [owners] themselves are not, nor never were in a Capacity to improve such large Tracts and other People will not become their Vassals or Tenants for one great reason: as people's (the better sort especially) [reasons for] leaving their native Country, was to avoid the dependence on landlords, and to enjoy in fee [simple land tenure] to descend to their posterity that their children may reap the benefit of their labor and Industry." Quoted in Irving Mark, *Agrarian Conflicts in Colonial New York, 1711–1775* (New York, 1940), 14.
107. Barbara L. Solow, "Slavery and Colonization," in Solow, ed., *Slavery and the Rise of the Atlantic System* (Cambridge, Engl., 1991), 32–37.
108. Emmanuel Downing to John Winthrop, [ca. August 1645], *Winthrop Papers,* 5:38.
109. The case against Fairbanks was eventually discharged, "it appearing that he did not wear them after the law was published." George Francis Dow, ed., *Records and Files of the Quarterly Courts of Essex County, Massachusetts,* 8 vols. (Salem, Mass., 1911–21; cited hereafter as *Essex Ct. Recs.*), 1:274.

CHAPTER 3: The Protestant Ethic and the Culture of Discipline

1. Weber, *Protestant Ethic,* 13–31; Joyce Appleby, "Value and Society," in Jack P. Greene and J. R. Pole, eds., *Colonial British America: Essays in the New History of the Early Modern Era* (Baltimore, 1984), 291.
2. Adam Smith, *Theory of Moral Sentiments* (1759) (Indianapolis, 1982), 50; John Locke, *An Essay Concerning Human Understanding,* Alexander Campbell Fraser, ed., 2 vols. (Oxford, 1894), 1:304.
3. Michael Walzer, *Spheres of Justice: A Defense of Pluralism and Equality* (New York, 1983), 186; Tocqueville and Malthus quoted in Gertrude Himmelfarb, *The Idea of Poverty: England in the Early industrial Age* (New York, 1984), 107, 149; Arthur Young, *Farmer's Tour* (London, 1771), 4:361.
4. Anthony Brewer, *A Guide to Marx's "Capital"* (Cambridge, Engl., 1984), 7; Leslie A. Mulholland, "Hegel and Marx on the Human Individual," in William Desmond, ed., *Hegel and His Critics: Philosophy in the Aftermath of Hegel* (Albany, 1989), 56–62.
5. Marx and Engels, *German Ideology,* in Eugene Kamenka, ed.,, *Portable Karl Marx* (New York, 1983), 164; E. J. Lieberman, *Acts of Will: The Life and Work of Otto Rank* (New York, 1985). For a pioneering academic

foray into some of these issues, see Frank Knight, "The Ethics of Competition," *Quarterly Journal of Economics,* 37 (1923), 579–624.

6. Norman F. Cantor and Peter L. Klein, eds., *Ancient Thought: Plato and Aristotle* (Waltham, Mass., 1969), 133 (quotation); Jane Jacobs, *Systems of Survival: A Dialogue on the Moral Foundations of Commerce and Politics* (New York, 1992); Ernest Barker, *The Political Thought of Plato and Aristotle* (New York, 1959), 242; Thomas L. Pangle, *The Spirit of Modern Republicanism: The Moral Vision of the American Founders and the Philosophy of Locke* (Chicago, 1988), 53–61; Walzer, *Spheres of Justice,* 53; Josef Pieper, *Leisure, The Basis of Culture* (New York, 1952); Eugene F. Rice, *The Renaissance Idea of Wisdom* (Westport, Conn., 1975); Isaac Kramnick, *Republicanism and Bourgeois Radicalism: Political Ideology in Late Eighteenth-Century England and America* (Ithaca, 1990), 1.
7. Hesiod, *Theogony & Works and Days,* M. L. West, trans. (Oxford, 1988), 37, 46, 49.
8. I am indebted to Vanessa Karahalios for her assistance in clarifying these issues.
9. John Boardman, Jasper Griffin, and Oswyn Murray, *The Oxford History of the Roman World* (Oxford, 1991), 90–118. I would like to thank Elizabeth Meyer for her assistance in these formulations.
10. John W. Baldwin, "The Medieval Theories of the Just Price: Romanists, Canonists, and Theologians in the Twelfth and Thirteenth Centuries," in *Pre-Capitalist Economic Thought: Three Modern Interpretations* (New York, 1972), 7; Keith Thomas, "Work and Leisure in Pre-Industrial Society," *Past and Present,* 29 (1964), 57, 59; Richard B. McBrien, *Catholicism,* 2 vols. (Minneapolis, 1980), 2:569–655.
11. J. E. Crowley, *This Sheba, Self: The Conceptualization of Economic Life in Eighteenth-Century America* (Baltimore, 1974), 40; E. Lipson, *The Economic History of England,* vol. 2, *The Age of Mercantilism* (London, 1956), lxxiv–lxxxvi; William Letwin, *The Origins of Scientific Economics: English Economic Thought, 1660–1776* (London, 1963), 136. Such thinking reached its apogee in the writings of Ferinando Galiani (1728–1787), who described labor as "the sole source of value," subject to scarcity, utility, and demand. Terence W. Hutchison, *Before Adam Smith: The Emergence of Political Economy, 1662–1776* (Oxford, 1988), 257.
12. D. C. Coleman, "Labor in the English Economy of the Seventeenth Century," in E. H. Carus-Wilson, ed., *Essays in Economic History,* 3 vols. (London, 1954–62), 2:294–295.
13. Joyce Appleby, *Capitalism and a New Social Order: The Republican Vision of the 1790s* (New York, 1984), 35. This is not to say, of course, that the ancient and aristocratic tendencies to disparage manual labor completely disappeared as a consequence of the Protestant Reformation. During the nineteenth century John Ruskin believed it was still necessary to make a conspicuous effort to eliminate "the dishonor of manual labor done. . . ." James Clark Sherburne, *John Ruskin, or the Ambiguities of Abundance: A Study in Social and Economic Criticism* (Cambridge, Mass., 1972), 283.
14. McBrien, *Catholicism,* 2:618; Cardinal Gasquet, *The Rule of St. Benedict* (London, 1925), chap. 48. David S. Landes has characterized the Cistercians, for example, as "as much an economic as a spiritual enterprise (they would not have recognized a difference). Their agriculture was the most advanced in Europe; their factories and mines, the most efficient. They made extensive use of hired labor, and their concern for

costs made them turn wherever possible to labor-saving devices. Their Rule enjoined them, for example, to build near rivers, so as to have access to water power; and they learned to use this in multifunctional, staged installations designed to exploit power capacity to the maximum." Landes, *Revolution in Time: Clocks and the Making of the Modern World* (Cambridge, Mass., 1983), 69.

15. Stephen Foster, *Their Solitary Way: The Puritan Social Ethic in the First Century of Settlement in New England* (New Haven, 1971), 108; Elizabeth Eisenstein, *The Printing Press as an Agent of Change: Communications and Cultural Transformations in Early Modern Europe,* 2 vols. (Cambridge, Engl., 1979), 1:384; Richard A. Goldthwaite, *The Building of Renaissance Florence: An Economic and Social History* (Baltimore, 1980); Winifred Barr Rothenberg, *From Market-Places to a Market Economy: The Transformation of Rural Massachusetts, 1750–1850* (Chicago, 1992), 9; Raymond De Roover, "Accounting Prior to Luca Pacioli," in A. C. Littleton and B. S. Yamey, eds., *Studies in the History of Accounting* (London, 1956), 114–174.
16. Baldwin, *Pre-Capitalist Economic Thought,* 7; Quentin Skinner, *The Foundations of Modern Political Thought,* 2 vols. (Cambridge, Engl., 1978), 2:323; Richard A. Goldthwaite, "Urban Values and the Entrepreneur: Values of the Marketplace; the Spirit of Corporatism, the Personality of the Monetary Nexus, Time—Civic Values—Consumerism—Class Ethos," in S. Cavaciocchi, ed., *L'impressa: Industria Commerico Bansa, secc. XIII–XVIII* (atti della Settimano di Studi e altri Convegni, no. 22 [Prato, 1991]), 647; Hutchison, *Before Adam Smith,* 100–103.

    The society of the Three Orders—those who pray, those who fight, and those who work—reached its peak on the Continent during the revival of both royal and episcopal authority in the late eleventh and early twelfth centuries. Natalie Davis, however, has argued that in France it was still "very much alive in the eighteenth century until the three estates came crashing down in the French Revolution." "Revolution and Revelation," *New York Review of Books* (2 February 1984), 33.
17. Robin Briggs, "The Catholic Puritans: Jansenists and Rigorists in France," in D. Pennington and K. Thomas, eds., *Puritans and Revolutionaries: Essays in 17th Century History* (Oxford, 1978), 333–357.
18. Gordon Marshall, *In Search of the Spirit of Capitalism: An Essay on Max Weber's Protestant Ethic Thesis* (New York, 1982), 71–72; David D. Hall, "On Common Ground: The Coherence of American Puritan Studies," *William and Mary Quarterly,* 3d Ser., 44 (1987), 210, 221; Daniel T. Rodgers, *The Work Ethic in Industrial America, 1850–1920* (Chicago, 1978), 8.
19. Helmut T. Lehmann and Jaroslav J. Pelikan, eds., *Luther's Works,* 55 vols. (New Haven, 1955–86), 44:189–190.
20. Christopher Hill, "Protestantism and the Rise of Capitalism," in F. J. Fisher, ed., *Essays in Economic and Social History of Tudor and Stuart England* (Cambridge, Engl., 1961), 30.
21. Michael Novak, *The Catholic Ethic and the Spirit of Capitalism* (New York, 1993), xv.
22. D. Hall, "On Common Ground," 210.
23. John Dillenberger, *Martin Luther: Selections from His Writings* (New York, 1962), Part One; Marshall, *Spirit of Capitalism,* 71–72.
24. Herbert Lüthy, "Once Again, Calvinism and Capitalism," in S.N. Eisenstadt, ed., *The Protestant Ethic and Modernization: A Comparative View*

(New York, 1968), 103; Bernard Bailyn, *The New England Merchants in the Seventeenth Century* (New York, 1964 [orig. 1955]), 20.

25. Charles L. Cohen, *God's Caress: The Psychology of Puritan Religious Experience* (New York, 1986), 111–133; Hall, "On Common Ground," 221–222.
26. Benjamin Nelson, "Self-Images and Systems of Spiritual Direction in the History of European Civilization," in Samuel Z. Klausner, ed., *The Quest for Self-Control: Classical Philosophies and Scientific Research* (New York, 1965), 49–103, esp. 69–75; Adam Seligman, "Inner-worldly Individualism and the Institutionalization of Puritanism in Late Seventeenth-Century New England," *British Journal of Sociology,* 41 (1990), 539.
27. Seligman, "Inner-worldly Individualism," 539.
28. Lüthy, "Calvinism and Capitalism," 103.
29. *Ibid.*
30. Edmund S. Morgan, *American Slavery–American Freedom: The Ordeal of Colonial Virginia* (New York, 1975), 295–296; Foster, *Their Solitary Way,* 108.

    Some have gone so far as to declare that the "work-in-the-world calling occupies the center of English Protestant attention—so much so that the particular calling comes very close to becoming the spiritual, salvation-working calling as well as the moral, socially utilitarian vocation." George and George, *The Protestant Mind,* 169. While the works righteousness implied in this comment failed to take hold in British America before the mid-eighteenth century, there is little doubt that the calling was not only among the most important elements of the European ethical heritage transmitted to America but also among the most long-lived.
31. Crowley, *Sheba, Self,* 54.
32. Edmund S. Morgan, "The Puritan Ethic and the American Revolution," *William and Mary Quarterly,* 3d Ser., 24 (1967), 4.
33. *Ibid.,* 4–5.
34. Raymond De Roover, "Scholastic Economics: Survival and Lasting Influence from the Sixteenth Century to Adam Smith," *Quarterly Journal of Economics,* 69 (1955), 179; George and George, *Protestant Mind,* 143; Crowley, *Sheba, Self,* 40–41; M. J. Kitch, ed., *Capitalism and the Reformation* (London, 1967), 90; E. A. J. Johnson, *Predecessors of Adam Smith: The Growth of British Economic Thought* (New York, 1937), 69; Laura Caroline Stevenson, *Praise and Paradox: Merchants and Craftsmen in Elizabethan Popular Literature* (Cambridge, Engl., 1984).
35. Letwin, *Scientific Economics,* 87; De Roover, "Scholastic Economics," 179; John White to John Winthrop, 1637, in *Winthrop Papers,* 3:336; Elizabeth Fox-Genovese, *The Origins of Physiocracy: Economic Revolution and Social Order in Eighteenth-Century France* (Ithaca, 1976), 100–102; Thomas K. McCraw, "The Trouble with Adam Smith," *American Scholar,* 61 (1992), 369.
36. Baxter quoted in Winthrop S. Hudson, "Puritanism and the Spirit of Capitalism," *Church History,* 18 (1949), 12n.
37. Eric G. Nellis, "Labor and Community in Massachusetts Bay, 1630–1660," *Labor History,* 18 (1977), 534; J. R. T. Hughes, *Social Control in a Colonial Economy* (Charlottesville, Va., 1976), 105.
38. *Mass. Recs.,* 4 (pt. 2):552.

39. Scholars either, in the manner of the new social historians, portray seventeenth-century New England as a traditionalist, market-averse society that did not embrace the Protestant ethic or, in the manner of Darrett Rutman's pioneering *Winthrop's Boston,* contend that the colony did embrace the Protestant ethic, but that it quickly gave way to the spirit of capitalism—indeed, in Rutman's case, even before the death of John Winthrop himself in 1649. Darrett B. Rutman, *Winthrop's Boston: Portrait of a Puritan Town, 1630–1649* (Chapel Hill, 1965), 279.
40. Miller, *The New England Mind,* 41; Perry Miller and Thomas H. Johnson, eds., *The Puritans: A Sourcebook of Their Writings,* 2 vols. (New York, 1963), 1:325–326, 319–320.
41. John Cotton, *Christ the Fountain of Life,* in Heimert and Delbanco, eds., *Puritans in America,* 30, 31.
42. Heimert and Delbanco, eds., *Puritans in America,* 30–31.
43. *Ibid.*
44. Richard Baxter, *The Poor Man's Family Book,* 6th edn (London, 1697), 290–291; Shepard quoted in Miller, *The New England Mind,* 44.
45. Richard Baxter, *A Christian Directory* (London, 1673), 277.
46. Cotton Mather, *Parentator,* 38; Bernard Bailyn, ed., "The Apologia of Robert Keayne, being the Last Will and Testament of Me, Robert Keayne, All of it Written with My Own Hands and Begun by Me, Mo: 6: 1: 1653. . . ," *Colonial Society of Massachusetts Transactions,* 42 (1964), 321–322.
47. Foster, *Their Solitary Way,* 122.
48. Thomas, "Work and Leisure," 62; Marshall, *Spirit of Capitalism,* 70–71. This cultural transformation did not, of course, end with Puritan New England. The historian G. M. Trevelyan once observed to his brother Charles of the Victorian "culture of altruism" that "we inherit the moral stamina produced in grandpa by religion or otherwise, and apply it straight off to our infidel sense of duty." David Cannadine, *G. M. Trevelyan: A Life in History* (New York, 1993), 51.
49. Antonio Gramsci, *Selections from the Prison Notebooks of Antonio Gramsci,* Quintin Hoare and Geoffrey Nowell Smith, eds. (New York, 1971), 281, 300; James Joll, *Gramsci* (Glasgow, 1977), 90. Even in the twentieth century, Gramsci writes, "there do not exist [in America] numerous classes without an essential function in the world of production, that is, totally parasitic classes. European 'tradition,' European 'civilization' is on the other hand characterized by the existence of such classes, created by the 'richness' and 'complexity' of past history, which has left a pile of passive sediment through the phenomena of saturation and fossilization of the state officials and of the intellectuals, of the clergy and the landed proprietors, of predatory commerce and of the army. We can say therefore that the older the history of a country, the more numerous and burdensome is this sedimentation of a mass of useless idlers who live on the 'inheritance' of their 'ancestors,' of these pensioners of economic history." *Prison Notebooks,* 281.

From the vantage point of Puritan republicanism during the Civil War period, it is also relatively easy to apply Gramsci's conception of civil society, in opposition to the state, as the prime locus for revolutionary praxis. *Prison Notebooks,* 12; Adam Seligman, *The Idea of Civil Society* (New York, 1992), x; Norberto Bobbio, "Gramsci and the Concept of Civil Society," in John Keane, ed., *Civil Society and the State: New European Perspectives* (London, 1988), 73–99.

50. Himmelfarb, *Idea of Poverty,* 27.
51. Historians of late sixteenth- and early seventeenth-century English Puritanism are increasingly emphasizing the influence of Reformed theologians from Heidelberg and Zurich (and the Rhineland generally). C. M. Dent describes William Perkins as the "English popularizer" of Theodorus Beza and Hieronymus Zanchius. Dent, *Protestant Reformers in Elizabethan Oxford* (Oxford, 1983), 91–100 (quotation, 100); Hall, "On Common Ground," 202–203.
52. Samuel Eliot Morison, *Builders of the Bay Colony* (Boston, 1958), 166–167; Miller, *New England Mind,* 41; Winton V. Solberg, *Redeem the Time: The Puritan Sabbath in Early America* (Cambridge, Mass., 1977), 44; Miller and Johnson, eds., *The Puritans,* 1:319, 323.
53. Foster, *Their Solitary Way,* 105 (quotation); Weber, *Protestant Ethic,* 13–31; Walzer, "Revolutionary Ideology," 62; Hall, "On Common Ground," 216.
54. Weber, *Protestant Ethic,* 111–112, 117, 172; Michael McGiffert, "Grace and Works: The Rise and Division of Covenant Theology in Elizabethan Puritanism," *Harvard Theological Review,* 75 (1982), 463–502; William K. B. Stoever, *"A Faire and Easie Way to Heaven": Covenant Theology and Antinomianism in Early Massachusetts* (Middletown, Conn., 1978), 8; David A. Weir, *The Origins of Federal Theology in Sixteenth-Century Reformation Thought* (New York, 1990), 154; John S. Coolidge, *The Pauline Renaissance in England: Puritanism and the Bible* (Oxford, 1970), 141–151.
55. Cohen, *God's Caress,* 55–63.
56. Stoever, *Faire and Easie Way to Heaven,* 8, italics added; Weir, *Origins of Federal Theology,* 154; Michael McGiffert, "William Tyndale's Conception of Covenant," *Journal of Ecclesiastical History,* 32 (1981), 169–170.
57. Robert G. Pope, *The Half-Way Covenant: Church Membership in Puritan New England* (Princeton, 1969), 3–5.
58. Edmund S. Morgan, *Visible Saints: The History of a Puritan Idea* (Ithaca, 1958), 69; Andrew Delbanco, *The Puritan Ordeal* (Cambridge, Mass., 1989), 149–150. I am profoundly indebted to John M. Murrin for redirecting my thoughts on these issues.
59. Edmund S. Morgan, *The Puritan Dilemma: The Story of John Winthrop* (Boston, 1958), 69; Miller, *New England Mind,* 69.
60. Samuel Willard, *A Compleat Body of Divinity in Two Hundred and Fifty Expository Lectures on the Assembly's Shorter Catechism* (Boston, 1726), as excerpted in David A. Hollinger and Charles Capper, eds., *The American Intellectual Tradition: A Sourcebook,* 2 vols. (New York, 1989), 1:21.
61. Dent, *Protestant Reformers in Elizabethan Oxford,* 99–100.
62. Morgan, *Visible Saints,* 68–71; Murrin, personal communication.
63. Morgan, *Puritan Dilemma,* 139 (quotation), 152.
64. Despite obvious cultural and economic contrasts, the specific connection between the Protestant ethic and commercial growth remains highly contested scholarly terrain. It is difficult to believe that the Protestant ethic did not have something to do with the contrasting economic destinies since 1600 of Holland and Belgium, England and Spain, and North and South America—not to mention the highly differentiated economic fortunes of the Protestant and Catholic regions of Germany and France. There is also the fact that Protestant minorities, but not Catholic minorities, served as the "yeast" for entrepreneurial developments in Northwest Europe during the sixteenth and seventeenth cen-

turies. Protestants in France, but not Catholics in England, were disproportionately represented in the ranks of successful inventors and entrepreneurs because Calvinistic Protestantism apparently fostered such endeavor and self-discipline more successfully than did Catholic doctrine.

To be sure, with the important exception of usury prohibitions, it was not Catholicism per se but rather the intolerance of the Counter-Reformation (the Index and Inquisition) that was most responsible for thwarting the economic growth of non-Protestant Europe. The purging of heretics, in Christianity's darkest century, was anything but casual; and it is not unreasonable to surmise that in such pogroms as the St. Bartholomew's Massacre (the three-day massacre of French Protestants in August 1572, sanctioned by Charles IX) a disproportionate number of economically talented people perished. In the Low Countries alone, something close to six thousand heretics were burned by order of Holy Roman Emperor Charles V during a reign that extended from 1516 to 1555. Over five thousand souls were executed in France during roughly the same period on orders of King Francis I and his son Henry II. As a result of the Counter-Reformation, early centers of Renaissance humanism such as Venice, Florence, and Antwerp—particularly in the areas of printing and bookmaking—became eclipsed by such rising Protestant centers as Amsterdam, Rotterdam, and London. By the mid-seventeenth century, Amsterdam had become the "central city of the Republic of Letters." Within the church, the liberalizing and reform tendencies that had begun with the Conciliarists and jurists failed to achieve their early promise. The Reformation's greatest consequence, it seems fair to argue, was not only to unleash the acquisitive impulse in Protestant Europe but to thwart the liberalizing impulse elsewhere. Lüthy, "Calvinism and Capitalism," 94; Baldwin Smith, *This Realm of England,* 154; Eisenstein, *Printing Press,* 1:409.

Though few historians today accept the caricatured Weberian "rational accummulator" image, and the Puritan insistence on "weaned affections" is widely recognized, Protestantism's contribution to the rise of capitalism remains fundamentally unresolved. On the one hand, we have Christopher Hill's famous declaration that "it was in fact the labour of generations of God-fearing Puritans that made England the leading industrial nation of the world—God, as His manner is, helping those who helped themselves." Protestantism, he observes more concretely, "gave a vital stimulus to productive efforts in countries where capitalism was developing, at a time when industry was small-scale, handicraft, unrationalized." Hill presents artisans, merchants, and small entrepreneurs as capitalism's greatest beneficiaries. Like Weber before him, he speaks of the "capitalist spirit," by which he means "an ethos which, within the framework of a market economy, emphasizes productive industry, frugality, and accumulation *as good in themselves.*" Hill's Marxian-Weberian interpretation has been vigorously assailed from a number of scholarly and theological quarters. The assaults of Charles and Katherine George, Michael Walzer, and Herbert Lüthy have been especially telling. With regard to Tudor-Stuart England, the Georges assert that "the Protestant vocational ethic [was] totally opposed to the individual social philosophy of the emerging and soon to be triumphant bourgeois society." The Georges, like Christopher Hill, take a dim view of the social effects of early capitalism, but absolve

Protestant Reform of responsibility for these depredations: "The spawning years of the lusty, ruthless English capitalism of the sixteenth and seventeenth centuries constituted a transformation in society which the English ministers—who lived through the epoch of lost villages, mass unemployment, hordes of beggars and vagrants, unprecedented inflation, and the dwindling of parish incomes—protested with a vehemence." For the Georges, the rise of capitalism is to be found in the growth of science, secularism, and the nation-state, all of which they believe (like Robert Brenner) were "in unique combinations from the seventeenth century." Far from serving as midwives to the new capitalist era, the painful preachers attacked everything from "unmercifull monopolies" to the unreasonable prices of merchants. Such specific manifestations of city capitalism as mercantile and industrial operations, according to the Georges, were all "brought under unfriendly scrutiny: they were the chief source of sabbath-breaking, inferior workmanship, 'private and secret conspiracies' to rig markets and control prices, and the nefarious practices of speculation in commercial instruments and products." Hill, "Protestantism and Capitalism," 16n (quotation, italics added), 31–32, 38–39; George and George, *Protestant Mind,* 148–149, 169, 65.

Herbert Lüthy, in what I regard as the most persuasive assessment to date, decries the overly Hegelian quality of much of this debate. Arguments and counterarguments, he points out, are arrayed according to doctrine and theory rather than according to existing social practice in historically finite circumstances. Sixteenth-century Geneva, low-country Scotland from 1580 to 1650, or seventeenth-century Massachusetts—the three societies in which Calvinist social ethics actually found expression in daily life—rarely receive direct scrutiny. The most hotly contested scholarly terrain continues to be what might be dubbed the "elective affinity" question. This is the degree to which Calvinism was a fitting system of beliefs—cosmological, theological, ethical—for the rise of the commercial and industrial capitalist middle classes. Weber, Tawney, Ernst Troeltsch, and Hill assert that the Protestant ethic fostered the competitive individualism of the businessman; Walzer, the Georges, and (more recently) Charles Lloyd Cohen denounce such views as an instrumental caricature. As a result, despite the fact that "few historical arguments have produced a greater wealth of intellectually fertile, subtle, and often deeply disturbing *aperçus,*" few have "born a richer crop of basic misunderstandings." Pointing to the meager harvest of definitive and unambiguous results, Lüthy declares that "The whole subject [of the Protestant ethic] is lit by the flickering light of the illuminating, frequently obvious, but equivocal relationship between categories of concepts that are remote from one another and, furthermore, are themselves essentially vague; the *ethic* of a religious belief and the *spirit* of an economic system, the cure of souls and the balancing of accounts." Lüthy, "Calvinism and Capitalism," 87–88.

65. William Hunt, *The Puritan Moment: The Coming of Revolution in an English County* (Cambridge, Mass., 1983), 79; Harry S. Stout, *The New England Soul: Preaching and Religious Culture in Colonial New England* (New York, 1986), 299.
66. Hunt, *Puritan Moment,* 79. For a parallel discussion of "moral discipline and the ethic of productivity" among sixteenth-century Lutherans, see William John Wright, *Capitalism, the State, and the Lutheran Reformation:*

Sixteenth-Century Hesse (Athens, Ohio, 1988), 161–181.

67. Hartmut Lehmann, "Ascetic Protestantism and Economic Rationalism: Max Weber Revisited after Two Generations," *Harvard Theological Review,* 80 (1987), 315–317; Hall, "On Common Ground," 198–199; Robert Zaller, "Parliament and the Crisis of European Liberty," in J. H. Hexter, ed., *Parliament and Liberty: From the Reign of Elizabeth to the English Civil War* (Stanford, 1992), 201–224.
68. Lehmann, "Ascetic Protestantism," 315–317; Hunt, *Puritan Moment,* 88–92; William Haller, *The Rise of Puritanism* (Philadelphia, 1938), 269–270; Emory Elliott, *Power and the Pulpit in Puritan New England* (Princeton, 1975), 13; Delbanco, *Puritan Ordeal,* 47–50.
69. Hunt, *Puritan Moment,* 79–80.
70. Peter Clark, *The English Alehouse: A Social History, 1200–1830* (London, 1983), chap. 7.
71. Mary Douglas and Baron Isherwood, *The World of Goods: Towards an Anthropology of Consumption* (New York, 1979), 203.
72. Hunt, *Puritan Moment,* 129.
73. Himmelfarb, *Idea of Poverty,* 368. As with much in colonial New England, the means to these ends often violated—sometimes profoundly—post-Enlightenment sensibilities. In 1634, in a Hawthorne-like decree, one Robert Cole, "oft punished for drunkenness," was "ordered to wear a red D about his neck for a year." *Winthrop's Journal,* 1:120; William Hutchinson and others to John Winthrop, 29 June 1640, in *Winthrop Papers,*4:259–260; *Essex Ct. Recs.,* 1:58; 2:57.
74. Jacques Le Goff, *Time, Work, and Culture in the Middle Ages* (Chicago, 1980), 48; Rodgers, *Work Ethic,* 9; George and George, *Protestant Mind,* 134; Solberg, *Redeem the Time,* 27–58. In 1634, Timothy Hawkins and John Vauhan were fined 20s. each for "mispending their tyme in company keeping, drinkeing stronge water, and selling other. . . ." *Mass. Recs.,* 1:112; see also 1:213; 2:195.
75. Cotton Mather, *Bonifacius: An Essay upon the Good* (1710), David Levin, ed. (Cambridge, Mass., 1966), 9.
76. Cotton Mather, *Early Piety, Exemplified in the Life and Death of Mr. Nathanael Mather* (London, 1689), 39; Franklin quoted in E. P. Thompson, "Time, Work-Discipline and Industrial Capitalism," *Past and Present,* 38 (1967), 89.
77. Le Goff, *Time, Work, and Culture,* 29, 69.
78. *Ibid.,* 50–51.
79. Landes, *Revolution in Time,* 404n.
80. Le Goff, *Time, Work, and Culture,* 49. It was in Renaissance Italy that wasting one's time first became a serious spiritual concern. The fundamental issue was one of accountability. Italian merchants became "accountants of time." The Dominican friar Domenico Calva of Pisa (d. 1342) devoted two chapters of his *Disciplina degli Spirituali* to the need to take careful account of one's time and avoid wasting it at all costs. Developing a spiritual calculus for the use of one's time, he portrayed it as the Lost Talent in the Gospel. The result was a more acute sense of time-consciousness, particularly for daily schedules. Leon Battista Alberti, a century later, wrote that "In the morning when I get up, the first thing I do is think . . . what am I going to do today? So many things: I count them, think about them, and to each I assign its time." As with merchant capitalism generally, such sentiments subsequently moved north and west—especially to Holland and England. David

Landes writes that "Italy, country of Dante and Dondi del' Orologio, declined over the next two hundred years to a position of chronometric laxity and horological dependence. Alberti was Italian and Catholic, but by the late sixteenth century, the typical watch wearer was North European and Protestant."

Advances in clock- and watchmaking coinciding with the Reformation allowed for the spread of such a calculating ethic beyond the urban mercantile classes of Northwest Europe. Both watchmaking and watch wearing took hold with greatest rapidity among European Protestants living north of the Alps. The watch, for the worldly ascetics of post-Reformation Europe, was what the clock had been to the cloistered ascetics of the medieval period. In the city of Augsburg, with a population equally divided between Protestants and Catholics, 87 percent of the clockmakers were Protestants. When Louis XIV revoked the Edict of Nantes in 1685, he nearly destroyed the French watch industry by forcing some two thousand Huguenots into exile. Many of these refugees, like Huguenot printers and papermakers, went to England or Switzerland, where they helped lay the foundation for the great Swiss watch industry of the next century. It was during the seventeenth century that watch dials began to show half-hour and then quarter-hour divisions. Improvements in accuracy that David Landes characterizes as "spectacular" came through replacing the balance-wheel regulator with a pendulum. The pendulum clock, conceived through the joint efforts of Galileo and Christian Huygens between 1637 and 1656, reduced daily time variations from the fifteen minutes typical of the verge with a balance to near-modern deviations of between ten or fifteen seconds.

The new equation clocks allowed the English to become the first Western nation to convert the solar time people had always lived by to the mean time now universal in the world. These technological advances in timekeeping, declares Landes, were pushed by such "eminently mercantile and bourgeois societies" as Holland and England. Englishmen in particular, he avers, "wanted to know the right time." For watchmaking, the introduction of the balance spring revolutionized personal time discipline. Robert Hooke, physicist, biologist, and member of the Robert Boyle circle, introduced the use of balance springs for watches. Accuracy improved as daily variations for watches were reduced from approximately thirty to approximately five minutes. Minute hands were introduced and then, in the 1690s, second hands.

The most popular London watch, represented among the material remains of seventeenth-century New England, was known, not surprisingly, as the Puritan watch. The new requirements of social time reflected by this austere and accurate timepiece are described by Landes. It was "presumably made for that pious faction of the middle class that in the best Calvinist tradition looked askance at decoration and accepted the watch only as a useful device. No group anywhere was quicker to adopt the watch as monitor and hence to focus on precision, simplicity, and reliability as against versatility, ingenuity, or appearance." The watchmakers serving this market, themselves often Puritans, naturally stressed the same virtues. Le Goff, *Time, Work, and Culture,* 50–51; Landes, *Revolution in Time,* 91–93, 102–103, 128–129; Eisenstein, *Printing Press,* 1:414; Joel Mokyr, *The Lever of Riches: Technological Creativity and Economic Progress* (New York, 1990), 73.

81. Perkins, *Works,* 3:654.

82. Richard Eaton, *A Sermon Preached at the Funerall of Thomas Durton* (London, 1616), 13.
83. John Preston, *Sermons Preached Before His Majesty* (London, 1630), 18; *Winthrop Papers,* 2:288. In Jan van der Spriett's oft-reproduced 1688 portrait of Increase Mather, the Puritan divine is shown holding a copy of the scriptures, with a watch located conspicuously on the table at which he is working.
84. *Essex Ct. Recs.,*1:35.
85. Joseph H. Smith, ed., *Colonial Justice in Western Massachusetts (1639–1702): The Pynchon Court Record* . . . (Cambridge, Mass., 1961), 310.
86. *Pynchon Court Rec.,* 323; *Essex Ct. Recs.,* 2:236–237.
87. Rodgers, *Work Ethic,* 9.
88. Eliot letter, in Thomas Shepard, "The Clear Sunshine of the Gospel Breaking Forth upon the Indians in New-England" (London, 1648) in *Massachusetts Historical Society Collections,* 3d Ser., 4 (1834), 57–58. The equation of time and work discipline with social mobility reached a new level during the next century in the writings of Benjamin Franklin. In his *Autobiography,* Franklin asserted that the "precept of Order" required that "every part of my business should have its alloted time"; therefore, "one page of my little book contain'd the following scheme of employment for the twenty-four hours of a natural day":

    4:30am— 7:30am: Rise, wash and address *Powerful Goodness!* Contrive day's business, and take the resolution of the day; prosecute the present study, and breakfast.

    8:00am—12:00pm: Work.

    12:00pm— 2:00pm: Read, or overlook my accounts, and dine.

    2:00pm— 6:00pm: Work.

    6:00pm—10:00pm: Put things in their places. Supper. Music or diversion, or conversation. Examination of the day.

    10:00pm— 4:30am: Sleep.

    Although rejecting a providentialist cosmology, Franklin retained the core of Puritan social ethics. Each of his mornings, he announced, began with the question, "What good shall I do this day?" and evenings concluded with the inquiry, "What good have I done to-day?" *The Autobiography of Benjamin Franklin,* Lewis Leary, intro. (New York, 1962), 86.

    The belief that such daily organization, not to say regimentation, was the key to worldly success became a staple of American middle-class and even elite culture by the nineteenth century. In 1880, Gifford Pinchot's mother Mary admonished her fifteen-year-old son that "I greatly fear you do not systematize your time sufficiently and for the present I wish you to write me every day what you have done the preceding day—from breakfast until bed time." She urged Gifford always to heed St. Paul's advice in Romans 12:11, to be "Not slothful in business; fervent in spirit; serving the Lord." Mary Pinchot to Gifford Pinchot, 17 October 1880, Family Correspondence, Gifford Pinchot Collection, Library of Congress, Washington, D.C. I am grateful to Brian Balogh for bringing this passage to my attention.
89. C. John Sommerville, *The Secularization of Early Modern England: From Religious Culture to Religious Faith* (New York, 1992), chap. 1.
90. Maurice Ashley, *The English Civil War* (Dover, N.H., 1993), 149.
91. Hunt, *Puritan Moment,* 131; Innes, *Work and Labor,* 40–41; Richard L.

Bushman, "American High-Style and Vernacular Cultures," in Greene and Pole, eds., *Colonial British America,* 371. Part of the Puritans' motivation to suppress traditional village rituals, as Keith Thomas has emphasized, derived from the Reformation's larger goal of curtailing magic and superstition generally. When the farmer was "dependent on circumstances outside of his control—the fertility of the soil, the weather, the health of his animals—he was more likely to accompany his labours with some magical precaution. There were all the traditional fertility rites and seasonal observances: Plough Monday to ensure the growth of corn; wassailing to bless the apple trees; Rogation procession and Midsummer fires for the crops; corn dollies at harvest time." Keith Thomas, *Religion and the Decline of Magic* (New York, 1971), 648.

92. Hunt, *Puritan Moment,* 134.
93. *Ibid.,* 175, 253; *Johnson's Wonder-Working Providence,* 23 (quotation).
94. Ashley, *English Civil War,* 28.
95. Maurice Lee, Jr., *Great Britain's Solomon: James VI and I in His Three Kingdoms* (Urbana, 1990); Lawrence Stone, *The Causes of the English Revolution, 1529–1642* (Oxford, 1972).
96. David Freeman Hawke, *Everyday Life in Early America* (New York, 1988), 91.
97. *Mass. Recs.,* 2:47.
98. Walzer, *Spheres of Justice,* 185, 192–193; Stephen Foster, *The Long Argument: English Puritanism and the Shaping of New England Culture, 1570–1700* (Chapel Hill, 1991), 81–82; Thomas Shepard, *Theses Sabbatical: Or, The Doctrine of the Sabbath* (London, 1649), 4; Solberg, *Redeem the Time,* 27–58.
99. Quoted in Hawke, *Everyday Life,* 89.
100. William B. Weeden, *Economic and Social History of New England, 1620–1789,* 2 vols. (Boston, 1891), 1:223.
101. *Mass. Recs.,* 4 (pt. 2):395.
102. Morgan, *The Puritan Family,* 7.
103. *Essex Ct. Recs.,* 1:133.
104. Hampshire County Probate Court Records, Hampden County Courthouse, Springfield, 1:7–9; Stephen Innes, *Labor in a New Land: Economy and Society in Seventeenth-Century Springfield* (Princeton, 1983), 96–97.
105. *Essex Ct. Recs.,* 1:113.
106. *Ibid.,*134; 4:24.
107. *Ibid.,* 3:269.
108. *Ibid.,* 1:134.
109. *Winthrop's Journal,* 2:44.
110. *Essex Ct. Recs.,* 1:135.
111. *Winthrop's Journal,* 2:354–355.
112. Walzer, *Spheres of Justice,* 188. Walzer bases his calculations for America on a five-day week, a two-week vacation, and four to seven legal holidays. In early modern France, journeymen usually worked a maximum of 250 days annually. Scholars estimate that in the Middle Ages, roughly 190 days were full work days, 70 partial, and 100 labor-free. After 1600, French artisans experienced a progressive reduction in the number of holidays, but even at the end of the seventeenth century there were still 38 work-free religious festivals and 52 Sundays. In the Chesapeake region of British America, hired hands were expected to labor 26 days each month, leading to a work year of over 300 days. Landes, *Revolution in Time,* 433n; James R. Farr, *Hands of Honor: Arti-*

sans and Their World in Dijon, 1550–1650 (Ithaca, 1988), 13–75; Robert Darnton, *The Great Cat Massacre, and Other Episodes in French Cultural History* (New York, 1984), 83–85; Thomas, "Work and Leisure," 63–64.

113. Hunt, *Puritan Moment,* 79–81.
114. Hawke, *Everyday Life,* 88–89.
115. William Bradford, *Of Plymouth Plantation, 1620–1647,* Samuel Eliot Morison, ed. (New York, 1952), 97; italics added.
116. *Mass. Recs.,* 1:405; William Nellis, "Labor and Community in Massachusetts Bay, 1630–1660," *Labor History,* 18 (1977), 534; Miller, *New England Mind,* 59; Morison, *Builders of the Bay Colony,* 167.
117. *Essex Ct. Recs.,* 1:15, 27, 34; *Early Records of the Town of Dedham,* 6 vols. (Dedham, Mass., 1886–1936; cited hereafter as *Dedham Recs.*), 5:111–112, 114; Henry M. Burt, ed., *The First Century of the History of Springfield: The Official Records from 1636–1736,* 2 vols. (Springfield, 1898–99; cited hereafter as *Springfield Town Recs.*), 2:147–148, 152–153; Nathaniel B. Shurtleff and David Pulsifer, eds., *Records of the Colony of New Plymouth in New England,* 12 vols. (Boston, 1855–61), 2:21; Innes, *Labor in a New Land,* 101–104. Even as late as the 1760s, as when Concord's William Hunt was reported to be "Loytering about from House to House Wasteing his time in a Sinfull maner," New England selectmen could be found intervening to take corrective action. Robert A. Gross, *The Minutemen and Their World* (New York, 1976), 11.
118. *Pynchon Court Rec.,* 276–277; Innes, *Labor in a New Land,* 132–133.
119. *Mass. Recs.,* 1:401; 3:375–376, quotation at 399.
120. *Mass. Recs.,* 4 (pt. 2):394–395; John Demos, *A Little Commonwealth: Family Life in Plymouth Colony* (New York, 1970), 62–81; J. R. T. Hughes, *Social Control in the Colonial Economy* (Charlottesville, Va., 1976), 101. Sanctions were also directed in 1651 against visiting mariners who, like local fishermen and ironworkers, rarely subscribed to the culture of discipline and were accordingly banned from "insinuat[ing] themselves into the fellowship of the younge people of this country, drawing them both by night and by day from theire callinges, studdies, honest occupations, and lodginge places. . . ." *Mass. Recs.,* 3:242; 5:62, 240–241. Behind all of these measures, as the dance critic Lincoln Kirstein has pointed out in an arresting commentary, was what amounted to a conservation of energy theory: "Faced with exile, a trackless continent, [Indian] enemies, starvation, an imponderable future, God-fearing pioneers needed every ounce of muscular energy just in order to survive. Jehovah had chastised a tribe frolicking in exile before a golden calf. Waste motion, especially that kindled by animal spirits, was not to be spent ecstatically or mindlessly." Kirstein, "Beliefs of a Master," *New York Review of Books* (15 March 1984), 17–23.
121. William Hutchinson and Others to John Winthrop, 29 June 1640, *Winthrop Papers,* 4:259–260; *Essex Ct. Recs.,* 1:15, 27, 34; *Mass. Recs.,* 5:240–241.
122. Arch, *Authorizing the Past,* chap. 1.
123. Milton, *Areopagitica* (London, 1644), in *Complete Prose Works of John Milton* (New Haven, 1959), 2:492; Michael G. Hall, *The Last American Puritan: The Life of Increase Mather* (Middletown, Conn., 1988), 152, 153. In 1695 England's Licensing Act was permitted to lapse, marking the formal end of censorship of the press by either Church or state. Barry Coward, *The Stuart Age: A History of England 1603–1714* (London, 1980), 306.

124. Chandler Robbins, *History of the Second Church, or Old North, in Boston* (Boston, 1852), 8ff.
125. John Morgan, *Godly Learning: Puritan Attitudes Toward Reason, Learning and Education, 1560–1640* (Cambridge, Engl., 1986), 172.
126. John White to John Winthrop, ca. 1637. *Winthrop Papers,* 3:336. See also the sentiments expressed in Dorothy Flute's letter to John Winthrop, 5 May 1640, *ibid.,* 4:236–237.
127. *Mass. Recs.,* 2:8–9, 203.
128. Gerald F. Moran and Maris A. Vinovskis, *Religion, Family, and the Life Course: Explorations in the Social History of Early America* (Ann Arbor, 1992), 124; Linda Auwers, "Reading the Marks of the Past: Exploring Female Literacy in Colonial Windsor, Connecticut," *Historical Methods,* 13 (1980), 209.
129. Michael G. Hall, ed., "The Autobiography of Increase Mather," *American Antiquarian Society Proceedings,* 71 (1961), 271; John Pynchon's Account Books, 6 vols., 1652–1702, Connecticut Valley Historical Museum, Springfield, Mass., 2:99; J. Trumbull, *History of Northampton* (Northampton, 1898); Richard I. Melvoin, *New England Outpost: War and Society in Colonial Deerfield* (New York, 1989), 154–155.
130. Kenneth A. Lockridge, *A New England Town, the First Hundred Years: Dedham, Massachusetts, 1636–1736* (New York, 1970), 10; *New Haven Town Recs., 1649–1662,* 97; *Springfield Town Recs.,* 2:197; Melvoin, *New England Outpost,* 157–158.
131. *Mass. Recs.,* 1:344; M. Hall, *Last American Puritan,* 136, 161.
132. Morison, *Builders of the Bay Colony,* 196–197; Peter Eisenstadt, "Weather Prediction in Seventeenth-Century Massachusetts Almanacs," in Karsky and Marienshas, eds., *Travail et Loisir* 85–87; M. Hall, *Last American Puritan,* 136, 161.
133. Laurel Thatcher Ulrich, "Vertuous Women Found: New England Ministerial Literature, 1668–1735," in Janet Wilson James, ed., *Women in American Religion* (Philadelphia, 1980), 67, 79 (quotation).
134. Moran and Vinovskis, *Religion, Family, and the Life Course, 120.* The quotation from Locke is from *Some Thoughts Concerning Education* (1693).
135. Increase Mather, "The Autobiography of Increase Mather," *American Antiquarian Society Proceedings,* 71 (1961), 278; Auwers, "Reading the Marks of the Past," 204. According to the family tradition of the Hosmers of eighteenth-century Concord, the unexpected eloquence of cabinetmaker Joseph Hosmer during the Revolutionary crisis was a result of his having "an old mother who sits in the chimney corner and reads English poerty all the day long. . . ." Cited in Gross, *Minutemen,* 65.
136. Kenneth A. Lockridge, *Literacy in Colonial New England: An Enquiry into the Social Context of Literacy in the Early Modern West* (New York, 1974), 78, 88, 93, 99; Auwers, "Reading the Marks of the Past," 204.
137. Henry F. May, *The Enlightenment in America* (New York, 1976), 35; Gloria L. Main, "An Inquiry into When and Why Women Learned to Write in Colonial New England," *Journal of Social History,* 24 (1991), 585; D. Hall, *Worlds of Wonder,* 34–35; James Axtell, *The School Upon a Hill: Education and Society in Colonial New England* (New York, 1976), 175; Lyle Koehler, *A Search for Power,* 41–42. Even in remote, relatively impoverished settlements like Deerfield, over half of the men owned books. Among the poorest rural households in southern New England during the years 1650–74, religious books were found listed in a third of probate inventories. Melvoin, *New England Outpost,* 326n; Main and

Main, "Living Standards in Colonial New England," 43.

138. Drawing on comparisons from Protestant populations in Scotland and Sweden during the seventeenth century, Lockridge emphasizes the critical role of public action at the local level. Throughout the Atlantic world he finds that "the only areas to show a rapid rise in literacy to levels approaching universality were small societies whose intense Protestantism led them widely to offer or to compel in some way the education of their people. In Calvinist Scotland, a system of compulsory elementary education appears to have raised adult male literacy from 33% around 1675 to nearly 90% by 1800, a pace surpassing the rate of improvement in male literacy in New England. Sweden provides a more dramatic example of the power of Protestant concern. . . . In parishes of Härnösand diocese . . . the proportion of males 'able to read' rose from 50% to 98% in the period 1645–1714." *Literacy in New England,* 78, 83, 88, 99; G. Main, "When and Why Women Learned to Write in Colonial New England," 585.
139. Lockridge, *Literacy in New England,* 88, 99; May, *Enlightenment in America,* 35; Auwers, "Reading the Marks of the Past," 204–214; D. Hall, "The Uses of Literacy," in Hall, *Worlds of Wonder,* 46; Moran and Vinovskis, *Religion, Family, and the Life Course,* 135; Joel Perlmann and Dennis Shirley, "Why Did New England Women Acquire Literacy?", *William and Mary Quarterly,* 3d Ser., 48 (1991), 66. Perlmann and Shirley believe that deeds, which exhibit higher signature rates than wills, are a more accurate reflector of literacy patterns. *Ibid.,* 61. James Farr has discovered that in Dijon, France, between 1562 and 1594 only a little more than a quarter (27%) of all artisans were fully literate, while almost half (46%) were completely illiterate. Although during the sixteenth century Calvinism and literacy were corrolated, by the mid-seventeenth century, when literacy rates among Dijon's artisans had risen to 44 percent, both Catholic and Calvinist efforts to reform popular education bore similar fruit. Farr, *Hands of Honor,* 239.
140. Lockridge, *Literacy in New England,* 27, 76–77.
141. Andrew Burnaby, *Travels Through the Middle Settlements in North-America in the Years 1759 and 1760* (Ithaca, 1960 [orig. 1775]), 61, 100–101.
142. Lockridge, *Literacy in New England,* 78, 83.
143. Robert E. Gallman, "Changes in the Level of Literacy in a New Community of Early America," *Journal of Economic History,* 48 (1988), 567; Gloria Main, "Why Women Learned to Write," 579–589.
144. Eisenstein, *Printing Press,* 1:423.
145. Cartwright quoted in D. Hall, *Worlds of Wonder,* 22; Axtell, *School Upon a Hill,* 175.
146. Morgan, *American Slavery–American Freedom,* 187.

CHAPTER 4: The Ethics of Exchange, Price Controls, and the Case of Robert Keayne

1. *Winthrop's Journal,* 1:215; *Mass. Recs.,* 1:281, 290; "Records of the First Church of Boston," *Colonial Society of Massachusetts Publications,* 39 (1961), 25, 29.
2. Bernard Bailyn, "The 'Apologia' of Robert Keayne," *William and Mary Quarterly,* 3d Ser., 7 (1950), 574; *Winthrop's Journal,* 1:315–318.

3. *Winthrop's Journal,* 2:64–65.
4. John Winthrop's Summary of the Case Between Richard Sherman and Robert Keayne, 15 July 1642, in *Winthrop Papers,* 4:349–350.
5. Samuel Eliot Morison, *Builders of the Bay Colony* (Boston, 1958), 93.
6. *Winthrop's Journal,* 2:64–66; Daniel Vickers, *Farmers and Fishermen: Two Centuries of Work in Essex County, Massachusetts 1630–1850* (Chapel Hill, 1994), 25–26.
7. *Mass. Recs.,* 3:65, 69, 278. After fining Keayne 20s., the House of Deputies, "upon his acknowledgment of his miscarriage therein," remitted the penalty. *Ibid.,* 69.
8. Morison, *Builders of the Bay Colony,* 92; Bailyn, "Apologia," (1950), 576.
9. Bernard Bailyn, "The Apologia of Robert Keayne . . ." *Colonial Society of Massachusetts Publications,* 42 (1964 [orig. 1952–54]), 280–286.
10. R. H. Tawney, *Religion and the Rise of Capitalism* (Gloucester, Mass., 1962), 128–129. The anti-capitalist portrayal has been followed by most subsequent scholars. Even Morison and Bailyn, whose interpretations of the economic development of Puritan New England are often shrewder than those of latter-day social historians, lumped the Bay Colonists with the Schoolmen on the issue of economic regulation. For Morison, it was clear that "the economic ideas of the New England puritans were medieval; and so far as their church had political power, it regulated rather than stimulated business enterprise." After reading the Reverend John Cotton's sermon on business ethics delivered during the proceedings against Keayne, Morison declared categorically that "John Cotton accepted the medieval doctrine of the just price. On economics he saw eye-to-eye with the greatest of medieval schoolmen, St. Thomas Aquinas." As with R. H. Tawney, Morison found that the classic instance of the just price policy was the case of Robert Keayne. Bailyn, the editor of Keayne's *Apologia pro vita sua,* finds him symbolizing the "divergence between the merchants and most of the rest of the Puritan population." For Bailyn, the import merchant was a lonely and persecuted avatar of the new capitalist ethics, a man whose sins were the classic ones of economic individualism: "malpractices in trade, particularly overcharging, usury, [and] taking advantage of a neighbor's need." Keayne and his fellow merchants, according to Bailyn, "read different lessons" from the Calvinist social teachings that formed the economic culture embraced by the vast majority of ministers, magistrates, and farmers. Along with most other scholars, Bailyn maintains that "in his scramble for profit," Keayne "trampled underfoot the notions of a just price." Morison, *Builders of the Bay Colony,* 160–161; Bernard Bailyn, *The New England Merchants in the Seventeenth Century* (New York, 1964), 41 43.

    More recently, the Keayne affair has been interpreted as a *Kulturkampf* between traditionalists and modernists—with more than a patina of class conflict being imputed to these categories. Ministers, magistrates, and "rural folk" prizing piety, reciprocity, and stability are pitted against bourgeois Boston merchant-capitalists seeking accumulation and mobility. Farmers and artisans adhering to "traditional communal notions of the 'just price,' " we are told in James Henretta's 1991 rendering of this view, contended against the free trade doctrines of merchants and shopkeepers. For Henretta, these binary opposites stand forth with especial clarity. He juxtaposes the "communal ethic of John Winthrop" to "the Protestant ethic of his merchant antagonists."

The Keayne censure, in this interpretation, is but one episode in the ongoing "protests of rural folk against mercantile capitalism." Henretta asserts that well into the eighteenth century, especially in the countryside, notions of "fair dealing" formed the core of New England's ethical outlook. The notions of inherent worth, and reasonableness (or "fair dealing"), are said by many scholars to be the governing rules for economic exchange in colonial New England. In pointing to the critical distinctions Puritan New Englanders drew between industry and avarice, Bailyn categorically asserts that Puritans made this differentiation—as had Catholics since before the twelfth century—according to the just price. The New Englanders "assumed that there existed an ideal standard of valuation applicable to every situation. *An unjust figure was the result not so much of the mechanical operation of an impersonal market as of some individual's gluttony.* A just charge was one willingly paid by a person experienced in such matters and in need of the article but under no undue compulsion to buy."

Supporting this perspective from the vantage point of law and jurisprudence, William E. Nelson asserts that customary standards of reasonableness governed wage and price levels in early New England. "The total picture of the law of exchanges that emerges" in colonial Massachusetts, he contends, "is one of a substratum of doctrine insuring that exchanges of goods and services would normally occur at the rates that were customary or otherwise reasonable at the time of the exchange." In his "*Mentalité* in Pre-Industrial America"—arguably the single most influential essay published in early American studies since 1970—James Henretta concedes that eighteenth-century farm account books reveal that an "impersonal price system figured prominently in these transactions"; yet he goes on to contend that, even this late into the colonial era, "goods were often bartered for their exchange value or for what was considered a 'just price.' "

Such interpretations are also applied to the Revolutionary period. Gary Nash, in his discussion of the urban laboring classes of Revolutionary America, declares that many among this group "clung to traditional ideas of a moral economy where the fair wage and just price rather than free competition and the laws of supply and demand ruled economic affairs." James A. Henretta, "The Weber Thesis Revisited: The Protestant Ethic and the Reality of Capitalism in Early America," in Henretta, *The Origins of American Capitalism* (Boston, 1991), 52, 56, 57–58; Bailyn, *New England Merchants,* 21, italics added; William E. Nelson, *Americanization of the Common Law: The Impact of Legal Change on Massachusetts Society, 1760–1830* (Cambridge, Mass., 1975), 61; James A. Henretta, "Families and Farms: *Mentalité* in Early America," *William and Mary Quarterly,* 3d Ser., 35 (1978), 19; Gary B. Nash, *The Urban Crucible: Social Change, Political Consciousness, and the Origins of the American Revolution* (Cambridge, Mass., 1979), 342.

11. M. J. Kitch, *Capitalism and the Reformation* (London, 1967), 90; John W. Baldwin, "The Medieval Theories of the Just Price: Romanists, Canonists, and Theologians in the Twelfth and Thirteenth Centuries," in *Pre-Capitalist Economic Thought: Three Modern Interpretations* (New York, 1972), 7.
12. *De justitia et juie,* as cited in Raymond De Roover, "Monopoly Theory Prior to Adam Smith: A Revision," *Quarterly Journal of Economics,* 65 (1951), 496n.

13. Baldwin, *Pre-Capitalist Economic Thought,* 8, 76–77.
14. Stephen Innes, *Labor in a New Land: Economy and Society in Seventeenth-Century Springfield* (Princeton, 1983), 17–43, 171–184.
15. Winthrop, "Modell of Christian Charity" (1630), *Winthrop Papers,* 2:283.
16. De Roover, "Monopoly Theory," 495–496; Stephen Foster, *Their Solitary Way: The Puritan Social Ethic in the First Century of Settlement in New England* (New Haven, 1971), 117; Cotton Mather, *Bonifacius: An Essay upon the Good,* David Levin, ed. (Cambridge, Mass., 1966), xxii.
17. De Roover, "Monopoly Theory," 496.
18. The bulk of twentieth-century scholarship on the just price has followed the interpretation offered by Werner Sombart in *Der moderne Kapitalismus* (2d rev. edn, 1916). The basic issue for Sombart was the relationship between profit margins and social mobility. He contrasted the capitalist age and its striving for unlimited acquisition *(Erwerbsprinzip)* with the putative medieval principle of merely providing for one's needs *(Bedarfsdeckungprinzip).* The gravamen of his argument was that price was *not* set for the purposes of accumulation or fostering upward mobility. According to De Roover's gloss on Sombart, "not only the medieval craftsmen but even the merchants [!] strove only to gain a livelihood befitting their rank in society and did not seek to accumulate wealth or to climb the social ladder." This attitude, declared Sombart, was most fundamentally rooted in the notion of the just price which he finds dominant throughout the medieval era. John Duns Scotus and a relatively minor nominalist philosopher named Heinrich von Langenstein (1325–1397) are invoked by Sombart to support this view. Langenstein had built his price theory on the cost of production, asserting that in the absence of public regulation, a producer should not charge more for his labor and costs than would be required to maintain him in his current station *(per quanto res suas vendendo statum sum continuare possit).*

    But this was decidedly a minority position, even at the height of classical scholasticism (1250–1400). To a striking degree, scholars of the early modern period have misconstrued just price theory and then applied their flawed insights to the sixteenth and seventeenth centuries. In truth, the writings of Thomas Aquinas, Albertus Magnus, Navarrus, Bernardino of Siena, and Luis de Molina form a line of intellectual descent that leads—after an important detour through Calvin's Geneva—directly to John Cotton's rules for trading in seventeenth-century Massachusetts. De Roover, "The Concept of the Just Price: Theory and Economic Policy," *Journal of Economic History,* 18 (1958), 419; Baldwin, *Pre-Capitalist Economic Thought,* 6. I am very grateful to Professor Thomas F. X. Noble for his assistance in these formulations.
19. De Roover, "Just Price," 423. See also John T. Noonan's *The Scholastic Analysis of Usury* (Cambridge, Mass., 1957).
20. De Roover finds a passage in Aquinas's *Summa theologica* that he believes "proves beyond doubt that [St. Thomas] considered the market price just." Aquinas, in providing what was essentially a gloss on Cicero's *De officiis,* tells the story of "a merchant who brings wheat to a country where there is dearth and knows that others are following with more. May this merchant, Aquinas asks, sell his wheat at the prevailing price *(pretium quod invenit)* or should he announce the arrival of fresh supplies and thus cause the price to fall? The answer is that *he may sell his wheat at the current price without infringing the rules of justice,* although, Aquinas

adds almost as an afterthought, he would act *more virtuously* by notifying the buyers." De Roover, "Just Price," 423, italics added.

21. *Ibid.*, 425.
22. Norman Jones, *God and the Moneylenders: Usury and Law in Early Modern England* (Oxford, 1989), 6–9; De Roover, "Just Price," 421; E. A. J. Johnson, *Predecessors of Adam Smith: The Growth of British Economic Thought* (New York, 1937), 46.
23. Darrett B. Rutman, *American Puritanism* (New York, 1970), 29.
24. *Winthrop's Journal,* 1:317–318, italics added.
25. Stephen Foster avers that this "was scarcely a very restrictive notion, whatever its medieval heritage." *Their Solitary Way,* 117.
26. *Mass. Recs.,* 1:331.
27. Mather, *Bonifacius,* xxii; De Roover, "Just Price," 418; Mary M. Schweitzer, *Custom and Contract: Household, Government, and the Economy in Colonial Pennsylvania* (New York, 1987), 60.
28. *Winthrop's Journal,* 1:316.
29. *Ibid.,* 2:20.
30. Winthrop, "Modell of Christian Charity," *Winthrop Papers,* 2:285.
31. *Ibid.,* 282–283, italics added.
32. *Ibid.,* 283–284; N. Jones, *God and the Moneylenders,* 151–152.
33. Winthrop, "Modell of Christian Charity," *Winthrop Papers,* 2:286.
34. Vickers, *Farmers and Fishermen,* 25.
35. As Eric Foner points out in his discussion of the failure of price controls in Revolutionary-era Philadelphia, tanners, shoemakers, and curriers—in addition to wealthy import merchants—voiced opposition to government control of the economy: "As urban consumers, all artisans shared an identity of interest with other groups in opposing high food prices, but as producers and retailers the masters felt obligated to pass on the increase in the cost of their raw materials to their consumers. The price of leather had increased more than sevenfold between May 1778 and July 1779, but the leather trades had been singled out as the first craft to be regulated by the [price control] Committee." Foner, *Tom Paine and Revolutionary America* (New York, 1976), 171.
36. De Roover, "Just Price," 418–419.
37. Richard B. Morris, *Government and Labor in Early America* (Boston, 1981 [orig. 1946]), 55.
38. *Mass. Recs.,* 1:74, 76.
39. *Ibid.,* 1:84.
40. *Ibid.,* 1:109, 111.
41. *Ibid.,* 1:111.
42. Morris, *Government and Labor,* 60.
43. Chapman promised to give "300 of 4-inch planke towards the sea fort." *Mass. Recs.,* 1:112.
44. Kenneth A. Lockridge, *A New England Town, the First Hundred Years: Dedham, Massachusetts, 1636–1736* (New York, 1970), 3–78; Stephen Innes, *Labor in a New Land: Economy and Society in Seventeenth-Century Springfield* (Princeton, 1983), 171–184.
45. *Mass. Recs.,* 1:115.
46. *Ibid.,* 1:127.
47. *Ibid.,* 1:159–160. The court warned that "if any man shall offend . . . against the true intent of this lawe, hee shalbe punished by fine or imprisionment." *Ibid.,* 160.
48. Morris, *Government and Labor,* 61; Alan Heimert and Andrew Delbanco,

The Puritans in America: A Narrative Anthology (Cambridge, Mass., 1985), 186.

49. *Mass. Recs.,* 1:183.
50. Vickers, *Farmers and Fishermen,* 26–27; Foster, *Their Solitary Way,* 119.
51. *Mass. Recs.,* 1:223.
52. E. A. J. Johnson, "Some Evidence of Mercantilism in the Massachusetts Bay," *New England Quarterly,* 1 (1928), 385.
53. *Winthrop's Journal,* 2:24.
54. *Mass. Recs.,* 1:326.
55. *Winthrop Papers,* 2:294; *Mass. Recs.,* 1:326.
56. *Mass. Recs.,* 1:340.
57. *Winthrop's Journal,* 2:91–92.
58. Vickers, *Farmers and Fishermen,* 26.
59. Stephen Foster, the one longstanding dissenter from the prevailing "just price" interpretation, pointed to the explanation some twenty years ago. Skeptical about the emerging *Kulturkampf* argument, Foster contended that an interpretation of the Keayne censure pitting a medieval oligarchy of magistrates against a modern class of bourgeois merchants was schematic and reductionist. Foster, *Their Solitary Way,* 116–117.
60. *Ibid.,* 119.
61. [William Wood?], *Good News from New-England (1648)* in *Massachusetts Historical Society Collections,* 4th Ser., 1 (1852), 204.
62. Bailyn, *New England Merchants,* 33, 41; Marion Gottfried, "The First Depression in Massachusetts," *New England Quarterly,* 9 (1936), 655–659.
63. Richard S. Dunn, *Puritans and Yankees: The Winthrop Dynasty of New England, 1630–1717* (New York, 1962), 87.
64. *Johnson's Wonder-Working Providence,* 209.
65. *Winthrop's Journal,* 2:17.
66. *Ibid.,* 2:6, 17, 19, 31 (quotation).
67. Rutman, *Winthrop's Boston,* 184. The 75 percent deflation in cattle prices was especially unsettling because cattle were the Bay Colony's principal staple product during the 1630s. Selling a surplus heifer at the end of the fattening season provided many households with their measure of surplus income. According to Edward Johnson, it was "the common practice of those that had any store of Cattel, to sell every year a Cow or two, which cloath'd their backs, fil'd their bellies with more varieties [of food and drink] than the Country of it self afforded, and put gold and silver in their purses beside." *Johnson's Wonder-Working Providence,* 209.
68. Edward L. Ayers, *The Promise of the New South* (New York, 1992), chap. 10.
69. Bailyn, "Apologia," (1950), 577.
70. Bailyn, "Apologia," (1964), 246.
71. *Ibid.,* 330.
72. *Ibid.,* 269.
73. *Ibid.,* 317.
74. *Ibid.,* 316. The memorandum books of Thomas Jefferson offer a revealing contrast to Robert Keayne's accounting practices. Although Jefferson displayed a Puritan-like zeal for recording even the most trivial daily financial transaction (including how much he lost in coin-flipping bets), he, astonishingly, failed to annually "cast up" his accounts—

calculate the overall profitability of his farms. Such neglect may have contributed to the indebtedness that dogged Jefferson for much of his adult life and ultimately led to the sale of his magnificant library, all his slaves, and his beloved Monticello to satisfy creditors. James A. Bear and Lucia C. Stanton, eds., *The Memorandum Books of Thomas Jefferson,* 2 vols. (forthcoming, Princeton University Press).

75. Bailyn, ed., "Apologia" (1964), 321.
76. Bailyn, "Apologia," (1950), 584–585.
77. Sylvia Thrupp, *The Merchant Class of Medieval London, 1300–1500* (Ann Arbor, 1948), 155–190, esp. 166–167. Summing up the changes brought by the advent of the Protestant ethic, Bernard Bailyn observes that "One of the elements that had been added to the merchant's creed in the course of the sixteenth century was the supernatural sanction that rigorized and steeled the personality traits originally engendered by the bourgeois occupations. The prudence that had once been accepted for its utility and stiffened by habit and custom was now further reinforced by revelation. The virtues that Keayne displayed to a hostile community would not have displeased a medieval merchant, but his ancestor might have been surprised at the conviction and self-righteousness with which he buttressed his actions." Bailyn, "Apologia," (1950), 585–586.
78. Barbara L. Solow, ed., *Slavery and the Rise of the Atlantic System* (Cambridge, Engl., 1991), 21–42; personal communication, Barbara L. Solow, 4 February 1993.
79. Bailyn, "Apologia," (1950), 585–586; Henry Adams, *The Education of Henry Adams,* intro. D. W. Brogan (Boston, 1961), 25; J. C. Levenson, *The Mind and Art of Henry Adams* (Stanford, 1957), 293–294; Weber, *Protestant Ethic,* 55.
80. Weber, *Protestant Ethic,* 17–18.
81. Heimert and Delbanco, *Puritans in America,* 187.
82. Bailyn, ed., "Apologia" (1964), 246.
83. *Ibid.,* 276, 254.
84. *Ibid.,* 264–265.

CHAPTER 5: "That Ancient Republican Independent Spirit"

1. Douglass C. North and Barry R. Weingast, "Constitutions and Commitment: The Evolution of Institutions Governing Public Choice in Seventeenth-Century England," *Journal of Economic History,* 49 (1989), 803–832.
2. *Mass. Recs.,* 1:115.
3. William Pynchon to John Haynes, 2 May 1639, *Massachusetts Historical Society Proceedings,* 48 (1915), 40–41. Covenanted societies, the actions of the Bay Colony leadership proclaimed, possessed an inherently republican dimension. In their own eyes, at least, these were free societies, acknowledging no sovereign authority except the Word of God. Harry S. Stout, *The New England Soul: Preaching and Religious Culture in Colonial New England* (New York, 1986), 298.
4. Karen Ordahl Kupperman, "Definitions of Liberty on the Eve of Civil War: Lord Saye and Sele, Lord Brooke, and the American Puritan Colonies," *Historical Journal,* 32 (1989), 19.

5. Quoted in Maurice Ashley, *The English Civil War* (Dover, N.H., 1993), 167.
6. Robert Heilbroner, "The World After Communism," *Dissent* (Fall 1990), 429–432.
7. Winifred Barr Rothenberg, *From Market-Places to a Market Economy: The Transformation of Rural Massachusetts, 1750–1850* (Chicago, 1992), 13–14.
8. Adam Seligman, *The Idea of Civil Society* (New York, 1992), 15–58.
9. Miller, *The New England Mind,* 483; Rothenberg, *Market-Places to a Market Economy,* 14–15.
10. Scott Michaelsen, "John Winthrop's 'Modell' Covenant and the Company Way," *Early American Literature,* 27 (1992), 85–86, 89; Mark Bond-Webster, "John Winthrop's 'Christian Charitie,' " 26. Cited with permission.
11. Winthrop, "Modell of Christian Charity" (1630), *Winthrop Papers,* 2:294, italics added; Michaelsen, "Winthrop's 'Modell' Covenant," 87. For the argument that the *Arbella* sermon was in fact first delivered in the port of Southampton, see Hugh J. Dawson, "John Winthrop's Rite of Passage: The Origins of the 'Christian Charitie' Discourse," *Early American Literature,* 26 (1991), 219–231.
12. Bond-Webster, "Christian Charitie," 27. See also David Zaret, *The Heavenly Contract: Ideology and Organization in Pre-Revolutionary Puritanism* (Chicago, 1985), for a still stronger statement of this position. During the period from Coke in the early seventeenth century to Blackstone in the mid-eighteenth—in Massachusetts, as throughout the Anglo-American world—contractualism grew increasingly potent as a check on state intervention into economic affairs. The obligations of contract were premised upon the existence of "the agenetic and autonomous individual." In their jurisprudence, public policy, and even within their gathered churches, the Bay Colonists believed, with Grotius, that "contracts were intended to promote a beneficial intercourse among mankind." In his *Commentaries,* Blackstone ratified almost two centuries of practice when he declared that "a contract for any valuable consideration, as for marriage, for money, for work done, or for reciprocal contracts, can never be impeached at law; and if it be of sufficient [and] adequate value, is never set aside in equity." Lorraine Daston, *Classical Probability in the Enlightenment* (Princeton, 1988), 21–22.
13. Daston, *Classical Probability,* 21; Daston, "Probabilistic Expectation and Rationality in Classical Probability Theory," *Historia Mathematica,* 7 (1980), 234–260.
14. Richard Ashcraft, "Liberalism and the Problem of Poverty," *Critical Studies,* 6, (1993), 495–496; Seligman, *Idea of Civil Society,* 19–20.
15. Grotius, *De Juri Belli ac Pacis,* Book I, chap. 1.
16. Quentin Skinner, *Foundations of Modern Political Thought,* 2 vols. (Cambridge, Engl., 1978), 2:339–342; Seligman, *Idea of Civil Society,* 19.
17. J. R. T. Hughes, *Social Control in the Colonial Economy* (Charlottesville, Va., 1976), 122; Thomas Hobbes, *Leviathan,* C. B. Macpherson, ed. (London, 1968), 201; Ames quoted in George and George, *The Protestant Mind,* 165–166. The distinction between the law of charity and the law of justice was the keystone to John Winthrop's *Arbella* sermon. Enforcement of this law of charity, however, was left to conscience, not a court of equity. Not surprisingly for a society based on the idea of

the covenant, contractualism was an early and permanent feature of Massachusetts jurisprudence. The terms of the agreement, not jury-determined notions of fairness, were normally the binding criteria in the Bay Colony's common law courts. Chancery courts, based on equitable, not contractual principles, were barred from the colony. Such sophisticated devices as penal bonds (laying out the penalties for unfulfilled contractual obligations) were employed as early as the 1640s as methods for guaranteeing contractual agreements. Even between ministers and their congregations, written contracts became nearly universal in Massachusetts from the 1660s onward. David D. Hall, *The Faithful Shepherd: A History of the New England Ministry in the Seventeenth Century* (Chapel Hill, 1972), 190–191; Stephen Innes, "Contract and Covenant in Seventeenth-Century Massachusetts," unpub. paper.

18. Perry Miller, *Errand into the Wilderness* (Cambridge, Mass., 1956), 146.
19. *The Book of General Lawes and Libertyes Concerning the Inhabitants of Massachusetts* (Boston, 1648), A2.
20. John Davenport [?], *A Discourse About Civil Government in a New Plantation Whose Design Is Religion* (Cambridge, Mass., 1663), 14–15.
21. David Thomas Konig, "The Virgin and the Virgin's Sister: Virginia, Massachusetts, and the Contested Legacy of Colonial Law," in Russell K. Osgood, ed., *The Massachusetts Supreme Judicial Court, 1692–1992* (Boston, 1992), 81–115; Stephen Foster, review, *William and Mary Quarterly,* 3d ser., 47 (1990), 293.
22. Mary Fulbrook, *Piety and Politics: Religion and the Rise of Absolutism in England, Wurttemberg, and Prussia* (Cambridge, Engl., 1983), 45.
23. Bernard Bailyn, *The Ideological Origins of the American Revolution* (Cambridge, Mass., 1967), 190. In its constitutionalism, as elsewhere, Massachusetts benefited from the ancient English fears of arbitrary power. Although what might be termed the "first industrialization" in Renaissance Italy and Germany had been accompanied by a marked expansion of state power, in England's industrial development during the sixteenth and seventeenth centuries the opposite occurred. After the Elizabethan Settlement in 1559, England could not be governed effectively without the cooperation of the rural-based gentry who dominated Parliament. J. U. Nef, *The Conquest of the Material World* (Chicago, 1964), 117.
24. Benjamin Nelson, "Conscience and the Making of Early Modern Cultures: *The Protestant Ethic* Beyond Max Weber," *Social Research,* 36 (1969), 17.
25. John A. Hall, *Liberalism: Politics, Ideology and the Market* (Chapel Hill, 1987), 53; Robert Brenner, "Bourgeois Revolution and Transition to Capitalism," in A. L. Beier, David Cannadine, and James M. Rosenheim, eds., *The First Modern Society: Essays in English History in Honour of Lawrence Stone* (Cambridge, Engl., 1989), 302; Bond-Webster, "Christian Charitie," 13.
26. George Lee Haskins, *Law and Authority in Early Massachusetts: A Study in Tradition and Design* (Boston, 1968), 121–123; E. Lipson, *The Economic History of England* vol. 2, *The Age of Mercantilism* (London, 1956), cxxi; Daniel Boorstin, *The Americans: The Colonial Experience* (New York, 1958), 28.
27. Peter Donald, *An Uncounselled King: Charles I and the Scottish Troubles, 1637–1641* (Cambridge, Engl., 1990); Allan I. MacInnes, *Charles I and*

the Making of the Covenanting Movement, 1625–1641 (Edinburgh, 1991), chap. 1.

28. During the revolution of the saints, the idea of popular sovereignty was propounded in unmistakable terms. Through such mechanisms as the Putney debates in Cromwell's New Model Army, the "ascending" ideal of politics was articulated as a rationale for Parliament's actions. The Levellers and other sectarians—the first bourgeois radicals—rejected corporate government and privilege on the grounds that it denied free-born Englishmen their natural rights to produce, buy, and sell on the open market. Even Charles I implicitly endorsed the principle of mixed government in *His Majesty's Answer to the Nineteen Propositions of Both Houses of Parliament* (1642). With such an acknowledgment, the regalist era in England effectively came to an end. Even to the King, the ancient notion of the "condescending" monarchy was no longer a tenable proposition. J. G. A. Pocock, *The Machiavellian Moment: Florentine Political Thought and the Atlantic Republican Tradition* (Princeton, 1975), 361–362.
29. Stout, *New England Soul,* 298. For the Massachusetts colonists during the seventeenth century, mercantilism was primarily an internal affair. Particularly before the 1660s, lip service was given to the colony's membership in the English imperial system, but compliance with the Acts of Navigation was in general done on the colonists' terms, not England's. When during the 1690s the Bay Colonists became more firmly integrated into the British Empire, it was—crucially—with revolutionary and Whig England that the New Englanders made their peace. Even here, primarily as a result of the negotiating skills of Increase Mather, the Bay Colonists' new charter guaranteed rights bequeathed to no other royal colony: the right to have the upper house elected by the lower house (rather than being appointed by the Crown) and the right of the upper house to provide "advice and consent" for executive actions.

    Although much more firmly enmeshed in the imperial system than before, the Bay Colonists continued to engage in the kind of independent behavior that drove royal officials to distraction. Having provided for *habeas corpus* by statute in 1692, and seeing the Privy Council then disallow it, Massachusetts repassed it again in 1695. The Bay Colony's flagrantly independent policy on paper money emissions from the 1720s onward was primarily responsible for Whitehall's mid-eighteenth-century currency restrictions. Rarely did imperial officials discuss the New England colonists during the eighteenth century without doing so in tones of frustration and disdain. A. H. Carpenter, "Habeas Corpus in the American Colonies," *American Historical Review,* 8 (1902), 18–27; Konig, "Contested Legacy," 92.
30. *Winthrop's Journal,* 2:24.
31. Bernard Bailyn, *The New England Merchants in the Seventeenth Century* (New York, 1961 [orig. 1955]), 92.
32. Thomas Hutchinson, *The Hutchinson Papers,* William H. Whitmore and William S. Appleton, eds., 2 vols. (Boston, 1865), 1:230–231.
33. *Ibid.,* 1:219.
34. *Mass. Recs.,* 2:109; Morison, *Builders of the Bay Colony,* 255. Although free trade sentiments were strongest in Massachusetts, they were not limited to the Bay Colony. Virginians likewise took the opportunities afforded by the English Civil War to affirm that free trade—in their

case, with the Dutch—was "the libertye of the Collony and a right of deare esteeme to free borne persons. . . ." Edmund S. Morgan, *American Slavery–American Freedom: The Ordeal of Colonial Virginia* (New York, 1975), 146–147.

35. *Mass. Recs.,* 2:109.
36. *Ibid.,* 5:200.
37. Calendar of State Papers, America and the West Indies (1661–68), 15.
38. E. A. J. Johnson, "Some Evidence of Mercantilism in the Massachusetts-Bay," *New England Quarterly,* 1 (1928), 380–381; Konig, "Contested Legacy," 104. As Konig points out: "With sterling valued at 6s. 8d. per ounce, these notes were to be equivalent to three ounces of silver and were to be redeemed promptly. Until 1710, they were; but the legislature kept placing later and later redemption dates on its emissions, and by 1717 the governor assailed the 'intolerable discount on the bills.' Although these bills were legal tender after 1692, creditors received them only reluctantly, and with good reason. Massachusetts bills continued to depreciate relative to silver (to the value of 20s. per ounce) because, like other colonial paper money, they outlived their statutory lifespan." *Ibid.*
39. "Representation of the Affairs of New England by Mr. Randolph," in Jack P. Greene, ed., *Settlements to Society: A Documentary History of the American Revolution* (New York, 1975), 141.
40. J. A. W. Gunn, *Politics and the Public Interest in the Seventeenth Century* (London, 1969), ix. Cambridge's Jonathan Mitchell (1624–1668) in *Nehemiah on the Wall* (1667) reminded the Massachusetts General Court that the "maxim of the Romans was, and is, a principle of right reason: *Salus populi suprema lex,* and is engraven on the forehead of the law and light of nature." From here, it was but a short step to Locke's assertions in the *Treatises of Government* that government was "only a fiduciary power to act for certain ends" and the "supreme power to remove or alter" the government rests with the people. J. Sanderson, *"But the People's Creatures": The Philosophical Basis of the English Civil War* (New York, 1989), 13; Mitchell's *Nehemiah on the Wall* quoted in Perry Miller, ed., *The American Puritans* (Garden City, N.J., 1956), 109.
41. *Mass. Recs.,* 5:201, 495; Innes, *Labor in a New Land,* 182.
42. Jonathan Sewall to General Frederick Haldimand, 30 May 1775, in Jack P. Greene, ed., *Colonies to Nation, 1763–1789: A Documentary History of the American Revolution* (New York, 1975), 266.
43. James Axtell, *Beyond 1492: Encounters in Colonial North America* (New York, 1992), 239. Respect for the rule of law did not translate into a respect for lawyers in Massachusetts. The *Body of Liberties* banned attorneys from taking fees for litigating disputes, an edict that was moderated into a ban on "Barratrie" (the offense of frequently stirring up lawsuits) in the 1648 *Laws and Libertys.*
44. John Dunn, *The Political Theory of John Locke* (Cambridge, Mass., 1969), 106; Seligman, *Idea of Civil Society,* 23.
45. *Winthrop's Journal,* 2:26.
46. Christopher Hill, "Protestantism and the Rise of Capitalism," in F. J. Fisher, ed., *Essays in Economic and Social History of Tudor and Stuart England* (Cambridge, Engl., 1961), 38; Miller, *Errand into the Wilderness,* 47.
47. David D. Hall, "Toward a History of Popular Religion in Early New England," *William and Mary Quarterly,* 3d Ser., 41 (1984), 49; Alexander

Hamilton, *Gentleman's Progress: The Itinerarium of Dr. Alexander Hamilton, 1744,* Carl Bridenbaugh, ed. (Chapel Hill, 1948), 163.

48. Lüthy, "Calvinism and Capitalism," 94; Seligman, *Idea of Civil Society,* 72.
49. Michael Novak, *The Catholic Ethic and the Spirit of Capitalism* (New York, 1993), 230–232; David Martin, *Tongues of Fire: The Explosion of Protestantism in Latin America* (Oxford, 1990), 290–291.
50. Georg Jellinek, *Die Erklärung der Menschen-und Bürgerrechte* (Leipzig, 1895); Hartmut Lehmann, "Ascetic Protestantism and Economic Rationalism: Max Weber Revisited After Two Generations," *Harvard Theological Review,* 80 (1987), 311.
51. William Perkins, *Cases of Conscience* (1613), *Works,* 3:11; Malynes, *Lex Consuetudo,* 220–221; William Hunt, *The Puritan Moment: The Coming of Revolution in an English County* (Cambridge, Mass., 1983), 231; William Riley Parker, *Milton: A Biography,* 3 vols. (Oxford, 1968), 1:267.
52. C. E. Mallet, *A History of the University of Oxford,* 3 vols. (Oxford, 1924–27), 2:235.
53. Laud quoted in Andrew Delbanco, *The Puritan Ordeal* (Cambridge, Mass., 1989), 44; Michael McGiffert, ed., *God's Plot: The Paradoxes of Puritan Piety, Being the Autobiography and Journal of Thomas Shepard* (Amherst, 1972), 49n.
54. Royal officials routinely described resistance to imperial authority as "the New England disease." Friends of the Crown, such as the royalist merchant John Usher of Boston, complained to William Blathwayt as late as 1692 that in Massachusetts, "itt's Comon Wealth and nott Kingly Government." William Dugdale, *A Short View of the Late Troubles* (Oxford, 1681), 37; Herbert Lüthy, "Once Again, Calvinism and Capitalism," in S. N. Eisenstadt, ed., *The Protestant Ethic and Modernization: A Comparative View* (New York, 1968) 103; Richard R. Johnson, *Adjustment to Empire: The New England Colonies, 1675–1715* (New Brunswick, N.J., 1981), 253, 277.
55. Byron quoted in Christopher Hibbert, *Cavaliers and Roundheads: The English at War, 1642–1649* (New York, 1993), 156.
56. James T. Kloppenberg, "The Virtues of Liberalism: Christianity, Republicanism, and Ethics in Early American Political Discourse," *Journal of American History,* 74 (1987), 12; Thomas Lechford, "Plain Dealing: or Newes from New England," (1642), *Massachusetts Historical Society Collections,* 3d Ser., 3 (1833), 74; David D. Hall, *Worlds of Wonder, Days of Judgment: Popular Religious Belief in Early New England* (Cambridge, Mass., 1990), 10; *Winthrop Papers,* 4:263–267; Kupperman, "Definitions of Liberty," 20–21. I am indebted here to Karen Kupperman's discussion of the exchange between Lord Saye and John Cotton in the 1630s over Non-separating Congregationalism. Kupperman's essay illuminates the English Puritans' concerns over the potentially tyrannical dimension of the Bay Colony's federal covenant ideology.

J. H. Elliott, in comparing the role of the state in British and Spanish America, was moved to comment that "New England, from the first, clearly represented a special case, and one of a kind that would not confront the Spanish crown. Captain John Smith wrote of the 'contempt of authority' displayed by the separatists in New England, and the determination displayed by John Winthrop and his successors to keep the crown's authority at arm's length in the name of a higher authority, that of God, had no parallel in Spanish America, a world in which holy experiments were based on the mutually reinforcing relationship of church and crown." Elliott notes in particular that Massachusetts Bay's decision to have its own flag—which it would continue to fly until the loss of the colony's charter in 1684—was "a degree of defiance that the Spanish crown would have regarded as intolerable." J. H. Elliott, "The Role of the State in British and Spanish Colonial America," Davis Center Seminar, Princeton University (27 April 1990), 21.

57. Seligman, *Idea of Civil Society,* 23.
58. Stephen Foster, "The Massachusetts Franchise in the Seventeenth Century," *William and Mary Quarterly,* 3d Ser., 24 (1967), 613; Bond-Webster, "Christian Charitie," 20; Robert G. Pope, *The Half-Way Covenant: Church Membership in Puritan New England* (Princeton, 1969), 5n.
59. John Frederick Martin, *Profits in the Wilderness: Entrepreneurship and the Founding of New England Towns in the Seventeenth Century* (Chapel Hill, 1991), 123, 134; Michaelsen, "John Winthrop's 'Modell' Covenant," 98n.
60. Bailyn, *Ideological Origins,* 190.
61. Kupperman, "Definitions of Liberty," 18; Karen Kupperman, "Errand to the West Indies: Puritan Colonization from Providence Island Through the Western Design," *William and Mary Quarterly,* 3d Ser., 45 (1988), 70–99.
62. *Mass. Recs.,* 1:87.
63. Stout, *New England Soul,* 21.
64. *Winthrop's Journal,* 2:24.
65. Kupperman, "Definitions of Liberty," 20–21; Edmund S. Morgan, ed., *Puritan Political Ideas, 1558–1794* (New York, 1965), intro.
66. Morison, *Builders of the Bay Colony,* 93. As J. H. Elliott noted after his comparative survey of Spanish and British America, "the 'fiction' of popular sovereignty was deeply rooted among the English emigrants," and nowhere "were its implications drawn out as fully as they were by John Winthrop in the Massachusetts of the 1630s." Elliott, "Role of the State," 18. For additional Anglo-Hispanic colonial comparisons, see James Lang, *Conquest and Commerce: Spain and England in the Americas* (New York, 1975), 25–45, 129–148; J. H. Elliott, *Spain and Its World, 1500–1700* (New Haven, 1989), 7–26; and Peter Bakewell, *Silver and Entrepreneurship in Seventeenth-Century Potosi: The Life and Times of Antonio López de Quiroga* (Albuquerque, 1988), 153–178.
67. Konig, "Contested Legacy," 92.
68. Morison, *Builders of the Bay Colony,* 83; Seligman, *Idea of Civil Society,* 73.
69. Contrary to common law practices, corporations in Massachusetts were in effect allowed to create other corporations. The Crown's justification for revoking the Massachusetts Bay charter in 1684 was officially based on the illegal incorporation of Harvard College in 1650. George Lee Haskins, *Law and Authority in Early Massachusetts: A Study in Tradition and Design* (Hamden, Conn., 1968), 26; Morgan, *The Puritan Dilemma,* 84–100; Foster, "The Massachusetts Franchise in the Seventeenth Century," 614; Daniel J. Boorstin, *The Americans: The Colonial Experience* (New York, 1958), 20; M. Hall, *Last American Puritan,* 13–14.
70. *Johnson's Wonder-Working Providence,* 146.
71. "Copy of a Letter from Mr. Cotton to Lord Say and Seal in the Year 1636," in Lawrence Shaw Mayo, ed., *The History of the Colony and Province of Massachusetts-Bay,* by Thomas Hutchinson, 3 vols. (Cambridge, Mass., 1936 [orig. 1764, 1767, 1828]), 1:416.

72. Stephen Foster, review, *William and Mary Quarterly*, 3d Ser., 47 (1990), 293; Wesley Frank Craven, *The Colonies in Transition, 1660–1713* (New York, 1968), 13; Morgan, *Puritan Dilemma*, 163; Loren Baritz, *City on a Hill: A History of Ideas and Myths in America* (New York, 1964), 33.
73. Morison, *Builders of the Bay Colony*, 261–262; *Winthrop's Journal*, 1:77–78, 151; *Mass. Recs.*, 1:147; Konig, "Contested Legacy," 90.
74. Barbara Aronstein Black, "The Concept of a Supreme Court: Massachusetts Bay, 1630–1686," in Russell K. Osgood, ed., *The History of the Law in Massachusetts: The Supreme Judicial Court, 1692–1992* (Boston, 1992), 43–79; Boorstin, *Colonial Experience*, 21–22. During the interim between the drawing up of the *Body of Liberties* in 1641 and their legislative publication in 1648, pressures from below for guarantees of "Naturall rights" continued unabated. Presbyterian Robert Child and his fellow "Remonstrants," in their 1646 demands for religious freedom and expansion of the franchise, sounded a strikingly Lockean note in demanding a "sure and comfortable enjoyment of [the settlers'] Lives, Liberties, and Estates, according to our due Naturall rights, as Freeborn subjects of the English nation." Child was fined £200 and sent back to England for his pains; but the Remonstrants' efforts paid off a year later, when the Massachusetts General Court voted to allow non-freemen to vote in all local elections. Greene, ed., *Settlements to Society*, 100.
75. Morris L. Cohen, "Legal Literature in Colonial Massachusetts," in *Law in Colonial Massachusetts, 1630–1800 (Colonial Society of Massachusetts Publications)*, 62 (Boston, 1984), 250–251. Cotton's *Moses His Judicials* was taken to New Haven, where it served as that rigorously Puritanical colony's fundamental code until New Haven was absorbed into Connecticut in 1662.
76. Baritz, *City on a Hill*, 26.
77. *Mass. Recs.*, 1:346; Konig, "Contested Legacy," 87; Thomas G. Barnes, "Thomas Lechford and the Earliest Lawyering in Massachusetts, 1638–1641," in *Law in Colonial Massachusetts*, 30–32; Barnes, "Law and Liberty (and Order) in Early Massachusetts," in Joseph H. Smith and Thomas G. Barnes, eds., *The English Legal System: Carryover to the Colonies* (Los Angeles, 1975), 63–89. The enshrining of the rule of law in Nathaniel Ward's 1641 *Body of Liberties* was early seen as one of the touchstone's of New England's "progressiveness." The man who rediscovered the original copy of Body of Liberties in the 1820s, art collector Francis Calley Gray (1790–1856), was especially impressed by the document's ban on husbands striking their wives. Marjorie B. Cohn, *Francis Calley Gray and Art Collecting for America* (Cambridge, Mass., 1986), 148–149. Compared by subsequent scholars to Magna Charta, the Petition of Right (1628), and the Instrument of Government (1653–57), the *Body of Liberties* has passed—surprisingly—into almost complete eclipse in recent scholarly literature. Since 1970, the repressiveness symbolized by the Salem witchcraft hysteria and the hanging of Quakers in 1659–61, not the rule of law embodied in the 1641 code, has been for many scholars the touchstone of New England's civic culture. Those emphasizing the repressiveness of Puritan New England include Paul Boyer and Stephen Nissenbaum, *Salem Possessed The Social Origins of Witchcraft* (Cambridge, Mass.); John Putnam Demos, *Entertaining Satan: Witchcraft and the Culture of Early New England* (New York, 1982); Carol F. Karlsen, *The Devil in the Shape of a Woman: Witchcraft in Colonial New England* (New York, 1987.

Sharply dissenting from the preoccupation with Puritan repressiveness, the legal historian Daniel Coquillette characterizes the *Body of Liberties* as "the most astonishing legal development of the [colony's] fruitful early period." The compilations, he declares, "were extraordinary—there was nothing like them in England or anywhere else in the colonies. They anticipated the parallel, but quite separate, law reform efforts during the English Civil War. Their most important feature was their inherent assumption that both ruling power and societal pluralism should be legally limited. In this sense, they reflected political developments in early seventeenth-century England, before the voyages of 1629–30, and also anticipated the 'modern scientific concept' of sovereignty." Daniel R. Coquillette, "The 'Countenance of Authoritie,' " in *Law in Colonial Massachusetts, 1630–1800* (Boston, 1984), xxviii–xix. Thomas Barnes, the editor of the most recent edition of the *Body of Liberties,* likewise characterizes the code as "a structured, rational, moderate, and compelling articulation of human rights." Barnes, "Law and Liberty," 71.

78. There remained limits to those who could enjoy the rule of law in Massachusetts, of course, particularly during the more intolerant first charter period. During most of the seventeenth century, those deemed as outsiders—Antinomians, Quakers, Baptists, and accused witches—fell beyond the pale of these protections. The principle of religious toleration, when it came, was forced on the Bay Colony by imperial authority. The 1691 charter extended legal protection to "all Christians" except Roman Catholics.
79. North and Weingast, "Constitutions and Commitment," 813–814. Recent scholars have insufficiently acknowledged that the political theory underlying the United States Constitution, although indebted to such Old World theorists as Locke, Montesquieu, and Hume, drew heavily—in my view, primarily—on colonial communal compacts such as the first and second Massachusetts charters. Some of the basic principles of American constitutionalism—the rule of law, representative government, separation of powers, freedom from taxation without consent—were, within the first decades of settlement, being institutionalized in religious covenants in Massachusetts and Connecticut. The 1629 Massachusetts charter has been characterized by one constitutional historian as "approximat[ing] a popular constitution more closely than any other instrument of government in actual use up to that time in America or elsewhere in modern times." C. H. McIlwain, "The Transfer of the Charter to New England, and Its Significance in American Constitutional History," *Massachusetts Historical Society Proceedings* (1929), 53–65, quotation at 62; Joseph Ellis, review, *American Historical Review,* 95 (1990), 903; Miller, *The New England Mind: The Seventeenth Century* (Boston, 1954), 397, 430; Donald S. Lutz, *The Origins of American Constitutionalism* (Baton Rouge, La., 1988), 31; Stout, *New England Soul,* 295; Bailyn, *Ideological Origins,* 190.
80. Quoted in Boorstin, *Colonial Experience,* 30–31.
81. Quoted in Haskins, *Law and Authority,* 129.
82. Kupperman, "Definitions of Liberty," 19.
83. William Bradford, *Of Plymouth Plantation 1620–1647,* Samuel Eliot Morison, ed. (New York, 1952), 120–121. Similarly, in 1991 Nataliya Yeromeeva, proprietor of a newly legalized housewares shop in the former Soviet Union, told a reporter: "It's in people's nature, that if some-

thing is theirs, it's theirs, and a person works with a totally different mind set if he has property." Novak, *Catholic Ethic,* 102.

84. Hunt, *Puritan Moment,* 213. It eventually fell to Locke, in the celebrated chapter V of the *Second Treatise,* to provide one of the most memorable rationales for the sanctity of property. In writing what many see as the founding document of liberalism, Locke declared that while the Lord may have created the earth for all to use, the expenditure of labor then became the price for securing its possession. Only in developing a natural resource—through the application of one's sweat and enterprise—does it become one's own, to use as one wishes. Locke wrote that "As much land as a man tills, plants, improves, and can use the product of, so much is his property." Thus the enjoyment of property, notes Donald Greene, "became inseparable from the second member of the trinity, Liberty." Greene, "The Reader Replies," *American Scholar,* 59 (1990), 476–478.
85. J. A. Leo Lemay, *The American Dream of Captain John Smith* (Charlottesville, Va., 1991), 213.
86. *The Colonial Laws of Massachusetts,* William Whitmore, ed. (Boston, 1889), 35.
87. R. M. Hartwell, *Industrial Revolution and Economic Growth* (London, 1971), 250.
88. The legal theorist James Kent, during the nineteenth century, was only slightly exaggerating when he declared that free socage tenure "laid the seed" of American capitalism. Lawrence M. Friedman, *A History of American Law* (New York, 1973), 51–57.
89. Adam Smith, *Wealth of Nations; Mass. Recs.,* 1:114; Christine Leigh Heyrman, *Commerce and Culture: The Maritime Communities of Colonial Massachusetts, 1690–1750* (New York, 1984), 58–59; Hughes, *Social Control,* 67; Martin, *Profits in the Wilderness,* 186–253. In France during the Middle Ages, the system of mortmain severely restricted opportunities to buy and sell land. By the early sixteenth century in regions such as Burgundy land had become enfranchised and thus was alienable. James R. Farr, *Hands of Honor: Artisans and Their World in Dijon, 1550–1650* (Ithaca, 1988), 98.
90. Konig, "Contested Legacy," 95; C. Ray Keim, "Primogeniture and Entail in Colonial Virginia," *William and Mary Quarterly,* 3d Ser., 35 (1968), 551–561.
91. Toby L. Ditz, *Property and Kinship: Inheritance in Early Connecticut, 1750–1820* (Princeton, 1986), 163–167. The 1641 *Body of Liberties* also included a pro-commercial clause that guaranteed equal justice under law to every person within the jurisdiction of Massachusetts, "whether Inhabitant or foreiner," an indication of the eventual role commerce would play in subverting Puritan exclusiveness. "Stranger's courts" were ordered set up to accommodate this need. Unless commercial disputes, particularly those relating to debt and contract, could be expeditiously resolved, merchants and entrepreneurs would be less likely to venture their capital. In 1672 the General Court guaranteed access to the regular common law courts to all non-native merchants and mariners, ordering that "all strangers coming into this country shall and may henceforth have liberty to sue one another in any Courts of the colony that have propper cognizance of such cases, and that any inhabitant may be sued by any strangers who are on immediate employ by navigation, marriner, or merchant. . . ." *Mass. Recs.,* 4 (pt. 2):532.

In Bay Colony jurisprudence, a tendency to treat land as an economic commodity was also reflected in the decisions of both judges and juries. With respect to debtor-creditor law, Massachusetts, unlike Virginia (where after 1705 both land and slaves were regarded as inviolate real property), allowed the taking of land by execution to satisfy obligations unsecured by mortgage. Throughout the colonial period, Bay Colony jurisprudence favored creditors over debtors, bringing real hardship to some, but also making the accumulation of capital easier by reducing risk. Massachusetts lawmakers, as David Konig has pointed out, recognized that because land was the primary source of wealth in colonial America, it had to be made more liquid as an economic commodity. Konig emphasizes that "Massachusetts law was particularly harsh on mortgagors seeking to exercise their equitable right of redemption to prevent foreclosure of mortgaged property, and the colony (and later commonwealth) pioneered methods for facilitating a lender's recovery of such property." From the seventeenth century onward, the colony allowed judgment creditors to take real property not pledged by mortgage in satisfaction of public as well as private debts. Konig, "Contested Legacy," 102.

In 1647, in an effort to facilitate commercial exchange, the Bay Colony passed a law of negotiable instruments that anticipated by three decades some of the key provisions of England's Statute of Frauds. This was technically known as the "contractual power of the holder in due course of a financial instrument." The law, especially with its elaborate defenses against fraud, was intended to foster predictability and reliability in the commercial marketplace by allowing debt to be created, transferred, and collected through government guarantee. It mandated that "any debt, or debts due upon bill or other specialty assigned to another, shall be as good a debt and estate to the Assignee, as it was to the assigner, at the time of its assignation; And that it shall be lawful for the said Assignee to sue for, and recover the said debt due upon bills, and so assigned, as fully as the original creditor might have done; provided the sayd assignment be made upon the back-side of the bill or specialtie."

Although, in the actual use of negotiable bills of exchange, Massachusetts lagged behind the Chesapeake tobacco colonies (the New Englanders preferring instead to employ depreciation-prone promissory notes), General Court officials recognized as early as the 1640s that public action would be required to provide an adequate "medium of exchange." J. R. T. Hughes, *The Governmental Habit: Economic Controls from Colonial Time to the Present* (New York, 1977), 47; Hughes, *Social Control,* 123; Friedman, *History of American Law,* 69; Konig, "Contested Legacy," 102ff.

The economic crisis of 1640 also led to the development of a corpus of maritime law. In 1650 the General Court appointed a committee to "peruse and duly consider" Gerard de Malynes's *Lex Mercatoria,* the most widely used merchant's handbook in the early seventeenth century, for the purpose of determining what "may be necessarily, usefully, and beneficially improved for the dividing of maritime affaires in this jurisdiction." The juridical foundations necessary for a commercialized economy were in place in the Bay Colony in relatively short order. *Mass. Recs.,* 4 (pt. 1), 10; Haskins, *Law and Authority,* 116, 129; Morgan, *Puri-*

tan Dilemma, 166–173; Bailyn, *New England Merchants,* 104; *Mass. Recs.,* 4 (pt. 2):532.

92. Vickers, *Farmers and Fishermen,* 325–327; Konig, "Contested Legacy," 90.
93. John Winthrop to John Winthrop, Jr., [ca. 1643], *Winthrop Papers,* 4:366–367; 5:289; Winthrop, "Modell of Christian Charity," *ibid.,* 2:285; *Johnson's Wonder-Working Providence,* 234–235. Before the Massachusetts version of the Glorious Revolution in 1689, common ownership of unallocated town land continued to prevail, but by the 1720s most towns had completed the conversion from joint to private land ownership.

    To improve the land, in the New England context, was to do anything that would make it more productive, useful, or habitable. Jack P. Greene, although downplaying its religious genealogy, contends that it was the concept of improvement that "enabled settlers in colonial British America as in early modern Ireland to think of the societies they were creating in developmental terms." Pointing out that the language of improvement was "ubiquitous in the early-modern British world," Greene ties it to the myriad projects for agricultural and manufacturing innovation in late Tudor and early Stuart England. In the new societies of colonial America, of which New England assuredly was the most obvious example, settlers "sought to 'improve' their situations by securing the necessary capital and labor to develop their lands and fortunes; towns that would facilitate trade; roads, bridges, and ferries that would provide them with better access to markets." Greene, "Changing Identity in the British Caribbean: Barbados as a Case Study," in Nicholas Canny and Anthony Pagden, eds., *Colonial Identity in the Atlantic World, 1500–1800* (Princeton, 1987), 228–229.
94. McCusker and Menard, *Economy of British America,* 95, 342. This tradition of activist government, based on Puritan covenantalism, took quick and lasting root in New England. Tom Paine, during the Revolutionary crisis, described government as a "necessary evil . . . produced by our wickedness," whereas James Otis of Massachusetts described it as a "necessary good, produced by our wants."
95. Michael Mann, "The Autonomous Power of the State: Its Origins, Mechanisms and Results," in John A. Hall, ed., *States in History* (New York, 1986), 109–136; Hall, *Liberalism,* 52–53.
96. Donald J. Pisani, "Promotion and Regulation: Constitutionalism and the American Economy," *Journal of American History,* 74 (1987), 757–758.
97. McCusker and Menard, *Economy of British America,* 95–96. The Massachusetts state, of course, was no Leviathan, particularly when compared with the modern regulatory state. The Puritan state lacked both the bureaucratic experience and financial resources to enforce the broad regulatory powers it putatively enjoyed. The end result was that statutes could be effective only if they reflected local sentiments. Lawrence M. Friedman, *A History of American Law* (New York, 1973), 29–90.
98. Miller, *New England Mind,* 41–42.
99. Seligman, *Idea of Civil Society,* x.
100. McCusker and Menard, *Economy of British America,* 95–96; George B. Langdon, Jr., *Pilgrim Colony: A History of New Plymouth, 1620–1691* (New Haven, 1966), 145; William B. Weeden, *Economic and Social His-*

tory of New England, 1620–1789, 2 vols. (Boston, 1891), 1:80–81; Henry W. Belknap, *Trades and Tradesmen of Essex County* (Salem, Mass., 1929), 63; Seligman, *Idea of Civil Society*, 73.

101. McCusker and Menard, *Economy of British America*, 342.
102. Richard S. Dunn, *Puritans and Yankees: The Puritan Dynasty of New England, 1630–1717* (New York, 1971), 59, 75.
103. *Springfield Town Recs.*, 1:261; Innes, *Labor in a New Land*, 85–87.
104. The town originally gave Pynchon a five-year limit for constructing the mill. In January 1663, the town meeting voted to grant Pynchon "thirty acres of land . . . and . . . the privilege of the said brook . . . on Condition that he build a Saw Mill . . . within five yeeres." *Springfield Town Recs.*, 1:303–304, 352–355.
105. *Ibid.*, 2:263–264.
106. Gunn, *Politics and the Public Interest in the Seventeenth Century* ix.
107. Edward Byers, *The Nation of Nantucket: Society and Politics in an Early American Commercial Center, 1660–1820* (Boston, 1987), 4; E. N. Hartley, *Ironworks on the Saugus: The Lynn and Braintree Ventures of the Company of Undertakers of the Ironworks in New England* (Norman, Okla., 1957), 61. The central issue here is the relationship of the public sphere to the private sphere. Walker Percy, in seeking to explain the "hypertrophy of pleasant familial space at the expense of a truly public sector" that he believes accounts for the "extraordinary apposition in Mississippi of kindliness and unspeakable [racial] violence," observes that "Though Faulkner liked to use such words as 'cursed' and 'doomed' in speaking of his region, it is questionable that Mississippians are very different from other Americans. It is increasingly less certain that Minnesotans would have performed better under the circumstances [of racial desegregation]. There is, however, one peculiar social dimension wherein the state does truly differ. It has to do with the distribution as Mississipians see it, of what is public and what is private. More precisely, it is the absence of a truly public zone, as the word is understood in most places." Seventeenth-century Massachusetts, one might argue, was in some ways a mirror-opposite of the Mississippi here described by Percy. Walker Percy, *Signposts in a Strange Land* (New York, 1991), 47–49.
108. Lipson, *Age of Mercantilism*, cxix; Mary D. Harris, ed., *The Coventry Leet Book: or Mayor's Register* (London, 1907–13), 673; Emory Battis, *Saints and Sectaries: Anne Hutchinson and the Antinomian Controversy in Massachusetts Bay Colony* (Chapel Hill, 1962), 97.
109. Smith, *Wealth of Nations*, 222, 227.
110. Smith, *Wealth of Nations*, 225.
111. *Ibid;* Child quoted in Lipson, *Age of Mercantilism*, cxxix.
112. *Mass Recs.*, 2:133.
113. "Orders of the Coopers," (ca. 26 December 1648), *Winthrop Papers*, 5:294–295.
114. Quoted in Darrett B. Rutman, *Winthrop's Boston, Portrait of a Puritan Town, 1630–1649* (Chapel Hill, 1965), 250.
115. *Mass Recs*, 4 (pt. 2):377.
116. *Ibid.*, 3:284.
117. Mary Roys Baker, "Anglo-American Trade Union Roots, 1130–1790," *Labor History*, 14 (1973), 366.
118. *Ibid.*
119. Belknap, *Trades and Tradesmen of Essex County*, 82.

120. Jean-Pierre Hirsch, "Revolutionary France, Cradle of Free Enterprise," *American Historical Review,* 94 (1989), 1286. By the sixteenth century, Lyon had moved toward a free labor system; but in Paris, Rouen, and most of the rest of France's many large provincial cities, only the smallest and newest of trades were not organized into guilds. Philip Benedict, *Rouen During the Wars of Religion* (Cambridge, Engl., 1981), 17; Farr, *Hands of Honor,* 13–75.
121. David Galenson, "The Rise of Free Labor, 1351–1875," in John James and Mark Thomas, eds., *Capitalism in Context: Essays on Economic Development and Cultural Change in Honor of R. M. Hartwell* (Chicago, 1994). The political economic consequences of the elimination of guilds were far-reaching. Marx, building on the insights of Adam Smith, used this change to illustrate the triumph of "movable capital" over "natural capital": "With guild-free manufacture, property relations also quickly changed. The first advance beyond naturally derived estate capital was provided by the rise of merchants, whose capital was from the beginning movable, capital in the modern sense as far as one can speak of it, given the circumstances of those times. The second advance came with manufacture, which again mobilised a mass of natural capital, and altogether increased the mass of movable capital as against that of natural capital." Marx and Engels, *Collected Works* (New York, 1976), 6:68.
122. Mather quoted in Miller, *New England Mind,* 307, 308.
123. *Mass. Recs.,* 2:29, 169; 3:265–266.
124. *Ibid.,* 4 (pt. 2):400.
125. Max Hartwell, "Education and Law," 250; Friedman, *History of American Law,* 69–70.
126. Galenson, "Rise of Free Labor."
127. *Ibid.* As Keith Thomas points out, until the nineteenth century, an English servant who killed his master stood accused not of murder, but petty treason. "Work and Leisure," 52.
128. Hunt, *Puritan Moment,* 64; Galenson, "Rise of Free Labor"; Morgan, *American Slavery–American Freedom,* 66.
129. Ashley, *English Civil War,* 10.
130. Smith, *This Realm of England,* 176–177.
131. North and Weingast, "Constitutions and Commitment," 810–811. According to North and Weingast, monopoly grants disrupted existing economic interests because the grants "acted as a tax that, since it expropriated the value of existing investment as well as future profits, was considerably greater at the margin than a 100 percent tax on profits." *Ibid.,* 811.
132. Hartley, *Ironworks on the Saugus,* 86.
133. Thirsk, *Projects,* 53; Lipson, *Age of Mercantilism,* cxii–cxiv.
134. Lewes Roberts, *The Treasure of Trafficke, Or a Discourse of Forraigne Trade* (London, 1641), 91.
135. Thirsk, *Projects,* 53; Hartley, *Ironworks on the Saugus,* 86.
136. North and Weingast, "Constitutions and Commitment," 813.
137. Joyce Oldham Appleby, *Economic Thought and Ideology in Seventeenth-Century England* (Princeton, 1978), 33; Smith, *This Realm of England,* 177; Hill, *Century of Revolution,* 32 (quotation).
138. London artisans quoted in Carl Bridenbaugh, *Vexed and Troubled Englishmen, 1590–1642* (New York, 1976), 171; Kupperman, "Definition of Liberty," 31.
139. Thirsk, *Projects,* 100.

140. Joel Mokyr, *The Lever of Riches: Technological Creativity and Economic Progress* (New York, 1990), 70.
141. *Winthrop's Journal,* 2:164.
142. Innes, *Labor in a New Land,* 11–12.
143. John H. Smith, ed., *Colonial Justice in Western Massachusetts (1639–1702): The Pynchon Court Record . . .* (Cambridge, Mass. 1961), 203.
144. *Discourse* quoted in Jacob Viner, "English Theories of Foreign Trade Before Adam Smith," *Journal of Political Economy,* 38 (1930), 417. During the seventeenth century, it became the practice of the Bay Colony to raise public revenues by farming out short-term monopoly licenses for various trading activities. In the spring of 1668 the Massachusetts treasurer was authorized to "rent, set, or to farme let, for the use of, and in behalfe of the country, for one or more yeares, not exceeding three years," the following:

    1. The impost of wine, brandy, and rum.
    2. The benefit of beaver, furrs, and peltry with the Indians.
    3. The rates of drawing of wines from vintners.
    4. The rates upon beere, cider, ale, [and] rum, from publick sellers.
    5. The benefit of selling amunition to the Indians.

    Mass. Recs., 4 (pt. 2):366.
145. *Winthrop's Journal,* 2:164.
146. *Mass. Recs.,* 1:331.
147. *Ibid.,* 1:327.
148. *Winthrop's Journal,* 2:164; *Mass. Recs.,* 3:53–54.
149. *Mass. Recs.,* 2:62, 81–82, 125–128.
150. *Ibid.,* 2:149.
151. *Ibid.,* 3:386.
152. *Ibid.,* 3:401.

CHAPTER 6: The Puritan Ironworks

1. Smith, *Wealth of Nations,* 116; Joel Mokyr, *The Lever of Riches: Technological Creativity and Economic Progress* (New York, 1990), 62; *Johnson's Wonder-Working Providence,* 73. The placid and pious agricultural villages that form typical images of seventeenth-century New England have little place for a belching, clanging, round-the-clock industrial operation requiring huge outlays of capital and worked by often ruffianly laborers. As Susan Geib notes, "nineteenth-century caricatures of seventeenth-century New England have fixed in the minds of most Americans an image of a people deprived of the basic necessities of life by 'frontier conditions.' " Flatly stating that "Nothing could be further from the truth," Geib points to New England's major export industries in processed fish, milled lumber, and oceangoing ships, as well as the colony's prominence in the Atlantic-Caribbean carrying trade. For Geib, however, the "supreme monument of seventeenth-century New England's swift economic expansion, built and operated on a level equal to that of the most heavily capitalized industries in England, was a factory now known as the Saugus Ironworks." Susan Geib, "Hammersmith: The Saugus Ironworks as an Example of Early Industrialization," in Jonathan L. Fairbanks and Robert F. Trent, eds., *New England*

Begins: The Seventeenth Century, 3 vols. (Boston, 1982), 2:352.

2. Douglas R. McManis, *Colonial New England: A Historical Geography* (New York, 1975), 129.
3. Albert O. Hirschman, *Rival Views of Market Society, and Other Recent Essays* (New York, 1986), 56–76.
4. Joseph A. Goldenberg, *Shipbuilding in Colonial America* (Charlottesville, Va., 1976), 16–17.
5. David Levine and Keith Wrightson, *The Making of an Industrial Society: Whickham, 1560–1765* (Oxford, 1991), 3–4, 76–81. Levine and Wrightson contend that "Tyneside might lay claim to the distinction of having been the first thoroughly industrialized local economy in Britain, one based as much on capital investment as on the use of wage-labour, and in which the agrarian economy, far from existing in symbiosis with industry, had been thoroughly subordinated to its demands." *Ibid.,* ix.
6. Barry Coward, *The Stuart Age: A History of England, 1603–1714* (Cambridge, Engl., 1980), 7, 16–17.
7. *Ibid.,* 16–17.
8. Ralph Davis, *The Rise of the English Shipping Industry in the Seventeenth and Eighteenth Centuries* (London, 1962), 1, 4, 10; J. U. Nef, *The Rise of the British Coal Industry,* 2 vols. (London, 1932), Appendix D; John J. McCusker and Russell R. Menard, *The Economy of British America, 1607–1789* (Chapel Hill, 1985), 98; Charles F. Carroll, *The Timber Economy of Puritan New England* (Providence, R.I., 1973), 8.
9. Joan Thirsk, *Economic Policy and Projects: The Development of a Consumer Society in Early Modern England* (Oxford, 1978), 49; J. U. Nef, *The Conquest of the Material World* (Chicago, 1964), 132.
10. David Kiernan, *The Derbyshire Lead Industry in the Sixteenth Century* (Chesterfield, Engl., 1989), 3–39, 264–270.
11. Wallace Notestein, *The English People on the Eve of Colonization* (New York, 1954), 21.
12. Maurice Aymard, ed., *Dutch Capitalism and World Capitalism* (Cambridge, Engl., 1982).
13. Paul Slack, "A Divided Society," in Christopher Haigh, ed., *The Cambridge Historical Encyclopaedia of Great Britain and Ireland* (Cambridge, Engl., 1985), 185–186.
14. Carroll, *Timber Economy,* 6–7, 9, 11; Slack, "Divided Society," 186.
15. Carroll, *Timber Economy,* 11 (quotation); Nef, *Rise of the British Coal Industry,* 1:158; Nef, *Conquest,* 263, 265.
16. Vaughan quoted in E. N. Hartley, *Ironworks on the Saugus: The Lynn and Braintree Ventures of the Company of Undertakers of the Ironworks in New England* (Norman, Okla., 1957), 26.
17. Carroll, *Timber Economy,* 14.
18. *Ibid.,* 9–10, 17.
19. "Saugus Iron Works," National Park Service Pamphlet, Saugus Iron Works National Historic Site.
20. Francis Bacon, "Of Plantations" (1625), repr. in Jack P. Greene, ed., *Settlements to Society, 1607–1763: A Documentary History of Colonial America* (New York, 1975), 10; William Cronon, *Changes in the Land: Indians, Colonists, and the Ecology of New England* (New York, 1983), 19–33; Carroll, *Timber Economy,* 32.
21. Samuel Eliot Morison, *Builders of the Bay Colony* (Boston, 1958), 276.
22. National Park Service pamphlet.
23. Smith, *Complete Works,* 1:336–337.

24. Thomas Morton, *New English Canaan* (1634–35), Charles Francis Adams, ed. (Boston, 1883), 219.
25. Richard Saltonstall to Emmanuel Downing, 4 February 1631/32, in Everett Emerson, ed., *Letters from New England: The Massachusetts Bay Colony, 1629–1638* (Amherst, Mass., 1976), 92.
26. *Johnson's Wonder-Working Providence,* 245–246.
27. Bailyn, *New England Merchants,* 61.
28. *Mass. Recs.,* 1:28; Joseph B. Felt, *Annals of Salem,* 2 vols. (Boston, 1845–49), 1:50.
29. Henry W. Belknap, *Trades and Tradesmen in Essex County* (Salem, Mass., 1929), 3; *Mass. Recs.,* 1:28, 30.
30. *Winthrop's Journal,* 2:222; *Mass. Recs.,* 2:103–104.
31. Dunn, *Puritans and Yankees,* 70.
32. *Mass. Recs.,* 1:327; 2:61–62. Such governmental grants had ample precedent in "pre-industrial" England. An Act of Parliament in 1629 gave exclusive rights to trade in coal from the Tyne to the citizens of Newcastle. Levine and Wrightson, *Making of an Industrial Society,* 16.
33. *Mass Recs.,* 1:327; 2:61–62, 81, 125–128; Bailyn, *New England Merchants,* 63.
34. Bailyn, *New England Merchants,* 63.
35. *Ibid.,* 62–63.
36. The two pioneers in charting New England's economic history, Bernard Bailyn and Darrett Rutman, both postulate a Puritan / commercialist division from the 1640s onward. On the one hand, we are told, there were the Puritan-minded country gentlemen such as Governor Winthrop, Thomas Dudley, John Endecott, and Roger Harlackenden, who dominated the colony during its first two decades. Their control of the colony's destiny is said to have been increasingly challenged after midcentury by such royalist Anglican merchants as Thomas Breedon, Thomas Temple, and Richard Wharton, at which point New England is declared to be succumbing to the twin processes of commercialization and secularization. Rutman, *Winthrop's Boston,* 252–255; Bailyn, *New England Merchants,* 62–63.
37. Paul R. Lucas, "Colony or Commonwealth: Massachusetts Bay, 1661–1666," *William and Mary Quarterly,* 3d Ser., 24 (1967), 90–91; Alan Heimert and Andrew Delbanco, eds., *The Puritans in America: A Narrative Anthology* (Cambridge, Mass., 1985), 186.
38. John Endecott to John Winthrop, 1 December 1643, *Winthrop Papers,* 4:417.
39. Dunn, *Puritans and Yankees,* 93; Franklin B. Dexter, ed., *New Haven Town Records, 1649–1662* (New Haven, 1917), 235, 260–261.
40. Morison, *Builders of the Bay Colony,* 278; Peter Bulkeley's Last Will and Testament, Middlesex County Records, 1:204. I am grateful to Sarah Redfield of Brandeis University for bringing Bulkeley's will to my attention.
41. National Park Service Pamphlet.
42. Hartley, *Ironworks on the Saugus,* 176–177; Geib, "Hammersmith," 352–360.
43. Susan Geib finds the establishment in early Massachusetts of "such a highly regulated operation for a product that could be obtained from England by merchants at little expense . . . altogether remarkable . . . ." Geib, "Hammersmith," 2:356.

44. Dunn, *Puritans and Yankees,* 87–88.
45. Bailyn, *Voyagers to the West: A Passage in the Peopling of America on the Eve of the Revolution* (New York, 1986), 250.
46. Vickers, *Farmers and Fishermen,* 189; *Essex Ct. Recs.,* 1:170.
47. In the words of Hammersmith's modern historian, by "encouraging the setting up of ironworks, the Puritan magistrates were opening up a Pandora's box, whose contents would undercut many of the things for which they stood." Hartley, *Ironworks on the Saugus,* 7.
48. Daniel Vickers, "Maritime Labor in Colonial Massachusetts: A Case Study of the Essex County Cod Fishery and the Whaling Industry of Nantucket, 1630–1675" (Ph.D. diss., Princeton University, 1981), 13.
49. Daniel Vickers declares apropos of the cod fisheries, "most fishermen were quite ready to reach for the nearest weapon at hand—a rock, a stick, an ax-handle, or even a soup ladle—and bloody their neighbor's heads if ever they were crossed." Vickers, *Farmers and Fishermen,* 138.
50. Thomas Welde to his former parishioners at Tarling, June–July 1632, in Emerson, ed., *Letters from New England,* 97.
51. H. R. Schubert, *History of the British Iron and Steel Industry, from ca. 450 B.C. to A.D. 1775* (London, 1957), 190.
52. Joshua Foote to John Winthrop, Jr., 20 September 1643, *Winthrop Papers,* 4:415–416.
53. Joshua Foote to John Winthrop, Jr., 20 May 1643, *ibid.,* 4:379–380.
54. Robert Child to John Winthrop, Jr., 27 June 1643, *ibid.,* 4:395–396.
55. Petition of John Winthrop, Jr., to Parliament [ca. 1644], *ibid.,* 4:424–425.
56. The Promoters of the Ironworks to John Winthrop, Jr., 13 March 1647/48, *ibid.,* 5:209.
57. Bradford, *Of Plymouth Plantation,* ed. Morrison, 100. The sixty "lusty men" had apparently been sent over by Weston to establish a new plantation at Wessagusset (Weymouth). They remained in Plymouth through July and August, and lived up to their reputation for fractiousness and disorderliness, before departing for Wessagusset. George D. Langdon, Jr., *Pilgrim Colony: A History of New Plymouth, 1620–1691* (New Haven, 1966), 17–18.
58. Morgan, *Visible Saints,* 67–68; Stephen Foster, *The Long Argument: English Puritanism and the Shaping of New England Culture, 1570–1700* (Chapel Hill, 1991), 69.
59. *Essex Ct. Recs.,* 1:292; 2:402–403; "Lynn Ironworks Papers," Baker Library, Harvard University, 115.
60. Hartley, *Ironworks on the Saugus,* 174.
61. *Ibid.,* 170.
62. *Essex Ct. Recs.,* 1:136.
63. *Ibid.,* 1:184.
64. *Ibid.,* 1:136.
65. "Lynn Ironworks Papers," Baker Library, 86, 98, 108, 130, 165.
66. National Park Service pamphlet.
67. *Essex Ct. Recs.:* 1:133–135.
68. *Ibid.,* 1:134.
69. *Ibid.,* 1:173.
70. Hartley, *Ironworks on the Saugus,* 287.
71. Rollin G. Osterweis, *Three Centuries of New Haven, 1638–1938* (New Haven, 1953), 71.

72. Hartley, *Ironworks on the Saugus,* 297.
73. Paul Boyer and Stephen Nissenbaum, *Salem Possessed: The Social Origins of Witchcraft* (Cambridge, Mass., 1974), 124.
74. Hartley, *Ironworks on the Saugus,* 275–276.
75. Massachusetts Archives, Statehouse, Boston, 41:670; Hartley, *Ironworks on the Saugus,* 272–276.
76. Hartley, *Ironworks on the Saugus,* 272.
77. Douglas R. McManis, *Colonial New England: A Historical Geography* (New York, 1975), 127–128; Hartley, *Ironworks on the Saugus,* 273.
78. McManis, *Historical Geography,* 127–128; Hartley, *Ironworks on the Saugus,* 274–275; Langdon, *Pilgrim Colony,* 144.
79. Langdon, *Pilgrim Colony,* 144.
80. *Ibid.,* 144–145; Hartley, *Ironworks on the Saugus,* 274–275.
81. Hartley, *Ironworks on the Saugus,* 276.
82. Oscar and Mary F. Handlin, *Commonwealth; A Study of the Role of Government in the American Economy: Massachusetts, 1774–1861,* revised ed. (Cambridge, Mass., 1969), 76; Hartley, *Ironworks on the Saugus,* 275–276.
83. Morison, *Builders of the Bay Colony,* 279–280.
84. In Hartley's understated lexicon, the careers of the family were truly "more than a little checkered." Hartley, *Ironworks,* 97.
85. *Essex Ct. Recs.,* 5:354.
86. *Ibid.,* 5:326, 351–353.
87. Hartley, *Ironworks on the Saugus,* 276.
88. Lester J. Cappon, ed., *The Adams-Jefferson Letters: The Complete Correspondence between Thomas Jefferson and Abigail and John Adams* (Chapel Hill, 1988), 402.
89. *Essex Ct. Recs.,* 7:237–238.
90. *Springfield Town Recs.,* 2:288, 346; Pynchon Account Books, 6:61; Innes, *Labor in a New Land,* 37, 368.
91. Belknap, *Trades and Tradesmen,* 86.
92. *Mass. Recs.,* 4 (pt. 1):311–312; Mary M. Schweitzer, *Custom and Contract: Household, Government, and the Economy in Colonial Pennsylvania* (New York, 1987), 49–53; Hartley, *Ironworks on the Saugus,* 272–305.

CHAPTER 7: The Making of Maritime New England

1. Joseph A. Goldenberg, *Shipbuilding in Colonial America* (Charlottesville, Va., 1976), 37; *Dictionary of American Biography,* Thomas Coram entry; Hamilton Andrews Hill, "Thomas Coram in Boston and Taunton," *American Antiquarian Society Proceedings,* 8 (1892), 134–145; Thomas Coram appeal to Massachusetts Superior Court, 2 September 1701, *Massachusetts Historical Society Proceedings,* 41 (1907–08), 16–17.
2. Bernard Bailyn and Lotte Bailyn, *Massachusetts Shipping, 1697–1714: A Statistical Study* (Cambridge, Mass., 1959), 105; Lawrence A. Harper, "The Effect of the Navigation Acts on the Thirteen Colonies," in Richard B. Morris, ed., *The Era of the American Revolution: Studies Inscribed to Evarts Boutell Greene* (New York, 1939), 8–10.
3. Bailyn and Bailyn, *Massachusetts Shipping,* 20; Ralph A. Davis, *The Rise of the English Shipping Industry in the Seventeenth and Eighteenth Centuries*

(London, 1962); Mary Roys Baker, "Anglo-American Trade Union Roots, 1130–1790," *Labor History,* 14 (1973), 394.

4. E. B. O'Callaghan and B. Fernow, eds., *Documents Relating to the Colonial History . . . of New York,* 11 vols. (Albany, 1856–87), 4:790; Bailyn and Bailyn, *Massachusetts Shipping,* 21.
5. Bailyn and Bailyn, *Massachusetts Shipping,* 22.
6. Samuel Maverick, "A Briefe Description of New England . . . ," (1660) *Massachusetts Historical Society Proceedings,* 2 (1885), 248.
7. Goldenberg, *Shipbuilding,* 19; William Avery Baker, "Vessel Types of Colonial Massachusetts," *Seafaring in Colonial Massachusetts, Colonial Society of Massachusetts Publications,* 52 (Boston, 1980), 3–29.
8. Bailyn and Bailyn, *Massachusetts Shipping,* 42.
9. James F. Shepherd and Gary M. Walton, *Shipping, Maritime Trade and the Economic Development of Colonial North America* (Cambridge, Engl., 1972), 241–245; Goldenberg, *Shipbuilding,* 42; Christine L. Heyrman, *Commerce and Culture: The Maritime Communities of Colonial Massachusetts, 1690–1750* (New York, 1984), 57.
10. Sewall quoted in Perry Miller, *The New England Mind: From Colony to Province* (Boston, 1961 [orig. 1953]), 483.
11. John J. McCusker and Russell R. Menard, *The Economy of British America, 1607–1789* (Chapel Hill, 1985), 320–321; Jacob M. Price, "A Note on the Value of Colonial Exports of Shipping," *Journal of Economic History,* 36 (1976), 704–724.
12. McCusker and Menard, *Economy of British America,* 320–321; Price, "Colonial Exports," 719; Ralph Davis, *The Rise of the English Shipping Industry* (London, 1962), 18.
13. Braudel, *Wheels of Commerce,* 241.
14. McCusker and Menard, *Economy of British America,* 319. As the pioneering economic historian William Weeden declared epigrammatically a century ago: "Without ships, no industries; without industries, agriculture would have languished, society would have dwindled, the state would have died." William B. Weeden, *Economic and Social History of New England, 1620–1789,* 2 vols. (Boston, 1891), 1:123.
15. Price, "Colonial Exports," 711; Goldenberg, *Shipbuilding,* 16; Douglas R. McManis, *Colonial New England: A Historical Geography* (New York, 1975), 117; Hartley, *Ironworks on the Saugus,* 48; Susan Geib, "Hammersmith: The Saugus Ironworks as an Example of Early Industrialization," in Jonathan L. Fairbanks and Robert F. Trent, eds., *New England Begins: The Seventeenth Century,* 3 vols. (Boston, 1982), 2:351–352.
16. John White, *The Planter's Plea* (1630), in *Massachusetts Historical Society Proceedings,* 62 (1929), 386.
17. Goldenberg, *Shipbuilding,* 16; Vickers, *Farmers and Fishermen,* 85–141.
18. Albert O. Hirschman, *The Strategy of Economic Development* (New Haven, 1958), 98–104; Hirschman, *Rival Views of Market Society,* 57. Hirschman contends that the creation of backward and forward linkages produces an economic dynamic that is considerably greater than the sum of its parts. These linkages Hirschman defines as follows: "1. The input-provision, derived demand, or *backward linkage effects,* i.e., every nonprimary economic activity will induce attempts to supply through domestic production the inputs needed in that activity. 2. The output-utilization or *forward linkage effects,* i.e., every activity that does not by its nature cater exclusively to final demands will induce attempts to utilize its out-

puts as inputs in some new activities." A backward linkage, in other words, relates to the impact of secondary on primary production. It pertains, as Hirschman put it in a subsequent publication, to "the direction of the stimulus toward further investment flows from the finished article back to the semiprocessed or raw materials from which it is made or to the machines which help make it." An example of backward linkage in the seventeenth-century New England setting would be the stimulus that a shipyard gave toward the creation of ropewalks, canvas works, smithies, and joineries. An example of forward linkage would be the stimulus that an ironworks gave to shipyards, smithies, naileries, and any enterprise involving a significant element of metal fabrication.

Moreover, the fact that these activities have typically taken place in cities suggests why Massachusetts offered a more dynamic economic environment than did Connecticut, which lacked an urban counterpart to Boston. As Hirschman contends, the dynamic element in the linkage process derives from productivity gains that are larger than the sum of their individual parts. "The fact that the linkage effects of two industries viewed in combination are larger than the sum of the linkage effects of each industry in isolation helps to account for the cumulative character of development." When "industry A is first set up, its satellites will soon follow; but when industry B is subsequently established, this may help to bring into existence not only its own satellites but some firms which neither A nor B in isolation could have called forth. And with C coming into play some firms will follow that require the combined stimuli not only of B and C but of A, B, and C. This mechanism may go far toward explaining the *acceleration* of industrial growth which is so conspicuous during the first stages of a country's development."

Hirschman's principal argument in *Strategy of Economic Development* was to favor enterprises with strong backward and forward linkages. In challenging the then widely held notion that industrialization was most successful when centrally planned, large-scale, and balanced, he advocated a policy he wryly dubbed "import-substituting industrialization." Countries, Hirschman declared, "tend to develop a comparative advantage in the articles they *import*." In an argument that applies well to what we know of the economic history of seventeenth-century Massachusetts, he emphasized the particular importance of consumption linkages in the developmental process. Increased imports of consumer goods such as textiles and ironwares into newly developing countries have "often been blamed for the decay of local handicraft and artisanal production." Yet Hirschman contends that these imports "must be correspondingly credited with laying the groundwork for local industry through consumption linkages." Imports, according to a line of reasoning that John Locke would have understood, will generate rising expectations, especially as erstwhile luxuries are redefined as necessities. And so it happened in early New England. A rising calculus of expectations among the settler population, along with the symbiotic effect of linked development in the productive sector, resulted in an accelerated level of economic growth. Hirschman, *Rival Views of Market Society*, 56–57; *Strategy of Economic Development*, 100; and "A Generalized Linkage Approach to Development, with Special Reference to Staples," in *Economic Development and Cultural Change, Supplement*, 35 (1977), 67–98.

19. Heyrman, *Commerce and Culture*, 57–58; Weeden, *Economic History*,

1:159; John Josselyn, "An Account of Two Voyages to New England," *Massachusetts Historical Society Collections,* 3 (1833), 3d Ser., 318–319.

20. Child quoted in Goldenberg, *Shipbuilding,* 23; Hirschman, *Rival Views of Market Society,* 56.
21. [William Wood?], *Good News from New-England* (1648), in *Massachusetts Historical Society Collections,* 4th Ser., 1 (1852), 218; Larzar Ziff, *Puritanism in America: New Culture in a New World* (New York, 1973), 13; Vickers, "Maritime Labor in Colonial Massachusetts," 318–319.
22. Goldenberg, *Shipbuilding,* 24–25; James R. Perry, *The Formation of Society on Virginia's Eastern Shore, 1615–1655* (Chapel Hill, 1990), 45–46; T. H. Breen and Stephen Innes, *"Myne Owne Ground": Race and Freedom on Virginia's Eastern Shore, 1640–1676* (New York, 1980), 41.
23. Jack P. Greene, *Pursuits of Happiness: The Social Development of Early Modern British Colonies and the Formation of American Culture* (Chapel Hill, 1988), 3–5, 36–38; Darrett B. Rutman, *Small Worlds, Large Questions: Explorations in Early American Social History, 1600–1850* (Charlottesville, Va., 1994), 93–112, 287–304.
24. Massachusetts Archives, Statehouse, Boston, 67:290.
25. "Articles of Agreement," (1636) for Springfield, in *New England Historical and Genealogical Register,* 13 (1859), 295–297.
26. Darrett B. Rutman, "Governor Winthrop's Garden Crop: The Significance of Agriculture in the Early Commerce of Massachusetts Bay," *William and Mary Quarterly,* 3d Ser., 20 (1963), 407; *Mass. Recs.,* 2:228–229; McCusker and Menard, *Economy of British America,* 23–26; Vickers, *Farmers and Fishermen, 100–116.*
27. Virginia DeJohn Anderson, "The Cattle Economy of Seventeenth-Century New England," unpubl. paper.
28. *Ibid.*; Charles F. Carroll, *The Timber Economy of Puritan New England* (Providence, R.I., 1973), 62–63; George Langdon, Jr., *Pilgrim Colony: A History of New Plymouth, 1620–1691* (New Haven, 1966), 16; The Rev. Francis Higginson to his friends at Leicester, September 1629, in Emerson, ed., *Letters from New England,* 30–31; John [?] Pond to William Pond, 15 March 1630/31, in *ibid.,* 64–65; Bradford, *Of Plymouth Plantation,* Morison, ed., 143; David F. Hawke, *Everyday Life in Early America* (New York, 1988), 39.
29. *Winthrop's Journal,* 1:112; 2:6; Anderson, "Cattle Economy."
30. Anderson, "Cattle Economy"; *Mass. Recs.,* 3:241; *Winthrop's Journal,* 1:105; McManis, *Historical Geography,* 130.
31. Sumner Chilton Powell, *Puritan Village: The Formation of a New England Town* (Middletown, Conn., 1963), chap. 1.
32. Richard I. Melvoin, *New England Outpost: War and Society in Colonial Deerfield* (New York, 1989), 160.
33. Innes, *Labor in a New Land,* 9, 231; Melvoin, *New England Outpost,* 159.
34. Springfield "Articles of Agreement."
35. *Springfield Town Recs.,* 1:232; Innes, *Labor in a New Land,* 37.
36. *Springfield Town Recs.,* 1:280.
37. Anderson, "Cattle Economy." This is not to imply that New Englanders were alone in the practice of keeping a record of animal brands. In the Chesapeake colonies, such books were maintained by the county courts. For the location of Springfield's cow and sheep pastures, see Innes, *Labor in a New Land,* xiii, 8.
38. Anderson, "Cattle Economy"; Marion H. Gottfried, "The First Depression in Massachusetts," *New England Quarterly,* 9 (1936), 655; Pynchon

quoted in Mason Green, *Springfield, 1636–1886* (Springfield, Mass., 1888), 29–30.

39. John Pynchon Account Books, 1652–1702, 1:176; Innes, *Labor in a New Land,* 73.
40. John Pynchon Account Books, 3:172–173, 207; 5:161, 417–418, 546–547.
41. William Coddington to John Winthrop, 5 August 1644, *Winthrop Papers,* 4:489.
42. Robert A. Gross, *The Minutemen and Their World* (New York, 1976), 86.
43. Virginia DeJohn Anderson, *New England's Generation: The Great Migration and the Formation of Society and Culture in the Seventeenth Century* (Cambridge, Engl., 1991), 92–100; *Johnson's Wonder-Working Providence,* 105–106; *Winthrop's Journal,* 1:151; Miller, *The New England Mind,* 36–37; Roger Thompson, *Mobility and Migration: East Anglian Founders of New England, 1629–1640,* (Amherst Mass., 1994), 212–223.
44. *Winthrop's Journal,* 1:178; John Cotton quoted in Miller, *New England Mind,* 36.
45. Bradford, *Of Plymouth Plantation,* 252–254.
46. *Johnson's Wonder-Working Providence,* 96, 209.
47. Winthrop, Jr., quoted in Dunn, *Puritans and Yankees,* 87.
48. *Winthrop's Journal,* 1:70.
49. *Winthrop's Journal,* 1:111, 187; Goldenberg, *Shipbuilding,* 11–23, 55; Dunn, *Puritans and Yankees,* 87.
50. Morison, *Builders of the Bay Colony,* 34; *Winthrop's Journal,* 2:23–24.
51. Goldenberg, *Shipbuilding,* 11; *Winthrop's Journal,* 2:60.
52. Hugh Peter and Emmanuel Downing to John Winthrop, 13 January 1640/41, *Winthrop Papers,* 4:304–305.
53. John Endecott to John Winthrop, 28 January 1640/41, *Winthrop Papers,* 4:311–312.
54. *Springfield Town Recs.,* 1:164.
55. Heyrman, *Commerce and Culture,* 58; Handlin and Handlin, *Commonwealth,* 92.
56. *Mass. Recs.,* 1:337–338; 4 (pt. 2):345–346.
57. Eric G. Nellis, "Work and Social Stability in Pre-Revolutionary Massachusetts," *Canadian Historical Association Papers* (1981), 96; Downing quoted in Belknap, *Trades and Tradesmen,* 8–9.
58. Goldenberg, *Shipbuilding,* 35, 53; Philip S. Foner, *History of the Labor Movement in the United States,* 5 vols. (New York, 1947), 1:22; Rutman, *Winthrop's Boston,* 189.
59. Nellis, "Work and Social Stability in Massachusetts," 96.
60. Shepherd and Walton, *Shipping, Trade, and Economic Development,* 48.
61. Davis, *English Shipping,* 375; Price, "Colonial Exports," 719–720.
62. Bailyn and Bailyn, *Massachusetts Shipping,* 56.
63. *Ibid.,* 57.
64. Heyrman, *Commerce and Culture,* 67.
65. *Mass. Recs.,* 4 (pt. 2):388–389.
66. *Mass. Recs.,* 1:292; *Winthrop's Journal,* 2:176; Rutman, "Governor Winthrop's Garden Crop," 402.
67. *Winthrop's Journal,* 2:85.
68. Richard Vines to John Winthrop, 19 July 1647, *Winthrop Papers,* 5:172; Gottfried, "First Depression," 672; Rutman, *Winthrop's Boston,* 185; Morgan, *The Puritan Dilemma,* 204–205.

69. Gottfried, "First Depression," 672.
70. *Good News from New-England,* 218; John Hull to Benedict Arnold, 16 April 1677, John Hull Letterbook, American Antiquarian Society, Worcester, Mass.
71. *Johnson's Wonder-Working Providence,* 247–248; Barbara L. Solow, ed., *Slavery and the Rise of the Atlantic System* (Cambridge, Engl., 1991), 16–17; Shepherd and Walton, *Shipping, Maritime Trade, and Economic Development,* 115; David Richardson, "Slavery, Trade, and Economic Growth in Eighteenth-Century New England," in Solow, ed., *Slavery and the Rise of the Atlantic System,* 250.
72. Andrew Burnaby, *Travels Through the Middle Settlements in North America in the Years 1759 and 1760 . . .* (Ithaca, 1963 [orig. 1775]), 96, 105, 114. Burnaby contrasted Massachusetts' success in exporting codfish and ships with neighboring Rhode Island, which possessed no exports "except in a very trifling degree." *Ibid.,* 96.
73. John Smith, *Description of New England* (1616), in *Complete Works,* 1:331; William Wood, *New England's Prospect* (1635), Alden T. Vaughan, ed. (Amherst, Mass., 1977), 53.
74. *Winthrop's Journal,* 1:310; 2:42.
75. McCusker and Menard, *Economy of British America,* 99.
76. Vickers, *Farmers and Fishermen,* 100.
77. *Mass. Recs.,* 3:374–375; Bailyn, *New England Merchants,* 82.
78. Vickers, *Farmers and Fishermen,* 145–153. In prohibiting the export of all foodstuffs except fish during King Philip's War, the General Court also suspended the existing ban on imports of wheat, sea biscuit, and flour. *Mass. Recs.,* 5:65.
79. John Frederick Martin, *Profits in the Wilderness: Entrepreneurship and the Founding of New England Towns in the Seventeenth Century* (Chapel Hill, 1991), 32; Bailyn and Bailyn, *Massachusetts Shipping,* 104–105; Goldenberg, *Shipbuilding,* 35.
80. Vickers, *Farmers and Fishermen,* 152–154.
81. Shepherd and Walton, *Shipping, Maritime Trade, and Economic Development,* 211–212, 217, 220, 223–224, 227; McCusker and Menard, *Economy of British America,* 108; J. G. Lydon, "Fish for Gold: The Massachusetts Fish Trade with Iberia, 1700–1773," *New England Quarterly,* 54 (1981), 562–563.
82. Baker, "Anglo-American Trade Union Roots," 369.
83. Goldenberg, *Shipbuilding;* Dickinson's "Farmer's Letters" excerpted in Greene, ed., *Colonies to Nation,* 122–133, quotation at 127.

    Daniel Vickers, whose account of the New England fishing industry is both the most recent and the most comprehensive, links it not only to the Bay Colony's swift economic ascent, but to the nineteenth-century industrial revolution as well: "For the men it employed, the profits it earned, the vessels and provisions it consumed, and the shipping business it fostered, the [fishing] industry was without question the first leading sector in New England's remarkable history of economic development. It is hard to imagine how the carrying trades would have succeeded in Massachusetts without fish to ship, and equally hard to explain the colony's successful industrialization during the nineteenth century without the profits cleared in overseas shipping." Vickers, *Farmers and Fishermen,* 143.
84. Clark, *Eastern Frontier,* 65.

85. McCusker and Menard, *Economy of British America,* 323; Carroll, *Timber Economy,* 110.
86. *Essex Ct. Recs.,* 1:297; Carroll, *Timber Economy,* 200; Bailyn, *New England Merchants,* 100–101.
87. Carroll, *Timber Economy,* 95; *Johnson's Wonder-Working Providence,* 116; Josselyn, "Two Voyages," 320; Heyrman, *Commerce and Culture,* 59.
88. John Winthrop, Jr., to John Winthrop, 18 January 1629/30, *Winthrop Papers,* 2:193–194; John Winthrop to Thomas Graves, 5 June 1634, in Emerson, ed., *Letters from New England,* 118.
89. Bradford, *Of Plymouth Plantation,* 145n; *Mass. Recs.,* 1:114.
90. *Mass. Recs.,* 1:149.
91. *Mass. Recs.,* 3:256.
92. *Winthrop's Journal,* 1:190; Martin, *Profits in the Wilderness,* 300; *Dedham Town Recs.,* 3:9–10.
93. Weeden, *Economic History,* 1:103; Samuel Eliot Morison, "The Plantation of Nashaway: An Industrial Experiment," *Colonial Society of Massachusetts Transactions,* 27 (1927–30), 204–222; Innes, *Labor in a New Land,* 36; Langdon, *Pilgrim Colony,* 145.
94. Quoted in Belknap, *Trades and Tradesmen,* 57.
95. Joseph B. Felt, *Statistics of Taxation in Massachusetts, Including Valuation and Population* (Boston, 1847), 235; Winifred Barr Rothenberg, *From Market-Places to a Market Economy: The Transformation of Rural Massachusetts, 1750–1850* (Chicago, 1992), 231. Taxable polls included all males over sixteen years, with the exceptions of the governor and deputy governor of the colony, as well as all settled ministers, grammar school masters, and the faculty, officers, and students of Harvard College.
96. J. Hector St. John de Crèvecoeur, *Letters From an American Farmer* (1782), Albert E. Stone, ed. (Harmondsworth, Engl., 1981), 66–105. For Daniel Vickers, the eventual success of the Massachusetts fishery rested on the "fundamental character of the Bay Colony itself—from its very beginnings it possessed a complex and diversified economy, staffed with farmers and waterfront craftsmen who were capable of providing much of the victualing and tonnage that a resident fishery would require." Vickers, *Farmers and Fishermen,* 203.
97. From the beginning, the town possessed a strong entrepreneurial dimension. As John Frederick Martin writes: "There had been no such thing as a town before New Englanders invented it, no English precedent, no guide to instruct the colonists. In creating the town, colonists came up with a wholly new institution. It was part land company and part borough, part joint-stock company and part village. The entrepreneurial aspect of towns helped overcome the tremendous organizational and financial difficulties presented by settling the wilderness." *Profits in the Wilderness,* 248–249.
98. Linda Auwers Bissell, "From One Generation to Another: Mobility in Seventeenth-Century Windsor, Connecticut," *William and Mary Quarterly,* 3d Ser., 31 (1974), 80.
99. Alexis de Tocqueville, *Democracy in America,* Phillips Bradley, ed., 2 vols. (New York, 1945), quotations at 1:69, 67. With the New England town in mind, Tocqueville offered what would become one of his most famous pronouncements: "A nation may establish a free government, but without municipal institutions it cannot have the spirit of liberty." *Ibid.,* 63.

Conclusion

1. Gordon S. Wood, *The Radicalism of the American Revolution* (New York, 1992), 170–171.
2. Karen Ordahl Kupperman, "Errand into the Indies: Puritan Colonization from Providence Island Through the Western Design," *William and Mary Quarterly,* 3d Ser., 43 (1988), 80.
3. Writing in *Democracy in America,* Tocqueville declared: "That Providence has given to every human being the degree of reason necessary to direct himself in the affairs that interest him exclusively is the grand maxim upon which the civil and political society rests in the United States." *Democracy in America,* 1:435–436.
4. Richard Wrightman Fox and T. Jackson Lears, *Culture of Consumption* (New York, 1983); Roland A. Delattre, "The Culture of Procurement: Reflections on Addiction and the Dynamics of American Culture," in Charles H. Reynolds and Ralph V. Norman, eds., *Community in America: The Challenge of "Habits of the Heart"* (Berkeley, 1988), 60.
5. Paul Seaver, *Wallington's World: A Puritan Artisan in Seventeenth-Century London* (Stanford, 1985), 128.
6. Robert D. Putnam, "The Prosperous Community: Social Capital and Public Life," *The American Prospect,* 13 (1993), 36, 38.
7. Putnam, "Prosperous Community," 35–36; Encyclical quoted in Michael Novak, *The Catholic Ethic and the Spirit of Capitalism* (New York, 1993), 119–125.
8. Robert D. Putnam, *Making Democracy Work: Civic Traditions in Modern Italy* (Princeton, 1993), 163–185.
9. Preston, *The New Covenant* (London, 1630), 155–156.
10. Tocqueville, *Democracy in America,* 2:104.
11. David D. Hall, "On Common Ground: The Coherence of American Puritan Studies," *William and Mary Quarterly,* 3d Ser., 44 (1987), 215.
12. Even for worldly maritime settlements such as Gloucester and Marblehead, the rise of trade did not bring the decline of community. In providing one example of the workings of communal capitalism, Christine Heyrman declares that by the mid-eighteenth century, "the drive for profit did not dominate social relationships or redefine attitudes governing economic behavior. Forbearance toward local debtors, a cautious approach to investment, limited aspirations for expansion and innovation, and a concern for communal welfare characterized the outlook of all participants in local commerce, even major merchants and entrepreneurs. . . . Commerce created prosperity and afforded some families an improved standard of living, but the new affluence did not diminish the piety of port dwellers." Christine Leigh Heyrman, *Commerce and Culture: The Maritime Communities of Colonial Massachusetts, 1690–1750* (New York, 1984), 19.
13. Bernard Bailyn, "The 'Apologia' of Robert Keayne," *William and Mary Quarterly,* 3d Ser., 7 (1950), 586.
14. Sacvan Bercovich, *The American Jeremiad* (Madison, 1978), xi.
15. Perry Miller, *The New England Mind: From Colony to Province* (Boston, 1961 [orig. 1953]), 42.
16. M. G. Hall, ed., "The Autobiography of Increase Mather," *American Antiquarian Society Proceedings,* 71 (1961), 303, 311, 318. Nor did such lamentations end with the eclipse of Puritanism. On the eve of the

American Revolution, John Adams—that most prototypical of New Englanders—could be found admonishing himself to "Beware of idleness, luxury, and all vanity, folly, and vice!" Charles Francis Adams, ed., *The Works of John Adams,* 10 vols. (Boston, 1850–1856), 2:304. According to Peter Shaw, Adams "truly believed that his choice lay between dissipated indolence and stern self-discipline." Shaw, *The Character of John Adams* (Chapel Hill, 1976), 38.

Index

INDEX

Index

INDEX

Index